Shojo Beat

kimi ni todoke
From Me to You

Vol. 2
Story & Art by
Karuho Shiina

Volume 2

Contents

Story Thus Far

Sawako Kuronuma has always been a loner. Though not by choice, this optimistic 15-year-old can't seem to make any friends. Stuck with the unfortunate nickname "Sadako" after the haunting movie character, rumors about her summoning spirits have been greatly exaggerated. With her shy personality and scary looks, most of her classmates barely talk to her, much less look into her eyes for more than three seconds lest they be cursed. Except for Shota Kazehaya. Kazehaya's the most popular boy in class, and his friendly attitude toward Sawako bewilders their classmates. But this unlikely friendship has changed Sawako's life. Two of her classmates, Yoshida and Yano, have started being friendly to her too. Everything seems to be looking up for Sawako until the nasty rumors about Yoshida and Yano start spreading. And the person accused of being behind the rumors...is "Sadako" herself!

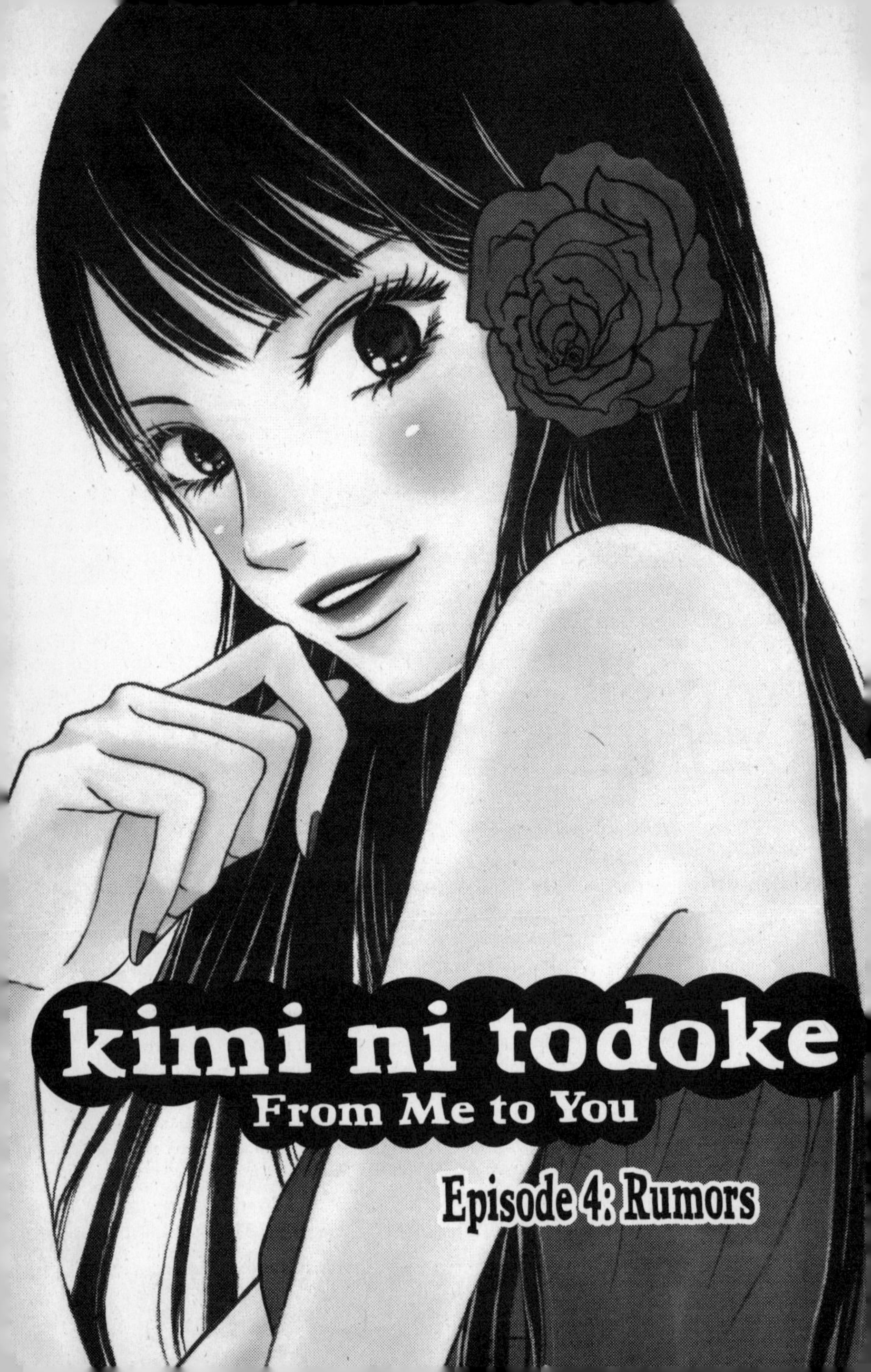
kimi ni todoke
From Me to You
Episode 4: Rumors

Motto

"Do one good deed each day."

character #1

Sawako Kuronuma

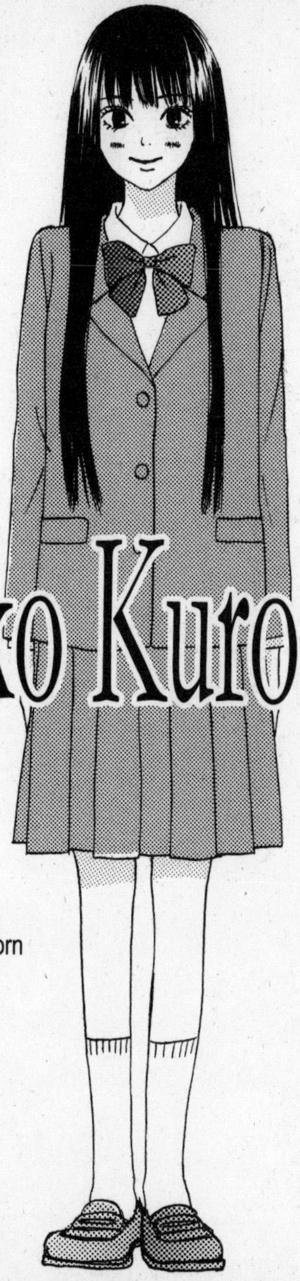

Nickname: Sadako
Height: 158 cm [5'2"]
Weight: 44 kg [97 lbs]
Blood type: O
Birthdate: December 31
Astrological sign: Capricorn

We asked her what television shows she likes to watch!

"I like shows about hot springs and traveling.

They make me feel like I'm right there with them.

Also shows that show craftsmen demonstrating their skills are exciting to watch..."

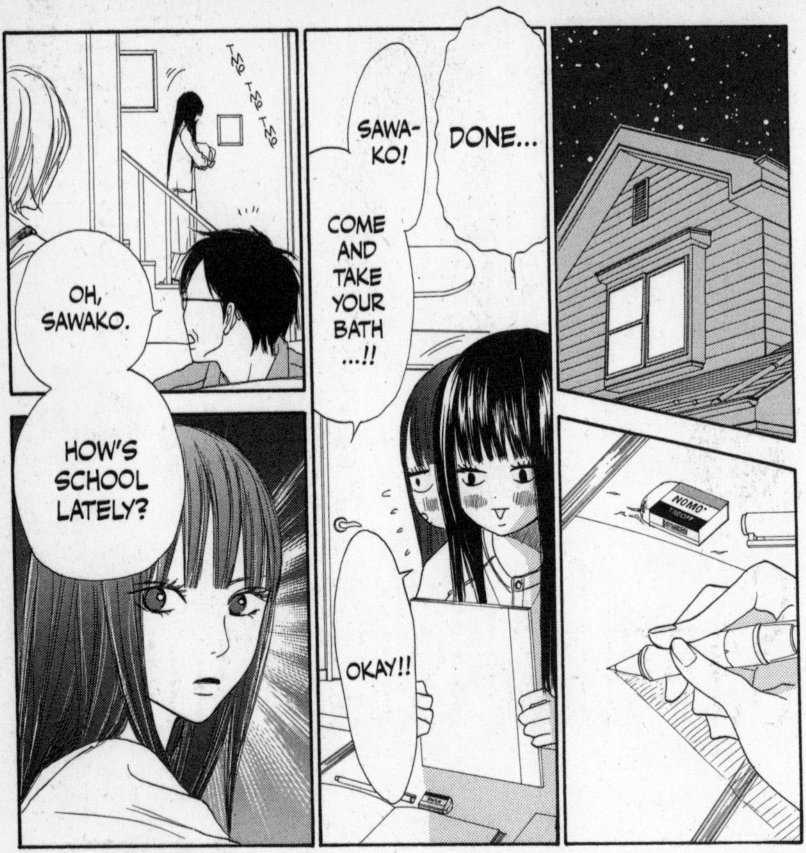
NOMO
DONE...
SAWAKO!
COME AND TAKE YOUR BATH ...!!
OKAY!!
TMP TMP TMP TMP
OH, SAWAKO.
HOW'S SCHOOL LATELY?

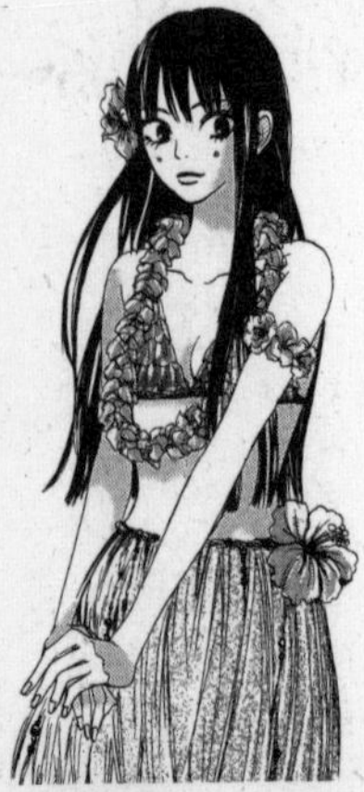

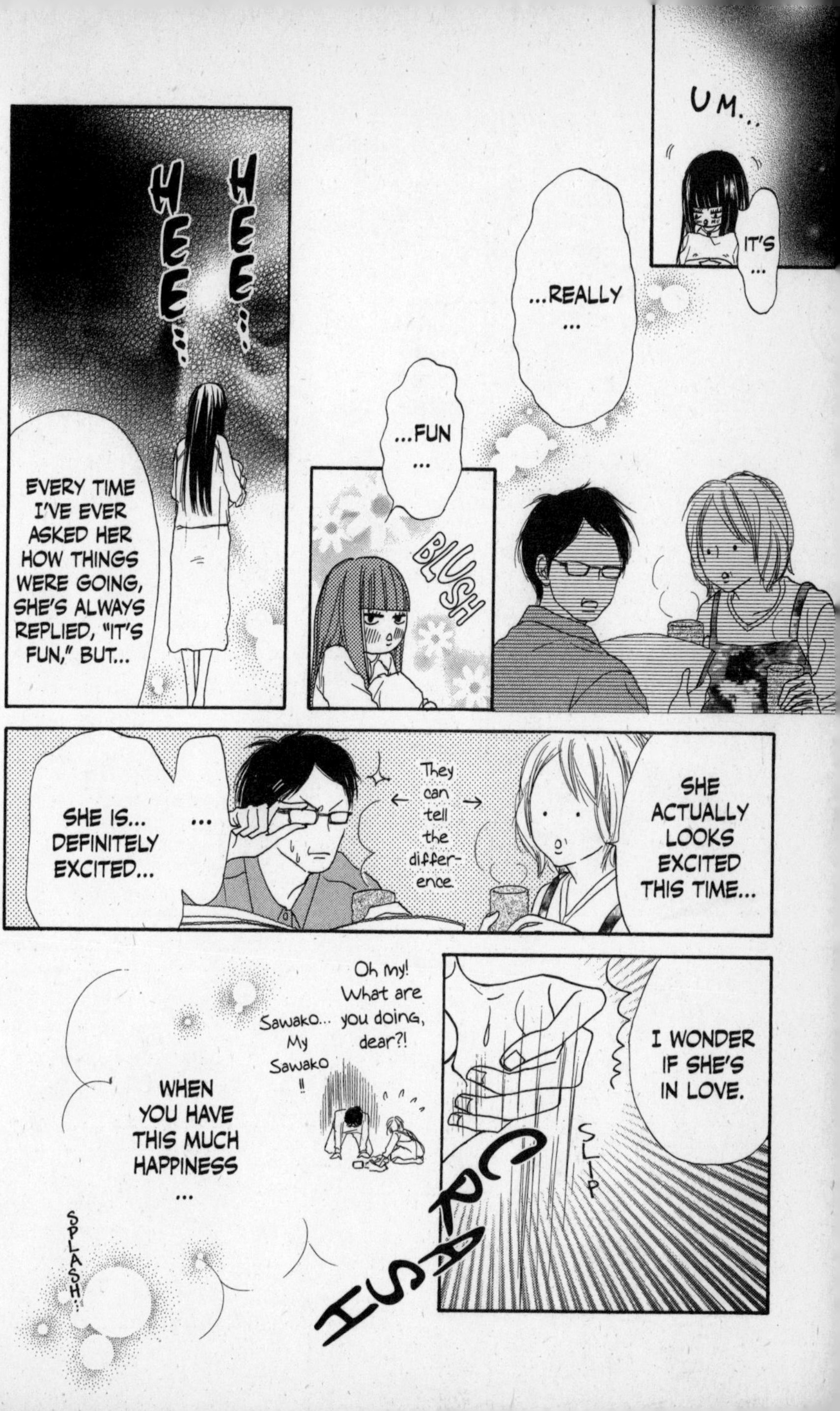
UM...
IT'S ...
...REALLY ...
...FUN ...
BLUSH
HEE... HEE...
EVERY TIME I'VE EVER ASKED HER HOW THINGS WERE GOING, SHE'S ALWAYS REPLIED, "IT'S FUN," BUT...
SHE ACTUALLY LOOKS EXCITED THIS TIME...
They can tell the difference.
SHE IS... DEFINITELY EXCITED...
...
I WONDER IF SHE'S IN LOVE.
SLIP
CRASH
Oh my! What are you doing, dear?!
Sawako... My Sawako!!
WHEN YOU HAVE THIS MUCH HAPPINESS ...
SPLASH!!

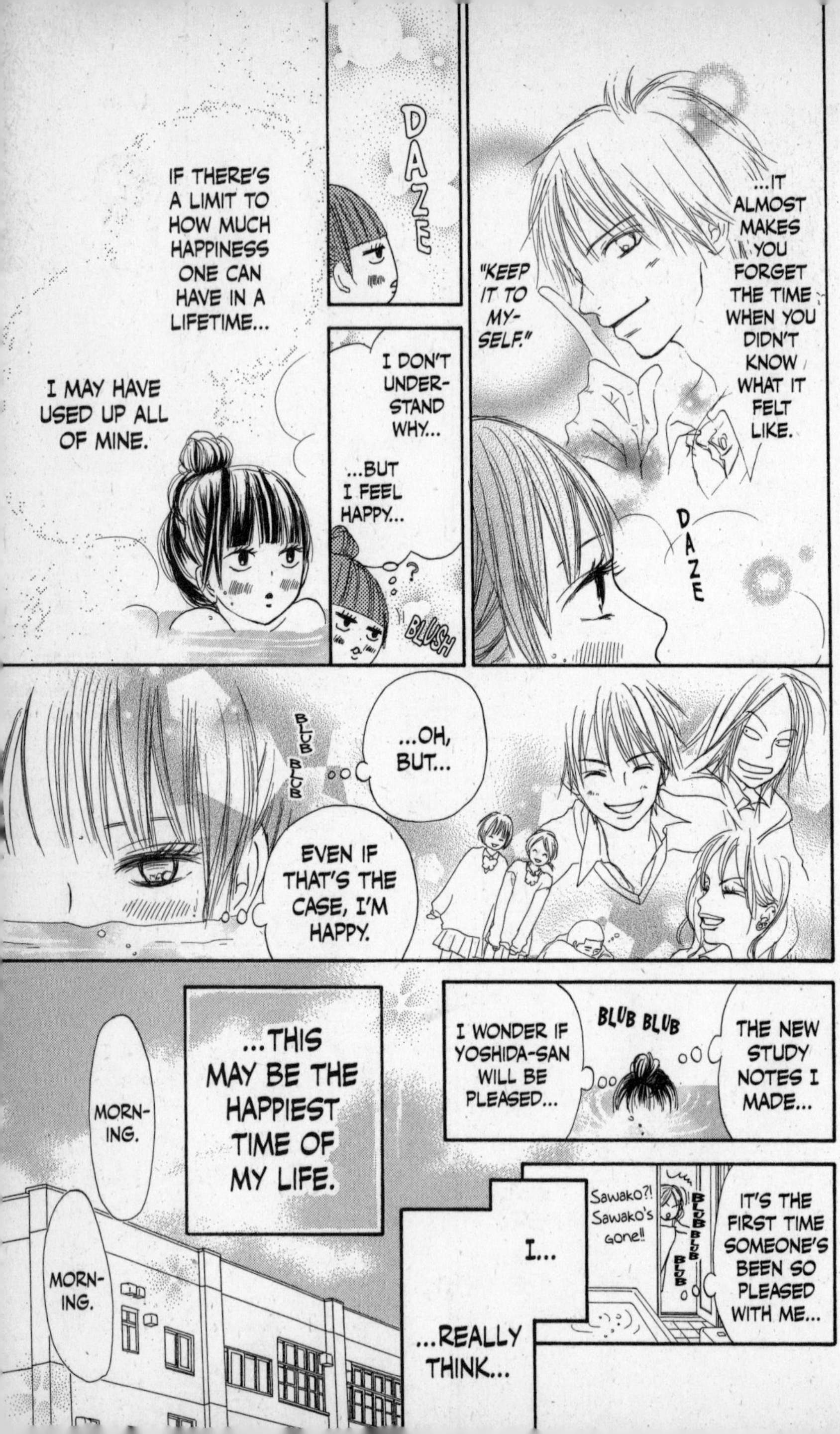
...IT ALMOST MAKES YOU FORGET THE TIME WHEN YOU DIDN'T KNOW WHAT IT FELT LIKE.
"KEEP IT TO MYSELF."
DAZE
DAZE
I DON'T UNDERSTAND WHY...
...BUT I FEEL HAPPY...
?
BLUSH
IF THERE'S A LIMIT TO HOW MUCH HAPPINESS ONE CAN HAVE IN A LIFETIME...
I MAY HAVE USED UP ALL OF MINE.
...OH, BUT...
BLUB BLUB
EVEN IF THAT'S THE CASE, I'M HAPPY.
THE NEW STUDY NOTES I MADE...
BLUB BLUB
I WONDER IF YOSHIDA-SAN WILL BE PLEASED...
IT'S THE FIRST TIME SOMEONE'S BEEN SO PLEASED WITH ME...
BLUB BLUB BLUB BLUB
Sawako?! Sawako's Gone!!
I...
...REALLY THINK...
...THIS MAY BE THE HAPPIEST TIME OF MY LIFE.
MORNING.
MORNING.

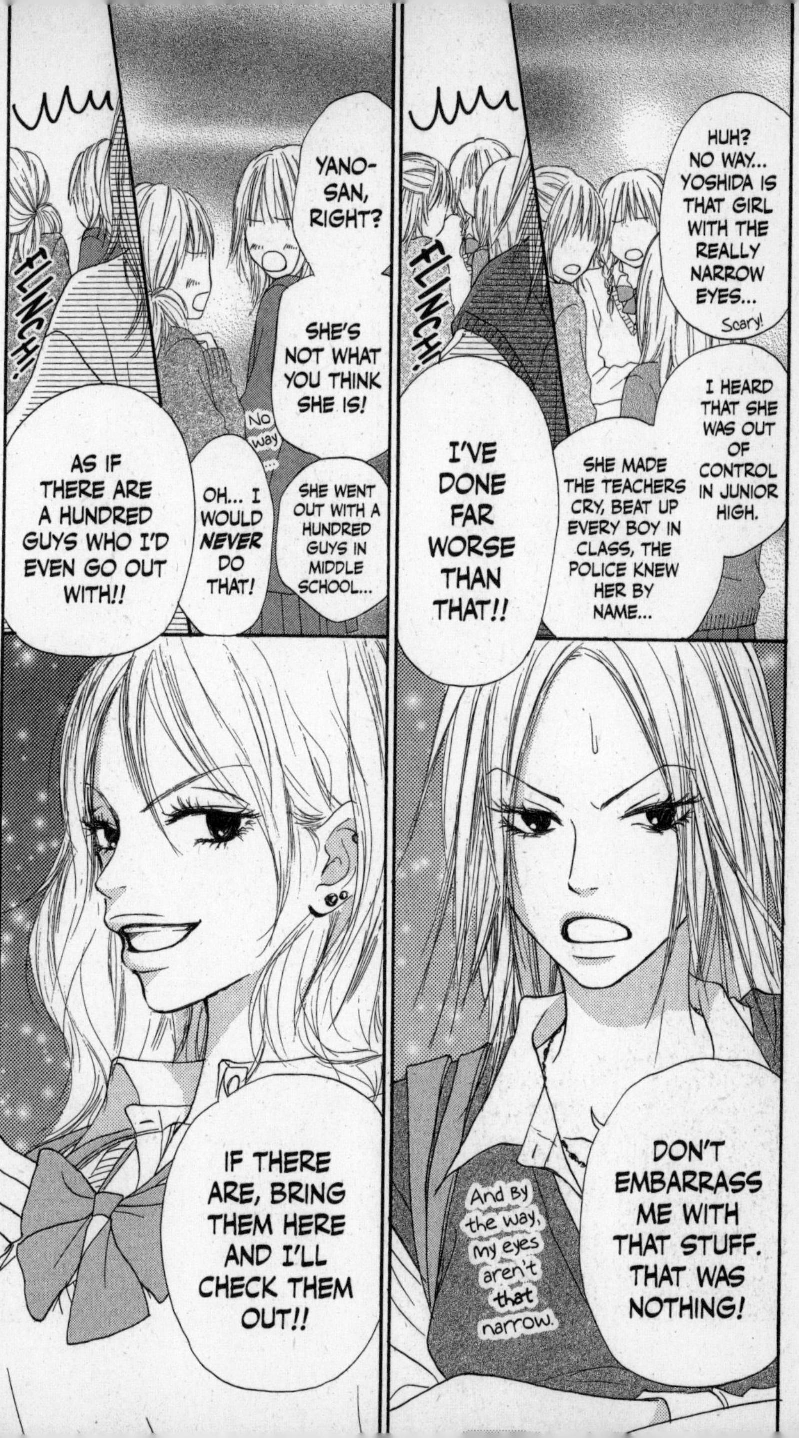
HUH? NO WAY... YOSHIDA IS THAT GIRL WITH THE REALLY NARROW EYES...
Scary!
I HEARD THAT SHE WAS OUT OF CONTROL IN JUNIOR HIGH.
SHE MADE THE TEACHERS CRY, BEAT UP EVERY BOY IN CLASS, THE POLICE KNEW HER BY NAME...
FLINCH!
I'VE DONE FAR WORSE THAN THAT!!
DON'T EMBARRASS ME WITH THAT STUFF. THAT WAS NOTHING!
And by the way, my eyes aren't *that* narrow.
YANO-SAN, RIGHT?
SHE'S NOT WHAT YOU THINK SHE IS!
No way...
SHE WENT OUT WITH A HUNDRED GUYS IN MIDDLE SCHOOL...
FLINCH!
OH... I WOULD ***NEVER*** DO THAT!
AS IF THERE ARE A HUNDRED GUYS WHO I'D EVEN GO OUT WITH!!
IF THERE ARE, BRING THEM HERE AND I'LL CHECK THEM OUT!!

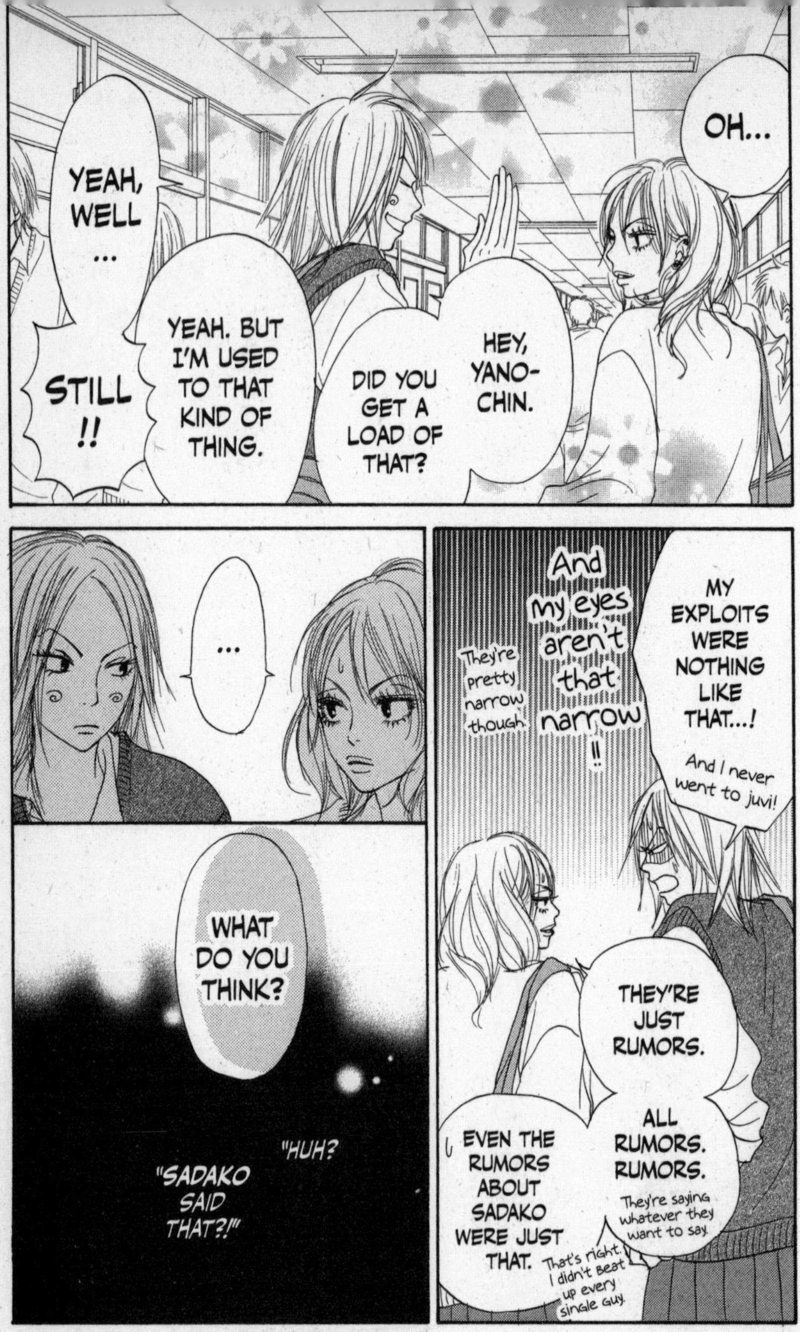
OH...
HEY, YANO-CHIN.
DID YOU GET A LOAD OF THAT?
YEAH. BUT I'M USED TO THAT KIND OF THING.
YEAH, WELL ...
STILL !!
MY EXPLOITS WERE NOTHING LIKE THAT...!
And I never went to juvi!
And my eyes aren't that narrow !!
They're pretty narrow though.
THEY'RE JUST RUMORS.
ALL RUMORS. RUMORS.
They're saying whatever they want to say.
EVEN THE RUMORS ABOUT SADAKO WERE JUST THAT.
That's right. I didn't beat up every single guy.
...
WHAT DO YOU THINK?
"HUH?
"SADAKO SAID THAT?!"

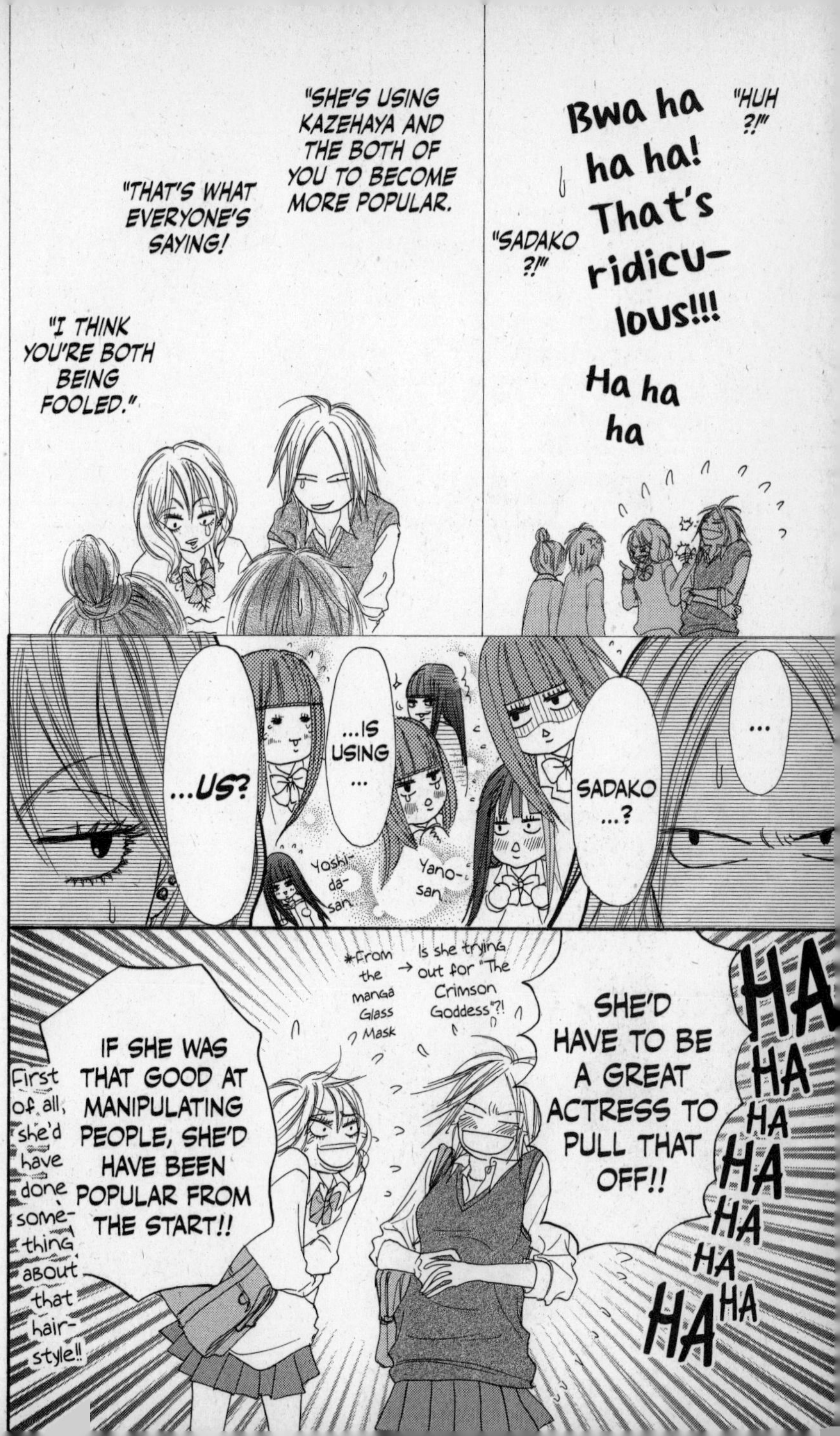

"HUH ?!"
Bwa ha ha ha! That's ridicu-lous!!!
"SADAKO ?!"
Ha ha ha
"SHE'S USING KAZEHAYA AND THE BOTH OF YOU TO BECOME MORE POPULAR.
"THAT'S WHAT EVERYONE'S SAYING!
"I THINK YOU'RE BOTH BEING FOOLED."
...
SADAKO ...?
...IS USING ...
...US?
Yano-san
Yoshi-da-san
HA HA HA HA HA HA HA HA HA
SHE'D HAVE TO BE A GREAT ACTRESS TO PULL THAT OFF!!
Is she trying out for "The Crimson Goddess"?!
*From the manga Glass Mask
IF SHE WAS THAT GOOD AT MANIPULATING PEOPLE, SHE'D HAVE BEEN POPULAR FROM THE START!!
First of all, she'd have done some-thing about that hair-style!!

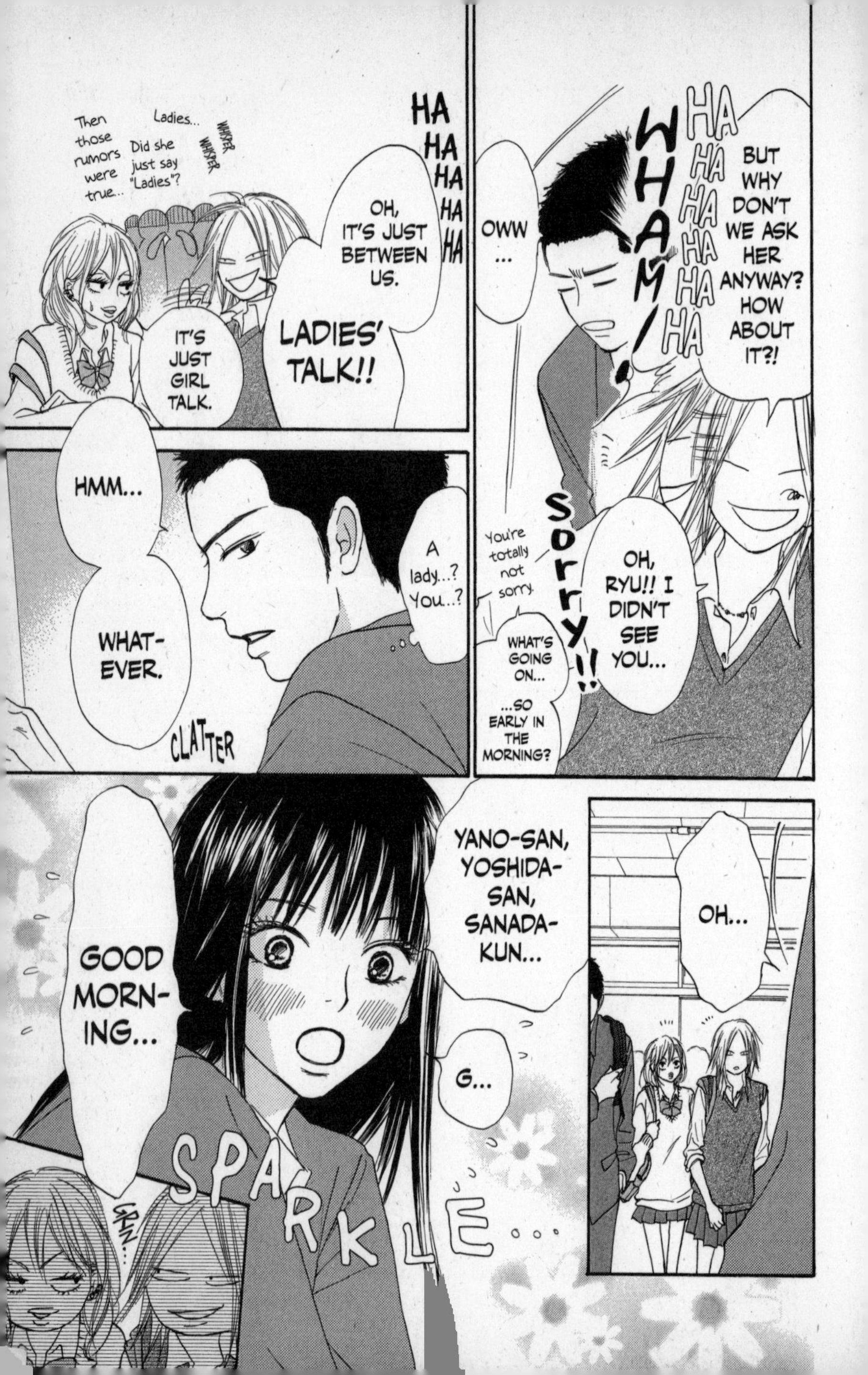
HA HA HA HA HA HA HA
BUT WHY DON'T WE ASK HER ANYWAY? HOW ABOUT IT?!
WHAM!
OWW...
OH, RYU!! I DIDN'T SEE YOU...
SORRY!!
You're totally not sorry.
WHAT'S GOING ON...
...SO EARLY IN THE MORNING?
HA HA HA HA HA
OH, IT'S JUST BETWEEN US.
LADIES' TALK!!
IT'S JUST GIRL TALK.
Ladies... Did she just say "Ladies"?
WHISPER WHISPER
Then those rumors were true...
A lady...? You...?
HMM...
WHAT-EVER.
CLATTER
OH...
YANO-SAN, YOSHIDA-SAN, SANADA-KUN...
G...
GOOD MORN-ING...
SPARKLE...
GRIN...

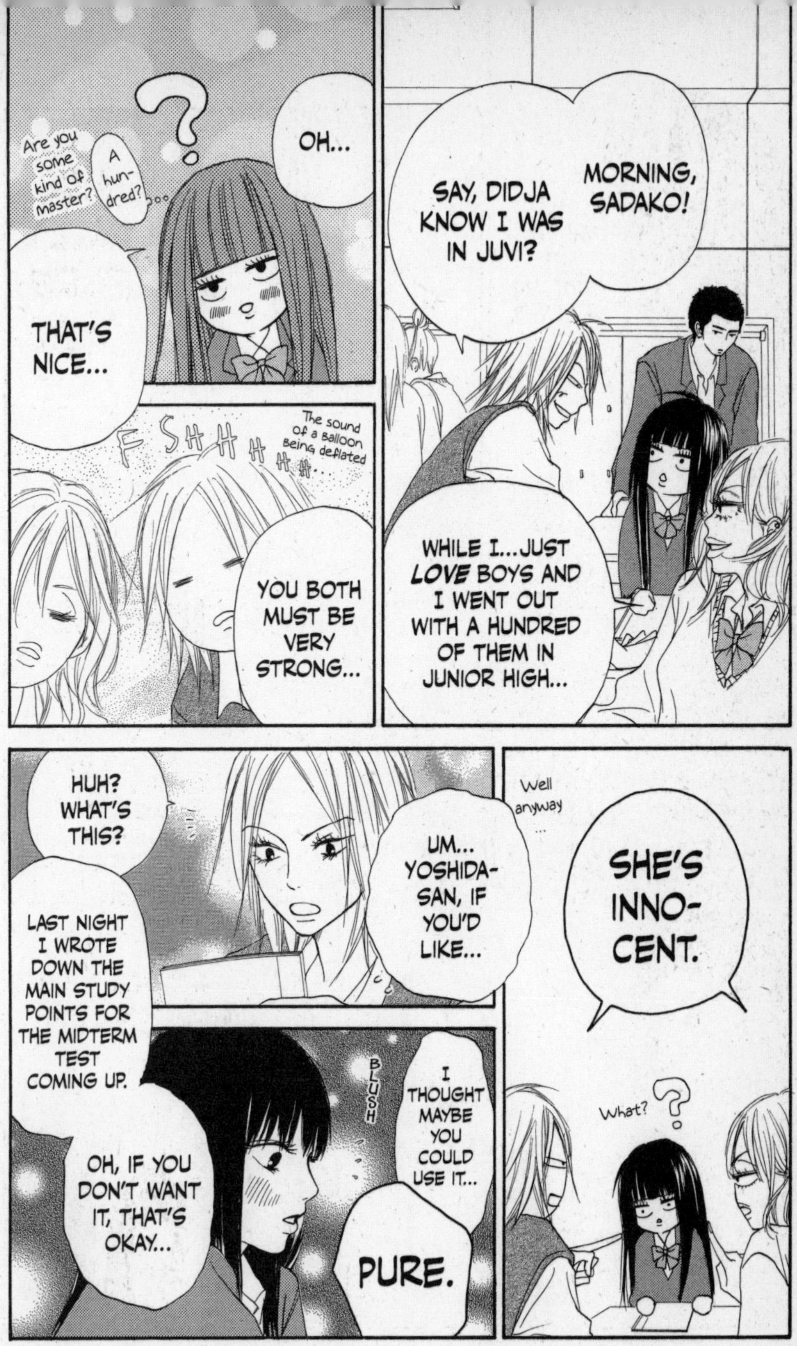
MORNING, SADAKO!
SAY, DIDJA KNOW I WAS IN JUVI?
WHILE I...JUST *LOVE* BOYS AND I WENT OUT WITH A HUNDRED OF THEM IN JUNIOR HIGH...
OH...
A hundred?...
Are you some kind of master?
THAT'S NICE...
FSHHHHH...
The sound of a Balloon Being deflated
YOU BOTH MUST BE VERY STRONG...
SHE'S INNO-CENT.
Well anyway...
What?
UM... YOSHIDA-SAN, IF YOU'D LIKE...
HUH? WHAT'S THIS?
LAST NIGHT I WROTE DOWN THE MAIN STUDY POINTS FOR THE MIDTERM TEST COMING UP.
I THOUGHT MAYBE YOU COULD USE IT...
BLUSH
OH, IF YOU DON'T WANT IT, THAT'S OKAY...
PURE.

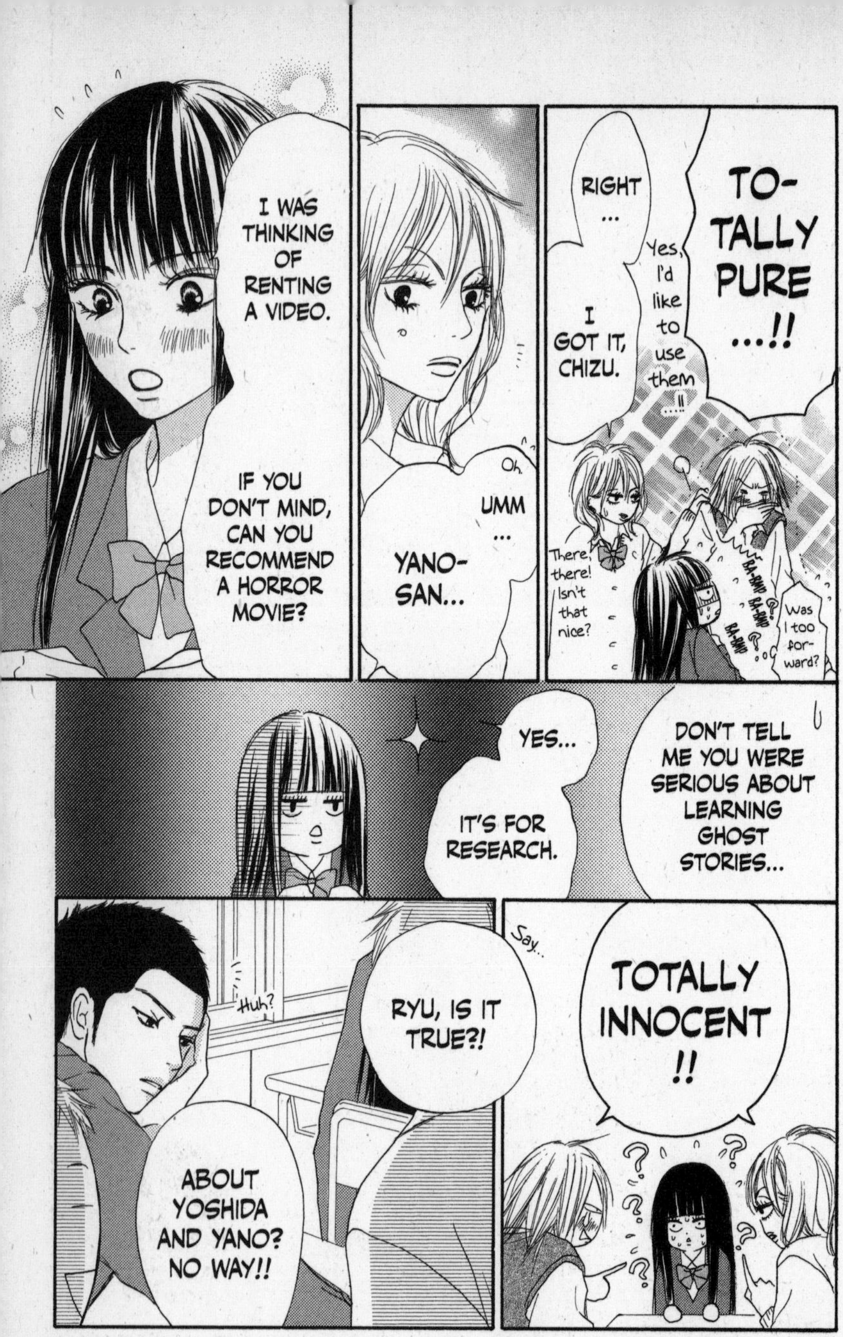
TO-TALLY PURE ...!!
Yes, I'd like to use them ...!!
RIGHT ... I GOT IT, CHIZU.
Was I too for-ward?
BA-BMP BA-BMP BA-BMP
There, there! Isn't that nice?
Oh.
UMM ...
YANO-SAN...
I WAS THINKING OF RENTING A VIDEO.
IF YOU DON'T MIND, CAN YOU RECOMMEND A HORROR MOVIE?
DON'T TELL ME YOU WERE SERIOUS ABOUT LEARNING GHOST STORIES...
YES...
IT'S FOR RESEARCH.
TOTALLY INNOCENT !!
Say...
RYU, IS IT TRUE?!
Huh?
ABOUT YOSHIDA AND YANO? NO WAY!!

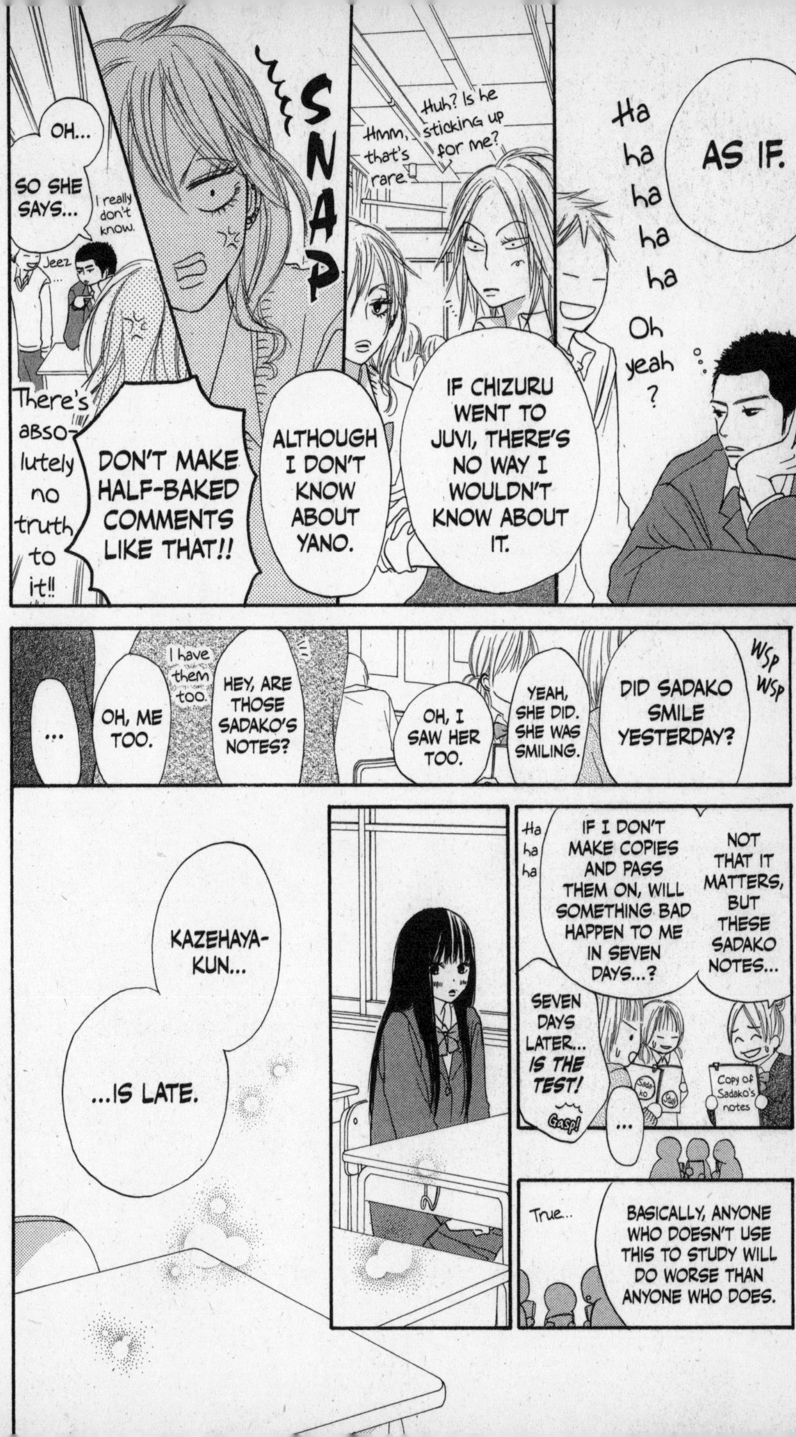
Ha ha ha ha ha
AS IF.
Oh yeah ?
Huh? Is he sticking up for me?
Hmm, that's rare.
IF CHIZURU WENT TO JUVI, THERE'S NO WAY I WOULDN'T KNOW ABOUT IT.
ALTHOUGH I DON'T KNOW ABOUT YANO.
SNAP
OH...
SO SHE SAYS...
I really don't know.
Jeez...
DON'T MAKE HALF-BAKED COMMENTS LIKE THAT!!
There's absolutely no truth to it!!
WSP WSP
DID SADAKO SMILE YESTERDAY?
YEAH, SHE DID. SHE WAS SMILING.
OH, I SAW HER TOO.
HEY, ARE THOSE SADAKO'S NOTES?
I have them too.
OH, ME TOO.
...
NOT THAT IT MATTERS, BUT THESE SADAKO NOTES...
IF I DON'T MAKE COPIES AND PASS THEM ON, WILL SOMETHING BAD HAPPEN TO ME IN SEVEN DAYS...?
Ha ha ha
Copy of Sadako's notes
SEVEN DAYS LATER... IS THE TEST!
Gasp!
...
BASICALLY, ANYONE WHO DOESN'T USE THIS TO STUDY WILL DO WORSE THAN ANYONE WHO DOES.
True...
KAZEHAYA-KUN...
...IS LATE.

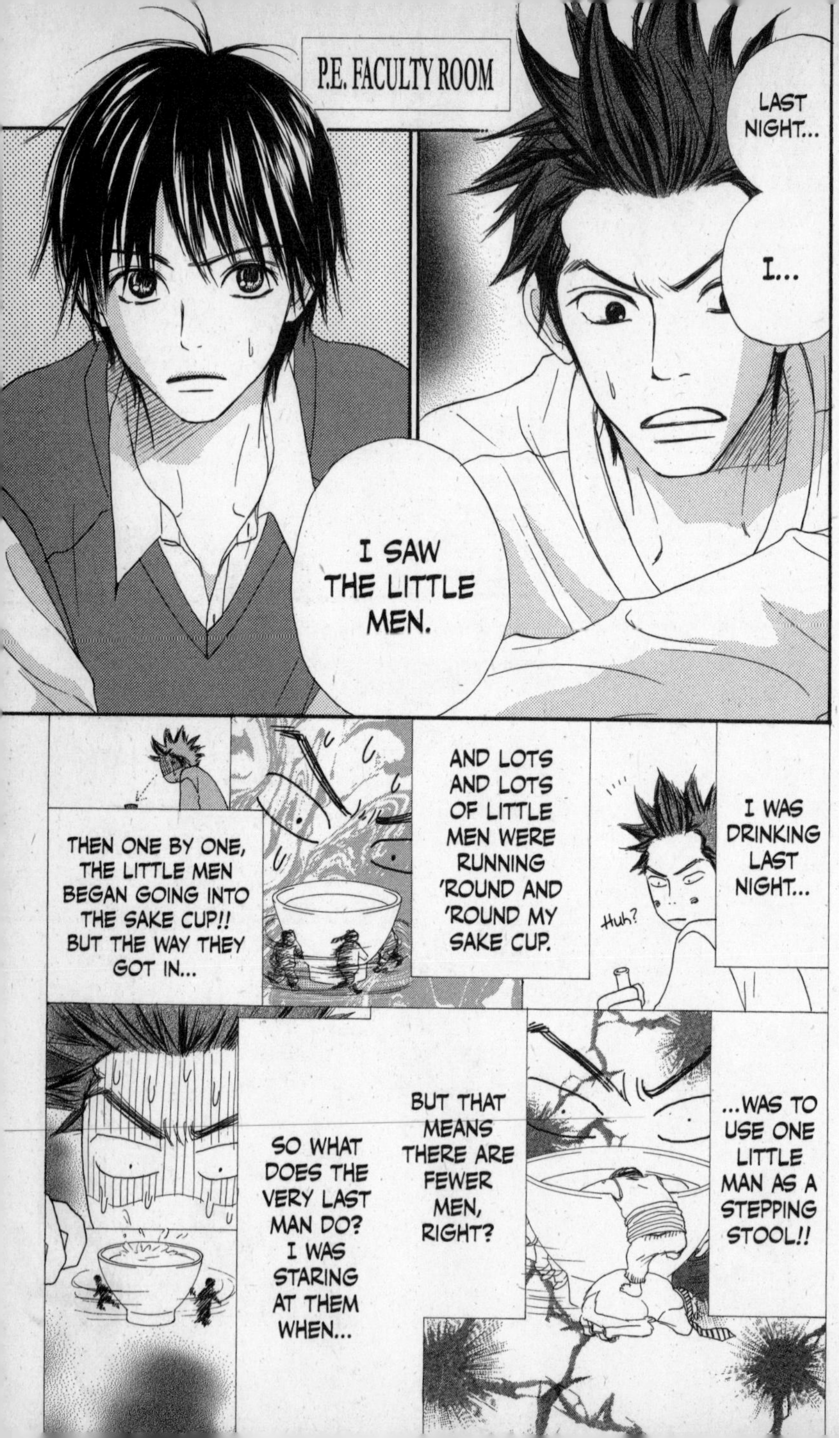
P.E. FACULTY ROOM
LAST NIGHT...
I...
I SAW THE LITTLE MEN.
I WAS DRINKING LAST NIGHT...
Huh?
AND LOTS AND LOTS OF LITTLE MEN WERE RUNNING 'ROUND AND 'ROUND MY SAKE CUP.
THEN ONE BY ONE, THE LITTLE MEN BEGAN GOING INTO THE SAKE CUP!! BUT THE WAY THEY GOT IN...
...WAS TO USE ONE LITTLE MAN AS A STEPPING STOOL!!
BUT THAT MEANS THERE ARE FEWER MEN, RIGHT?
SO WHAT DOES THE VERY LAST MAN DO? I WAS STARING AT THEM WHEN...

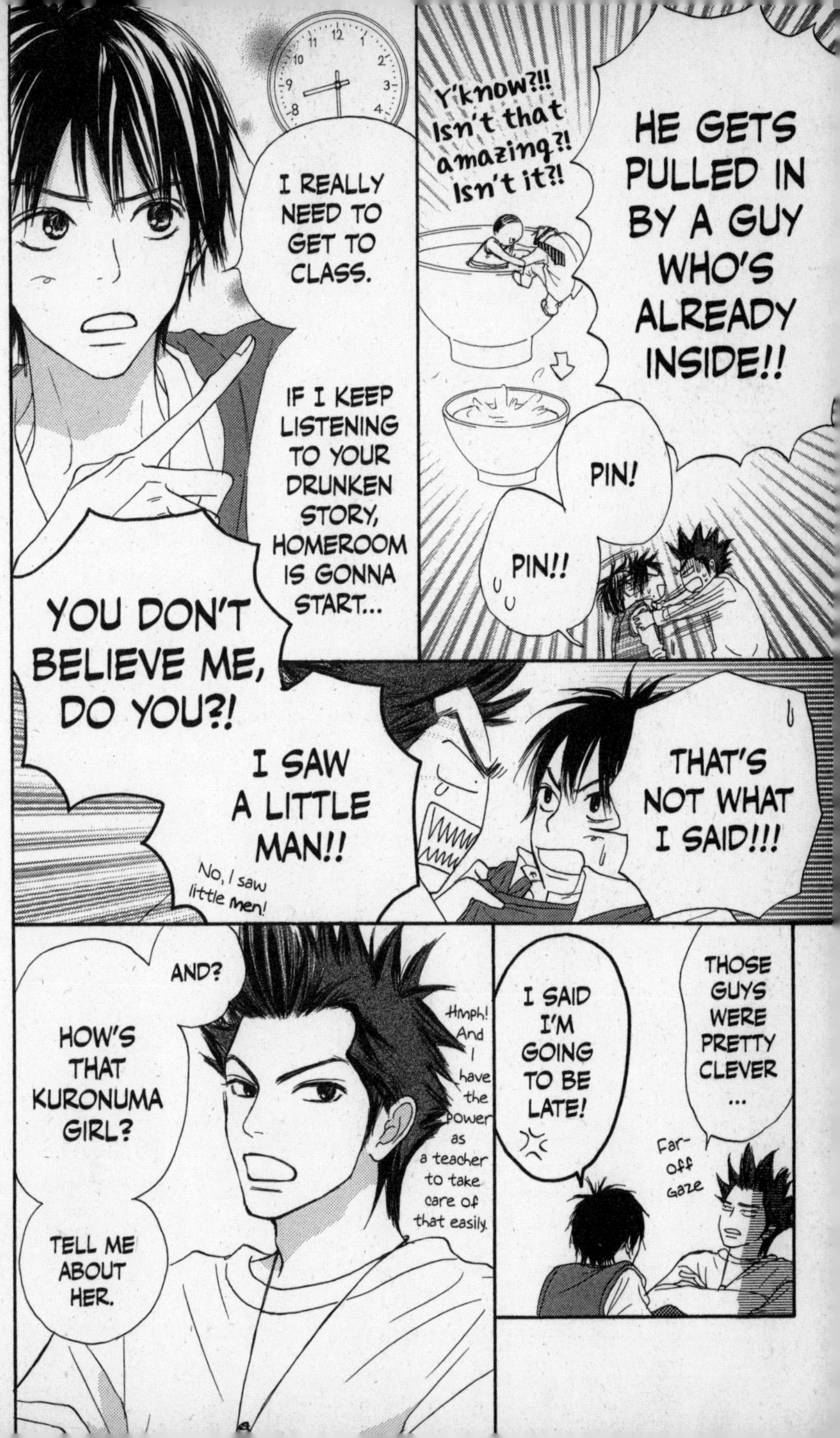
Y'know?!! Isn't that amazing?! Isn't it?!
HE GETS PULLED IN BY A GUY WHO'S ALREADY INSIDE!!
PIN!
PIN!!
I REALLY NEED TO GET TO CLASS.
IF I KEEP LISTENING TO YOUR DRUNKEN STORY, HOMEROOM IS GONNA START...
YOU DON'T BELIEVE ME, DO YOU?!
THAT'S NOT WHAT I SAID!!!
I SAW A LITTLE MAN!!
No, I saw little men!
THOSE GUYS WERE PRETTY CLEVER ...
Far-off Gaze
I SAID I'M GOING TO BE LATE!
Hmph! And I have the power as a teacher to take care of that easily.
AND?
HOW'S THAT KURONUMA GIRL?
TELL ME ABOUT HER.

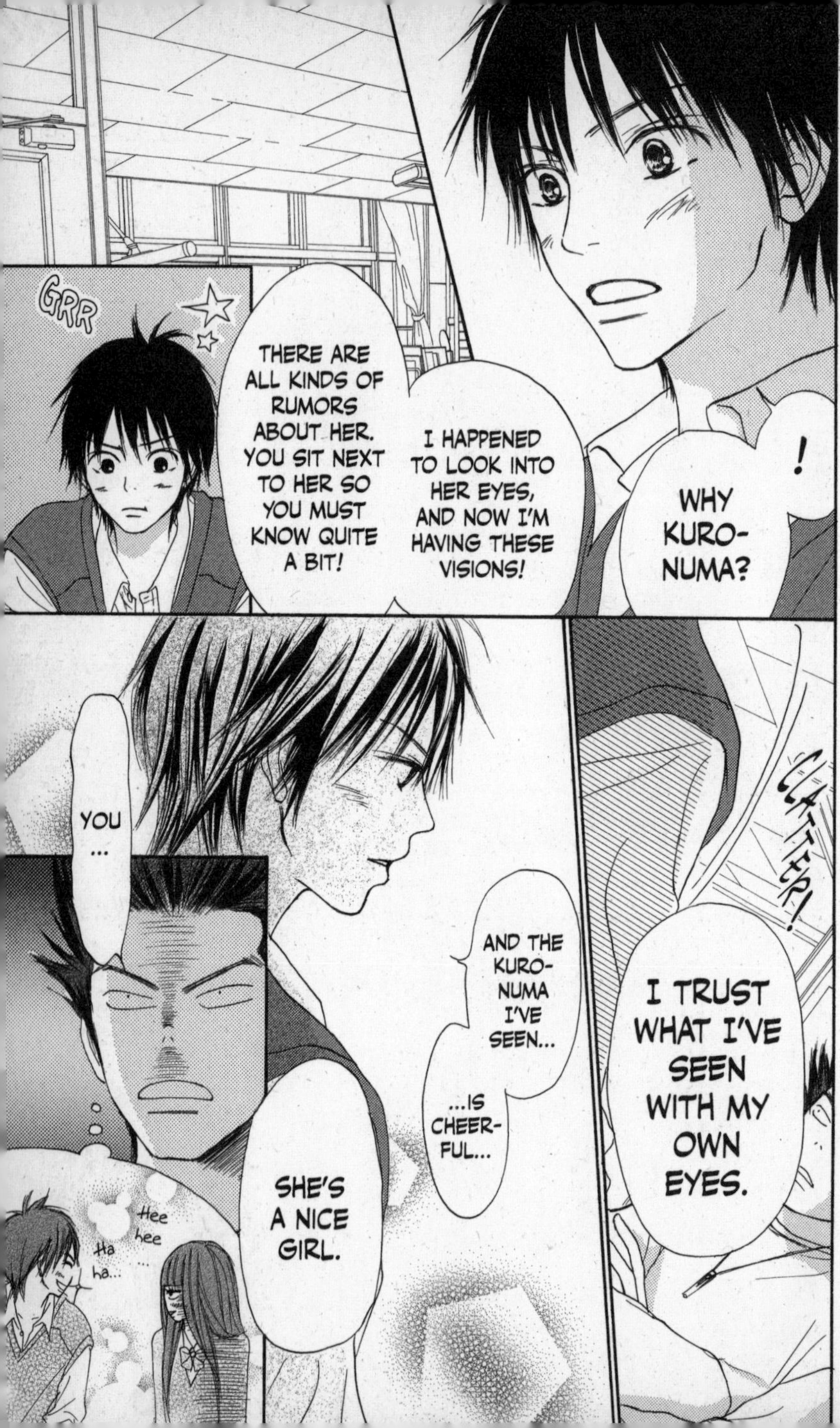
!
WHY KURO-NUMA?
I HAPPENED TO LOOK INTO HER EYES, AND NOW I'M HAVING THESE VISIONS!
THERE ARE ALL KINDS OF RUMORS ABOUT HER. YOU SIT NEXT TO HER SO YOU MUST KNOW QUITE A BIT!
GRR
CLATTER!
I TRUST WHAT I'VE SEEN WITH MY OWN EYES.
AND THE KURO-NUMA I'VE SEEN...
...IS CHEER-FUL...
SHE'S A NICE GIRL.
YOU ...
Hee hee ...
Ha ha...

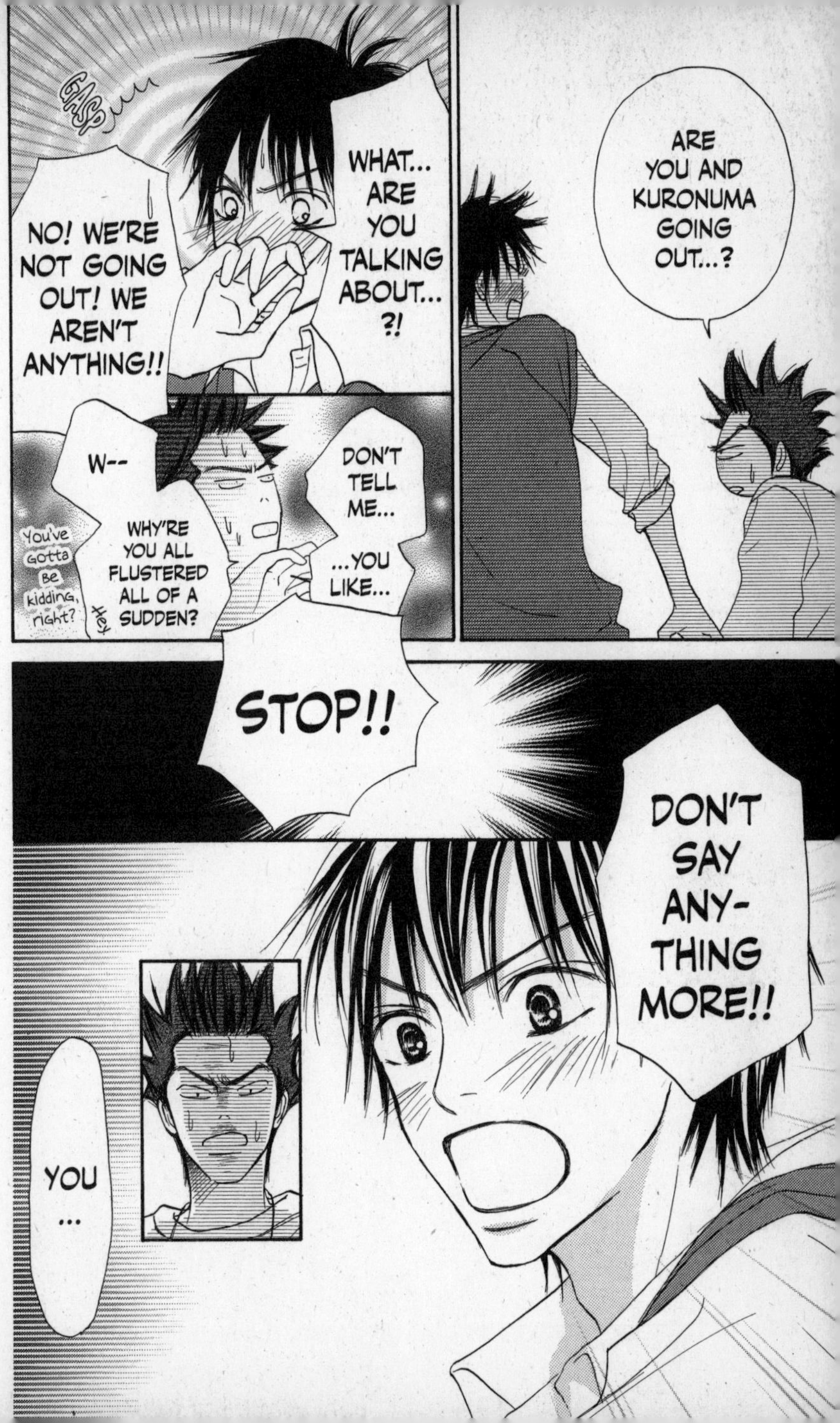
ARE YOU AND KURONUMA GOING OUT...?
WHAT... ARE YOU TALKING ABOUT...?!
GASP
NO! WE'RE NOT GOING OUT! WE AREN'T ANYTHING!!
DON'T TELL ME...
...YOU LIKE...
W--
WHY'RE YOU ALL FLUSTERED ALL OF A SUDDEN?
Hey
You've gotta be kidding, right?
STOP!!
DON'T SAY ANY-THING MORE!!
YOU ...

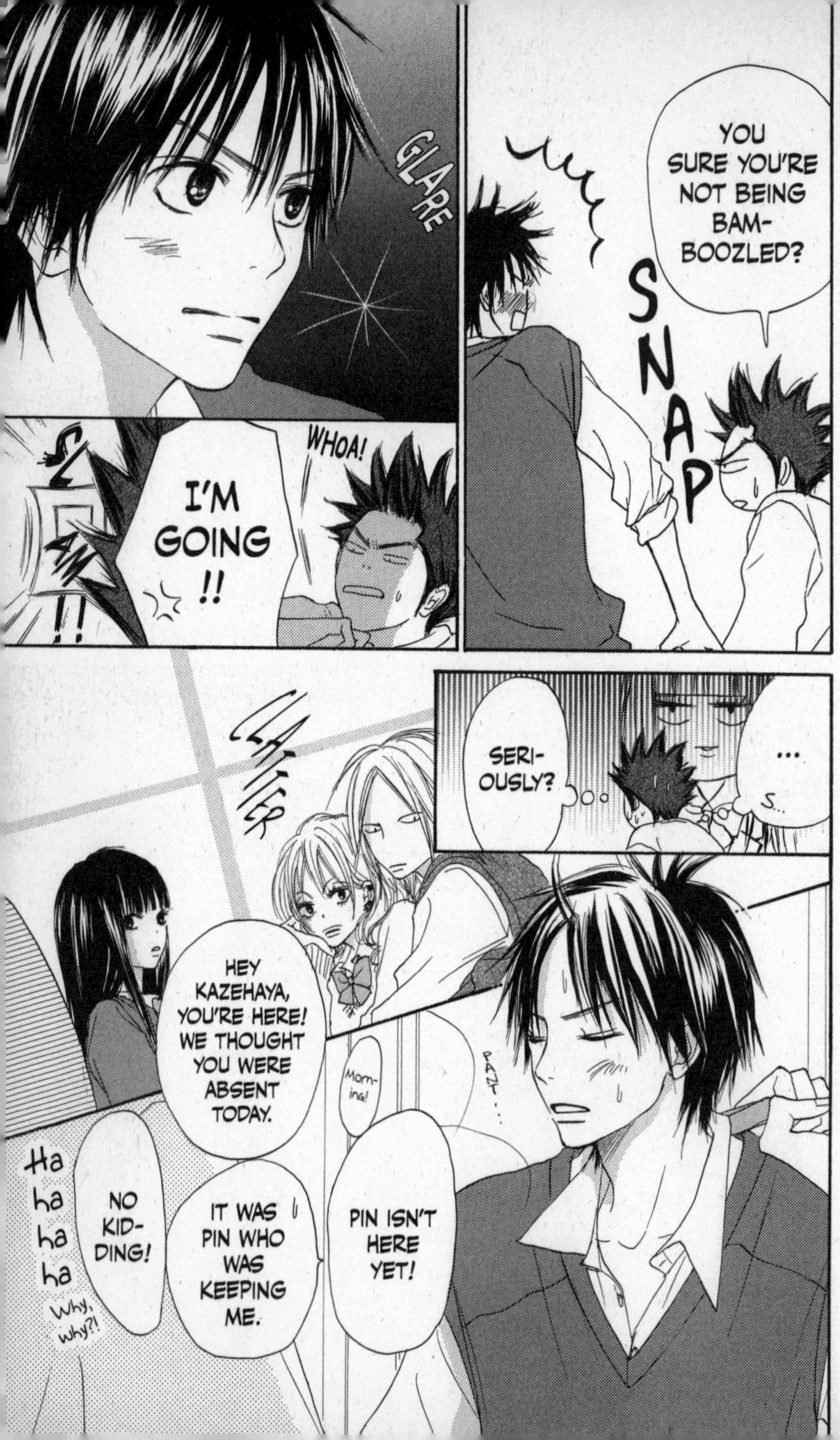
YOU SURE YOU'RE NOT BEING BAM-BOOZLED?
SNAP
GLARE
WHOA!
I'M GOING!!
SLAM!!
...
S...
SERI-OUSLY?
CHATTER
PIN ISN'T HERE YET!
PANT...
Morn-ing!
HEY KAZEHAYA, YOU'RE HERE! WE THOUGHT YOU WERE ABSENT TODAY.
IT WAS PIN WHO WAS KEEPING ME.
NO KID-DING!
Ha ha ha ha
Why, why?!

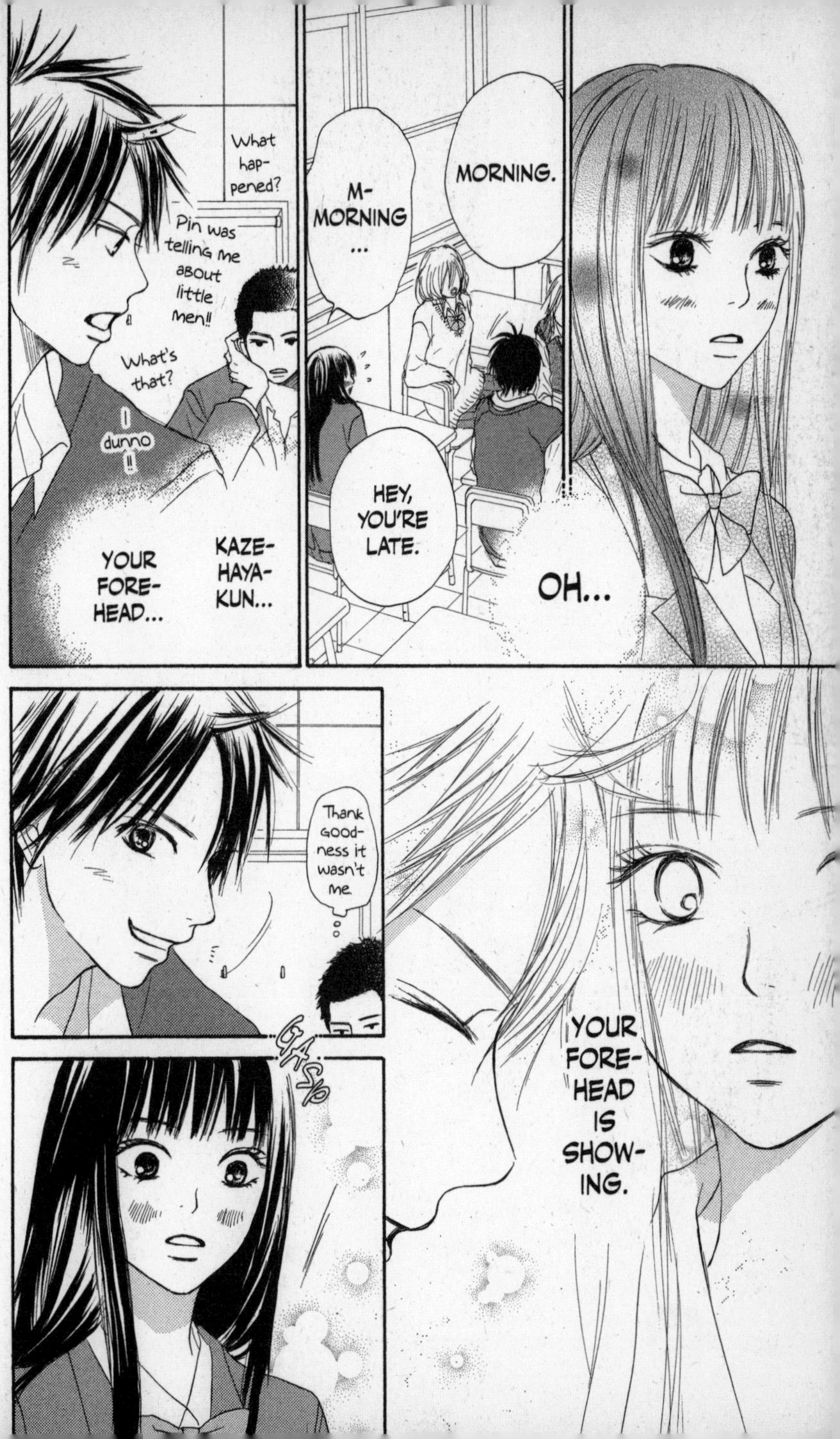
OH...
MORNING.
M-MORNING...
HEY, YOU'RE LATE.
What happened?
Pin was telling me about little men!!
What's that?
I dunno!!
KAZE-HAYA-KUN...
YOUR FORE-HEAD...
YOUR FORE-HEAD IS SHOW-ING.
Thank good-ness it wasn't me.
GASP

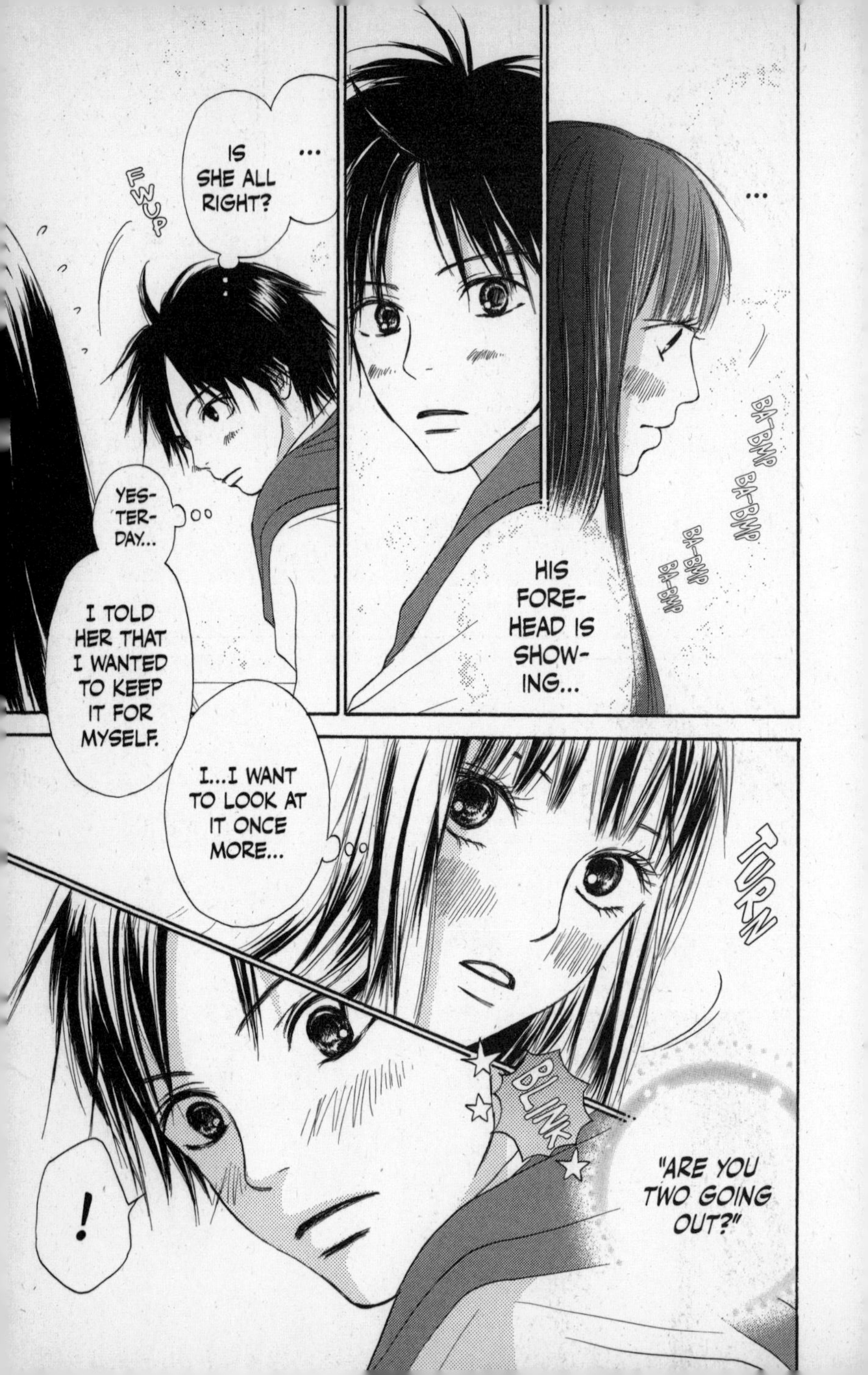
...
BA-BMP BA-BMP
BA-BMP BA-BMP
HIS FORE-HEAD IS SHOW-ING...
...
IS SHE ALL RIGHT?
FWUP
YES-TER-DAY...
I TOLD HER THAT I WANTED TO KEEP IT FOR MYSELF.
TURN
"ARE YOU TWO GOING OUT?"
BLINK
I...I WANT TO LOOK AT IT ONCE MORE...
!

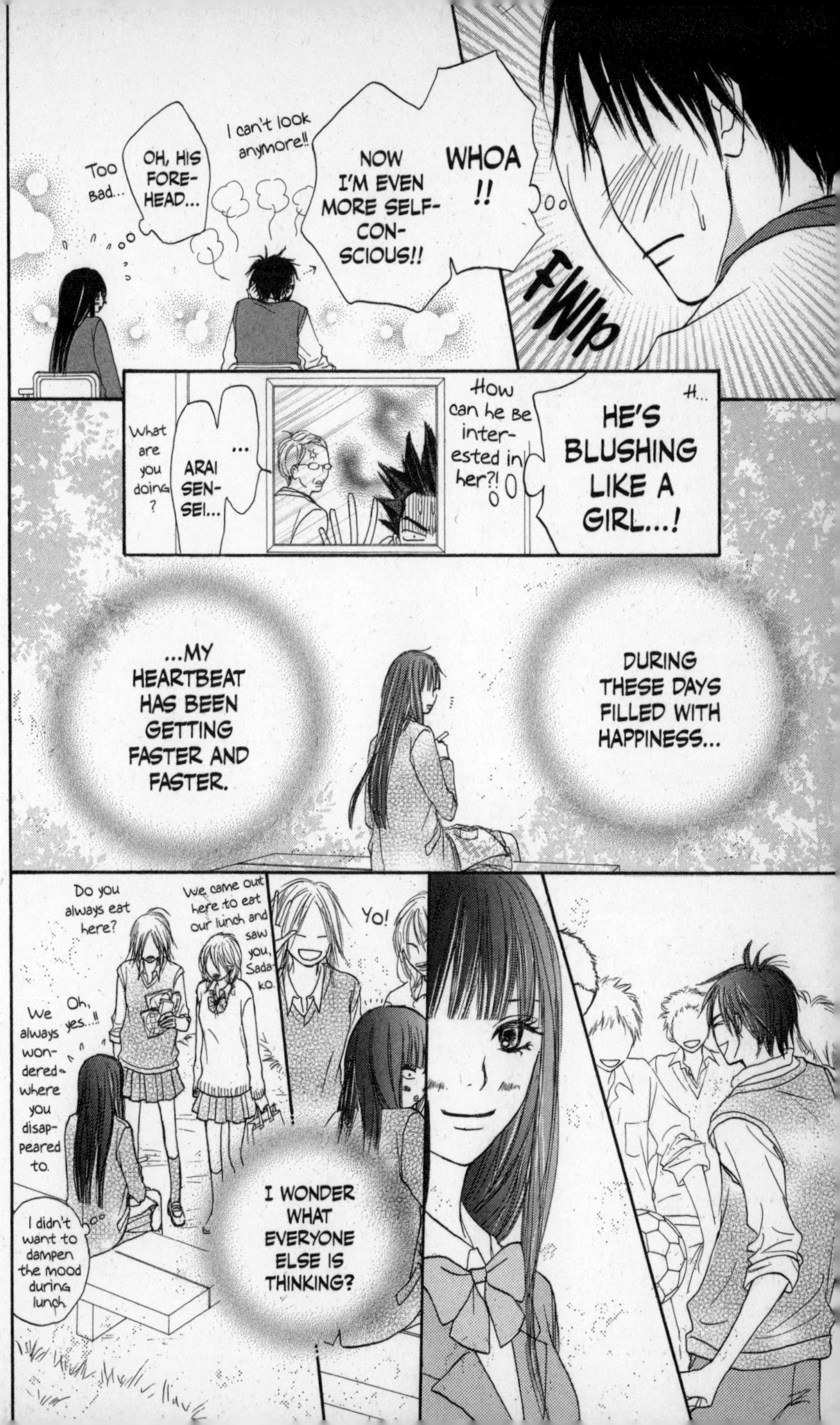
WHOA!!
NOW I'M EVEN MORE SELF-CONSCIOUS!!
FWIP
I can't look anymore!!
OH, HIS FOREHEAD...
Too bad...
H...
HE'S BLUSHING LIKE A GIRL...!
How can he be interested in her?!
ARAI SENSEI...
...
What are you doing?
DURING THESE DAYS FILLED WITH HAPPINESS...
...MY HEARTBEAT HAS BEEN GETTING FASTER AND FASTER.
I WONDER WHAT EVERYONE ELSE IS THINKING?
Yo!
We came out here to eat our lunch and saw you, Sadako.
Do you always eat here?
Oh, yes...!!
We always wondered where you disappeared to.
I didn't want to dampen the mood during lunch.

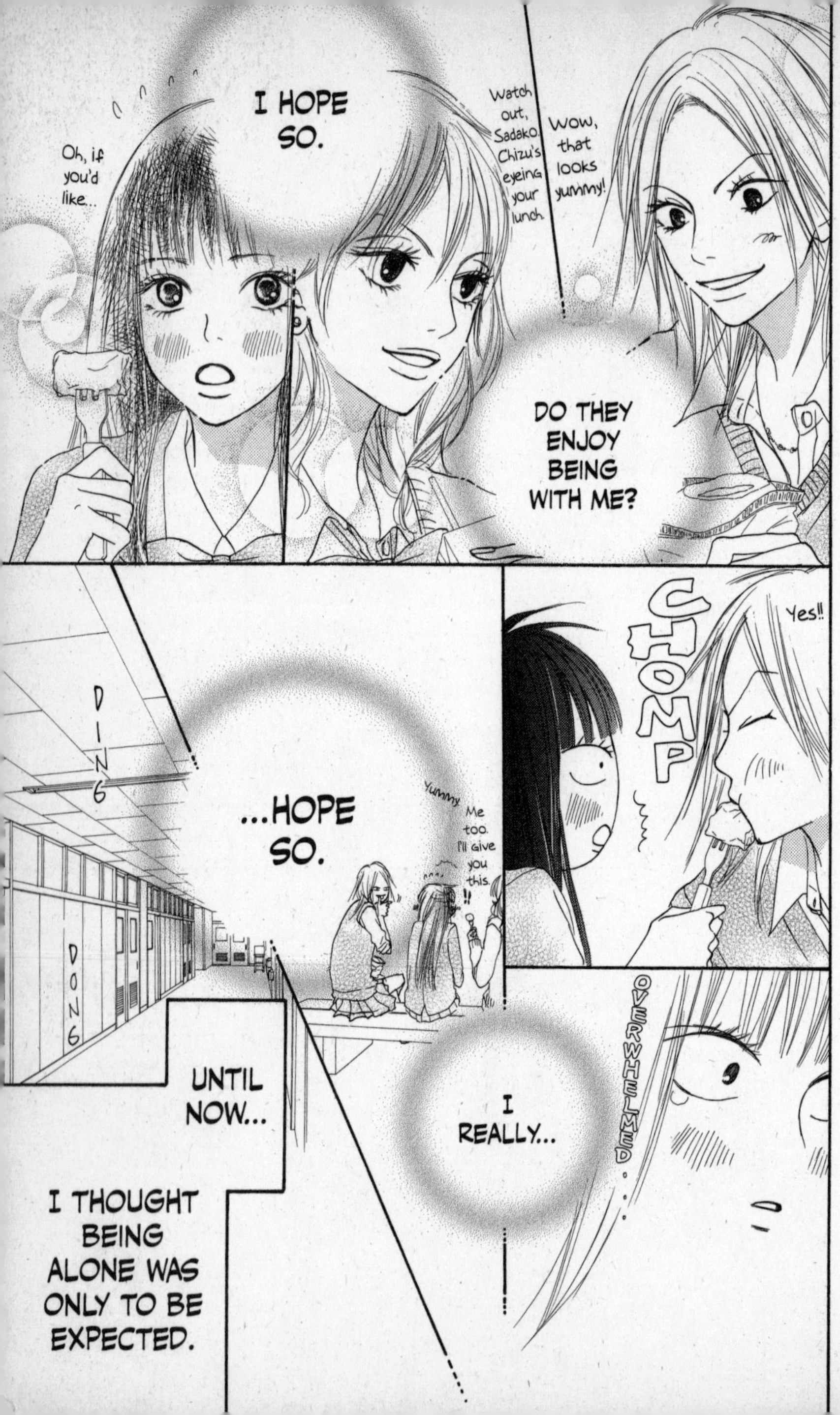
Wow, that looks yummy!
Watch out, Sadako. Chizu's eyeing your lunch.
DO THEY ENJOY BEING WITH ME?
I HOPE SO.
Oh, if you'd like...
CHOMP
Yes!!
...HOPE SO.
Yummy
Me too. I'll give you this.
!!
DING
DONG
OVERWHELMED...
I REALLY...
UNTIL NOW...
I THOUGHT BEING ALONE WAS ONLY TO BE EXPECTED.

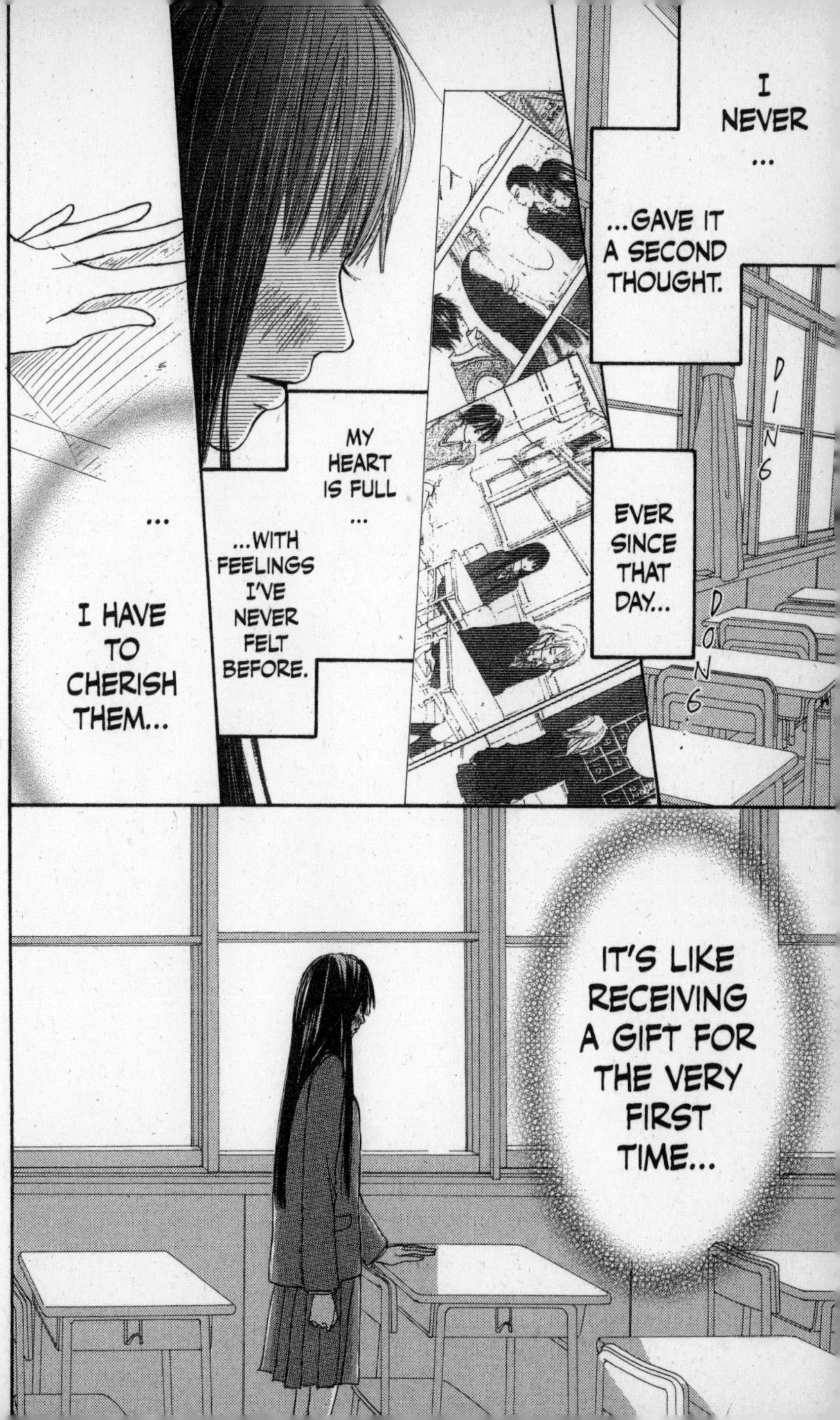
I NEVER ...
...GAVE IT A SECOND THOUGHT.
EVER SINCE THAT DAY...
DING
DONG
MY HEART IS FULL ...
...WITH FEELINGS I'VE NEVER FELT BEFORE.
...
I HAVE TO CHERISH THEM...
IT'S LIKE RECEIVING A GIFT FOR THE VERY FIRST TIME...

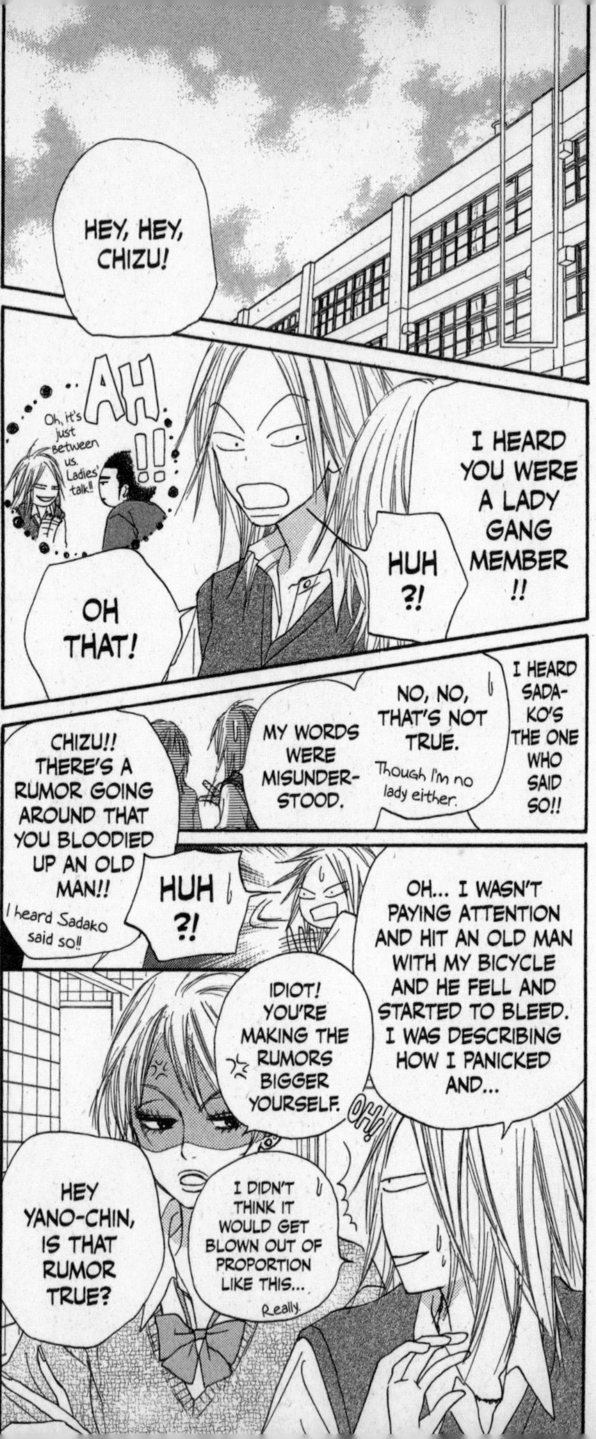
HEY, HEY, CHIZU!
I HEARD YOU WERE A LADY GANG MEMBER!!
HUH ?!
AH !!
Oh, it's just between us. Ladies' talk!!
OH THAT!
I HEARD SADAKO'S THE ONE WHO SAID SO!!
NO, NO, THAT'S NOT TRUE.
Though I'm no lady either.
MY WORDS WERE MISUNDERSTOOD.
CHIZU!! THERE'S A RUMOR GOING AROUND THAT YOU BLOODIED UP AN OLD MAN!!
I heard Sadako said so!!
OH... I WASN'T PAYING ATTENTION AND HIT AN OLD MAN WITH MY BICYCLE AND HE FELL AND STARTED TO BLEED. I WAS DESCRIBING HOW I PANICKED AND...
HUH ?!
IDIOT! YOU'RE MAKING THE RUMORS BIGGER YOURSELF.
OH!
I DIDN'T THINK IT WOULD GET BLOWN OUT OF PROPORTION LIKE THIS...
Really.
HEY YANO-CHIN, IS THAT RUMOR TRUE?

KARUPIN on JAPAN 1

Hello.
How are you?
Shiina here.
This is volume 2!
I'm so happy about it!

Yay!

By the way, between the first and second volumes, I cut my hair.

(Comparison from volume 1)

Long hair ⟷ Short hair ← Volume 2

For beauty? Uh-uh...
For fashion? Uh-uh...
It's only because it's easier to wash my hair!!
I'm such an old biddy...!!

Also, it's so hot, I don't want to use a hair dryer. You can wash short hair so quickly and it dries so fast!!

Wooo Ahhh.

You can dry it with a fan.
Huh? Are you saying no one cares about my hair?
Well, that's true.
Sorry!!

Popsicles are so yummy.

Everyone loves popsicles, right?
Huh? Who cares? Seriously?!
(Just play-acting by myself.)

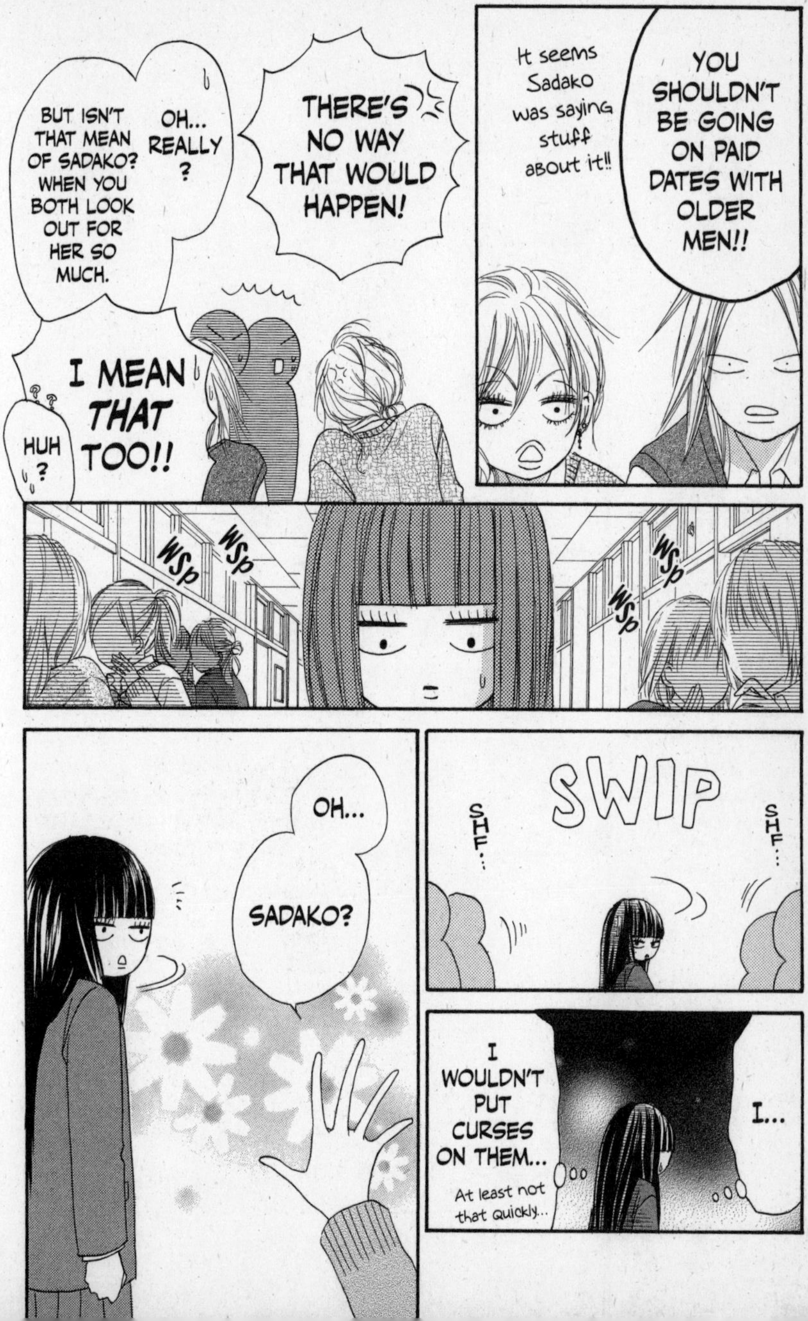
YOU SHOULDN'T BE GOING ON PAID DATES WITH OLDER MEN!!
It seems Sadako was saying stuff about it!!
THERE'S NO WAY THAT WOULD HAPPEN!
OH... REALLY?
BUT ISN'T THAT MEAN OF SADAKO? WHEN YOU BOTH LOOK OUT FOR HER SO MUCH.
I MEAN *THAT* TOO!!
HUH?
WSP
WSP
WSP
WSP
SHF...
SWIP
SHF...
I...
I WOULDN'T PUT CURSES ON THEM...
At least not that quickly...
OH...
SADAKO?

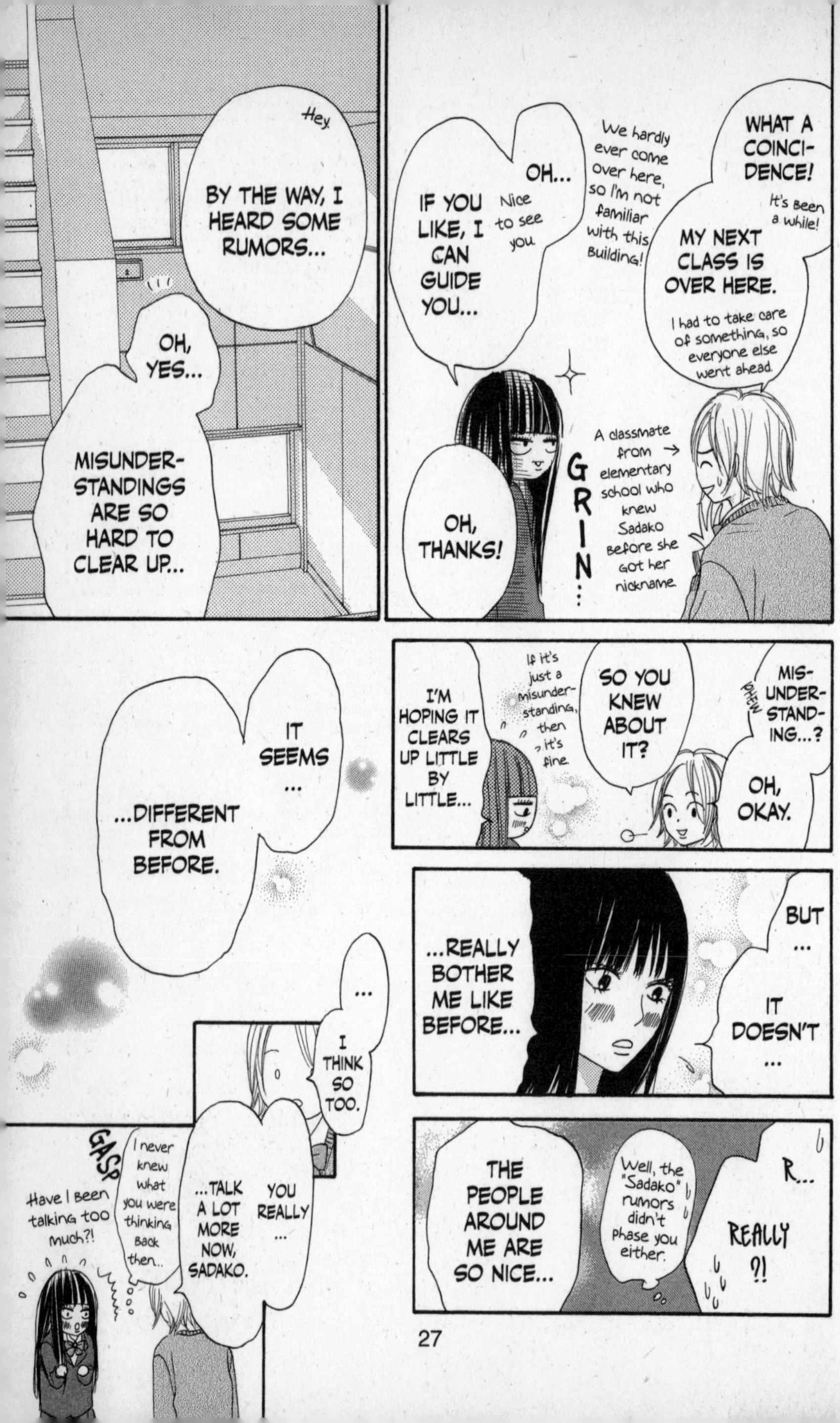
WHAT A COINCIDENCE!
It's been a while!
MY NEXT CLASS IS OVER HERE.
I had to take care of something, so everyone else went ahead.
We hardly ever come over here, so I'm not familiar with this building!
OH... IF YOU LIKE, I CAN GUIDE YOU...
Nice to see you.
A classmate from elementary school who knew Sadako before she got her nickname →
GRIN...
OH, THANKS!
Hey.
BY THE WAY, I HEARD SOME RUMORS...
OH, YES...
MISUNDERSTANDINGS ARE SO HARD TO CLEAR UP...
MISUNDERSTANDING...?
PHEW
OH, OKAY.
SO YOU KNEW ABOUT IT?
If it's just a misunderstanding, then it's fine.
I'M HOPING IT CLEARS UP LITTLE BY LITTLE...
BUT... IT DOESN'T...
...REALLY BOTHER ME LIKE BEFORE...
R... REALLY?!
Well, the "Sadako" rumors didn't phase you either.
THE PEOPLE AROUND ME ARE SO NICE...
IT SEEMS...
...DIFFERENT FROM BEFORE.
...
I THINK SO TOO.
YOU REALLY...
...TALK A LOT MORE NOW, SADAKO.
I never knew what you were thinking back then...
GASP
Have I been talking too much?!

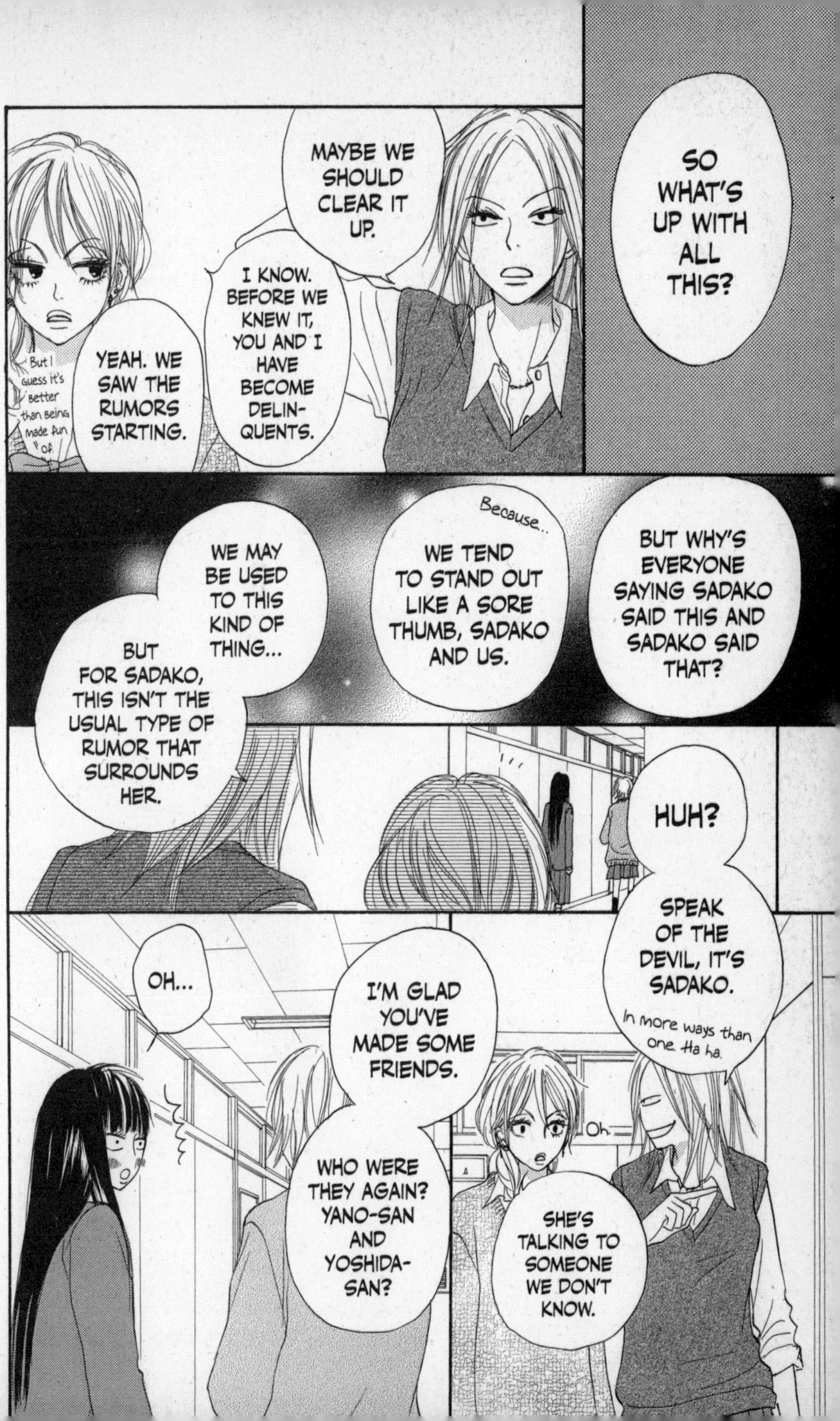
SO WHAT'S UP WITH ALL THIS?
MAYBE WE SHOULD CLEAR IT UP.
I KNOW. BEFORE WE KNEW IT, YOU AND I HAVE BECOME DELIN-QUENTS.
YEAH. WE SAW THE RUMORS STARTING.
But I guess it's better than being made fun of.
BUT WHY'S EVERYONE SAYING SADAKO SAID THIS AND SADAKO SAID THAT?
Because...
WE TEND TO STAND OUT LIKE A SORE THUMB, SADAKO AND US.
WE MAY BE USED TO THIS KIND OF THING...
BUT FOR SADAKO, THIS ISN'T THE USUAL TYPE OF RUMOR THAT SURROUNDS HER.
HUH?
SPEAK OF THE DEVIL, IT'S SADAKO.
In more ways than one. Ha ha.
Oh.
SHE'S TALKING TO SOMEONE WE DON'T KNOW.
I'M GLAD YOU'VE MADE SOME FRIENDS.
WHO WERE THEY AGAIN? YANO-SAN AND YOSHIDA-SAN?
OH...

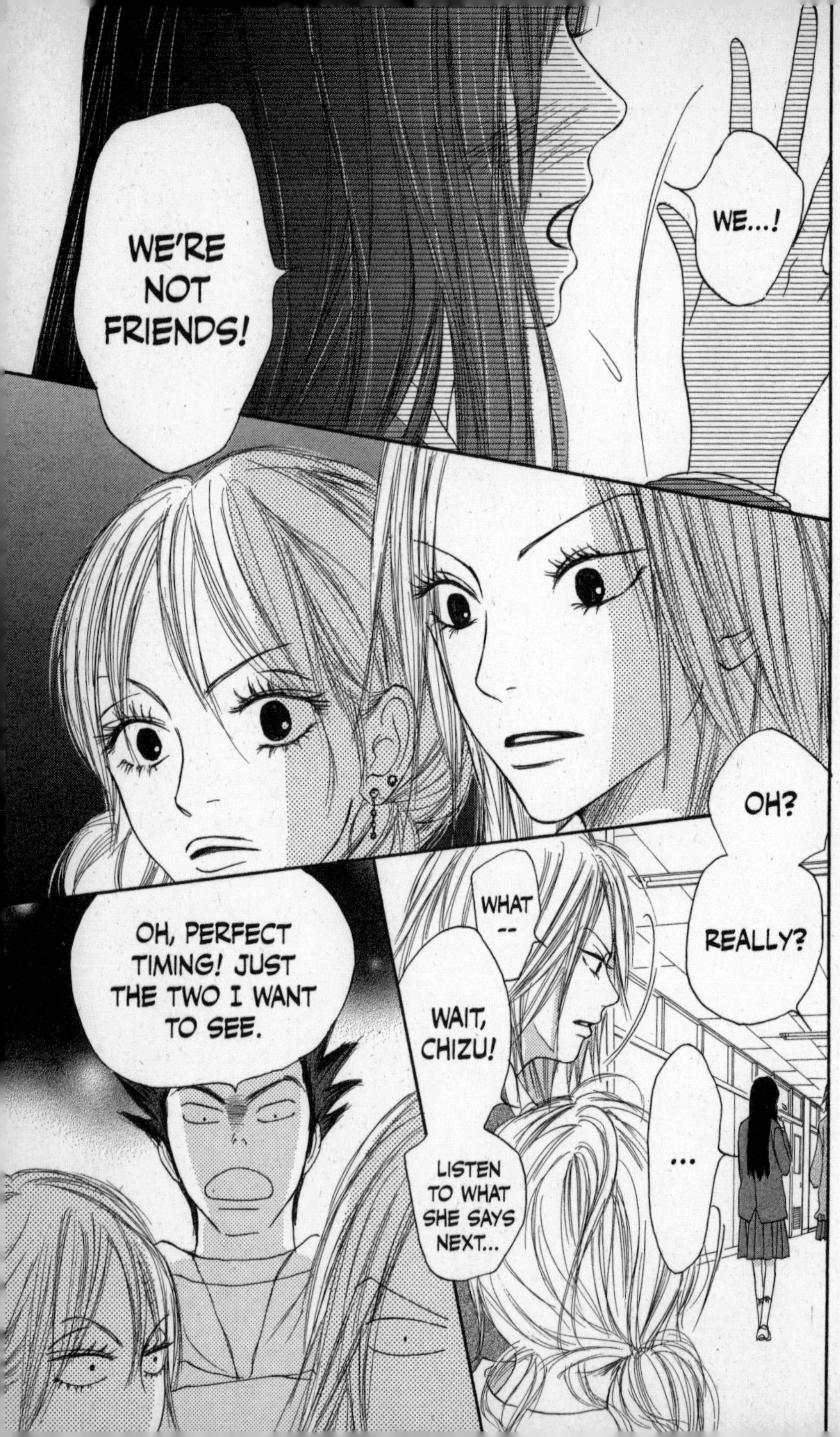
WE...!
WE'RE NOT FRIENDS!
OH?
REALLY?
...
WHAT --
WAIT, CHIZU!
LISTEN TO WHAT SHE SAYS NEXT...
OH, PERFECT TIMING! JUST THE TWO I WANT TO SEE.

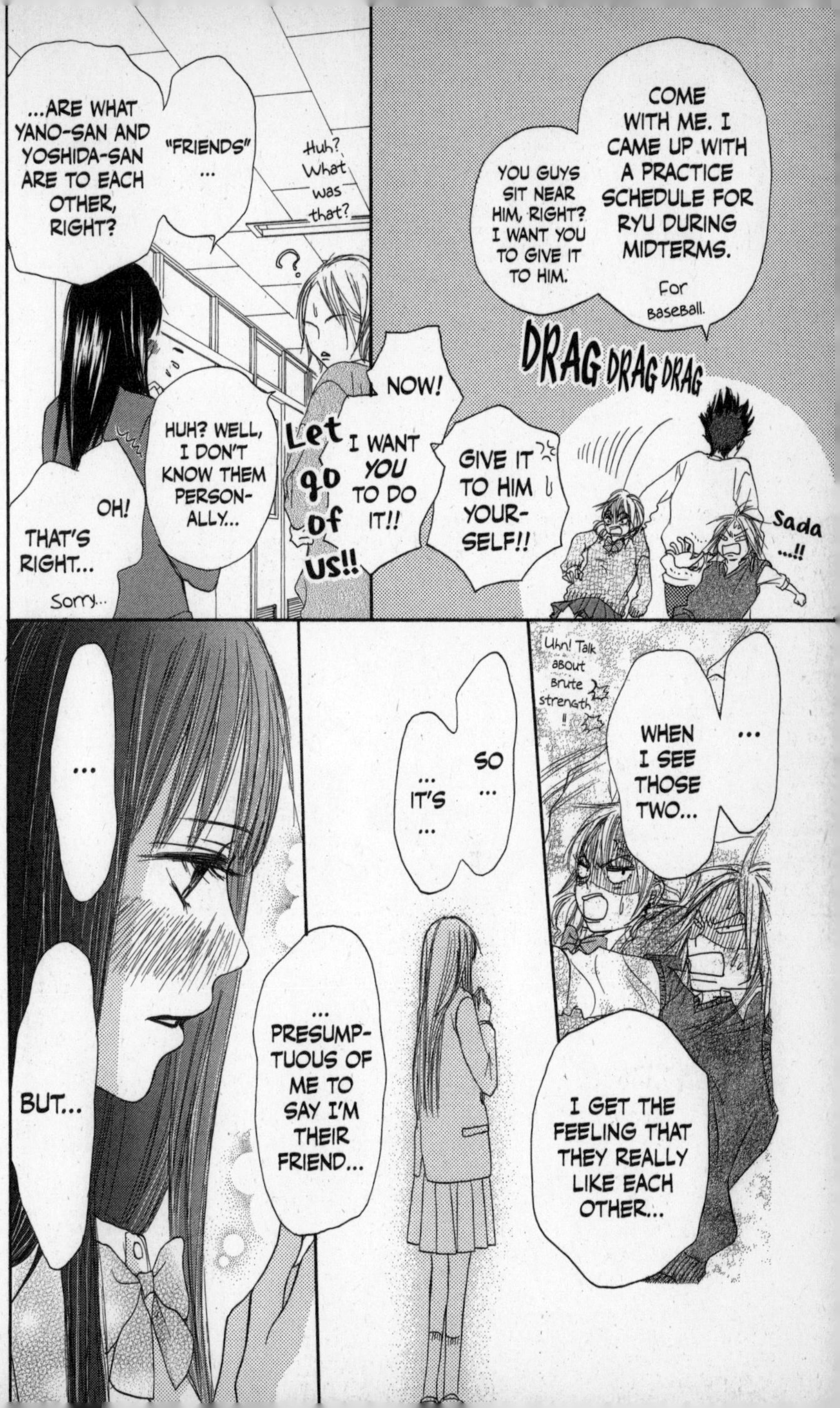
COME WITH ME. I CAME UP WITH A PRACTICE SCHEDULE FOR RYU DURING MIDTERMS.
For Baseball.
YOU GUYS SIT NEAR HIM, RIGHT? I WANT YOU TO GIVE IT TO HIM.
DRAG DRAG DRAG
Sada ...!!
GIVE IT TO HIM YOURSELF!!
I WANT YOU TO DO IT!!
NOW!
Let go of US!!
Huh? What was that?
"FRIENDS" ...
...ARE WHAT YANO-SAN AND YOSHIDA-SAN ARE TO EACH OTHER, RIGHT?
HUH? WELL, I DON'T KNOW THEM PERSON-ALLY...
OH! THAT'S RIGHT...
Sorry...
Uhn! Talk about Brute strength !!
...
WHEN I SEE THOSE TWO...
I GET THE FEELING THAT THEY REALLY LIKE EACH OTHER...
SO ...
... IT'S ...
... PRESUMP-TUOUS OF ME TO SAY I'M THEIR FRIEND...
...
BUT...

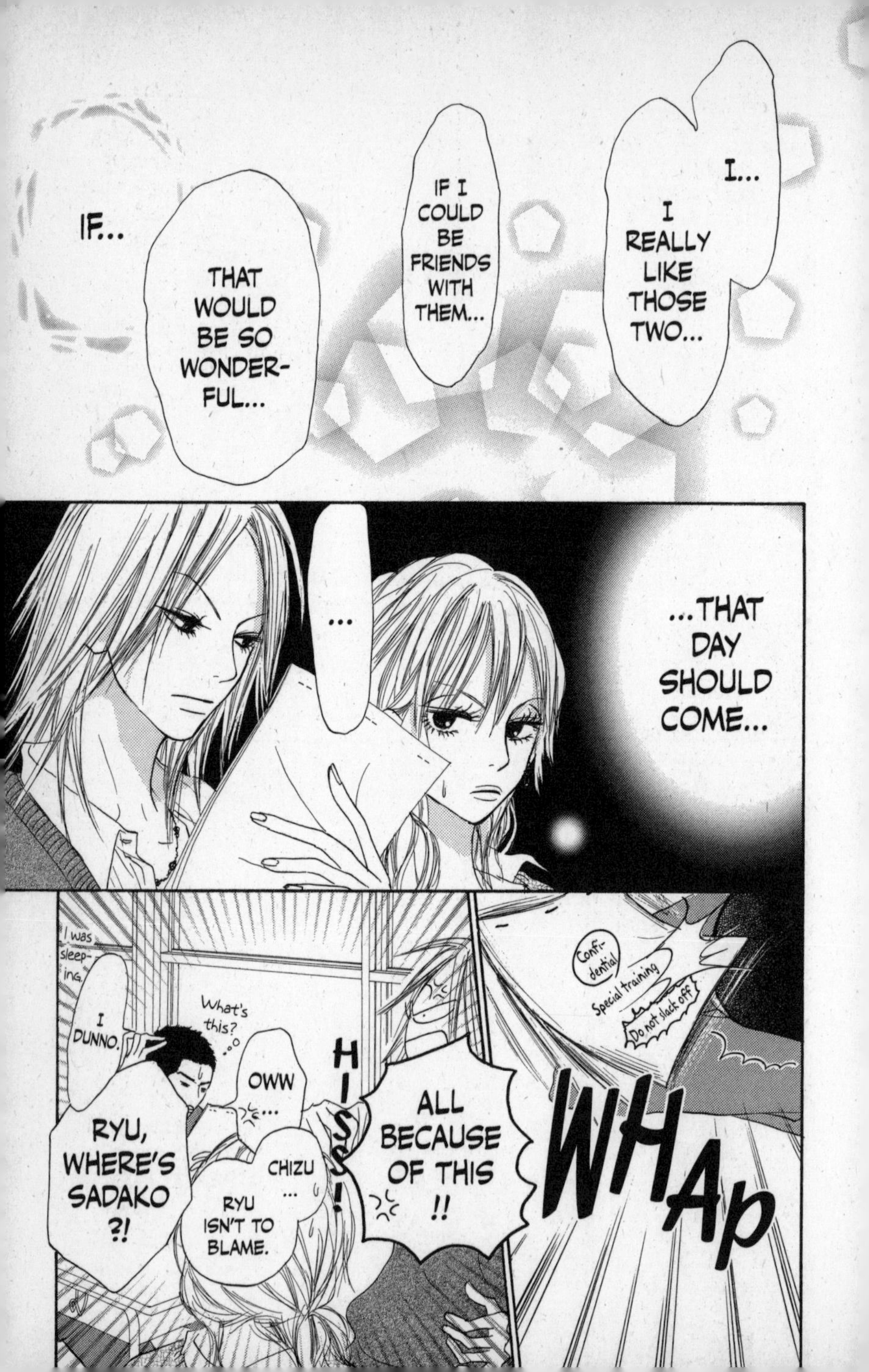
I...
I REALLY LIKE THOSE TWO...
IF I COULD BE FRIENDS WITH THEM...
THAT WOULD BE SO WONDER-FUL...
IF...
...THAT DAY SHOULD COME...
...
WHAp
Confi-dential
Special training
Do not slack off
ALL BECAUSE OF THIS !!
HISS!
OWW...
What's this?
I was sleep-ing.
I DUNNO.
CHIZU...
RYU ISN'T TO BLAME.
RYU, WHERE'S SADAKO ?!

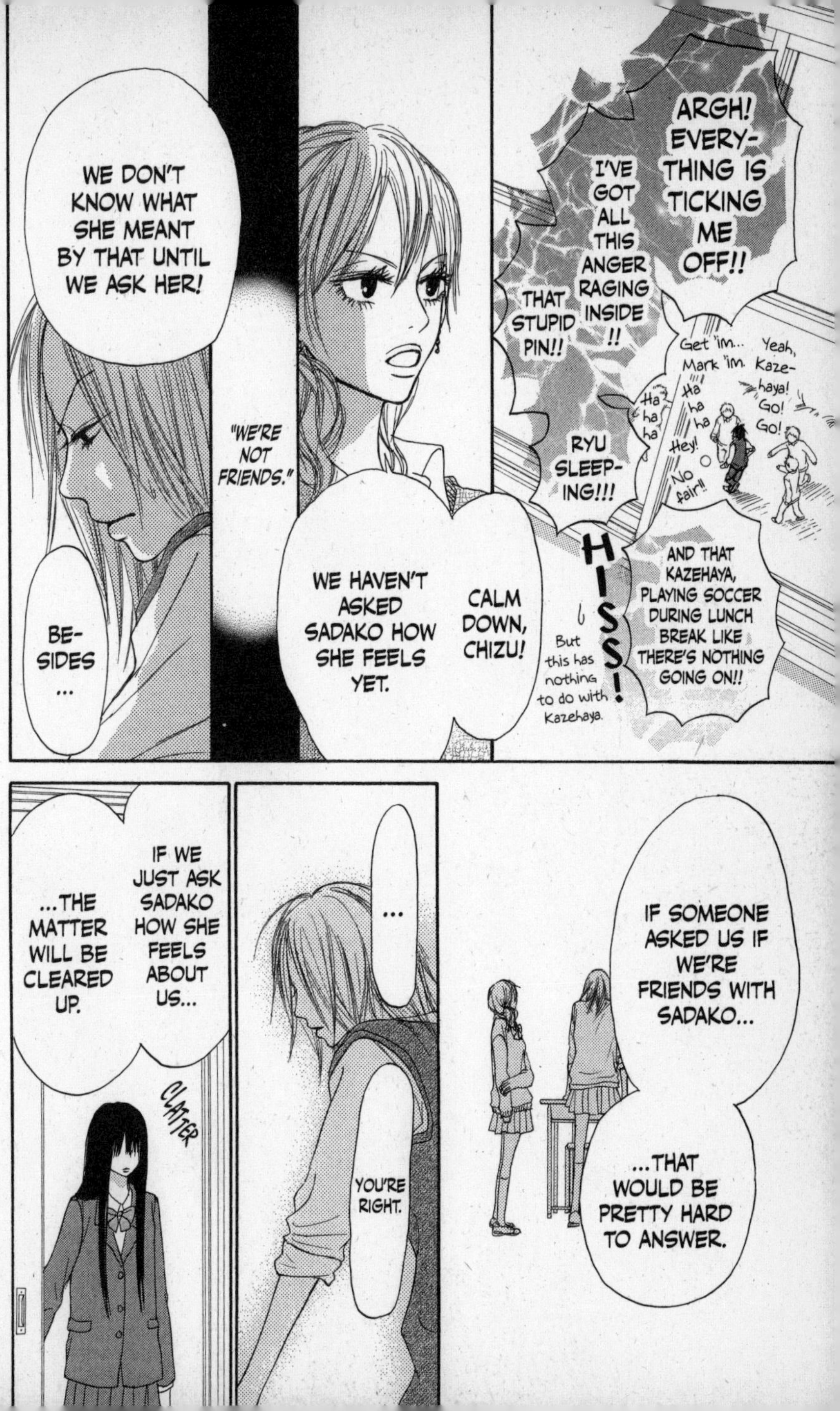
ARGH! EVERYTHING IS TICKING ME OFF!!
I'VE GOT ALL THIS ANGER RAGING INSIDE!!
THAT STUPID PIN!!
RYU SLEEPING!!!
Yeah, Kazehaya! Go! Go!
Get 'im... Mark 'im.
Ha ha ha
Ha ha ha
Hey!
No fair!!
AND THAT KAZEHAYA, PLAYING SOCCER DURING LUNCH BREAK LIKE THERE'S NOTHING GOING ON!!
HISS!
But this has nothing to do with Kazehaya.
CALM DOWN, CHIZU!
WE HAVEN'T ASKED SADAKO HOW SHE FEELS YET.
"WE'RE NOT FRIENDS."
WE DON'T KNOW WHAT SHE MEANT BY THAT UNTIL WE ASK HER!
BESIDES...
IF SOMEONE ASKED US IF WE'RE FRIENDS WITH SADAKO...
...THAT WOULD BE PRETTY HARD TO ANSWER.
...
YOU'RE RIGHT.
IF WE JUST ASK SADAKO HOW SHE FEELS ABOUT US...
...THE MATTER WILL BE CLEARED UP.
CLATTER

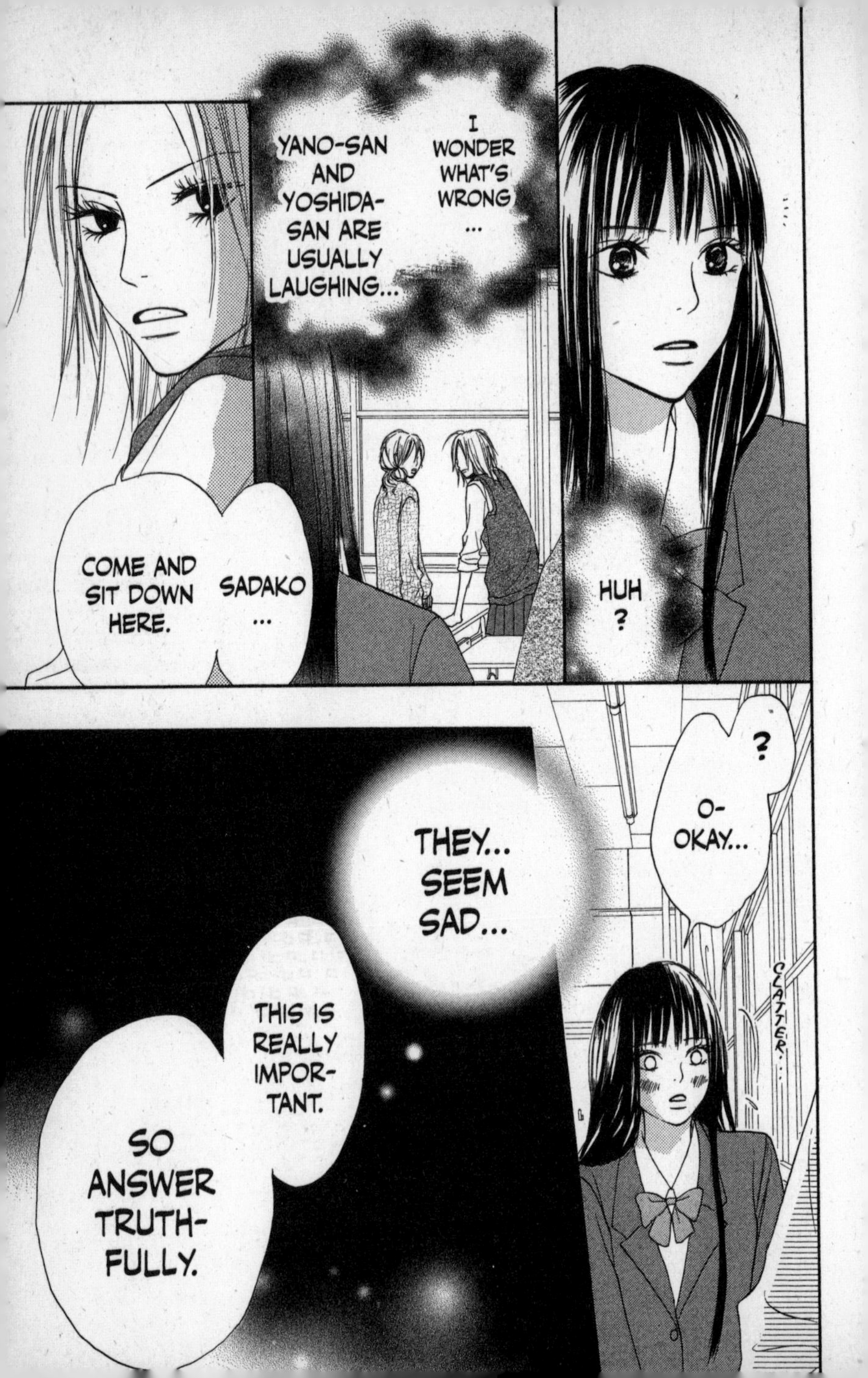
...
HUH ?
I WONDER WHAT'S WRONG ...
YANO-SAN AND YOSHIDA-SAN ARE USUALLY LAUGHING...
SADAKO ...
COME AND SIT DOWN HERE.
? O-OKAY...
CLATTER...
THEY... SEEM SAD...
THIS IS REALLY IMPOR-TANT.
SO ANSWER TRUTH-FULLY.

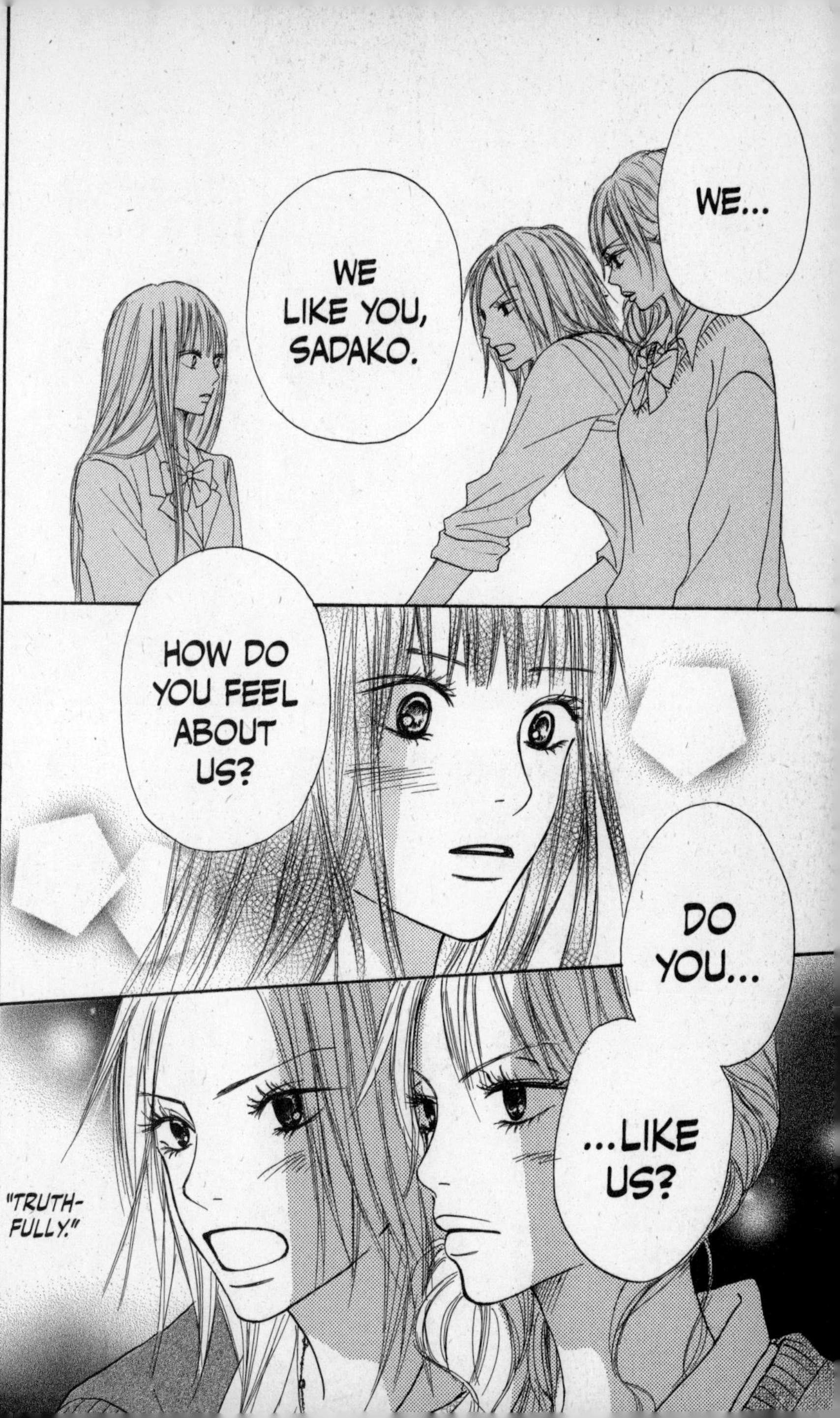
WE...
WE LIKE YOU, SADAKO.
HOW DO YOU FEEL ABOUT US?
DO YOU...
...LIKE US?
"TRUTH-FULLY."

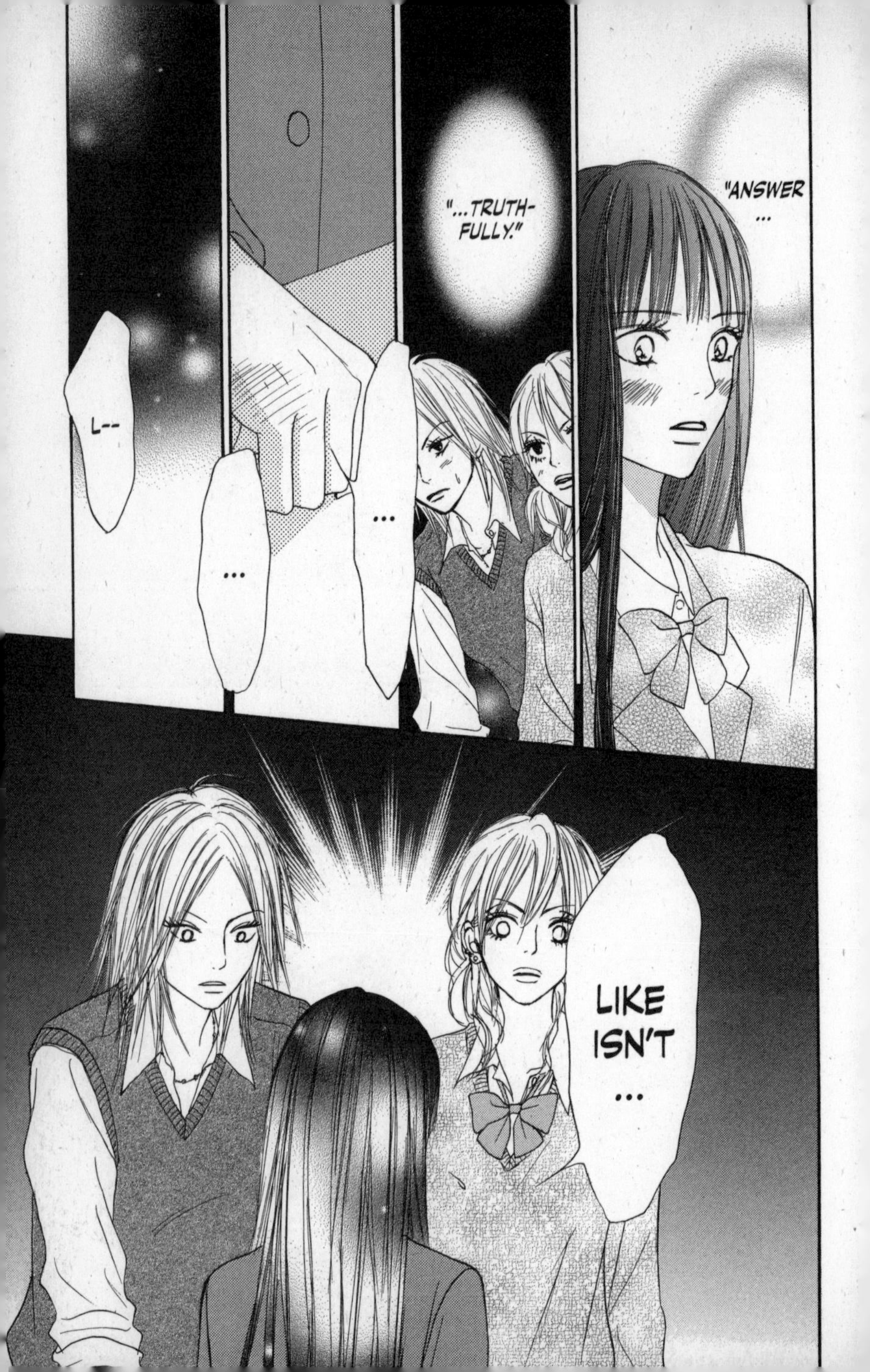
"ANSWER ...
"...TRUTHFULLY."
...
...
L--
LIKE ISN'T ...

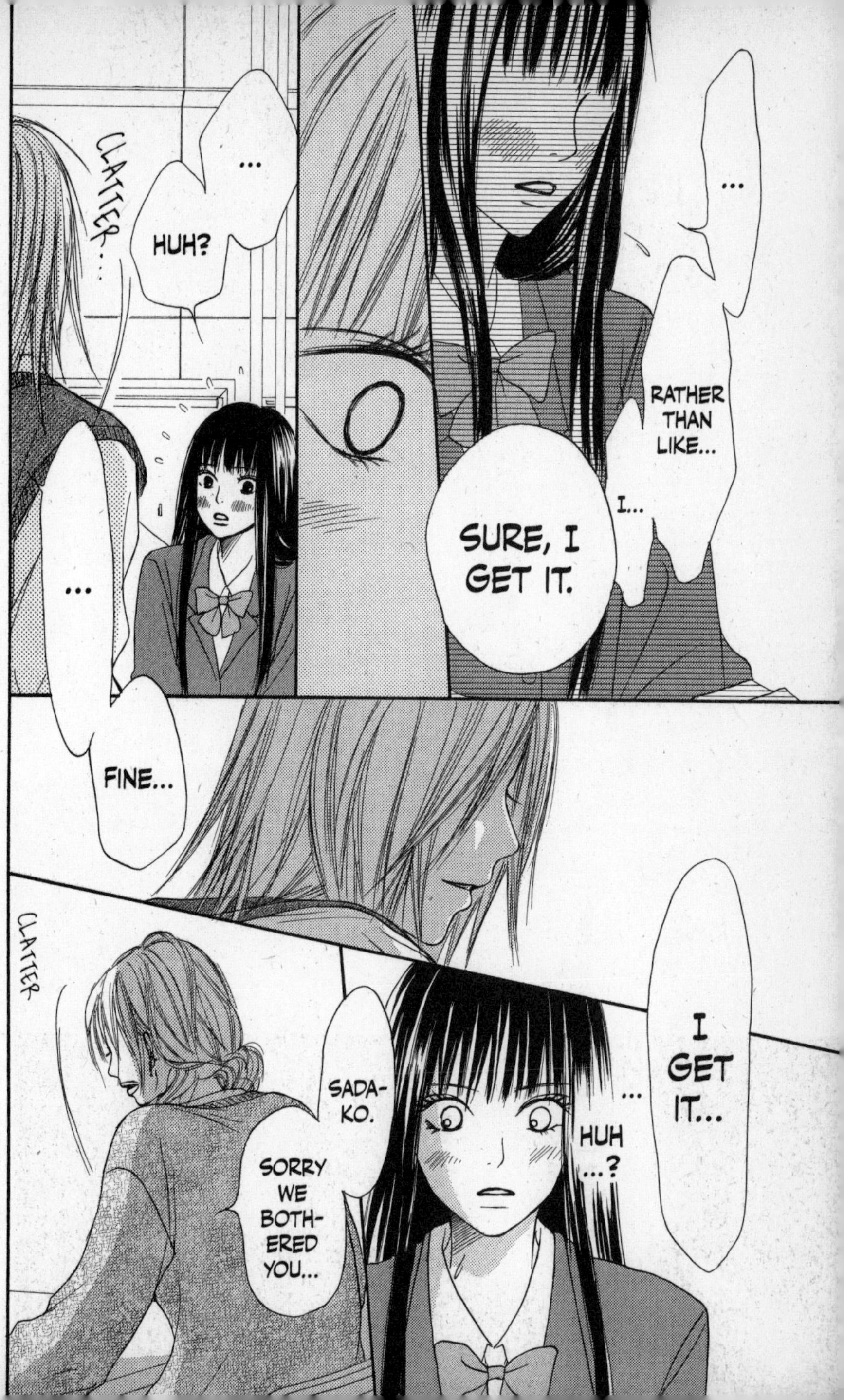
...
RATHER THAN LIKE...
I...
SURE, I GET IT.
...
HUH?
CLATTER...
...
FINE...
I GET IT...
...HUH ...?
SADAKO.
SORRY WE BOTHERED YOU...
CLATTER

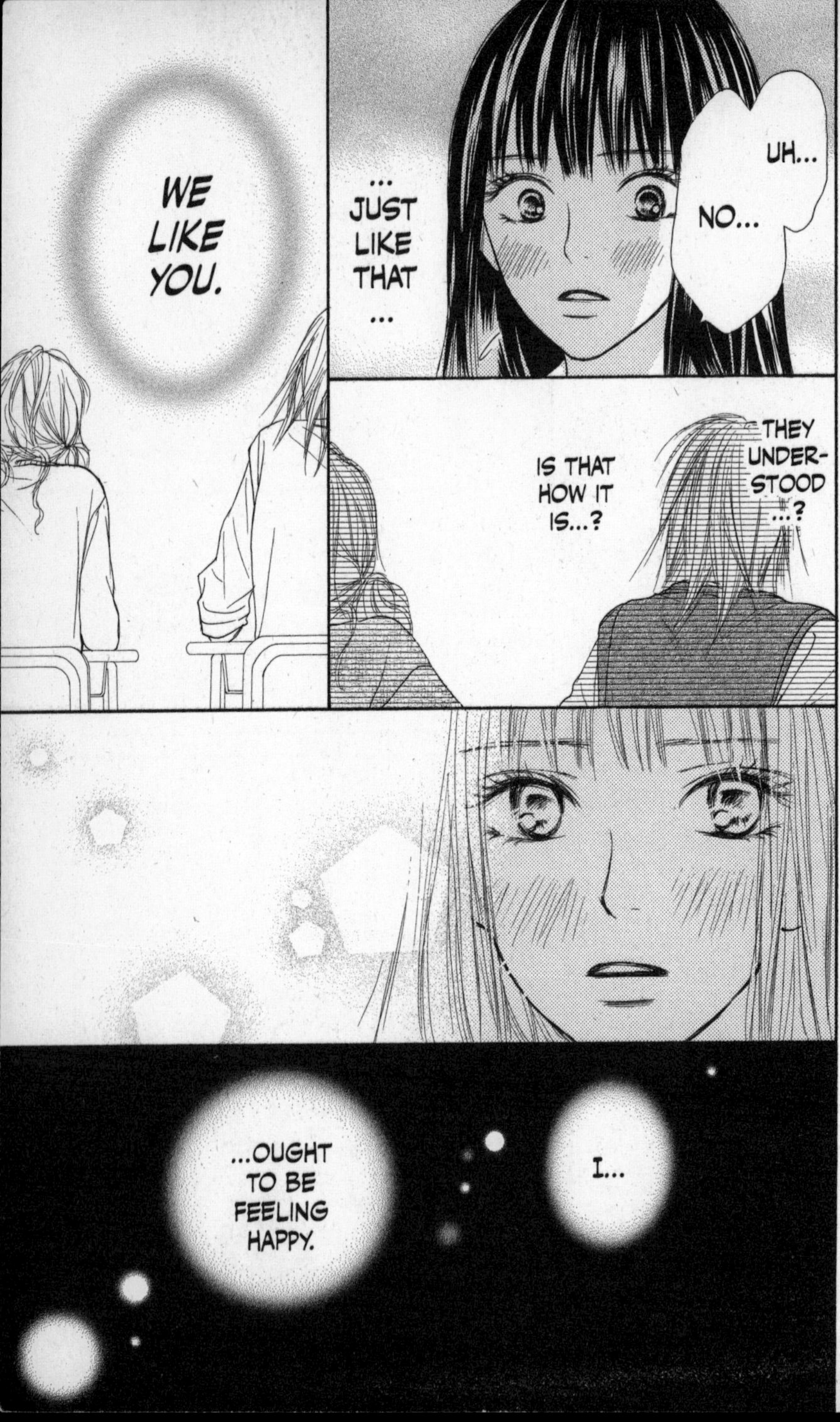
UH...
NO...
...JUST LIKE THAT...
THEY UNDER-STOOD ...?
IS THAT HOW IT IS...?
WE LIKE YOU.
I...
...OUGHT TO BE FEELING HAPPY.

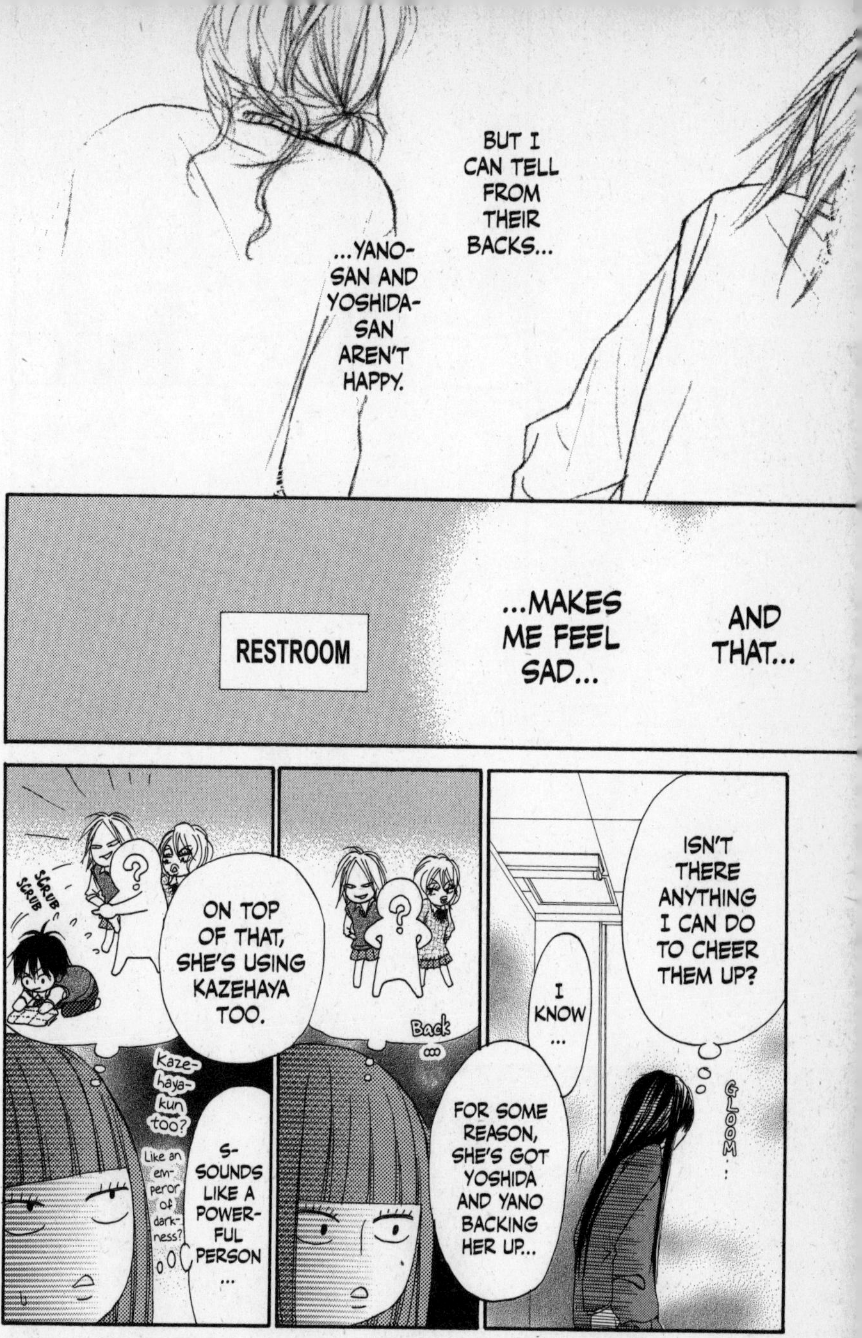
BUT I CAN TELL FROM THEIR BACKS...
...YANO-SAN AND YOSHIDA-SAN AREN'T HAPPY.
AND THAT...
...MAKES ME FEEL SAD...
RESTROOM
ISN'T THERE ANYTHING I CAN DO TO CHEER THEM UP?
GLOOM..
I KNOW...
FOR SOME REASON, SHE'S GOT YOSHIDA AND YANO BACKING HER UP...
Back...
SCRUB SCRUB
ON TOP OF THAT, SHE'S USING KAZEHAYA TOO.
Kaze-haya-kun too?
Like an emperor of darkness?
S-SOUNDS LIKE A POWERFUL PERSON...

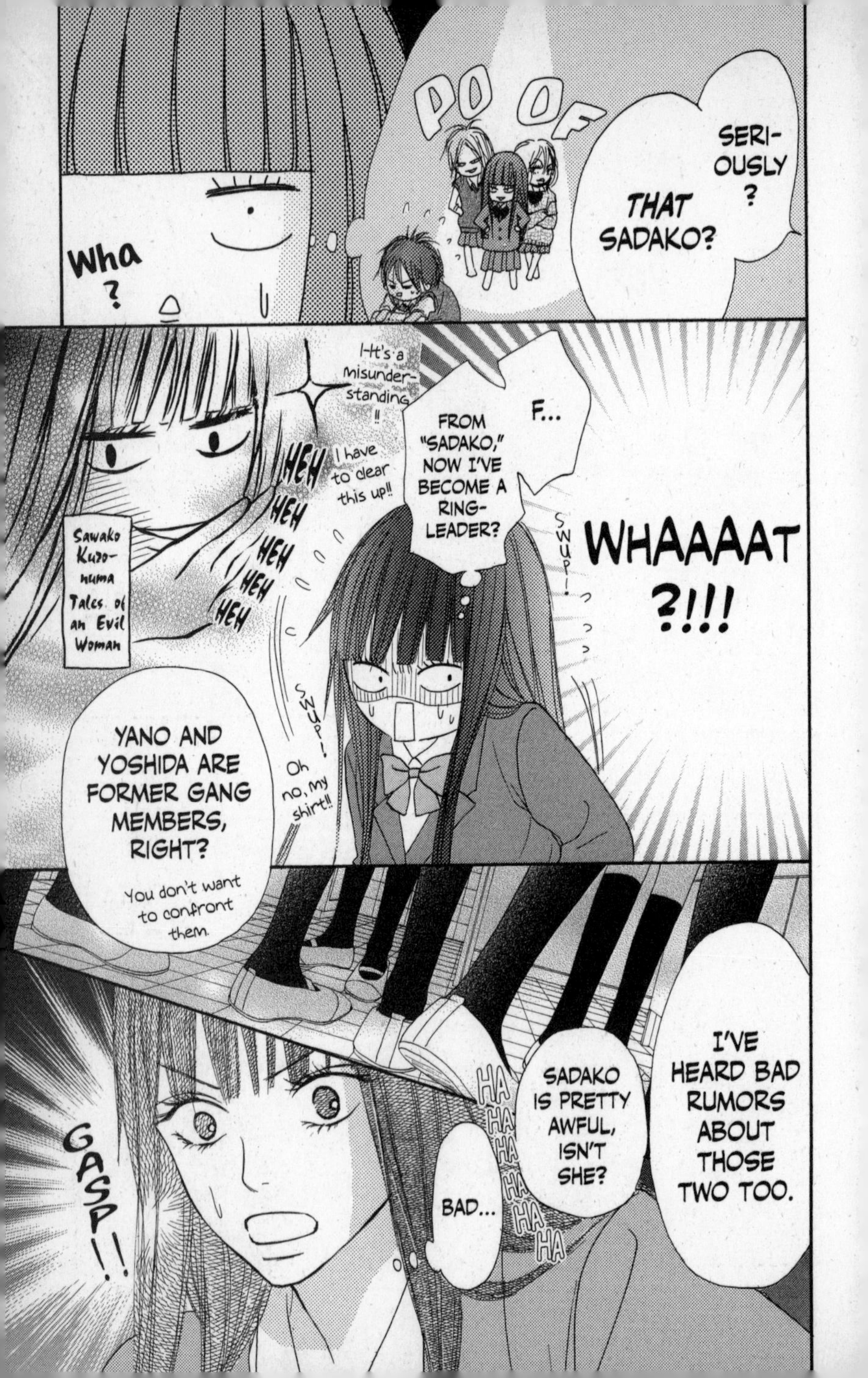
SERI-OUSLY? THAT SADAKO?
POOF
Wha?
WHAAAAT?!!!
F...
FROM "SADAKO," NOW I'VE BECOME A RING-LEADER?
SWUP!
I-It's a misunderstanding!!
I have to clear this up!!
HEH HEH HEH HEH HEH
Sawako Kuronuma Tales of an Evil Woman
SWUP!
Oh no, my shirt!!
YANO AND YOSHIDA ARE FORMER GANG MEMBERS, RIGHT?
You don't want to confront them.
I'VE HEARD BAD RUMORS ABOUT THOSE TWO TOO.
SADAKO IS PRETTY AWFUL, ISN'T SHE?
HA HA HA HA HA HA HA
BAD...
GASP!!

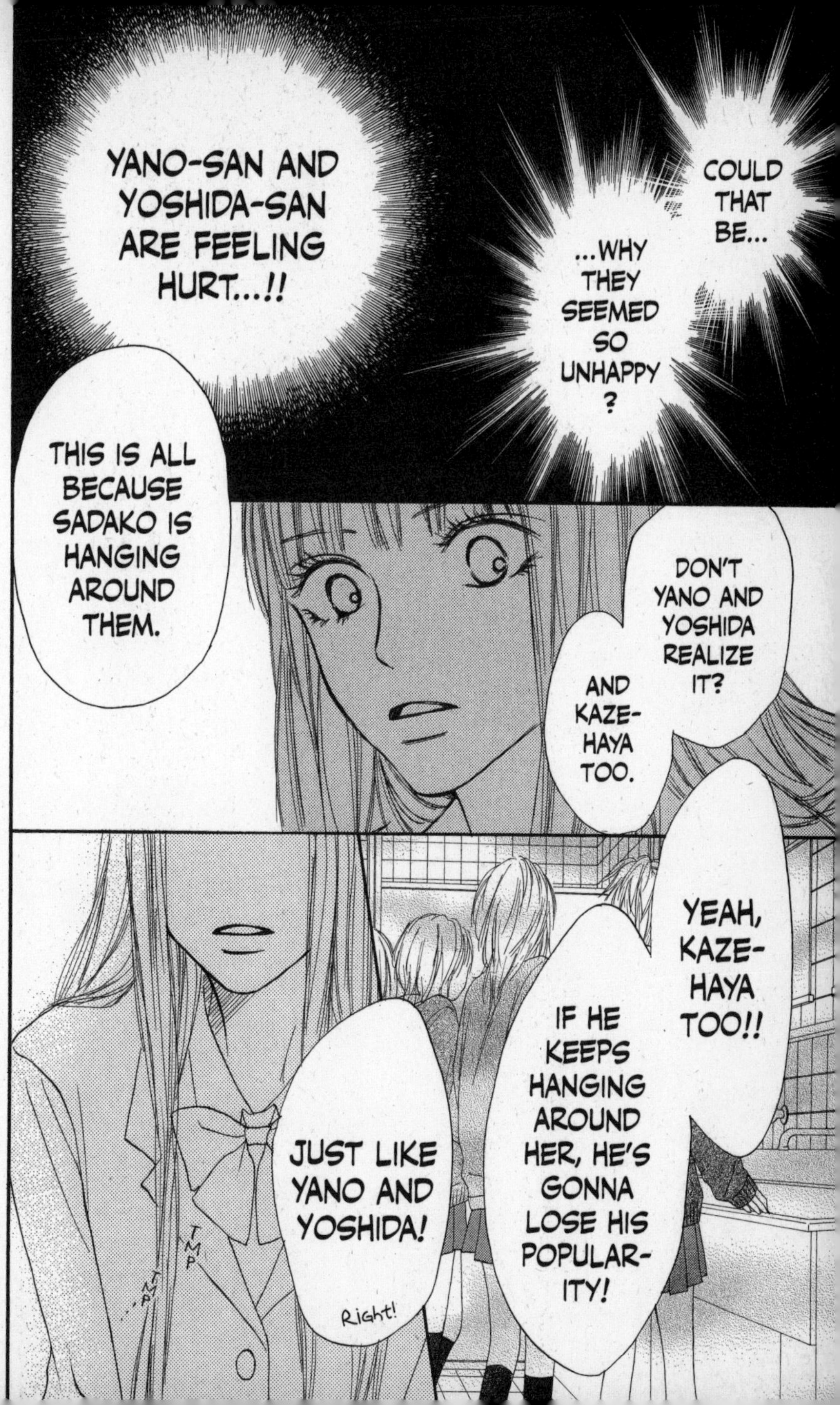
COULD THAT BE...
...WHY THEY SEEMED SO UNHAPPY?
YANO-SAN AND YOSHIDA-SAN ARE FEELING HURT...!!
THIS IS ALL BECAUSE SADAKO IS HANGING AROUND THEM.
DON'T YANO AND YOSHIDA REALIZE IT?
AND KAZE-HAYA TOO.
YEAH, KAZE-HAYA TOO!!
IF HE KEEPS HANGING AROUND HER, HE'S GONNA LOSE HIS POPULAR-ITY!
JUST LIKE YANO AND YOSHIDA!
Right!
TMP
TMP

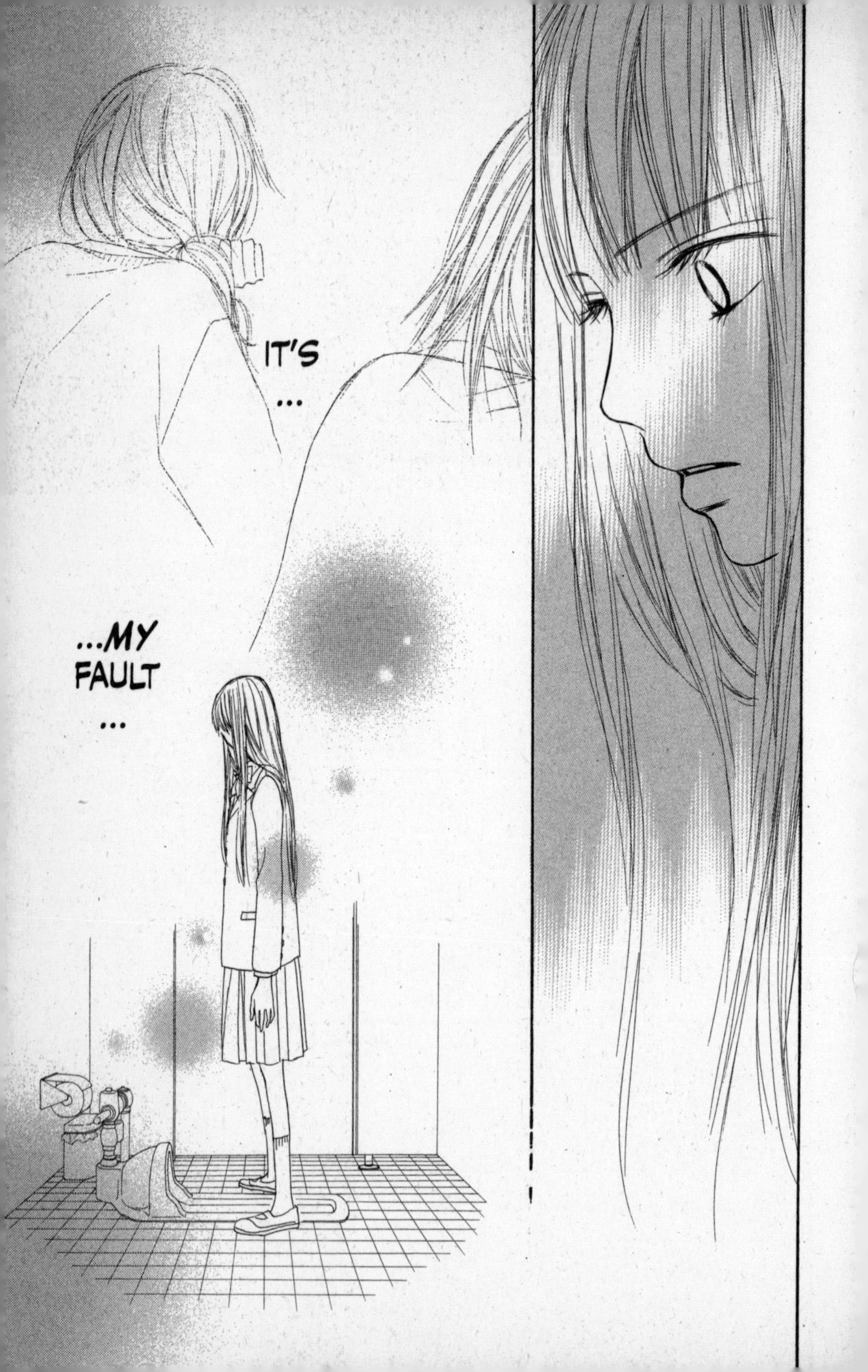
IT'S ...
...MY FAULT ...

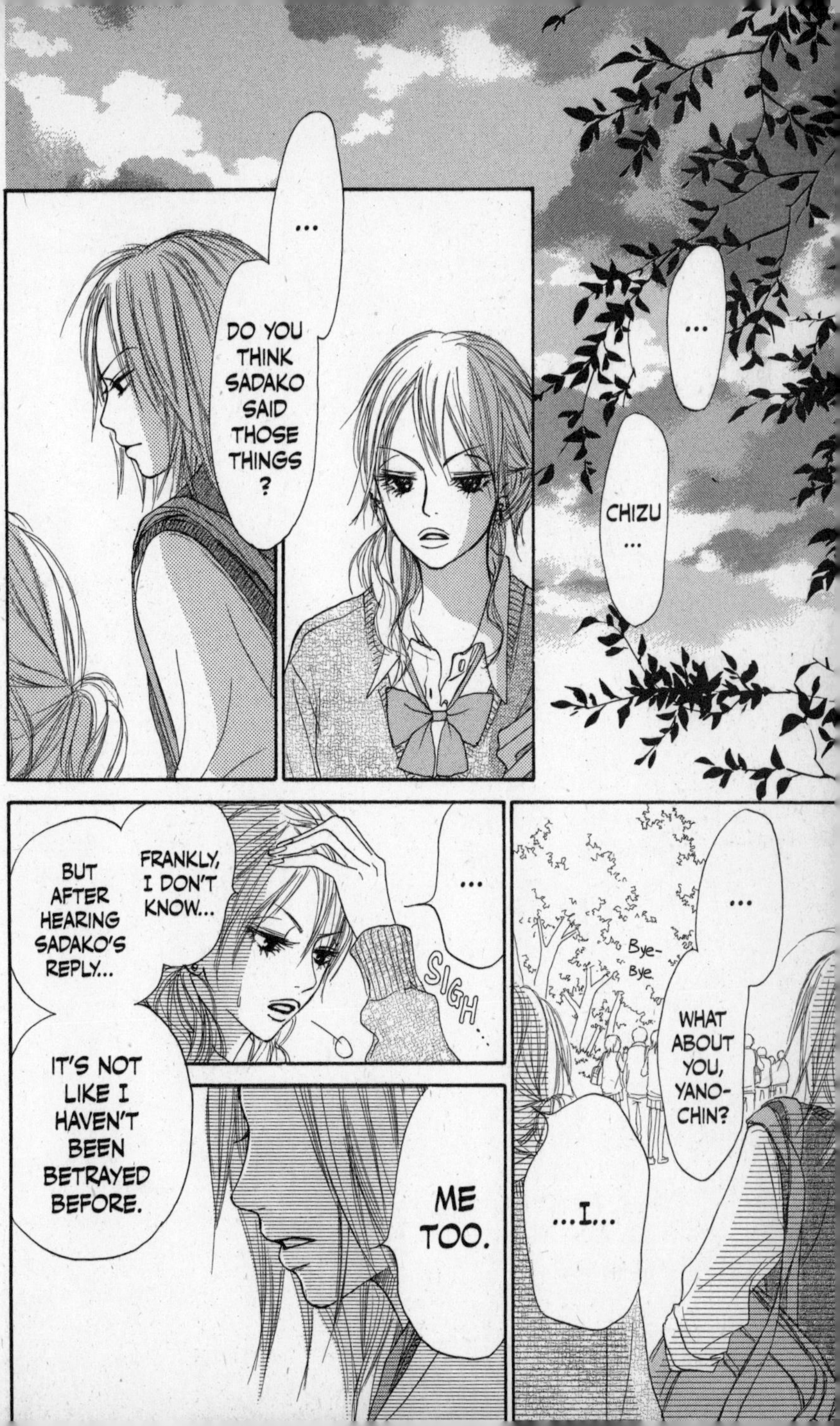
...
CHIZU ...
...
DO YOU THINK SADAKO SAID THOSE THINGS?
...
WHAT ABOUT YOU, YANO-CHIN?
Bye-Bye.
...I...
...
SIGH...
FRANKLY, I DON'T KNOW...
BUT AFTER HEARING SADAKO'S REPLY...
IT'S NOT LIKE I HAVEN'T BEEN BETRAYED BEFORE.
ME TOO.

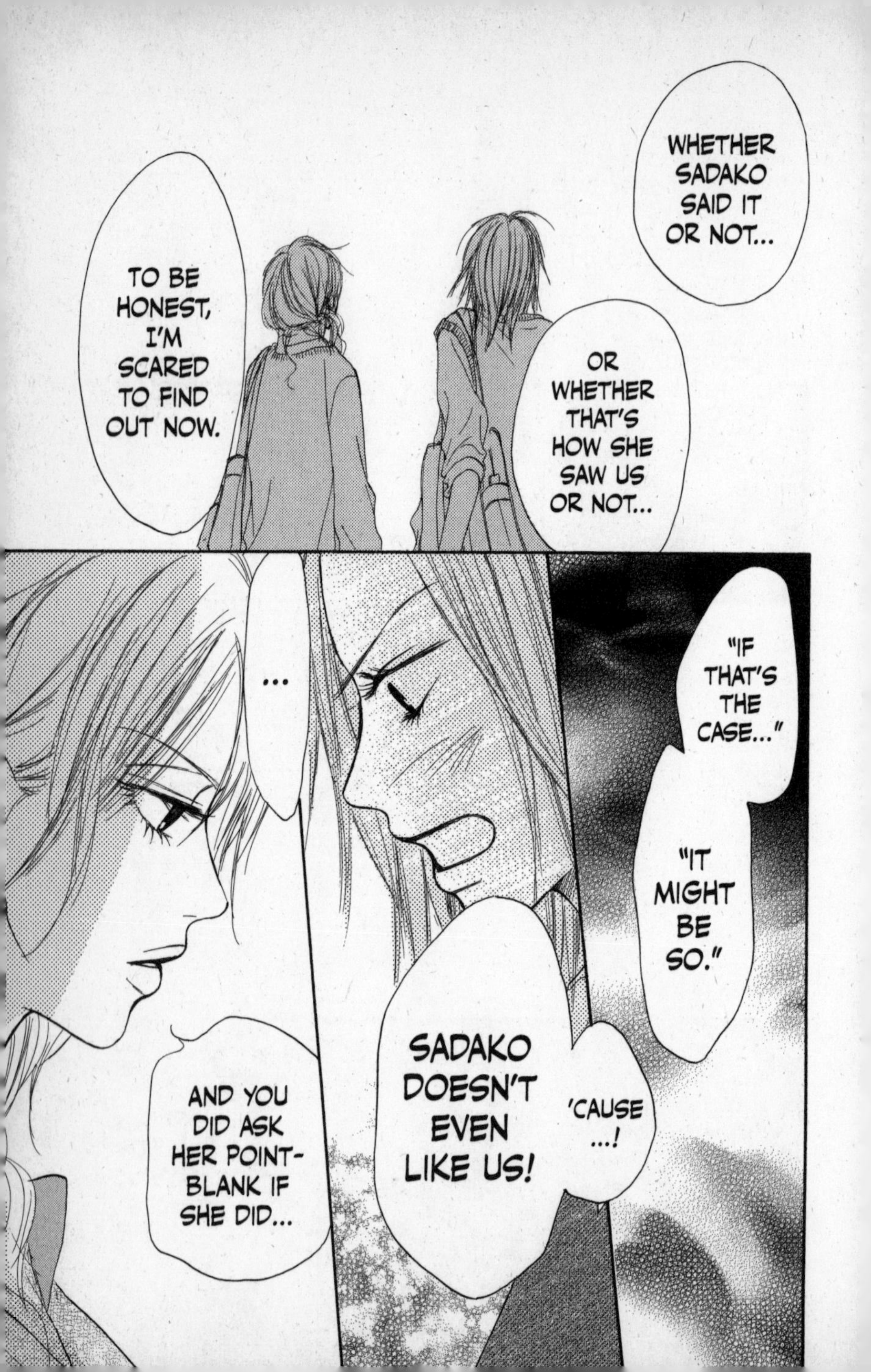
WHETHER SADAKO SAID IT OR NOT...
OR WHETHER THAT'S HOW SHE SAW US OR NOT...
TO BE HONEST, I'M SCARED TO FIND OUT NOW.
"IF THAT'S THE CASE..."
"IT MIGHT BE SO."
'CAUSE ...!
SADAKO DOESN'T EVEN LIKE US!
...
AND YOU DID ASK HER POINT-BLANK IF SHE DID...

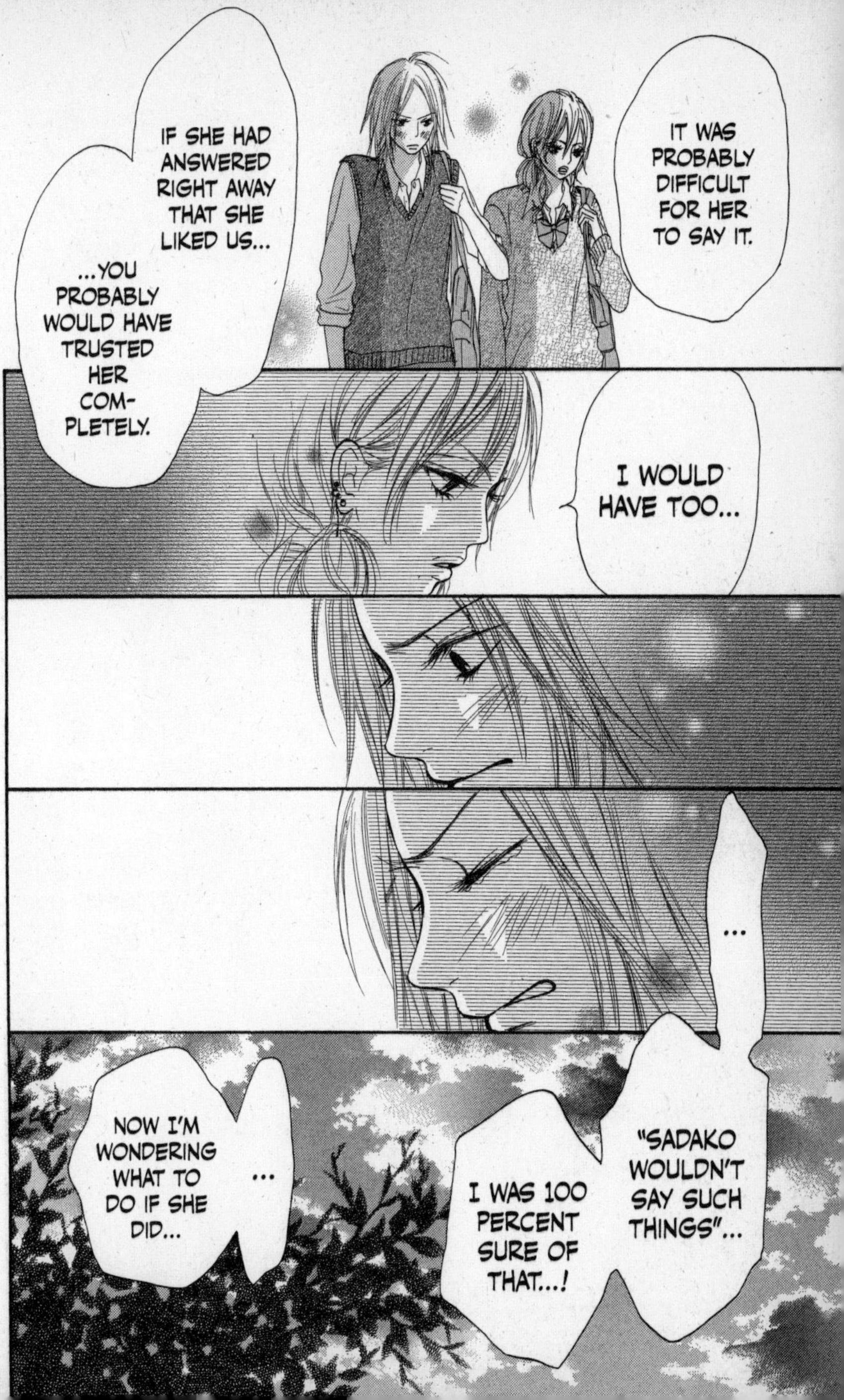
IT WAS PROBABLY DIFFICULT FOR HER TO SAY IT.
IF SHE HAD ANSWERED RIGHT AWAY THAT SHE LIKED US...
...YOU PROBABLY WOULD HAVE TRUSTED HER COM-PLETELY.
I WOULD HAVE TOO...
...
"SADAKO WOULDN'T SAY SUCH THINGS"...
I WAS 100 PERCENT SURE OF THAT...!
...
NOW I'M WONDERING WHAT TO DO IF SHE DID...

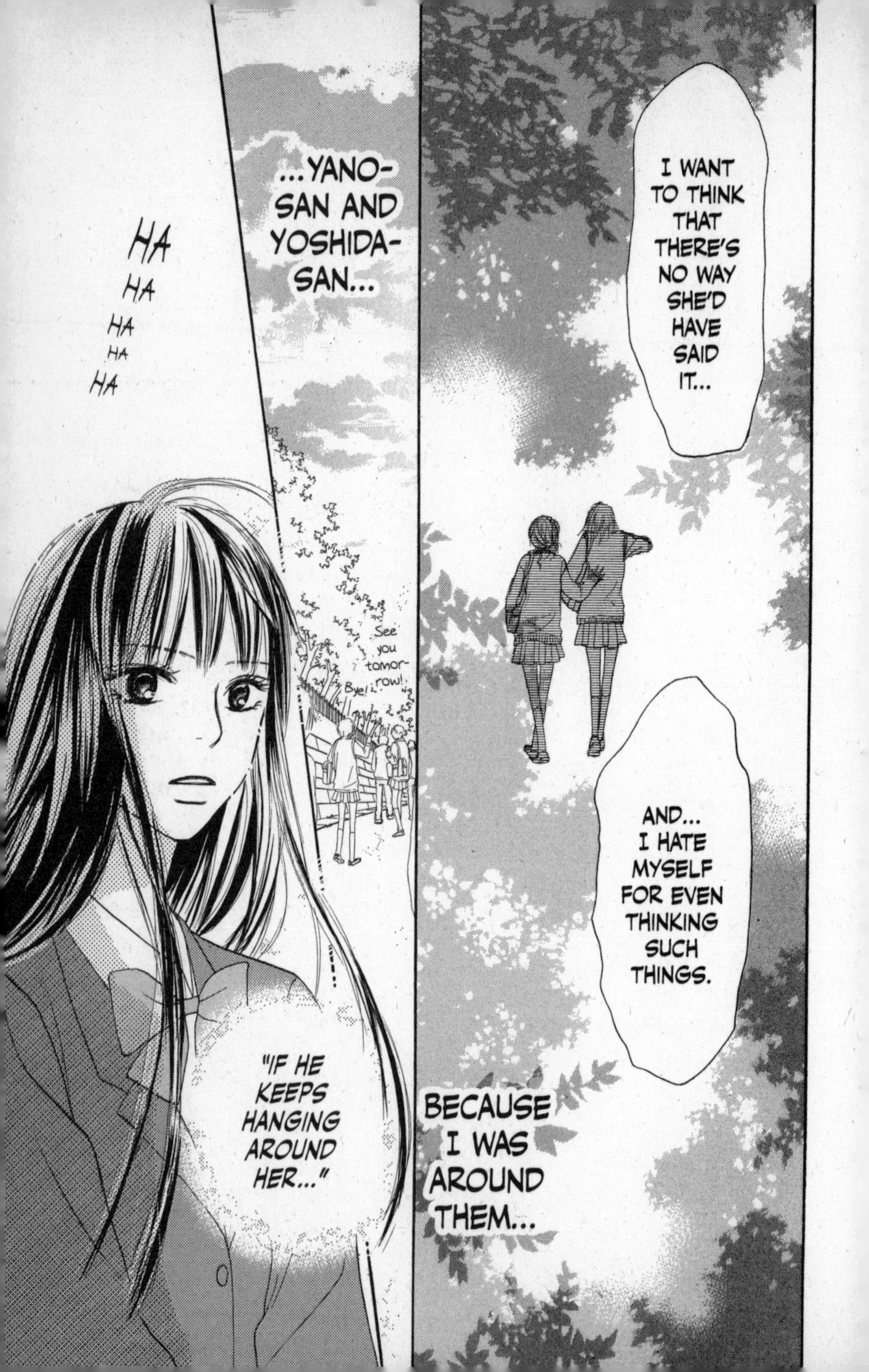
I WANT TO THINK THAT THERE'S NO WAY SHE'D HAVE SAID IT...
AND... I HATE MYSELF FOR EVEN THINKING SUCH THINGS.
BECAUSE I WAS AROUND THEM...
...YANO-SAN AND YOSHIDA-SAN...
HA HA HA HA HA
See you tomor-row!
Bye!
"IF HE KEEPS HANGING AROUND HER..."

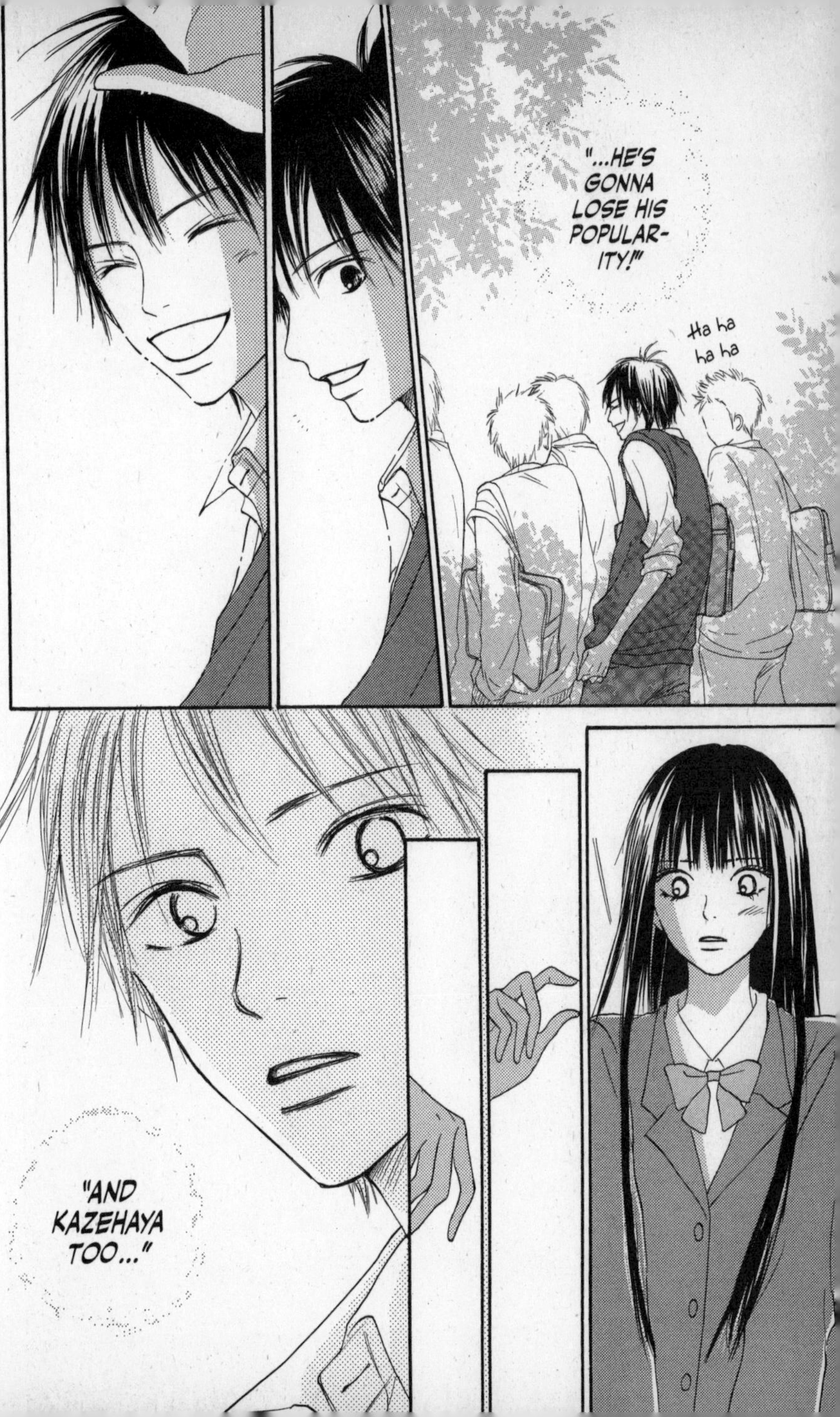
"...HE'S GONNA LOSE HIS POPULAR-ITY!"
Ha ha ha ha
"AND KAZEHAYA TOO..."

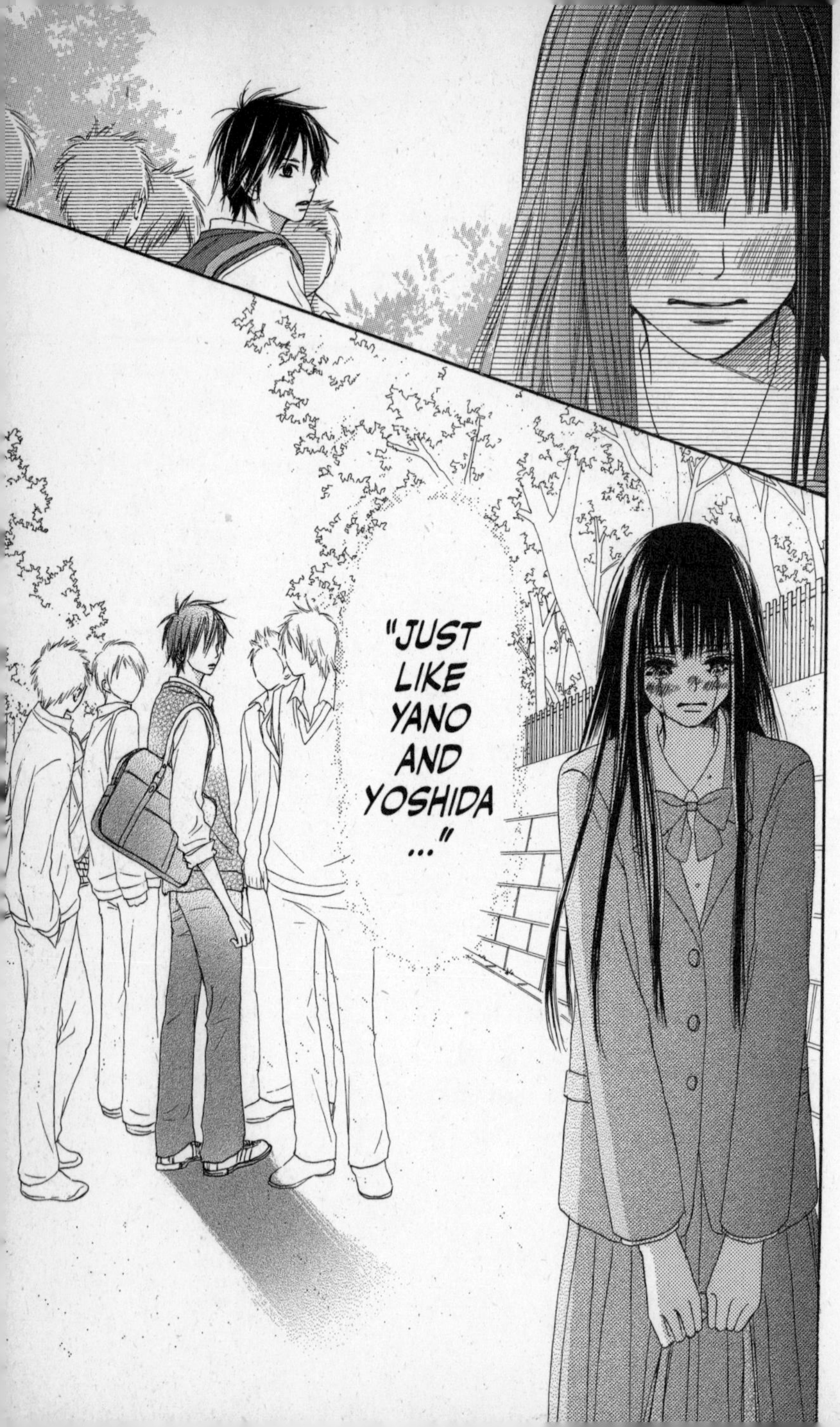
"JUST LIKE YANO AND YOSHIDA ..."

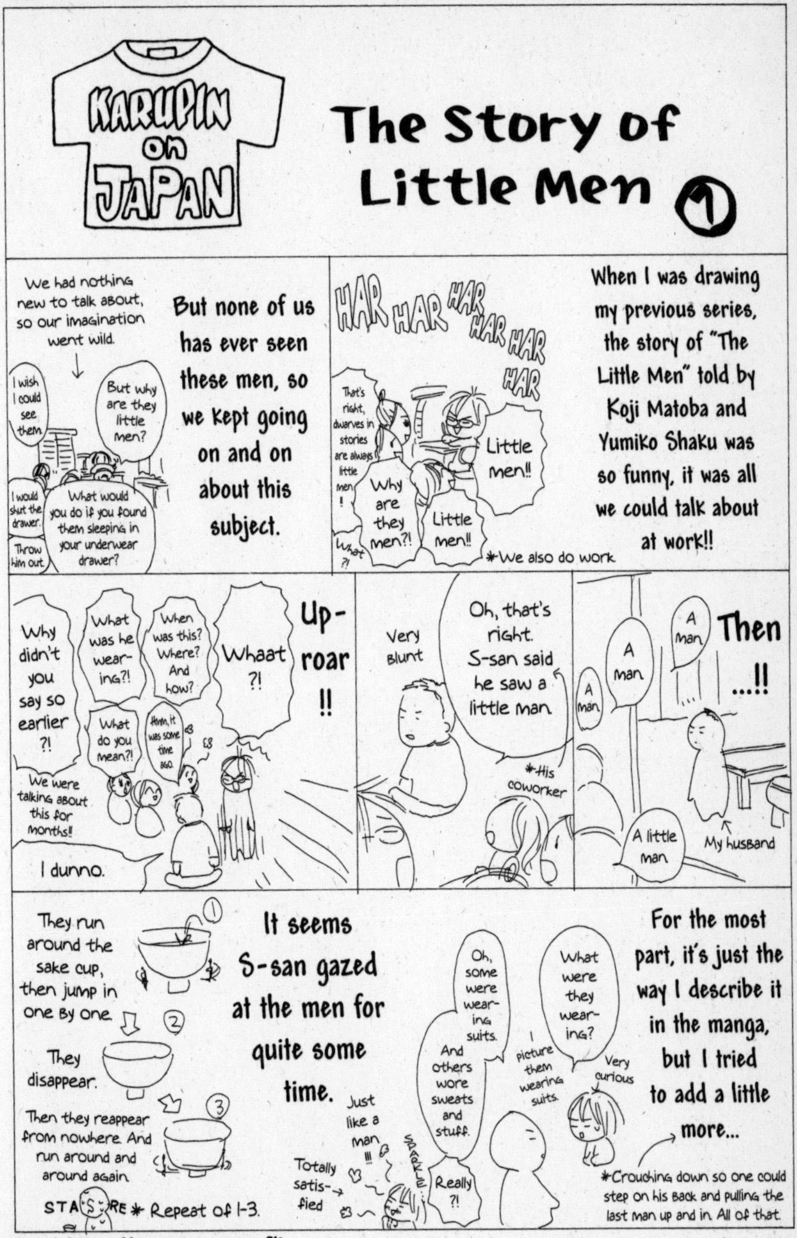
KARUPIN on JAPAN
The Story of Little Men 1
When I was drawing my previous series, the story of "The Little Men" told by Koji Matoba and Yumiko Shaku was so funny, it was all we could talk about at work!!
HAR HAR HAR HAR HAR HAR
Little men!!
That's right, dwarves in stories are always little men!
Why are they men?!
Little men!!
What ?!
*We also do work.
But none of us has ever seen these men, so we kept going on and on about this subject.
We had nothing new to talk about, so our imagination went wild.
But why are they little men?
I wish I could see them.
What would you do if you found them sleeping in your underwear drawer?
I would shut the drawer.
Throw him out.
Then ...!!
A man
A man
A man
A little man
My husband
Oh, that's right. S-san said he saw a little man.
Very blunt
*His coworker
Up-roar!!
Whaat ?!
When was this? Where? And how?
What was he wearing?!
Why didn't you say so earlier?!
Hmm, it was some time ago.
What do you mean?!
We were talking about this for months!!
I dunno.
For the most part, it's just the way I describe it in the manga, but I tried to add a little more...
*Crouching down so one could step on his back and pulling the last man up and in. All of that.
What were they wearing?
Very curious
I picture them wearing suits.
Oh, some were wearing suits.
And others wore sweats and stuff.
Really ?!
SPARKLE
Just like a man !!!
Totally satis-fied
It seems S-san gazed at the men for quite some time.
They run around the sake cup, then jump in one by one.
They disappear.
Then they reappear from nowhere. And run around and around again.
STARE * Repeat of 1-3.

Part 2 continues on page 94.

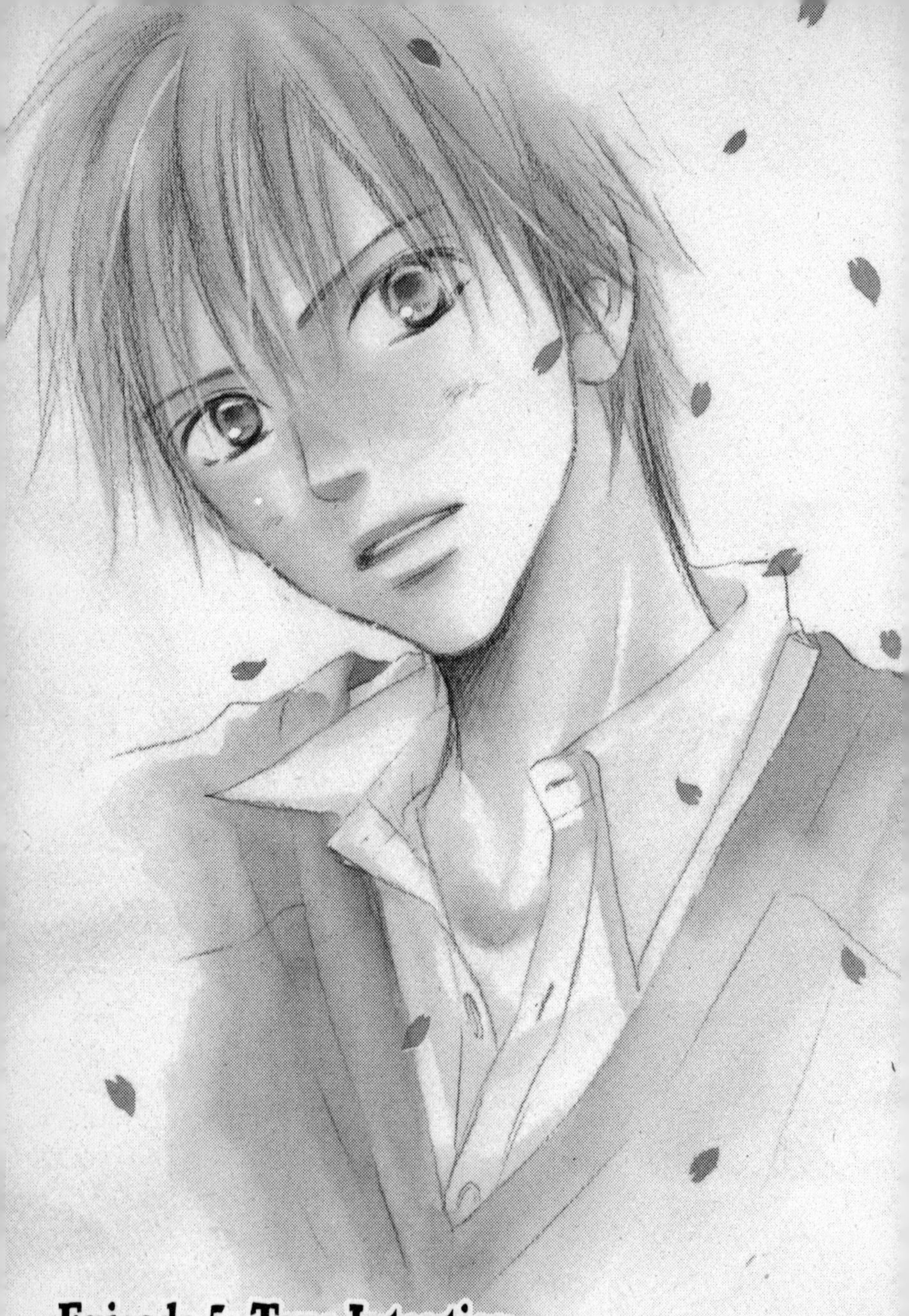

Episode 5: True Intention

Motto

"Be guided by the truth."

character #2

Shota Kazehaya

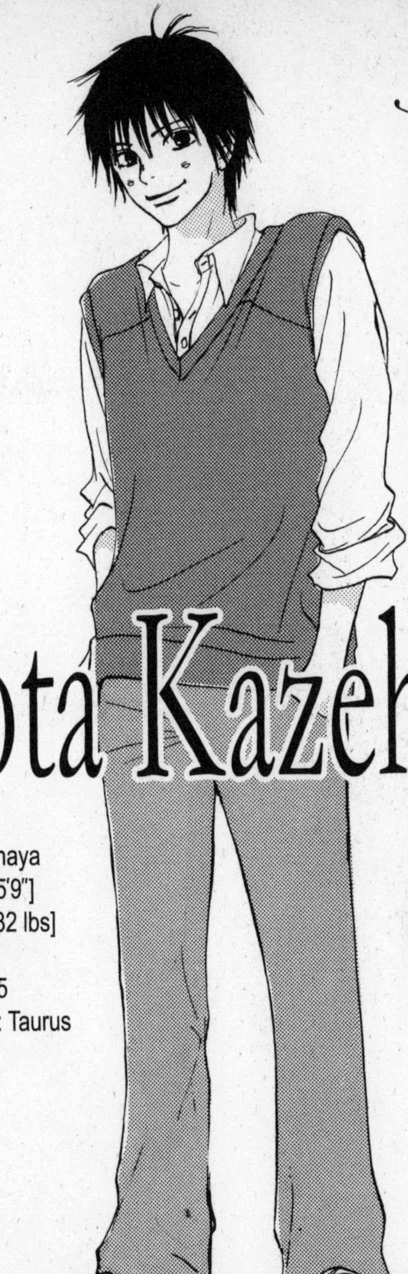

Nickname: Kazehaya
Height: 175 cm [5'9"]
Weight: 60 kg [132 lbs]
Blood type: O
Birthdate: May 15
Astrological sign: Taurus

We asked him what television shows he likes to watch!

"Everything and anything about sports!

Also, if there are any shows about the Egyptian pyramids or Machu Picchu or stuff like that, I'll definitely watch those!"

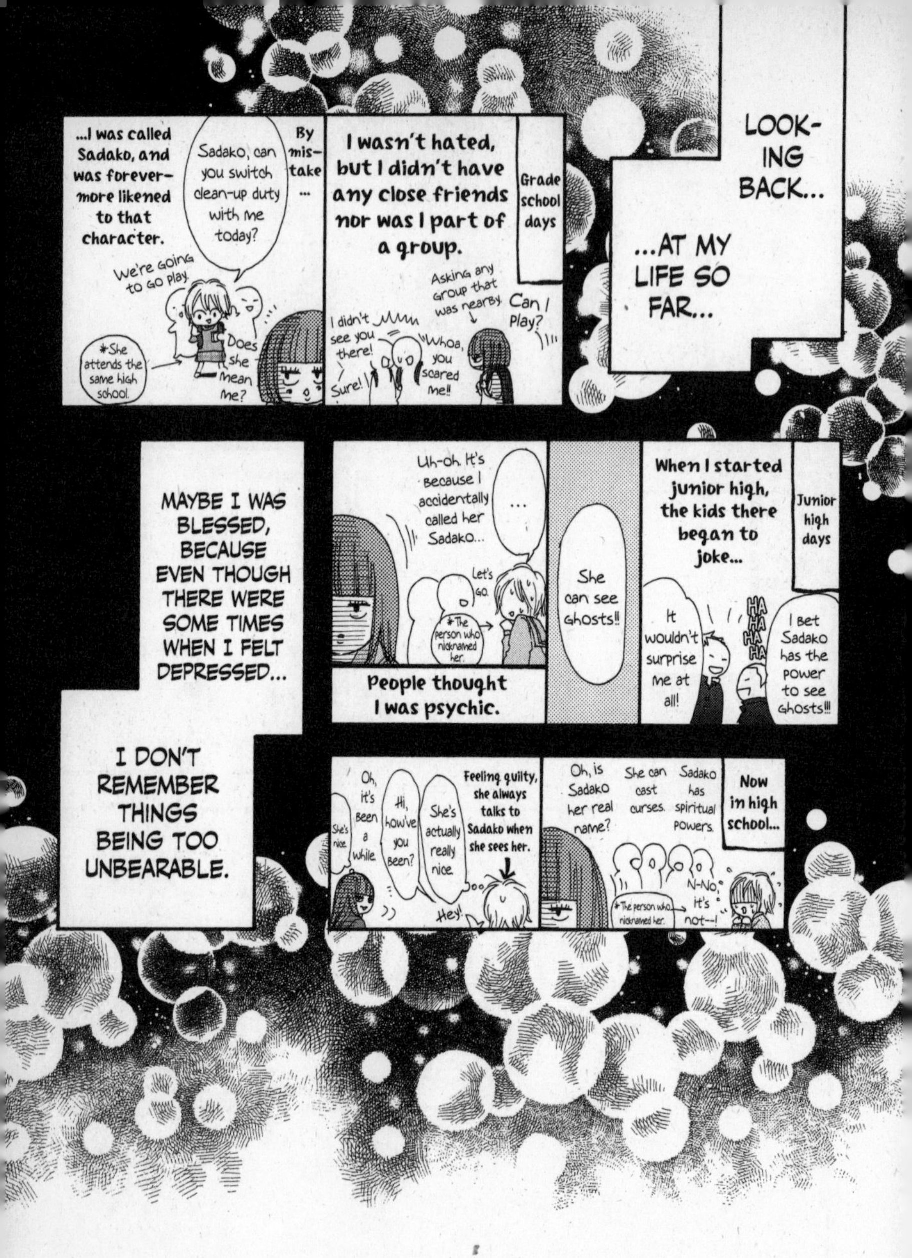
LOOKING BACK...
...AT MY LIFE SO FAR...
Grade school days
I wasn't hated, but I didn't have any close friends nor was I part of a group.
Asking any group that was nearby.
Can I play?
Whoa, you scared me!!
I didn't see you there!
Sure!
By mistake...
...I was called Sadako, and was forevermore likened to that character.
Sadako, can you switch clean-up duty with me today?
We're going to go play.
Does she mean me?
*She attends the same high school.
Junior high days
When I started junior high, the kids there began to joke...
I bet Sadako has the power to see ghosts!!!
HA HA HA HA
It wouldn't surprise me at all!
She can see ghosts!!
...
Uh-oh. It's because I accidentally called her Sadako...
Let's go.
*The person who nicknamed her.
People thought I was psychic.
MAYBE I WAS BLESSED, BECAUSE EVEN THOUGH THERE WERE SOME TIMES WHEN I FELT DEPRESSED...
Now in high school...
Sadako has spiritual powers.
She can cast curses.
Oh, is Sadako her real name?
N-No, it's not--!
*The person who nicknamed her.
Feeling guilty, she always talks to Sadako when she sees her.
She's actually really nice.
Hi, how've you been?
Oh, it's been a while.
She's nice.
Hey!
I DON'T REMEMBER THINGS BEING TOO UNBEARABLE.

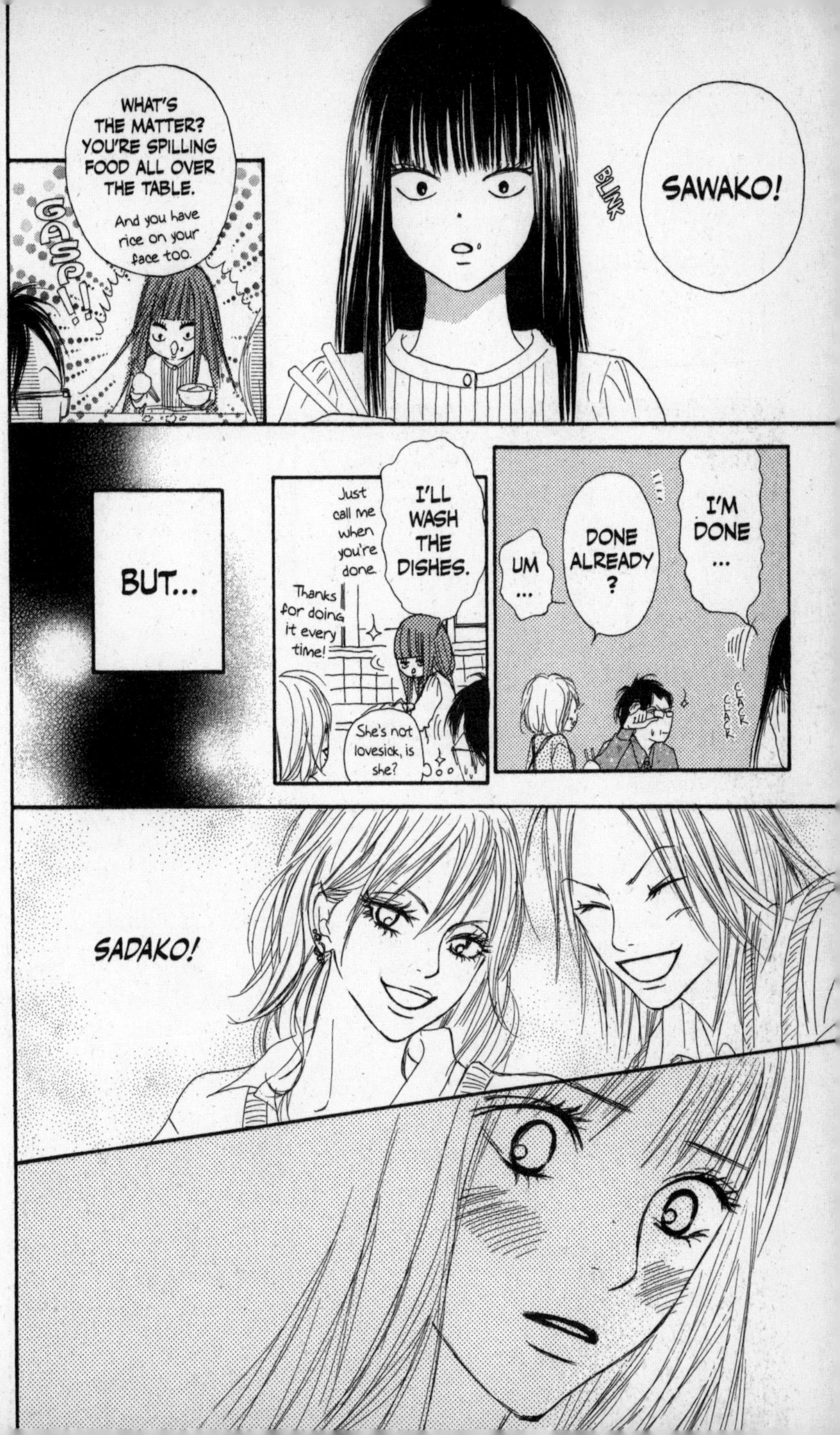
SAWAKO!
BLINK
WHAT'S THE MATTER? YOU'RE SPILLING FOOD ALL OVER THE TABLE.
And you have rice on your face too.
GASP!!
I'M DONE ...
DONE ALREADY ?
UM ...
CLACK CLACK
I'LL WASH THE DISHES.
Just call me when you're done.
Thanks for doing it every time!
She's not lovesick, is she?
BUT...
SADAKO!

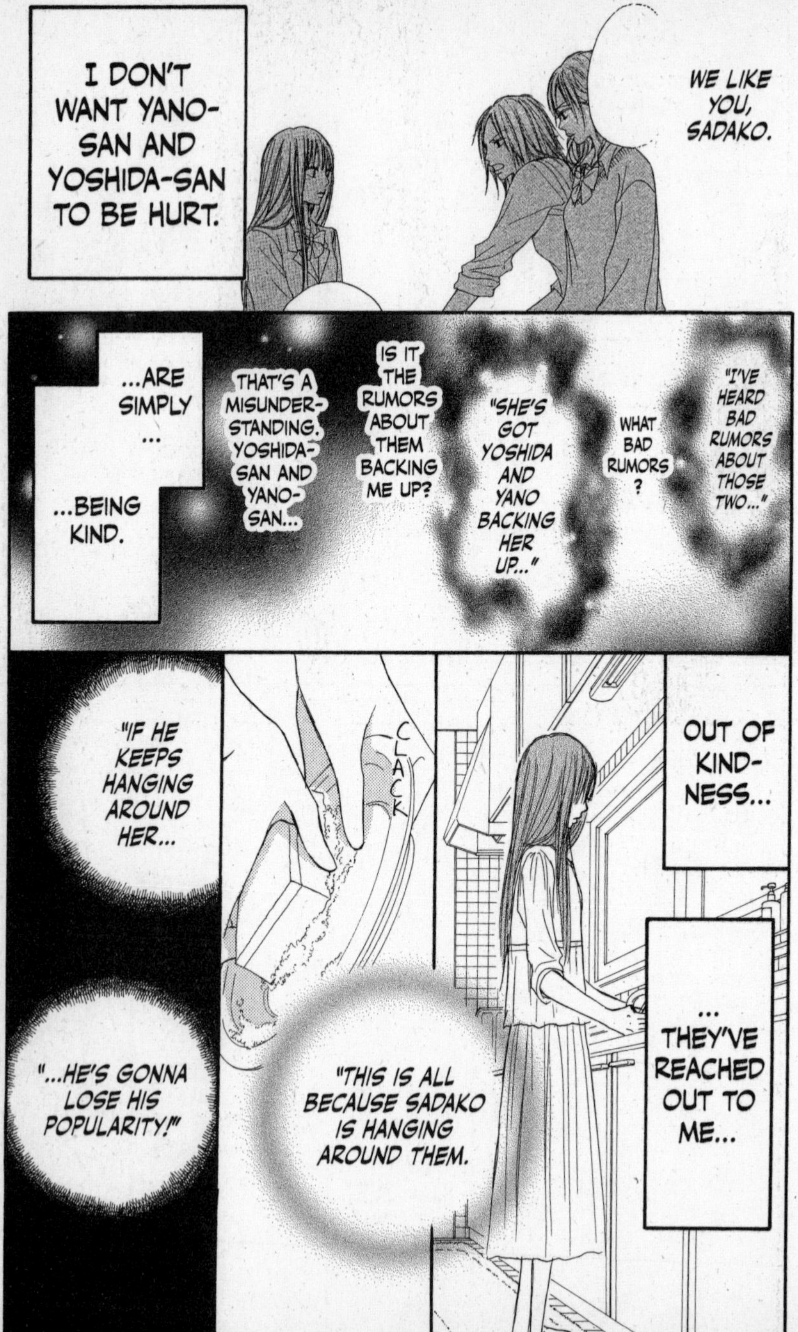
WE LIKE YOU, SADAKO.
I DON'T WANT YANO-SAN AND YOSHIDA-SAN TO BE HURT.
"I'VE HEARD BAD RUMORS ABOUT THOSE TWO..."
WHAT BAD RUMORS?
"SHE'S GOT YOSHIDA AND YANO BACKING HER UP..."
IS IT THE RUMORS ABOUT THEM BACKING ME UP?
THAT'S A MISUNDERSTANDING. YOSHIDA-SAN AND YANO-SAN...
...ARE SIMPLY...
...BEING KIND.
OUT OF KINDNESS...
...THEY'VE REACHED OUT TO ME...
"THIS IS ALL BECAUSE SADAKO IS HANGING AROUND THEM.
CLACK
"IF HE KEEPS HANGING AROUND HER...
"...HE'S GONNA LOSE HIS POPULARITY!"

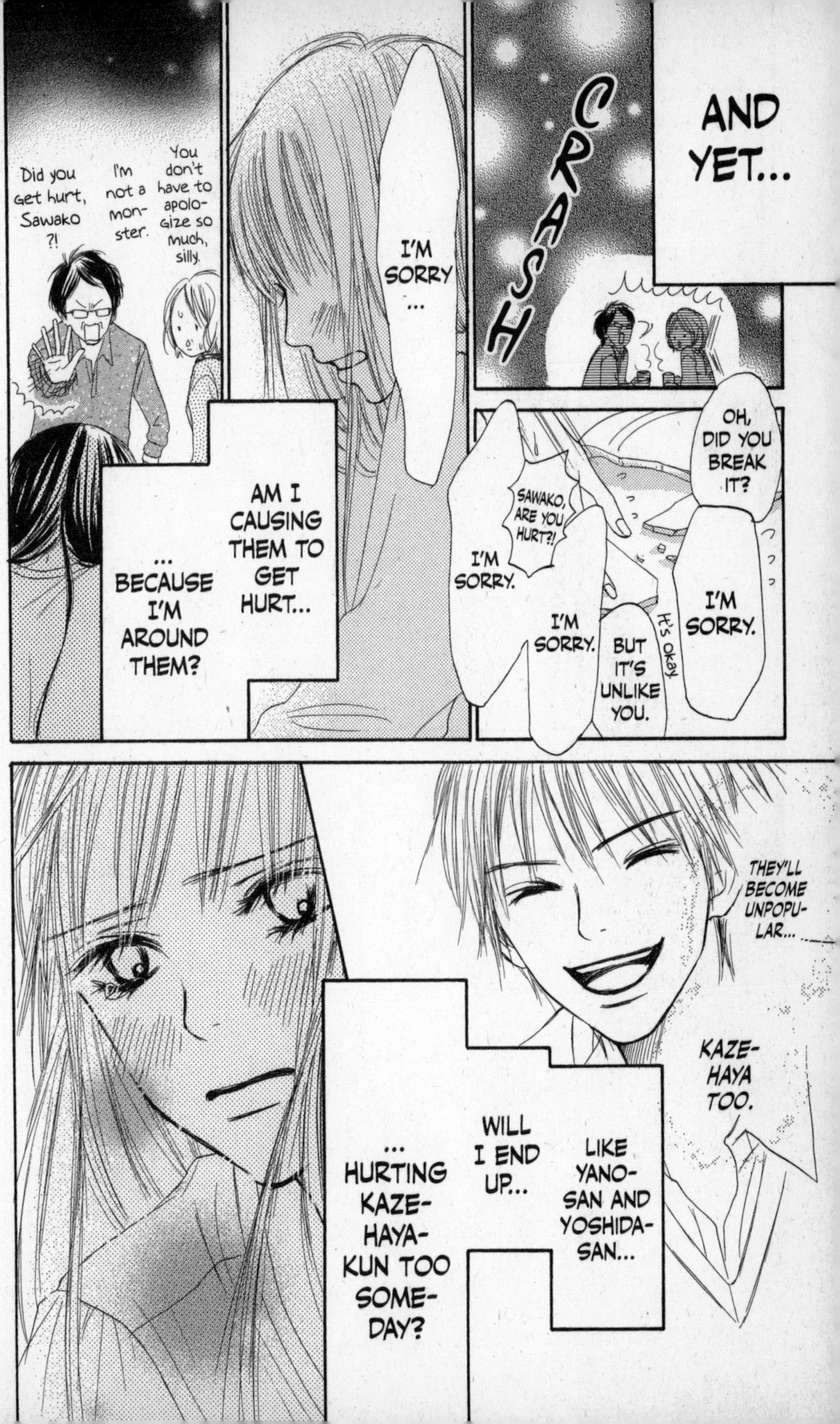
AND YET...
CRASH
OH, DID YOU BREAK IT?
I'M SORRY.
It's okay
BUT IT'S UNLIKE YOU.
I'M SORRY.
SAWAKO, ARE YOU HURT?!
I'M SORRY.
I'M SORRY...
AM I CAUSING THEM TO GET HURT...
You don't have to apologize so much, silly.
I'm not a monster.
Did you get hurt, Sawako?!
...BECAUSE I'M AROUND THEM?
THEY'LL BECOME UNPOPULAR...
KAZEHAYA TOO.
LIKE YANO-SAN AND YOSHIDA-SAN...
WILL I END UP...
...HURTING KAZEHAYA-KUN TOO SOMEDAY?

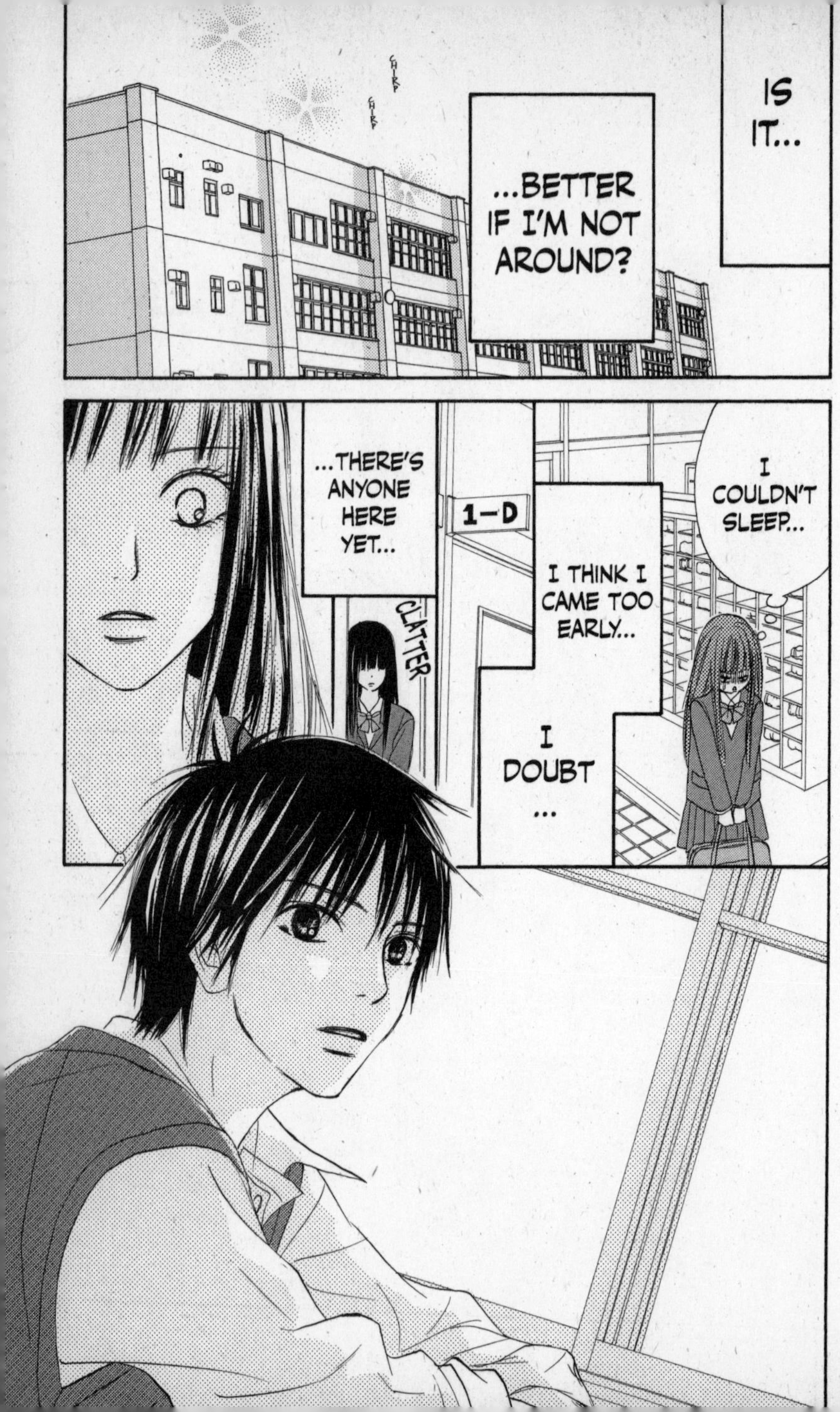
CHIRP
CHIRP
IS IT...
...BETTER IF I'M NOT AROUND?
I COULDN'T SLEEP...
I THINK I CAME TOO EARLY...
I DOUBT ...
...THERE'S ANYONE HERE YET...
1-D
CLATTER

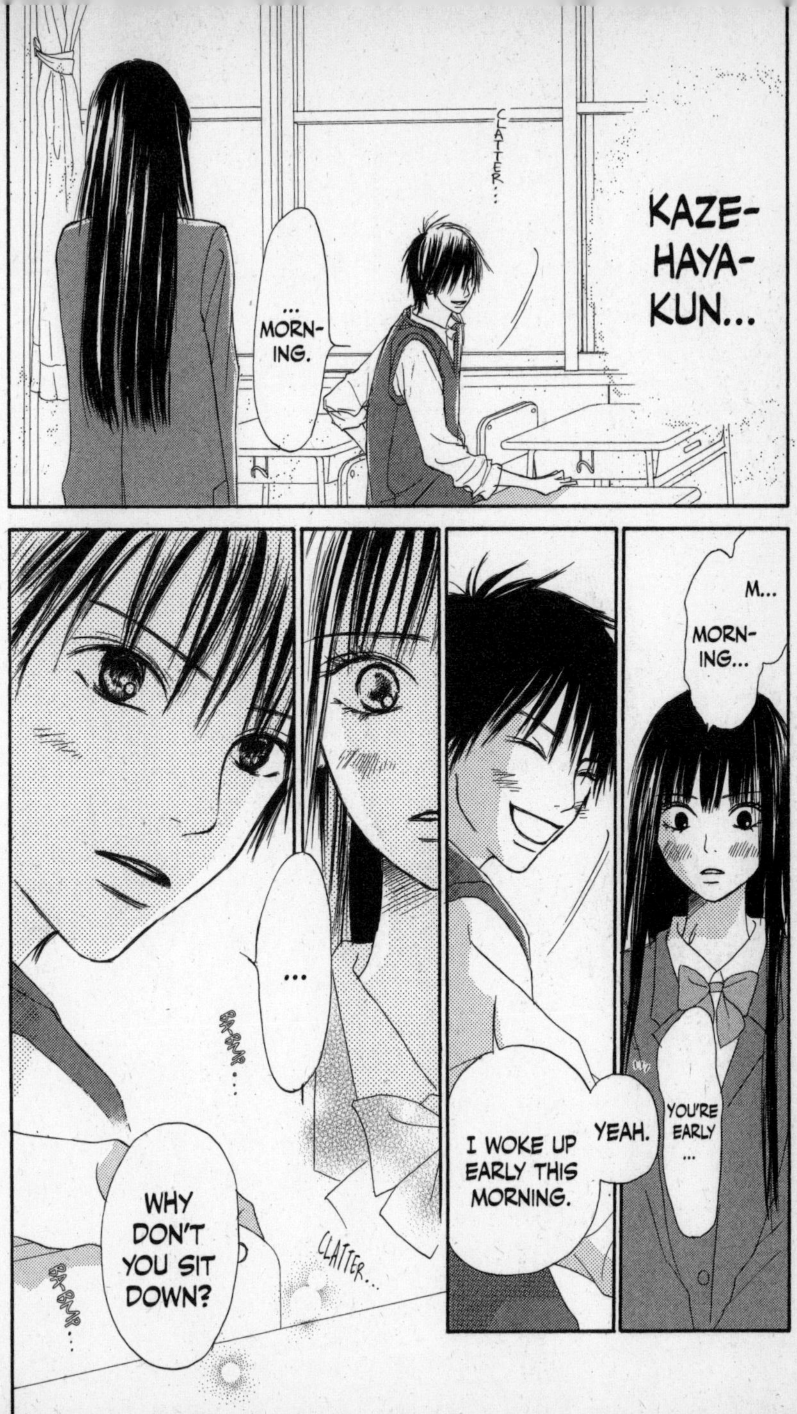
KAZE-HAYA-KUN...
CLATTER...
... MORNING.
M... MORNING...
YOU'RE EARLY ...
YEAH.
I WOKE UP EARLY THIS MORNING.
...
BA-BMP...
WHY DON'T YOU SIT DOWN?
CLATTER...
BA-BMP...

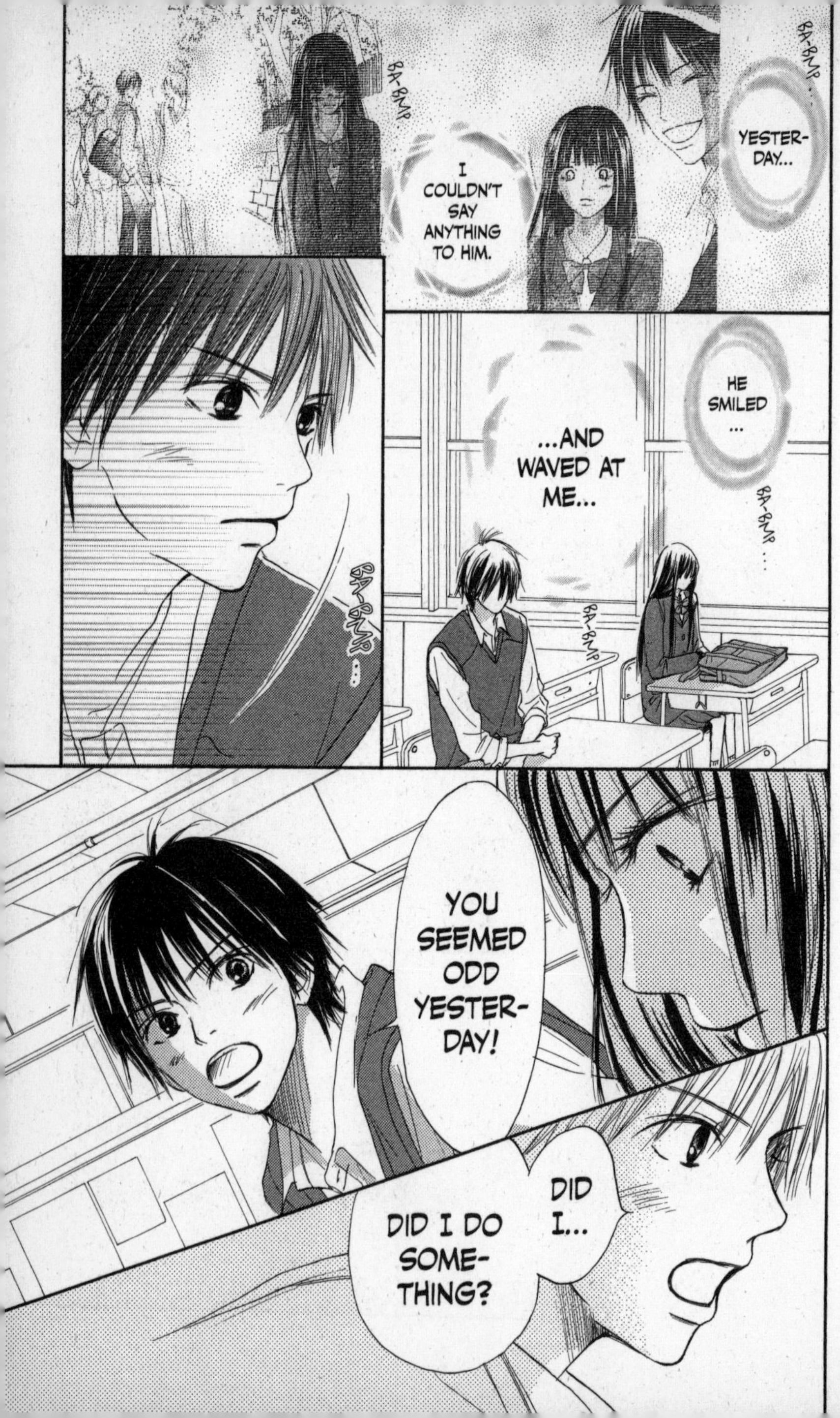
BA-BMP...
YESTER-DAY...
I COULDN'T SAY ANYTHING TO HIM.
BA-BMP
HE SMILED...
...AND WAVED AT ME...
BA-BMP...
BA-BMP
BA-BMP...
YOU SEEMED ODD YESTER-DAY!
DID I...
DID I DO SOME-THING?

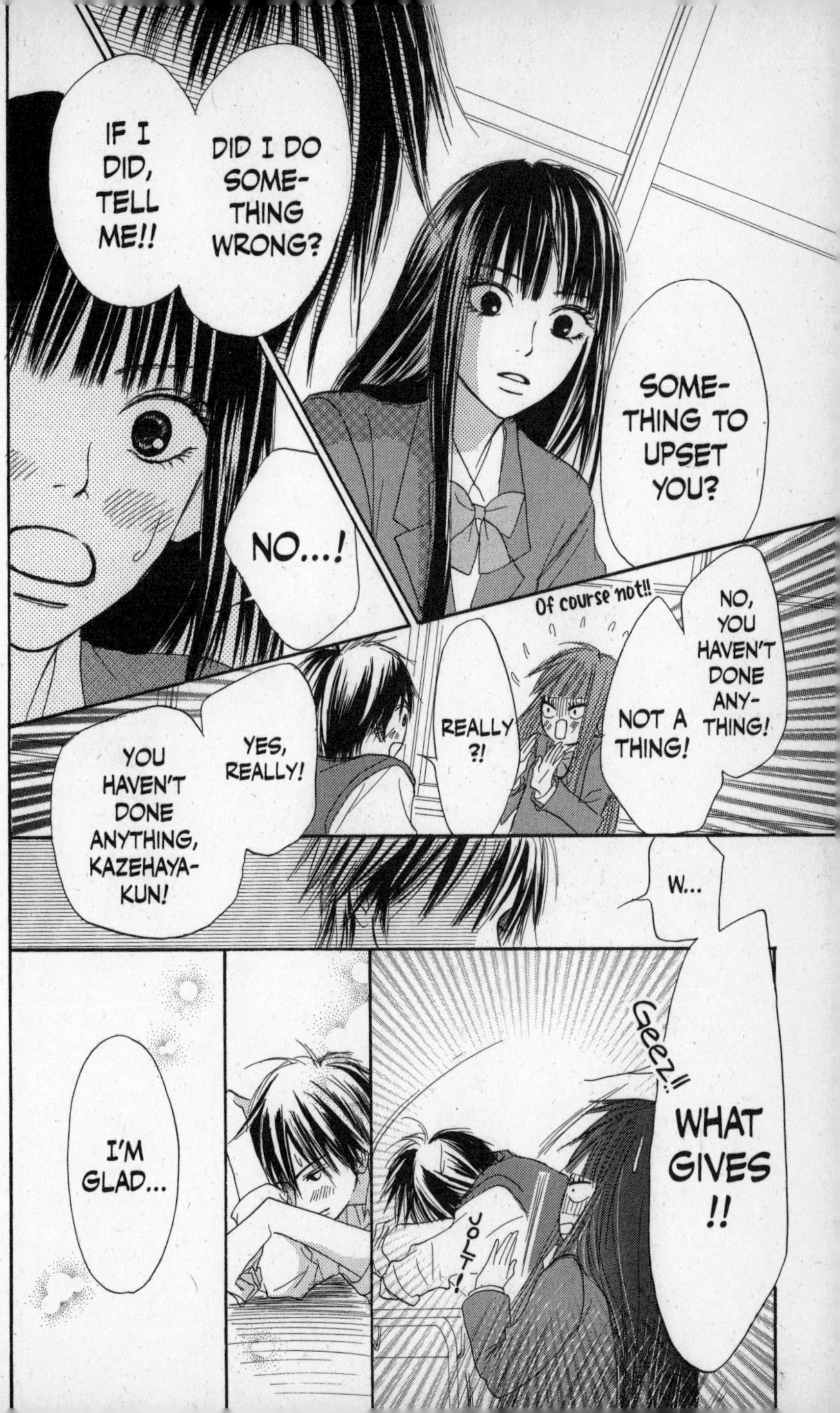
DID I DO SOME-THING WRONG?
IF I DID, TELL ME!!
SOME-THING TO UPSET YOU?
NO...!
NO, YOU HAVEN'T DONE ANY-THING!
NOT A THING!
Of course not!!
REALLY?!
YES, REALLY!
YOU HAVEN'T DONE ANYTHING, KAZEHAYA-KUN!
W...
Geez!!
WHAT GIVES!!
JOLT!
I'M GLAD...

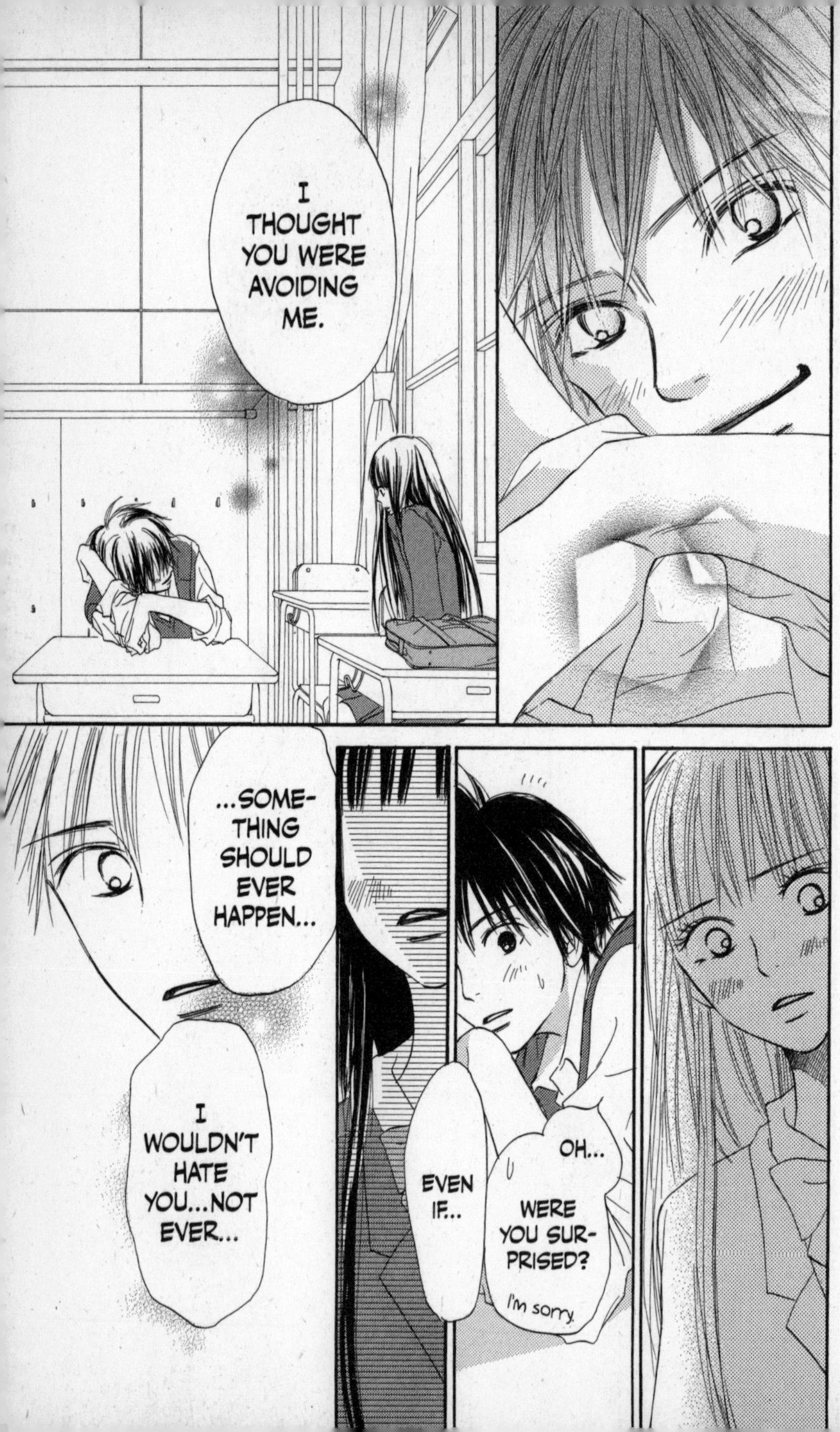
I THOUGHT YOU WERE AVOIDING ME.
OH...
WERE YOU SURPRISED?
I'm sorry.
EVEN IF...
...SOMETHING SHOULD EVER HAPPEN...
I WOULDN'T HATE YOU...NOT EVER...

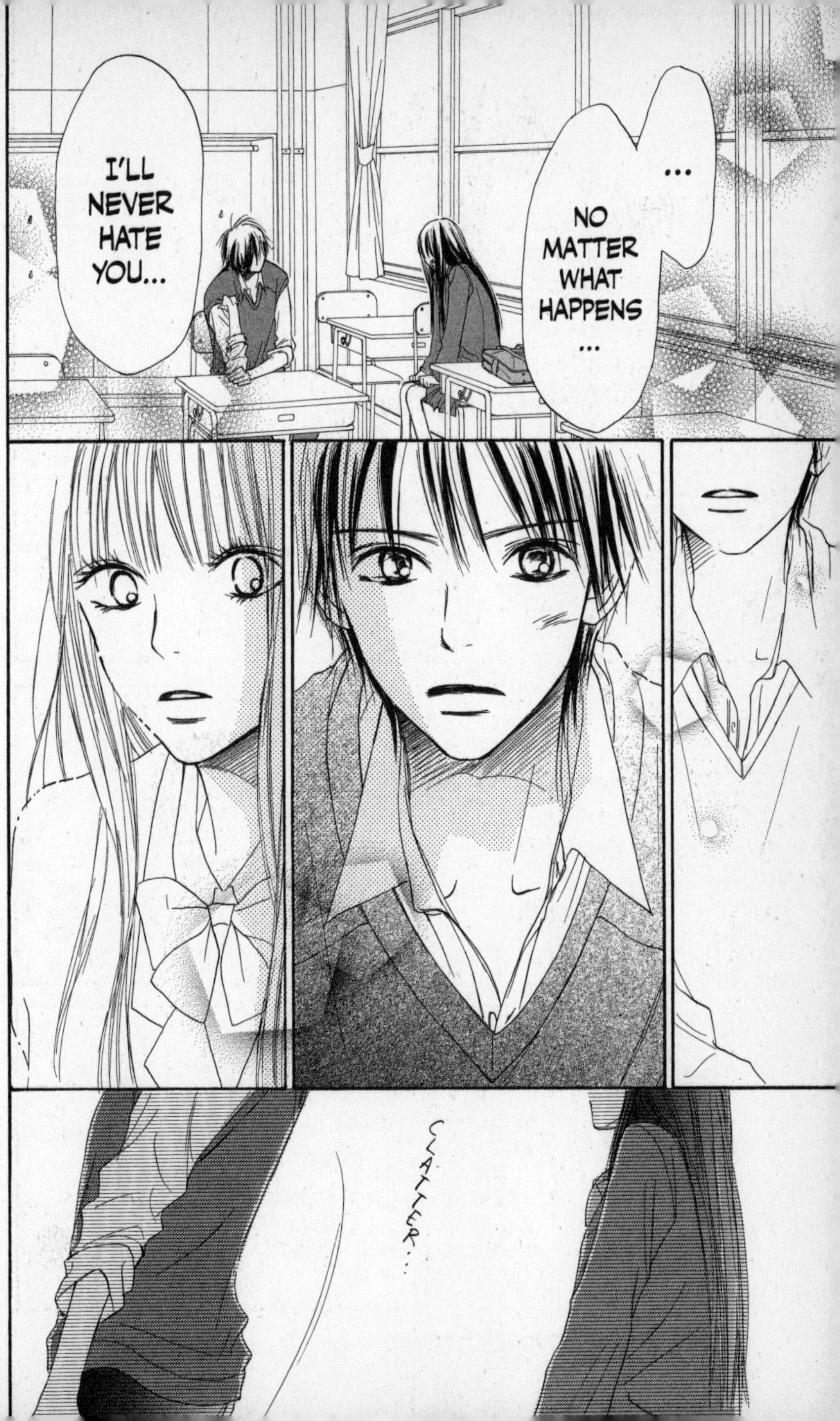
... NO MATTER WHAT HAPPENS ...
I'LL NEVER HATE YOU...
CLATTER...

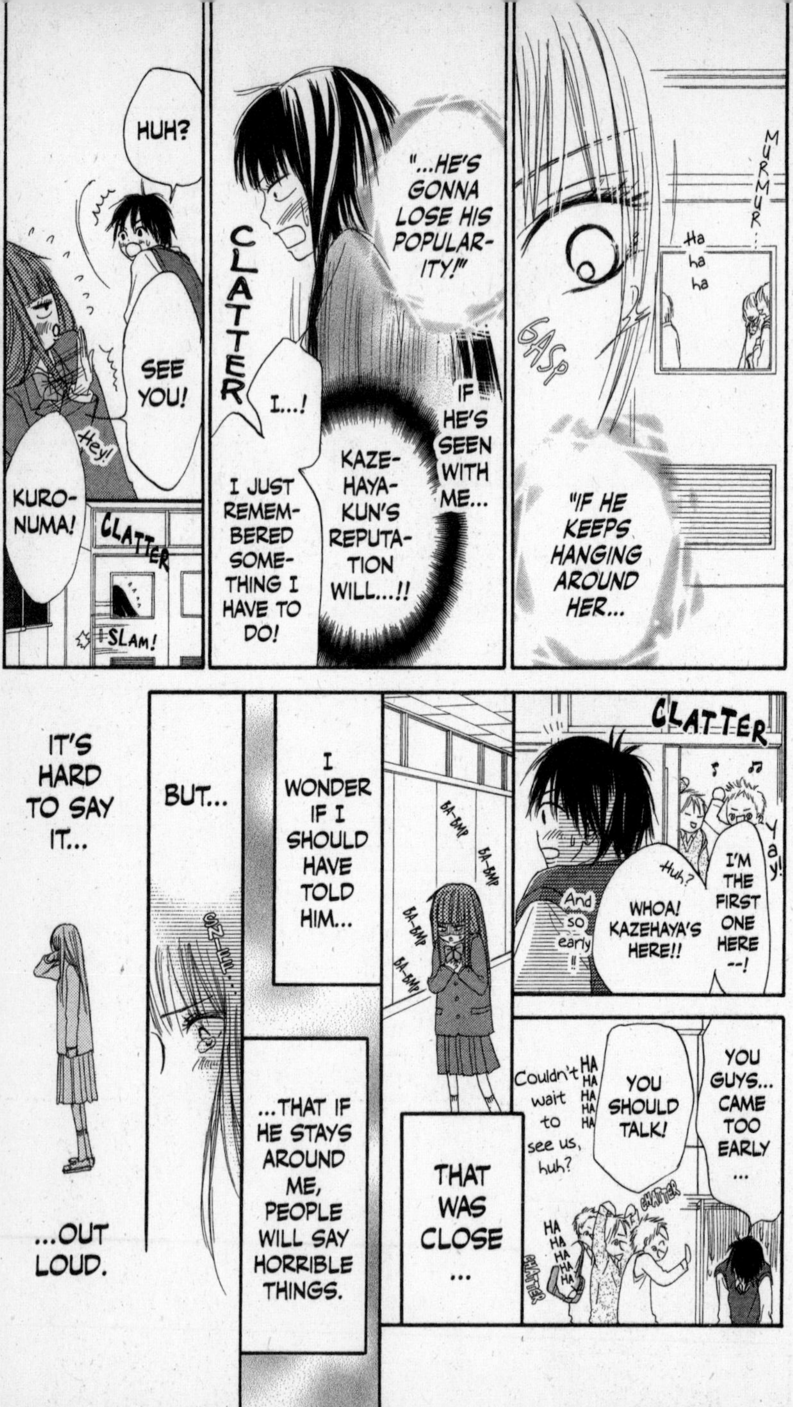
MURMUR...
Ha ha ha
GASP
"IF HE KEEPS HANGING AROUND HER...
"...HE'S GONNA LOSE HIS POPULARITY!"
IF HE'S SEEN WITH ME...
KAZEHAYA-KUN'S REPUTATION WILL...!!
CLATTER
I...!
I JUST REMEMBERED SOMETHING I HAVE TO DO!
HUH?
SEE YOU!
Hey!
KURONUMA!
CLATTER
SLAM!
CLATTER
I'M THE FIRST ONE HERE--!
Yay!
WHOA! KAZEHAYA'S HERE!!
Huh?
And so early!!
YOU GUYS... CAME TOO EARLY...
YOU SHOULD TALK!
HA HA HA HA HA
Couldn't wait to see us, huh?
CHATTER
HA HA HA HA HA
CHATTER
THAT WAS CLOSE...
I WONDER IF I SHOULD HAVE TOLD HIM...
BA-BMP
BA-BMP
BA-BMP
BA-BMP
...THAT IF HE STAYS AROUND ME, PEOPLE WILL SAY HORRIBLE THINGS.
BUT...
SNIFF
IT'S HARD TO SAY IT...
...OUT LOUD.

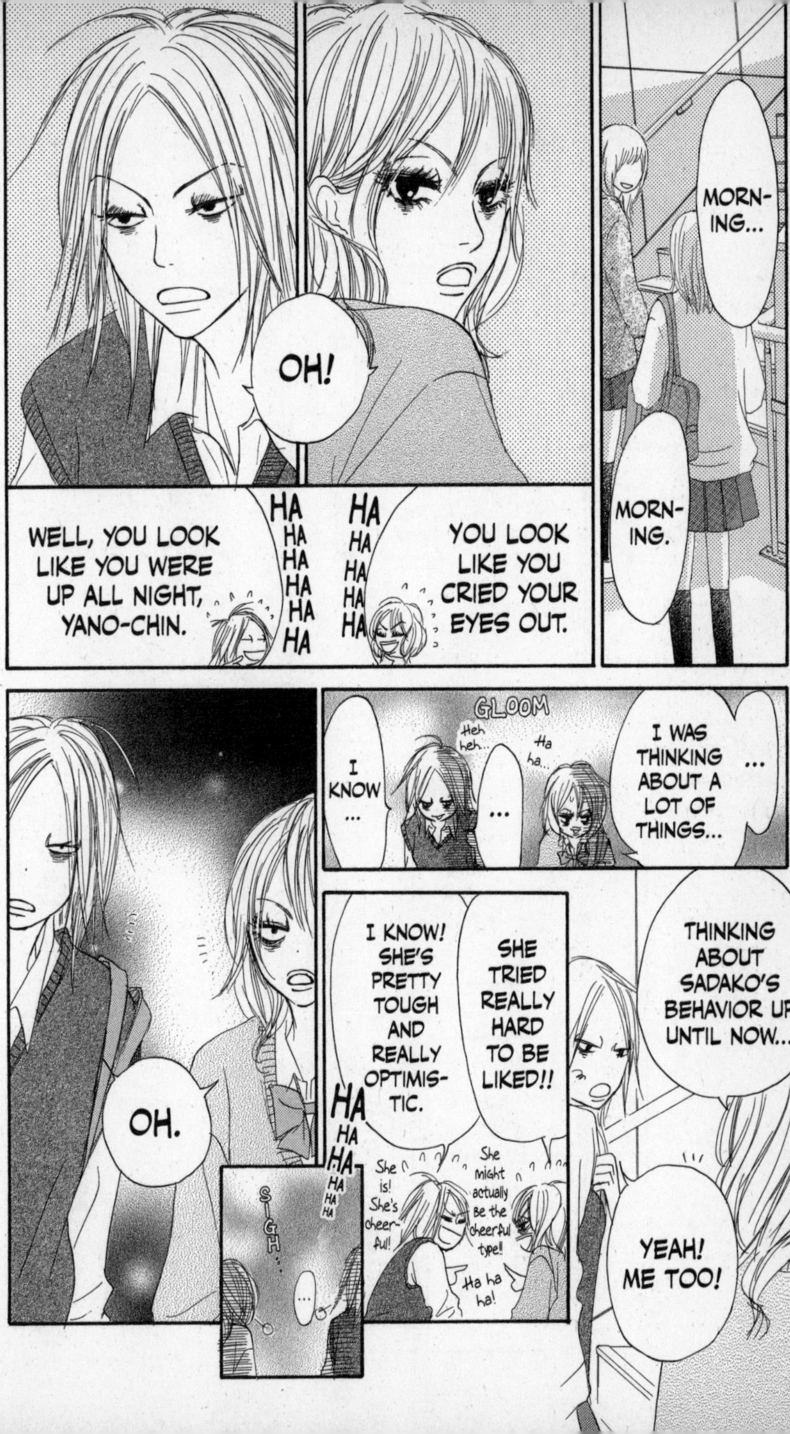

MORN-ING...
MORN-ING.
OH!
HA HA HA HA HA HA
YOU LOOK LIKE YOU CRIED YOUR EYES OUT.
HA HA HA HA HA HA
WELL, YOU LOOK LIKE YOU WERE UP ALL NIGHT, YANO-CHIN.
GLOOM
I WAS THINKING ABOUT A LOT OF THINGS...
...
Ha ha...
...
Heh heh...
I KNOW ...
THINKING ABOUT SADAKO'S BEHAVIOR UP UNTIL NOW...
YEAH! ME TOO!
SHE TRIED REALLY HARD TO BE LIKED!!
I KNOW! SHE'S PRETTY TOUGH AND REALLY OPTIMIS-TIC.
HA HA HA HA HA HA
She might actually be the cheerful type!!
Ha ha ha!
She is! She's cheer-ful!
SIGH...
...
OH.

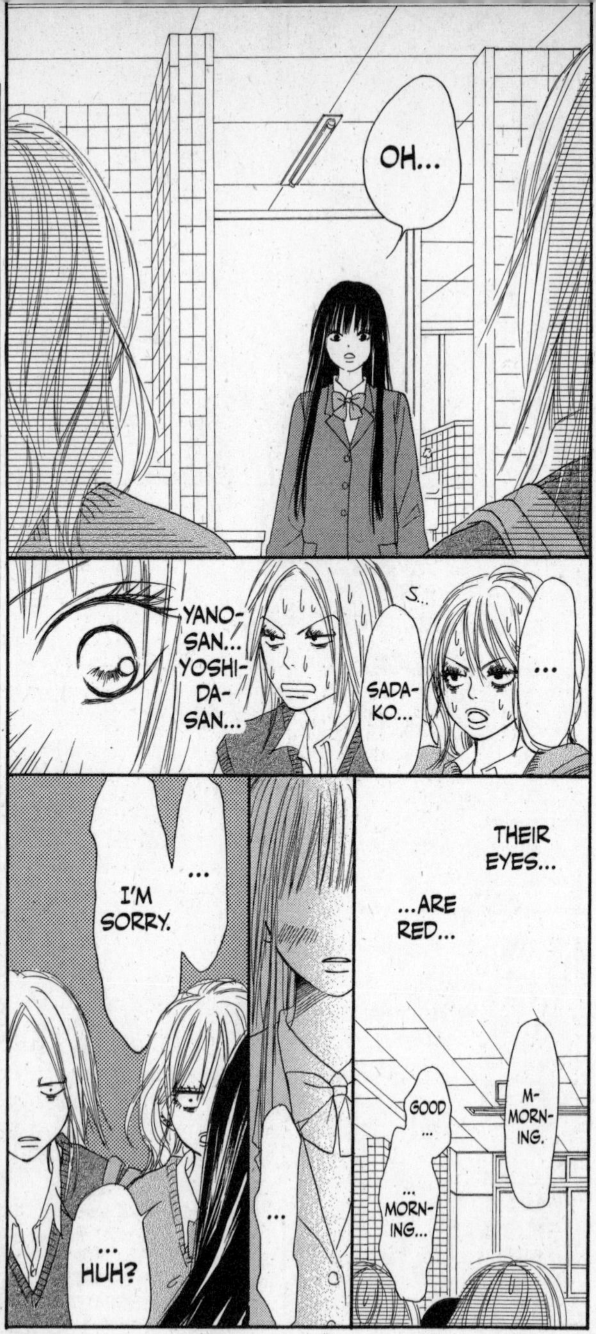

OH...
...
S...
SADA-KO...
YANO-SAN... YOSHI-DA-SAN...
THEIR EYES...
...ARE RED...
M-MORNING.
GOOD... ...MORNING...
...
... I'M SORRY.
... HUH?

KARUPIN on JAPAN 2

Since I began drawing this manga, I've received more letters (or is it emails?) from mothers telling me that that they're reading it with their daughters.

Warm fuzzy feeling

I grew up sharing shojo manga with my mother, so that makes me very happy.

I have two older brothers, so we shared shonen manga too!

We never got scolded that we were reading manga!

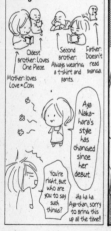

Oldest brother: Loves One Piece.

Second brother: Always wearing a t-shirt and pants.

Father: Doesn't read manga.

Mother: loves Love*Com.

Aya Nakahara's style has changed since her debut.

You're right, but who are you to say such things?

Ha ha ha. Aya-chan, sorry to bring this up all the time!!

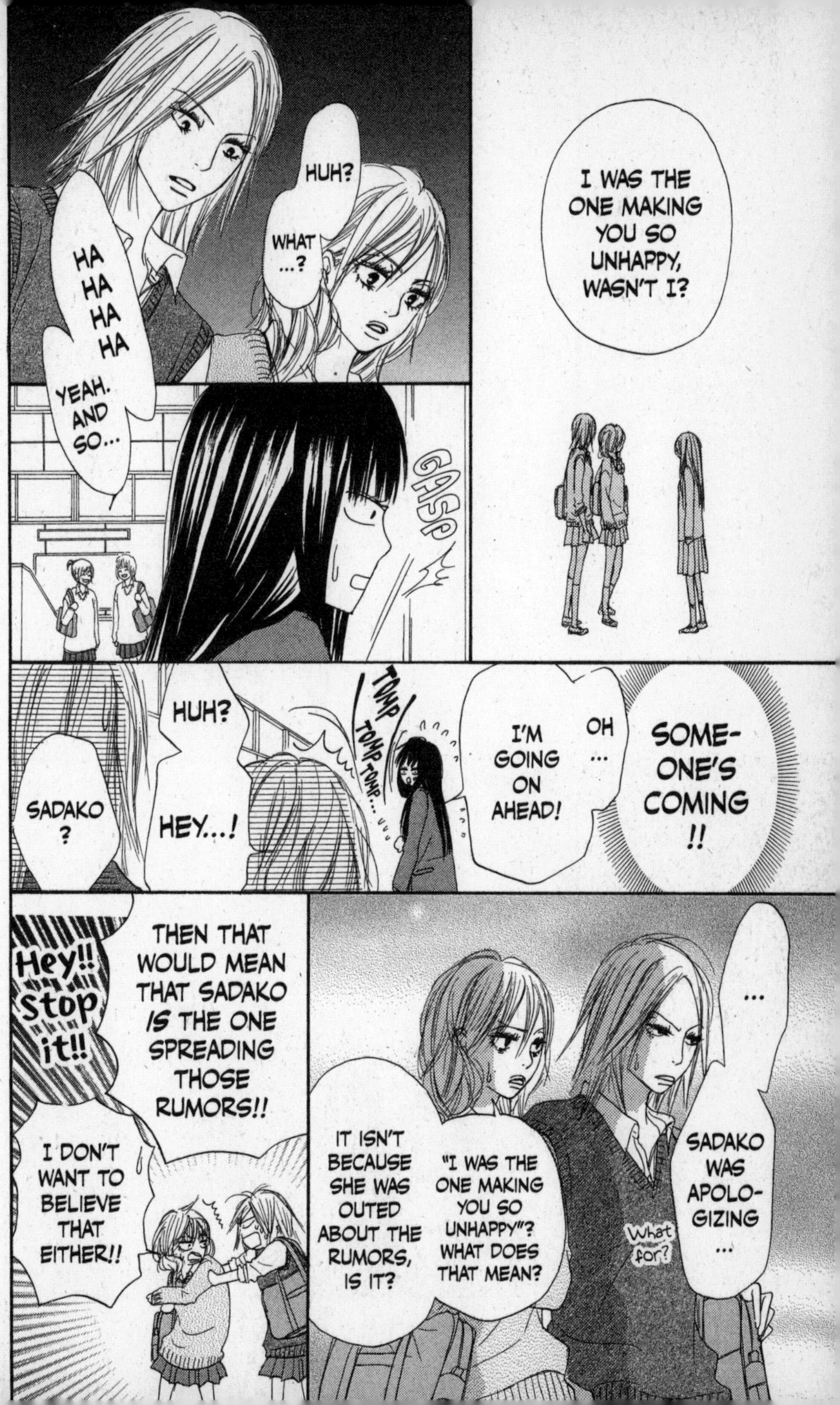
I WAS THE ONE MAKING YOU SO UNHAPPY, WASN'T I?
HUH?
WHAT ...?
HA HA HA HA
YEAH. AND SO...
GASP
SOME-ONE'S COMING !!
OH ...
I'M GOING ON AHEAD!
TOMP TOMP TOMP...
HUH?
HEY...!
SADAKO ?
...
SADAKO WAS APOLO-GIZING ...
What for?
"I WAS THE ONE MAKING YOU SO UNHAPPY"? WHAT DOES THAT MEAN?
IT ISN'T BECAUSE SHE WAS OUTED ABOUT THE RUMORS, IS IT?
THEN THAT WOULD MEAN THAT SADAKO *IS* THE ONE SPREADING THOSE RUMORS!!
Hey!! Stop it!!
I DON'T WANT TO BELIEVE THAT EITHER!!

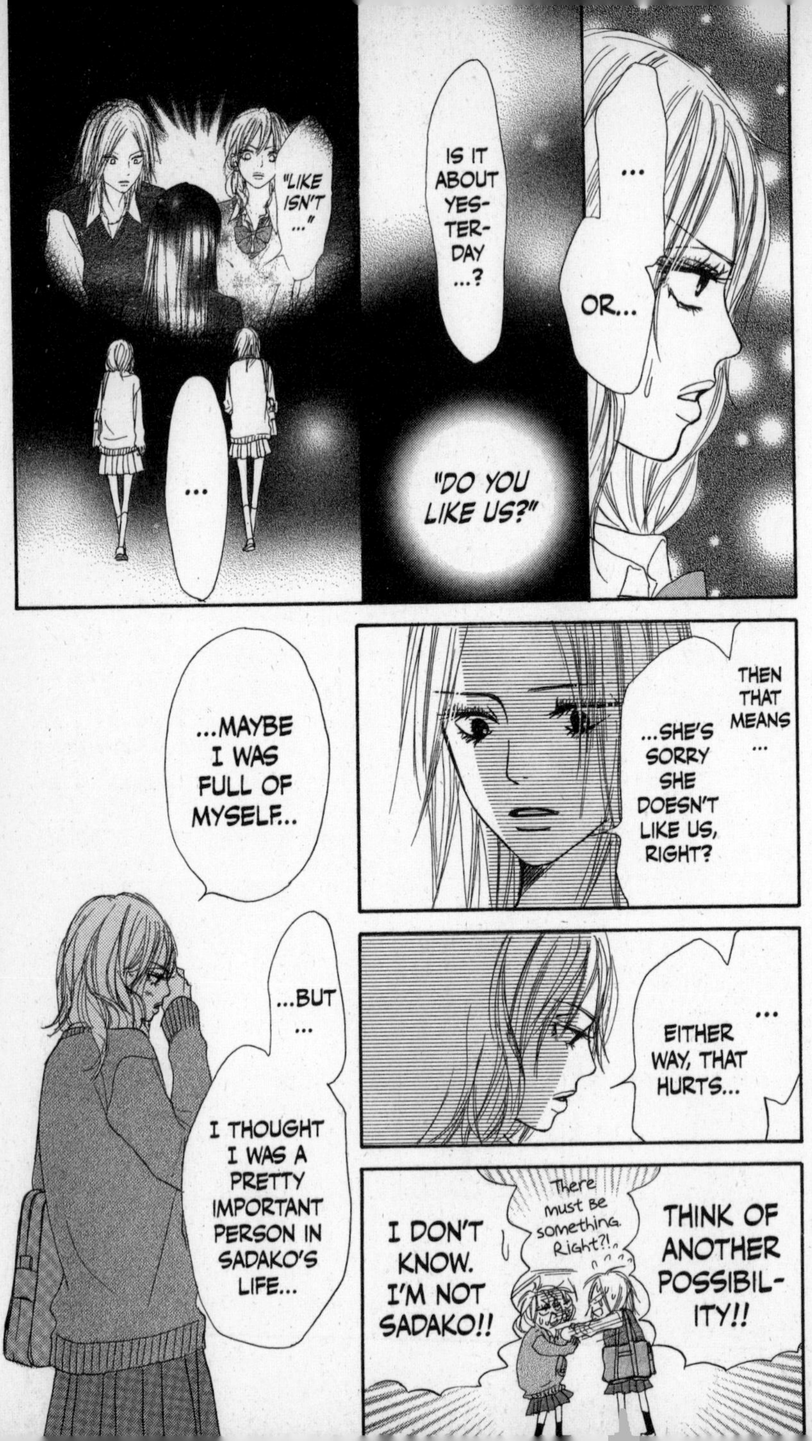
...
OR...
IS IT ABOUT YES-TER-DAY ...?
"DO YOU LIKE US?"
"LIKE ISN'T ..."
...
THEN THAT MEANS ...
...SHE'S SORRY SHE DOESN'T LIKE US, RIGHT?
...
EITHER WAY, THAT HURTS...
THINK OF ANOTHER POSSIBIL-ITY!!
There must be something. Right?!
I DON'T KNOW. I'M NOT SADAKO!!
...MAYBE I WAS FULL OF MYSELF...
...BUT ...
I THOUGHT I WAS A PRETTY IMPORTANT PERSON IN SADAKO'S LIFE...

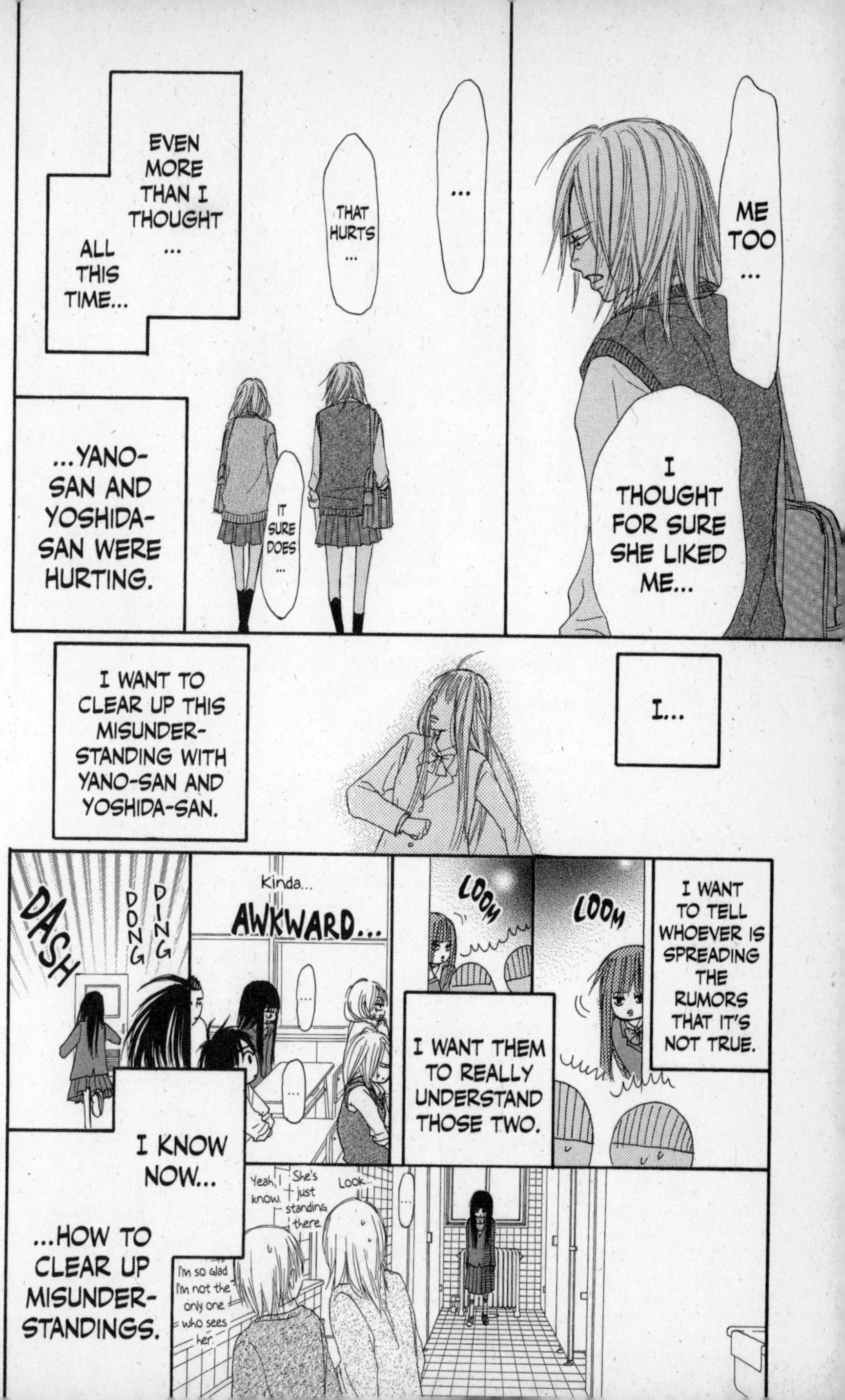
ME TOO...
I THOUGHT FOR SURE SHE LIKED ME...
...
THAT HURTS...
EVEN MORE THAN I THOUGHT...
ALL THIS TIME...
IT SURE DOES...
...YANO-SAN AND YOSHIDA-SAN WERE HURTING.
I...
I WANT TO CLEAR UP THIS MISUNDERSTANDING WITH YANO-SAN AND YOSHIDA-SAN.
I WANT TO TELL WHOEVER IS SPREADING THE RUMORS THAT IT'S NOT TRUE.
LOOM
LOOM
I WANT THEM TO REALLY UNDERSTAND THOSE TWO.
Kinda...
AWKWARD...
...
...
DING
DONG
DASH
...
Look...
She's just standing there
Yeah, I know.
I'm so glad I'm not the only one who sees her.
I KNOW NOW...
...HOW TO CLEAR UP MISUNDERSTANDINGS.

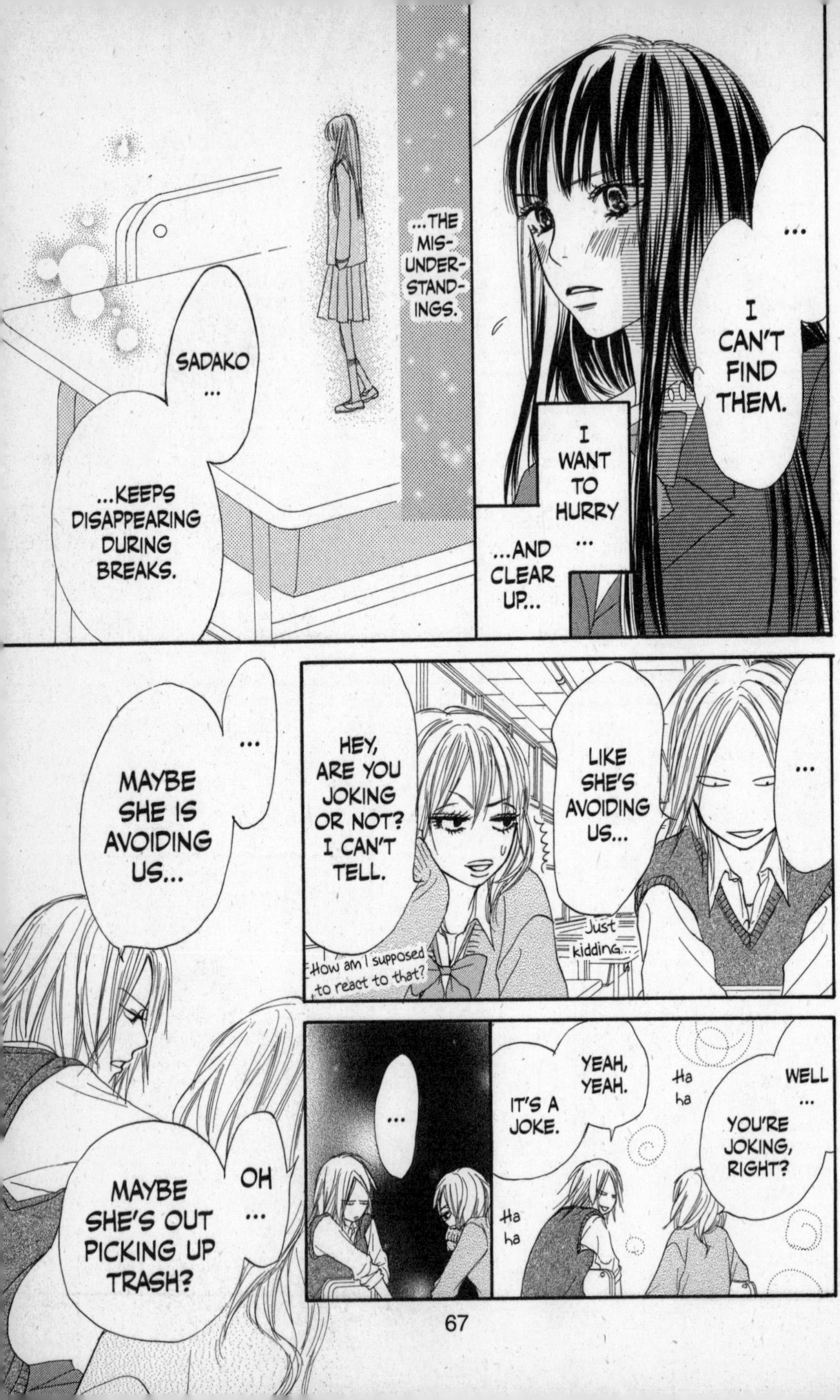
... I CAN'T FIND THEM.
I WANT TO HURRY ...
...AND CLEAR UP...
...THE MIS-UNDER-STANDINGS.
SADAKO ...
...KEEPS DISAPPEARING DURING BREAKS.
...
LIKE SHE'S AVOIDING US...
Just kidding...
HEY, ARE YOU JOKING OR NOT? I CAN'T TELL.
How am I supposed to react to that?
WELL ... YOU'RE JOKING, RIGHT?
Ha ha
YEAH, YEAH.
IT'S A JOKE.
Ha ha
...
... MAYBE SHE IS AVOIDING US...
OH ...
MAYBE SHE'S OUT PICKING UP TRASH?

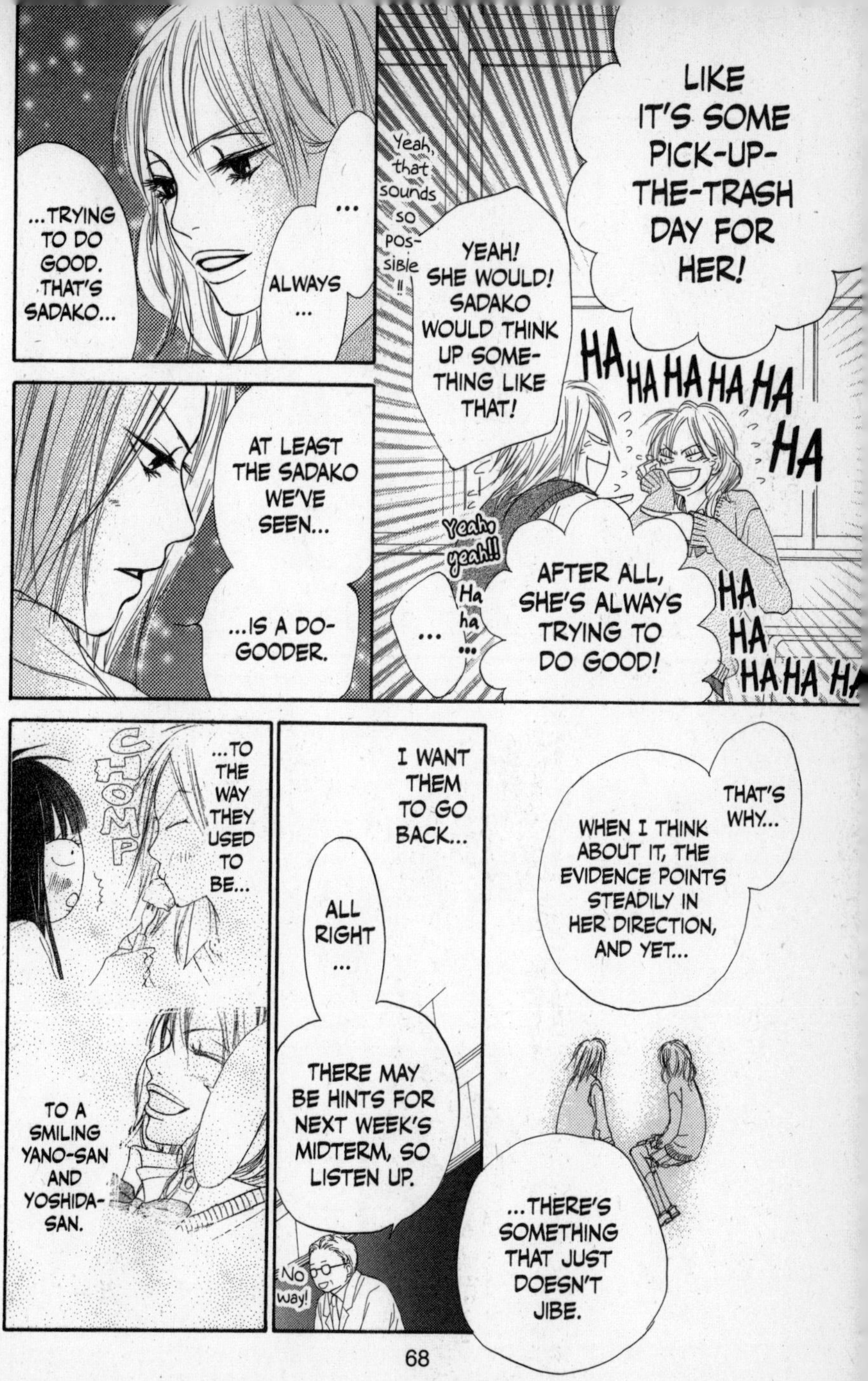
LIKE IT'S SOME PICK-UP-THE-TRASH DAY FOR HER!
Yeah, that sounds so pos-sible!!
YEAH! SHE WOULD! SADAKO WOULD THINK UP SOME-THING LIKE THAT!
HA HA HA HA HA HA HA
Yeah, yeah!!
AFTER ALL, SHE'S ALWAYS TRYING TO DO GOOD!
HA HA HA HA HA
Ha ha ...
...
... ALWAYS ...
...TRYING TO DO GOOD. THAT'S SADAKO...
AT LEAST THE SADAKO WE'VE SEEN...
...IS A DO-GOODER.
THAT'S WHY...
WHEN I THINK ABOUT IT, THE EVIDENCE POINTS STEADILY IN HER DIRECTION, AND YET...
...THERE'S SOMETHING THAT JUST DOESN'T JIBE.
I WANT THEM TO GO BACK...
ALL RIGHT ...
THERE MAY BE HINTS FOR NEXT WEEK'S MIDTERM, SO LISTEN UP.
No way!
CHOMP
...TO THE WAY THEY USED TO BE...
TO A SMILING YANO-SAN AND YOSHIDA-SAN.

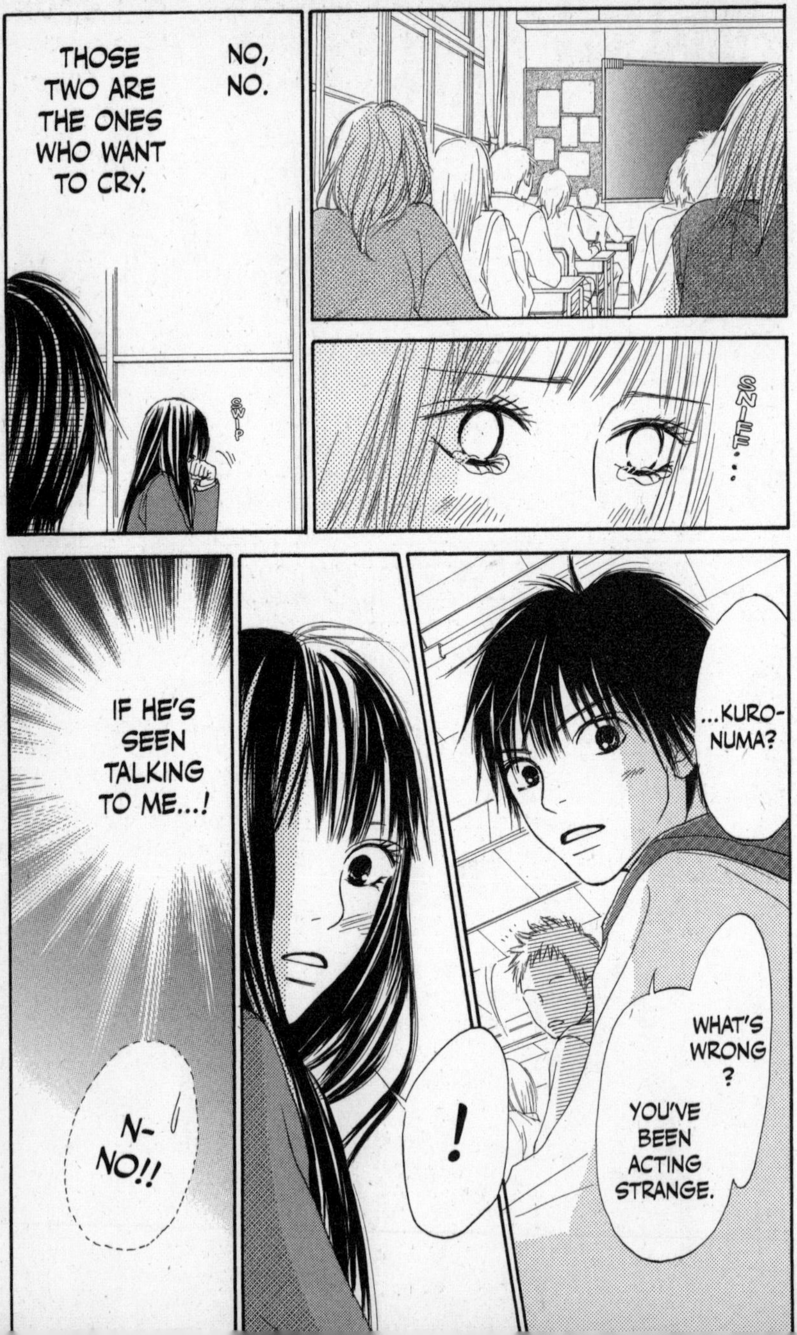
SNIFF...
NO, NO.
THOSE TWO ARE THE ONES WHO WANT TO CRY.
SWIP
...KURO-NUMA?
WHAT'S WRONG?
YOU'VE BEEN ACTING STRANGE.
!
IF HE'S SEEN TALKING TO ME...!
N-NO!!

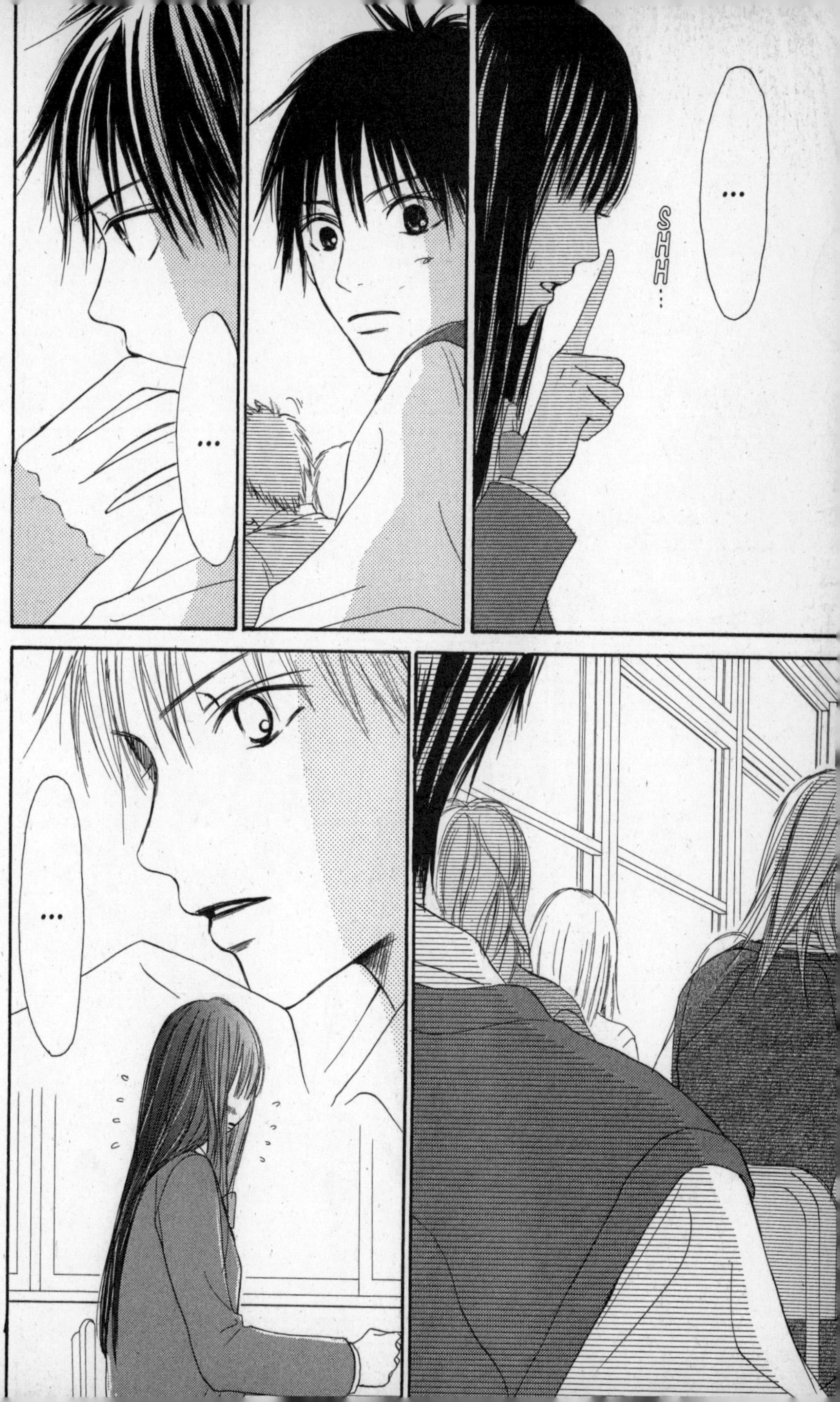
...
SHHH...
...
...

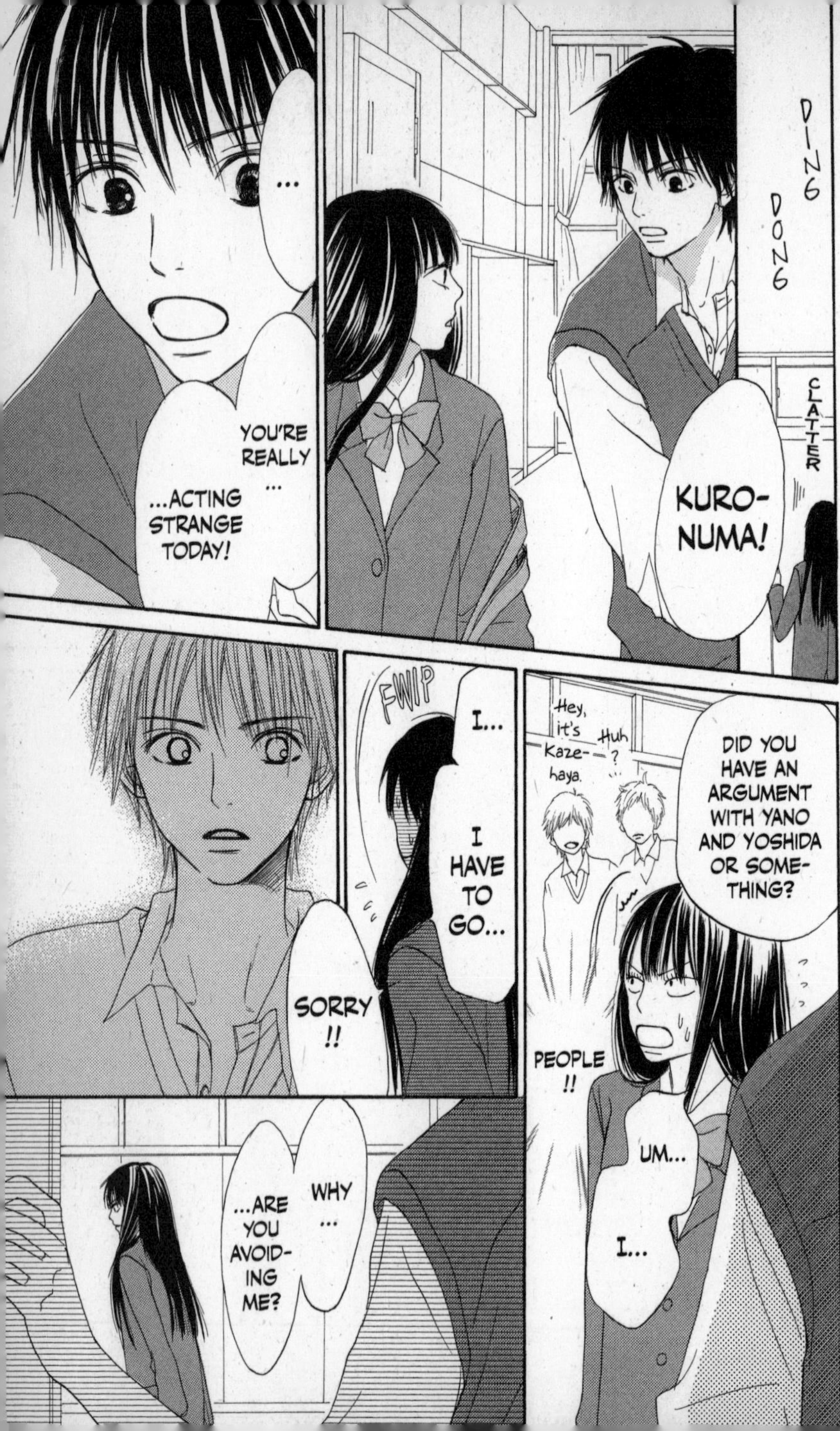
DING DONG
CLATTER
KURO-NUMA!
...
YOU'RE REALLY ...
...ACTING STRANGE TODAY!
DID YOU HAVE AN ARGUMENT WITH YANO AND YOSHIDA OR SOMETHING?
Huh?
Hey, it's Kaze-haya.
PEOPLE!!
UM...
I...
FWIP
I...
I HAVE TO GO...
SORRY!!
WHY ...
...ARE YOU AVOID-ING ME?

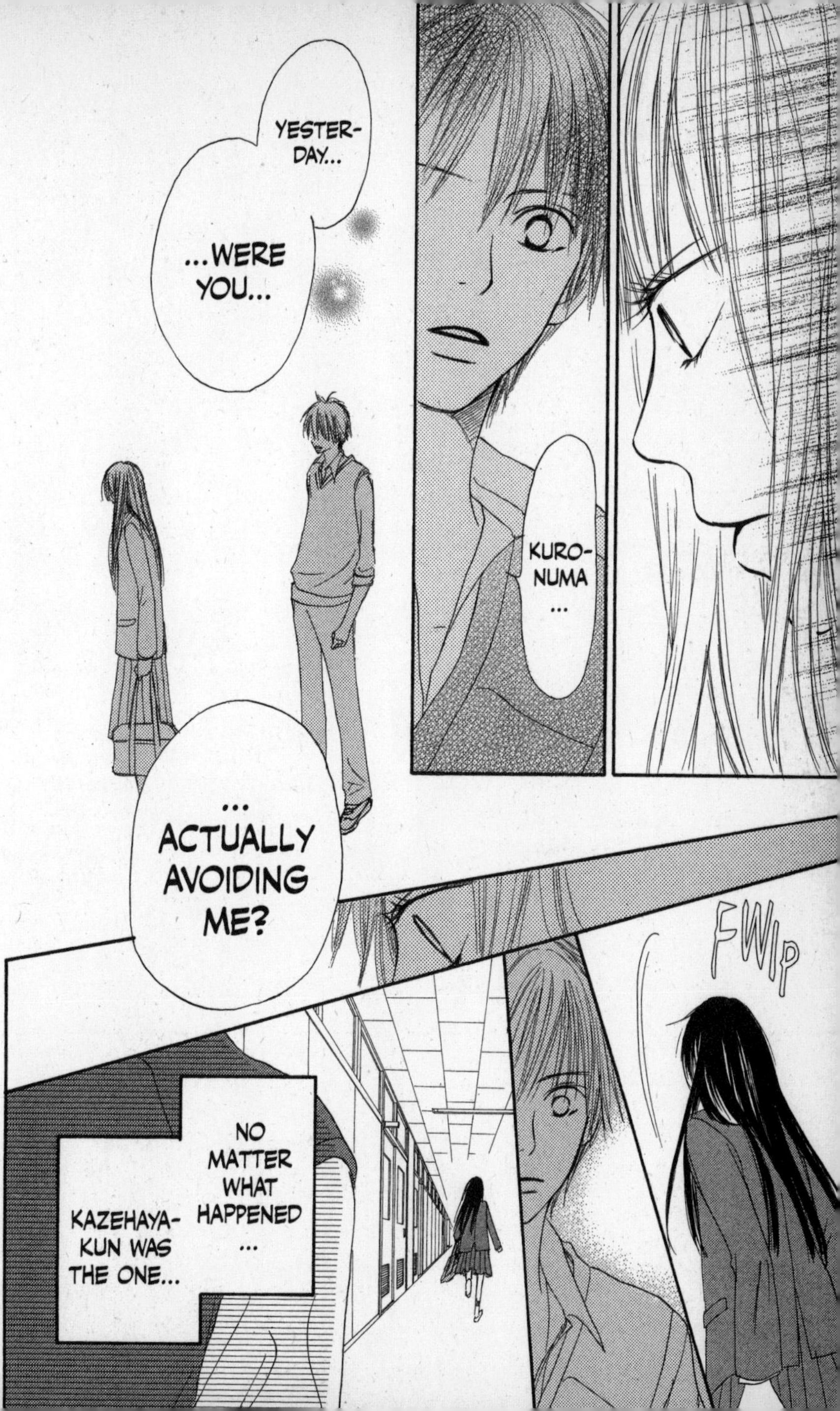
KURO-NUMA ...
YESTER-DAY...
...WERE YOU...
... ACTUALLY AVOIDING ME?
FWIP
NO MATTER WHAT HAPPENED ...
KAZEHAYA-KUN WAS THE ONE...

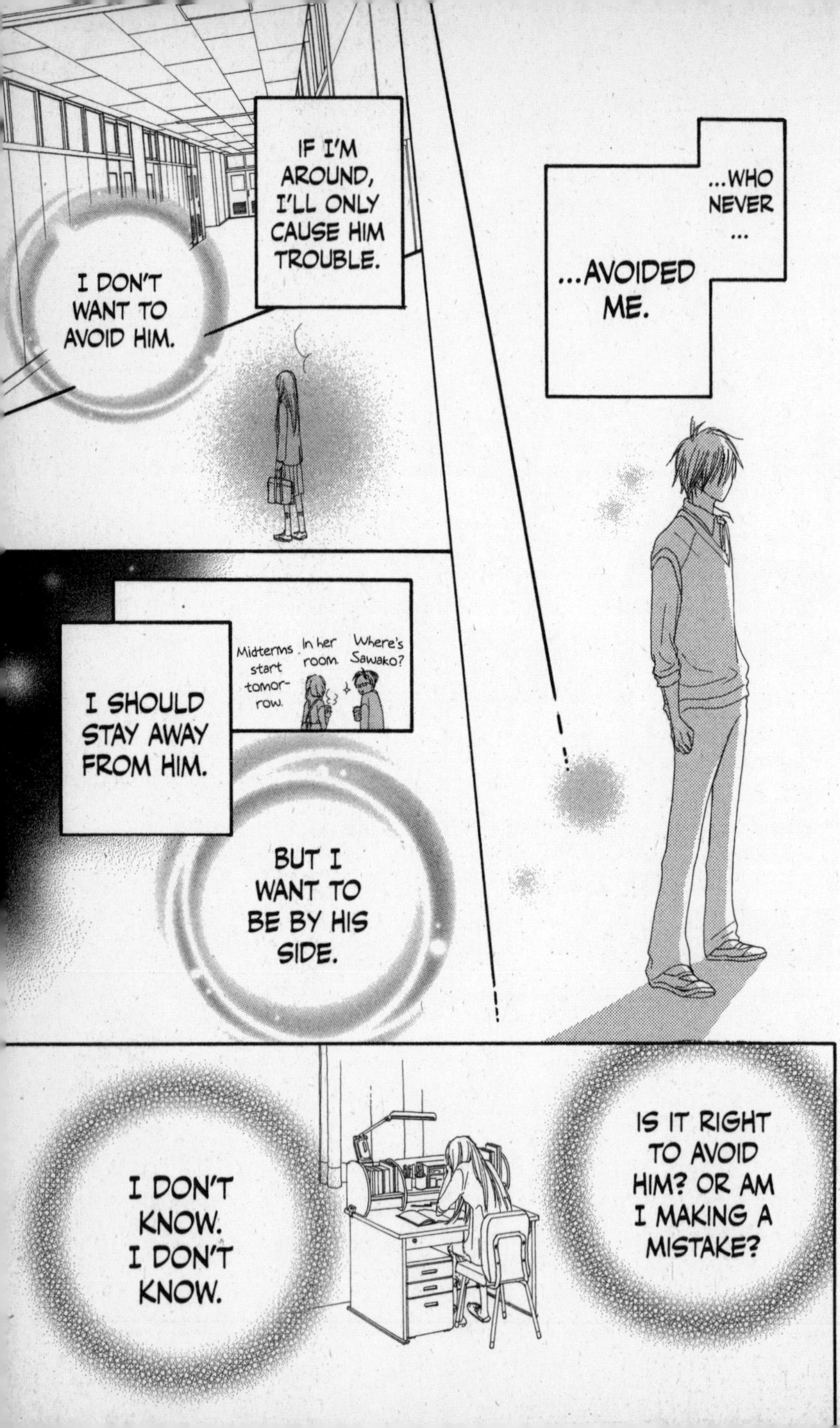

...WHO NEVER ...
...AVOIDED ME.
IF I'M AROUND, I'LL ONLY CAUSE HIM TROUBLE.
I DON'T WANT TO AVOID HIM.
Where's Sawako?
In her room.
Midterms start tomor-row.
I SHOULD STAY AWAY FROM HIM.
BUT I WANT TO BE BY HIS SIDE.
IS IT RIGHT TO AVOID HIM? OR AM I MAKING A MISTAKE?
I DON'T KNOW. I DON'T KNOW.

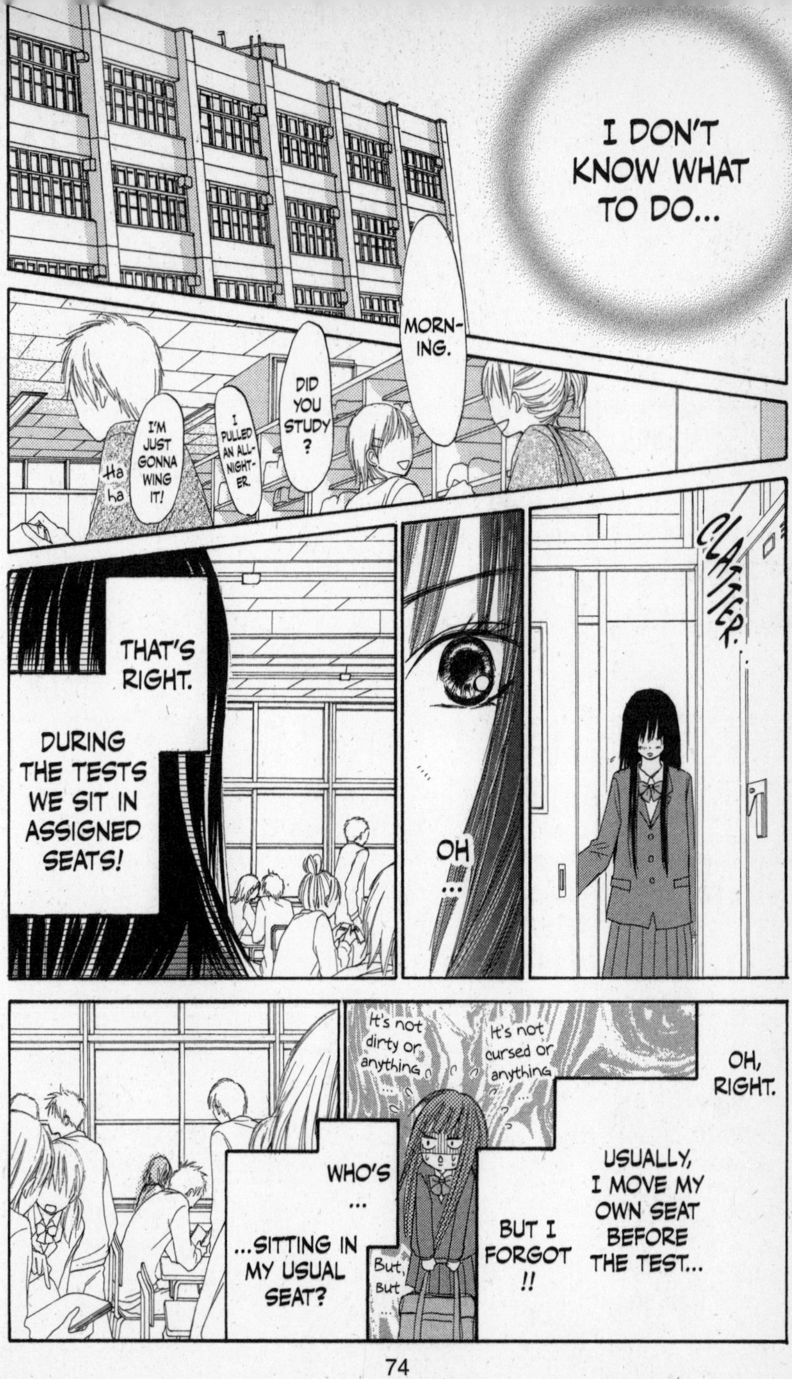
I DON'T KNOW WHAT TO DO...
MORN-ING.
DID YOU STUDY?
I PULLED AN ALL-NIGHT-ER.
I'M JUST GONNA WING IT!
Ha ha
CLATTER.
OH ...
THAT'S RIGHT.
DURING THE TESTS WE SIT IN ASSIGNED SEATS!
OH, RIGHT.
USUALLY, I MOVE MY OWN SEAT BEFORE THE TEST...
BUT I FORGOT !!
It's not cursed or anything ...
It's not dirty or anything ...
But, but
WHO'S ...
...SITTING IN MY USUAL SEAT?

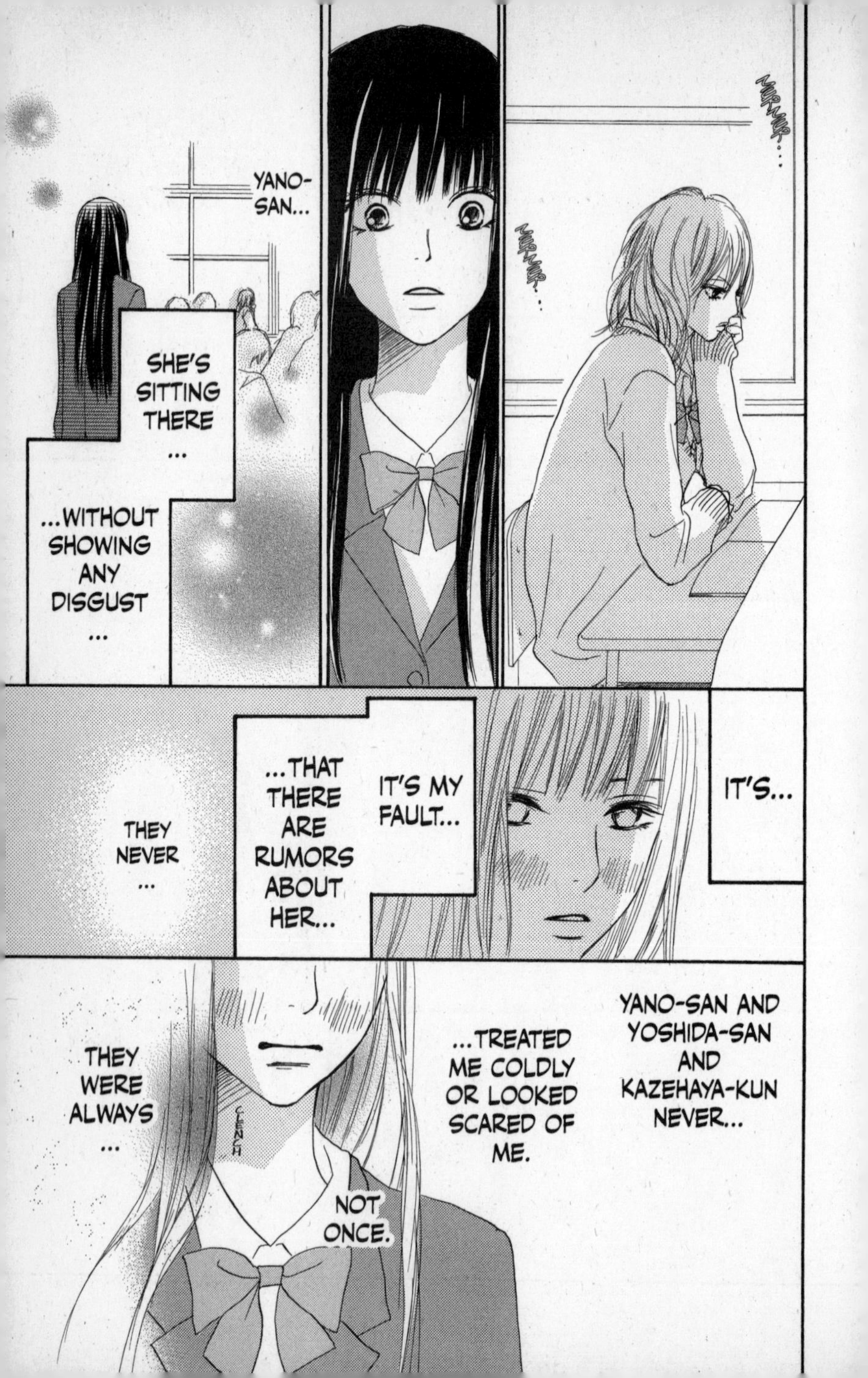
MURMUR...
MURMUR...
YANO-SAN...
SHE'S SITTING THERE...
...WITHOUT SHOWING ANY DISGUST...
IT'S...
IT'S MY FAULT...
...THAT THERE ARE RUMORS ABOUT HER...
THEY NEVER...
YANO-SAN AND YOSHIDA-SAN AND KAZEHAYA-KUN NEVER...
...TREATED ME COLDLY OR LOOKED SCARED OF ME.
NOT ONCE.
CLENCH
THEY WERE ALWAYS...

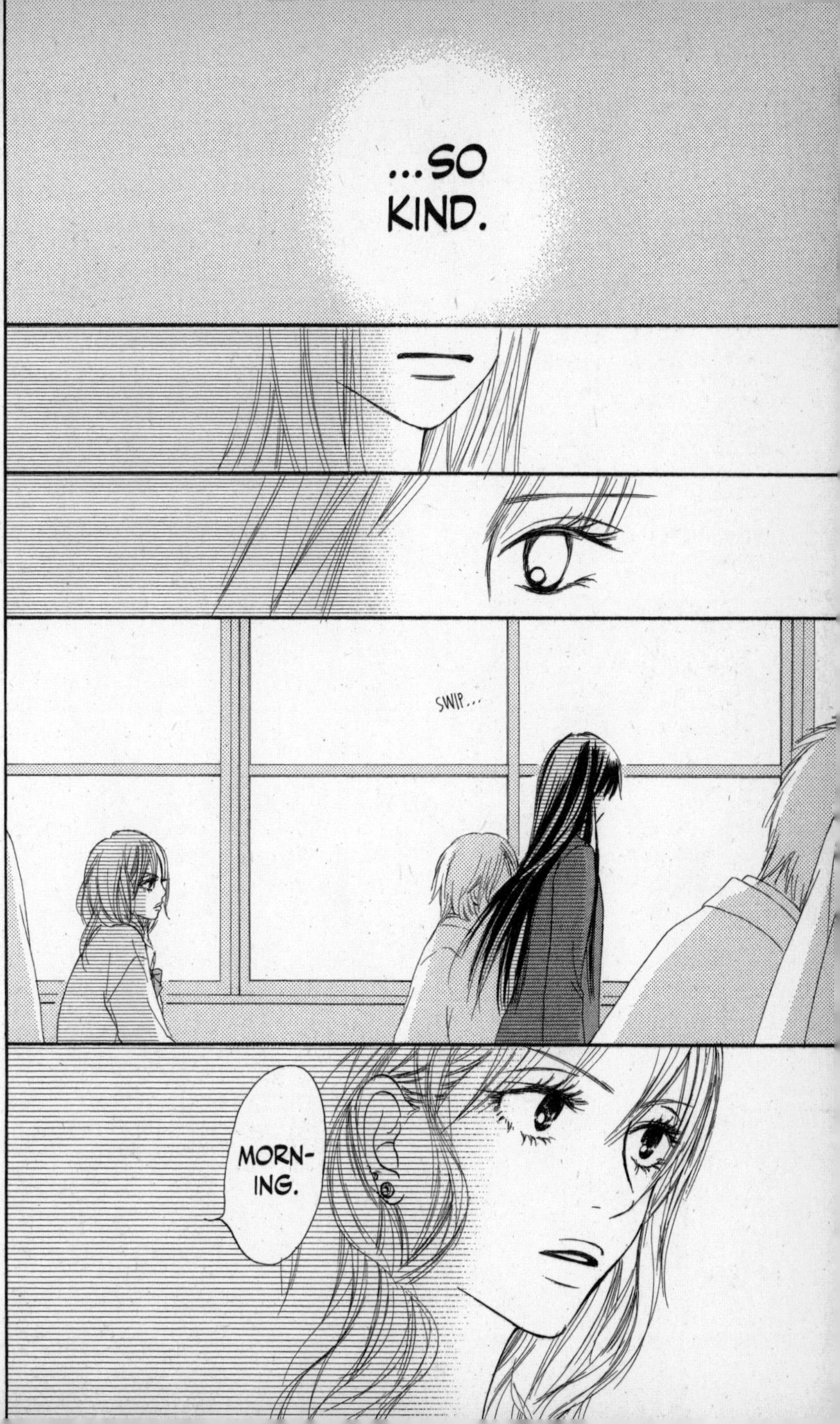
...SO KIND.
SWIP...
MORN-ING.

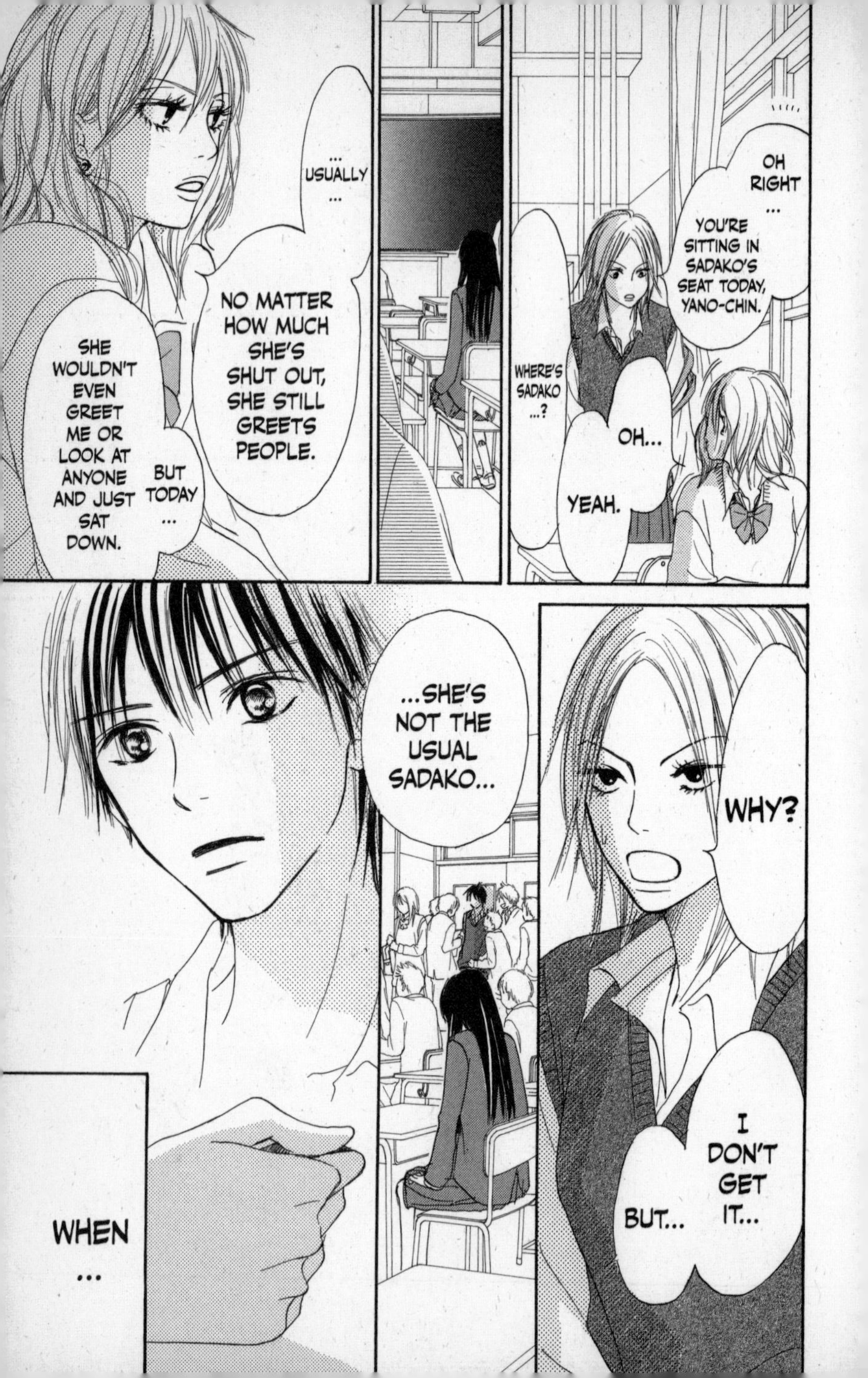

OH RIGHT ... YOU'RE SITTING IN SADAKO'S SEAT TODAY, YANO-CHIN.
WHERE'S SADAKO ...?
OH...
YEAH.
... USUALLY ...
NO MATTER HOW MUCH SHE'S SHUT OUT, SHE STILL GREETS PEOPLE.
BUT TODAY ...
SHE WOULDN'T EVEN GREET ME OR LOOK AT ANYONE AND JUST SAT DOWN.
WHY?
I DON'T GET IT...
BUT...
...SHE'S NOT THE USUAL SADAKO...
WHEN ...

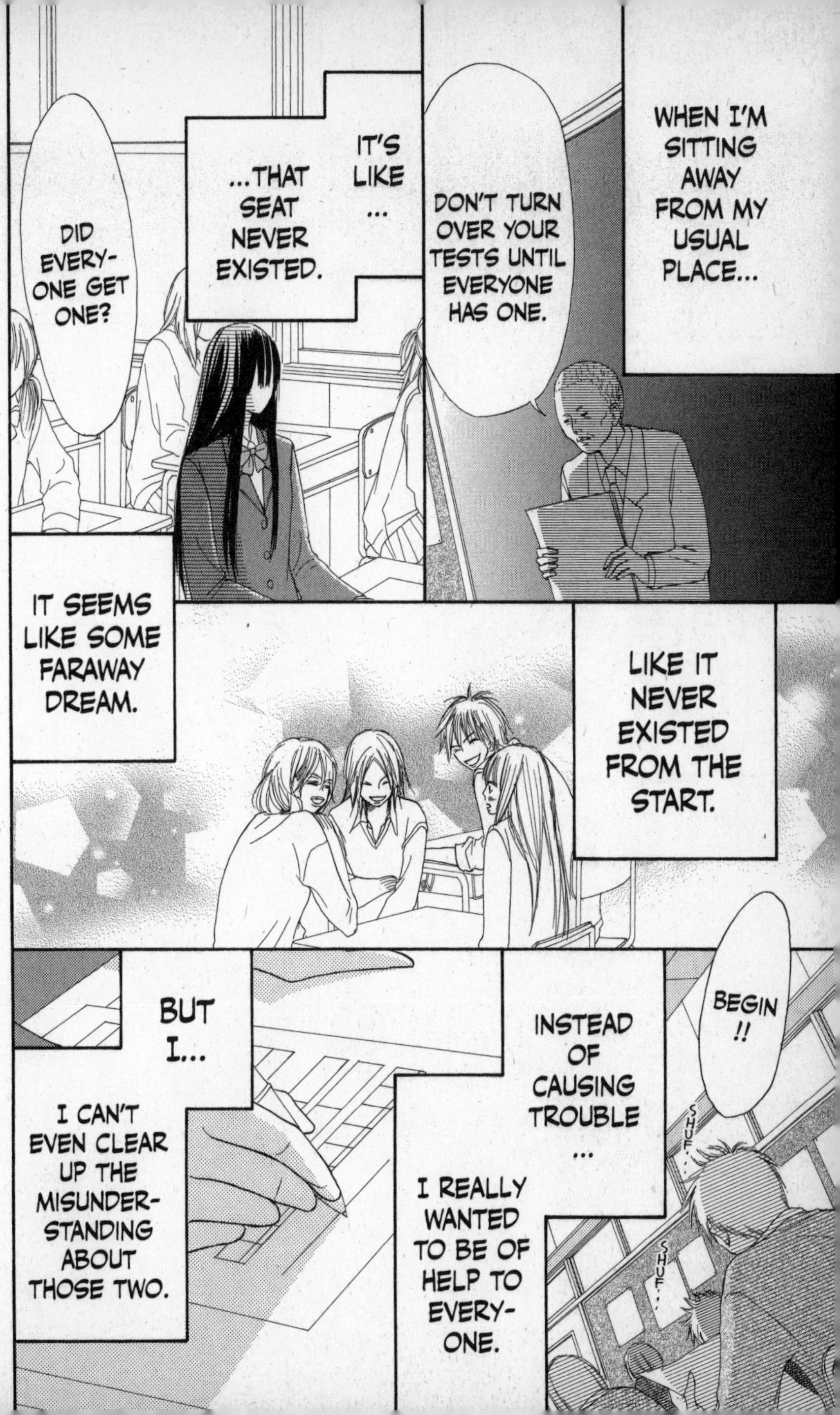
WHEN I'M SITTING AWAY FROM MY USUAL PLACE...
DON'T TURN OVER YOUR TESTS UNTIL EVERYONE HAS ONE.
IT'S LIKE...
...THAT SEAT NEVER EXISTED.
DID EVERY-ONE GET ONE?
LIKE IT NEVER EXISTED FROM THE START.
IT SEEMS LIKE SOME FARAWAY DREAM.
BEGIN!!
SHUF...
SHUF...
INSTEAD OF CAUSING TROUBLE...
I REALLY WANTED TO BE OF HELP TO EVERY-ONE.
BUT I...
I CAN'T EVEN CLEAR UP THE MISUNDER-STANDING ABOUT THOSE TWO.

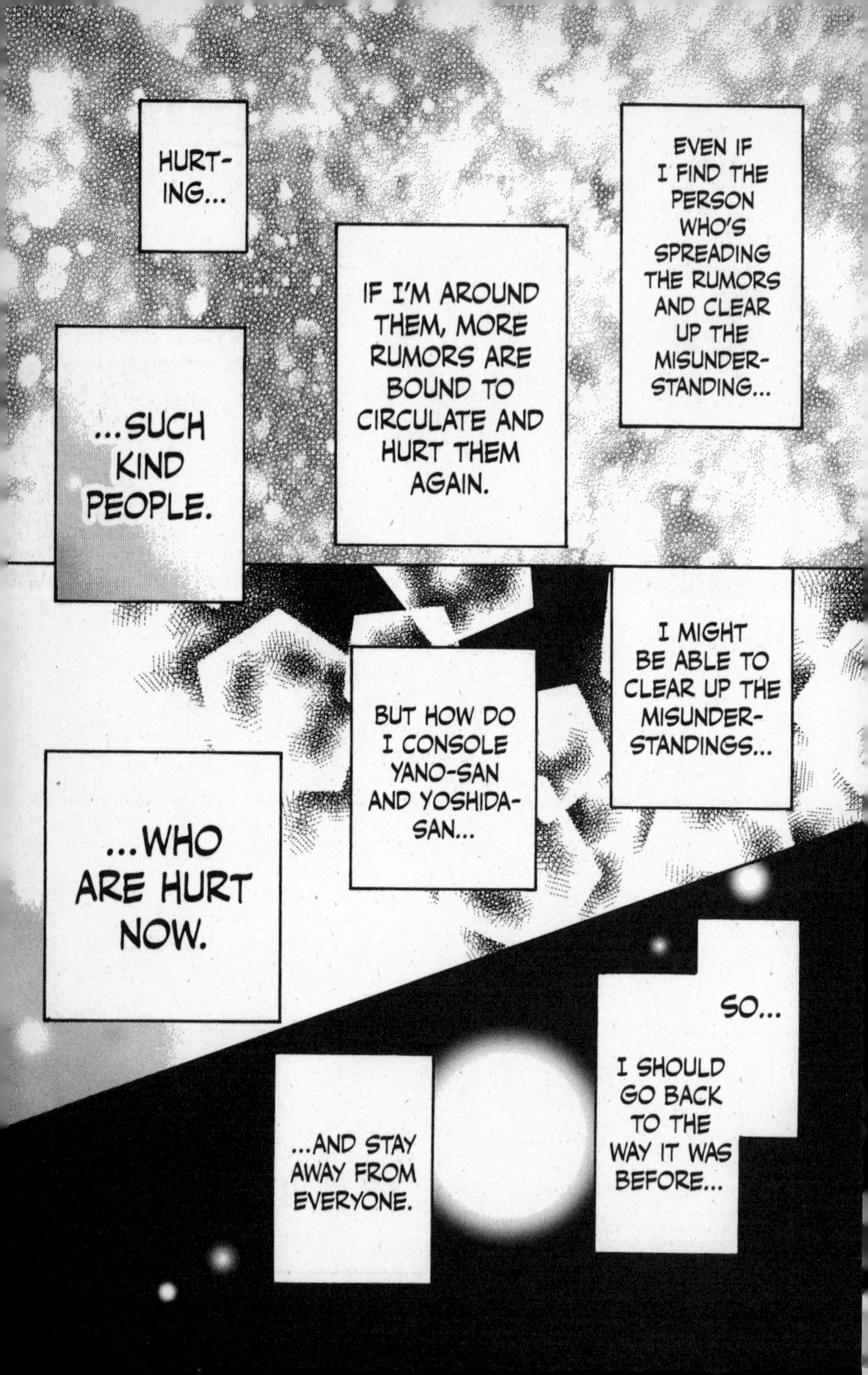
EVEN IF I FIND THE PERSON WHO'S SPREADING THE RUMORS AND CLEAR UP THE MISUNDER-STANDING...
IF I'M AROUND THEM, MORE RUMORS ARE BOUND TO CIRCULATE AND HURT THEM AGAIN.
HURT-ING...
...SUCH KIND PEOPLE.
I MIGHT BE ABLE TO CLEAR UP THE MISUNDER-STANDINGS...
BUT HOW DO I CONSOLE YANO-SAN AND YOSHIDA-SAN...
...WHO ARE HURT NOW.
SO...
I SHOULD GO BACK TO THE WAY IT WAS BEFORE...
...AND STAY AWAY FROM EVERYONE.

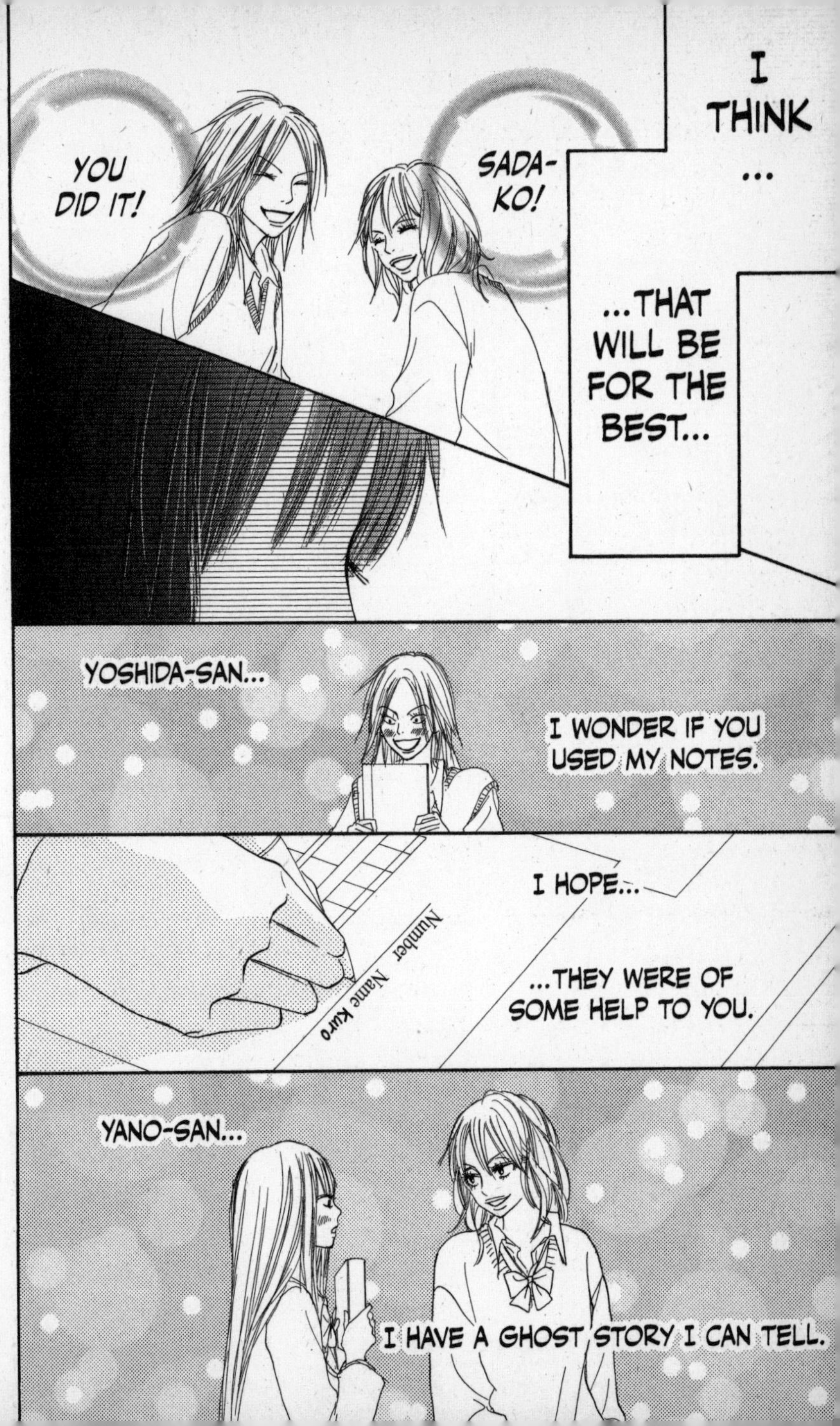
I THINK ...
...THAT WILL BE FOR THE BEST...
SADA-KO!
YOU DID IT!
YOSHIDA-SAN...
I WONDER IF YOU USED MY NOTES.
I HOPE...
...THEY WERE OF SOME HELP TO YOU.
Number
Name Kuro
YANO-SAN...
I HAVE A GHOST STORY I CAN TELL.

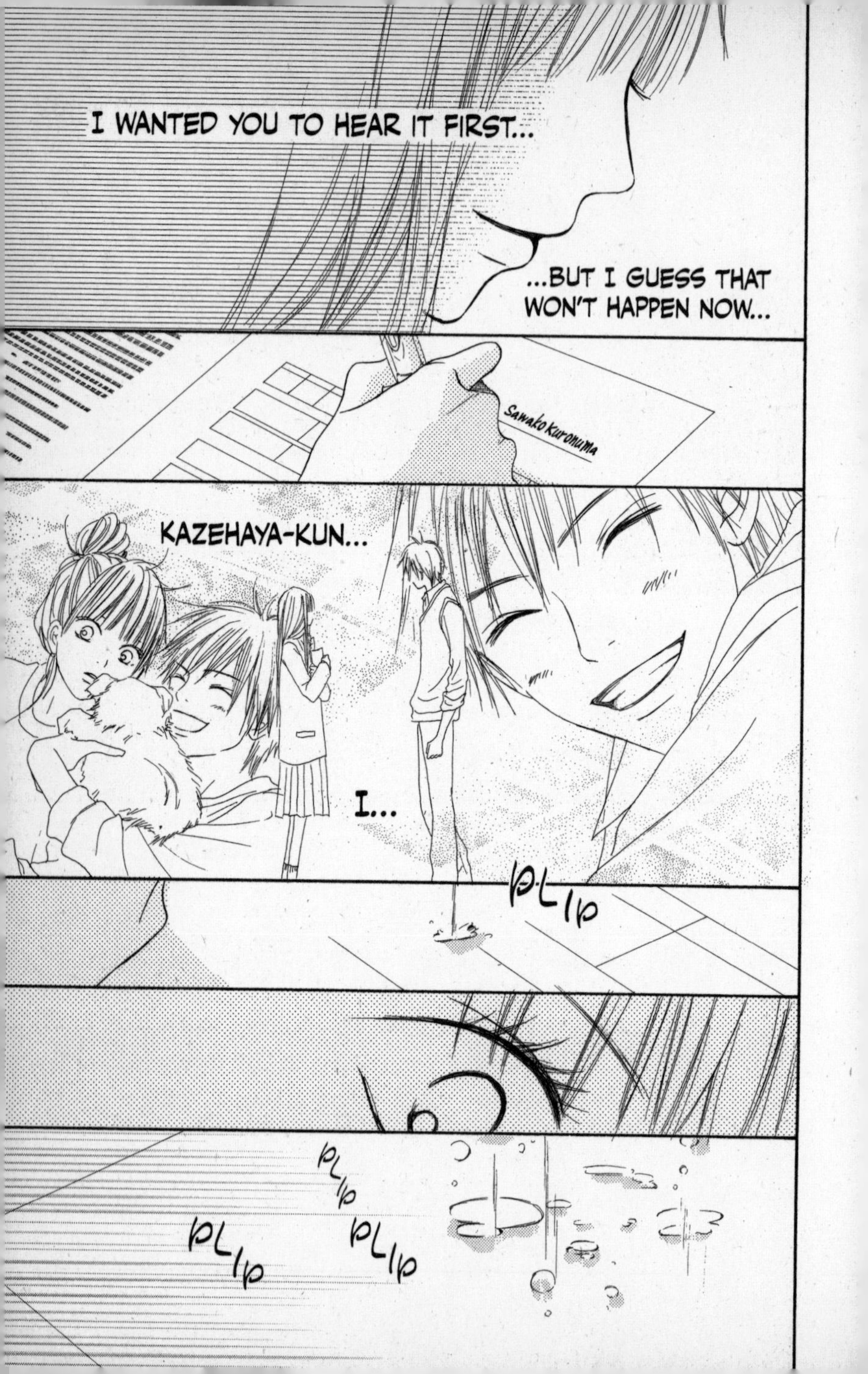
I WANTED YOU TO HEAR IT FIRST...
...BUT I GUESS THAT WON'T HAPPEN NOW...
Sawako Kuronuma
KAZEHAYA-KUN...
I...
PLIP
PLIP
PLIP
PLIP

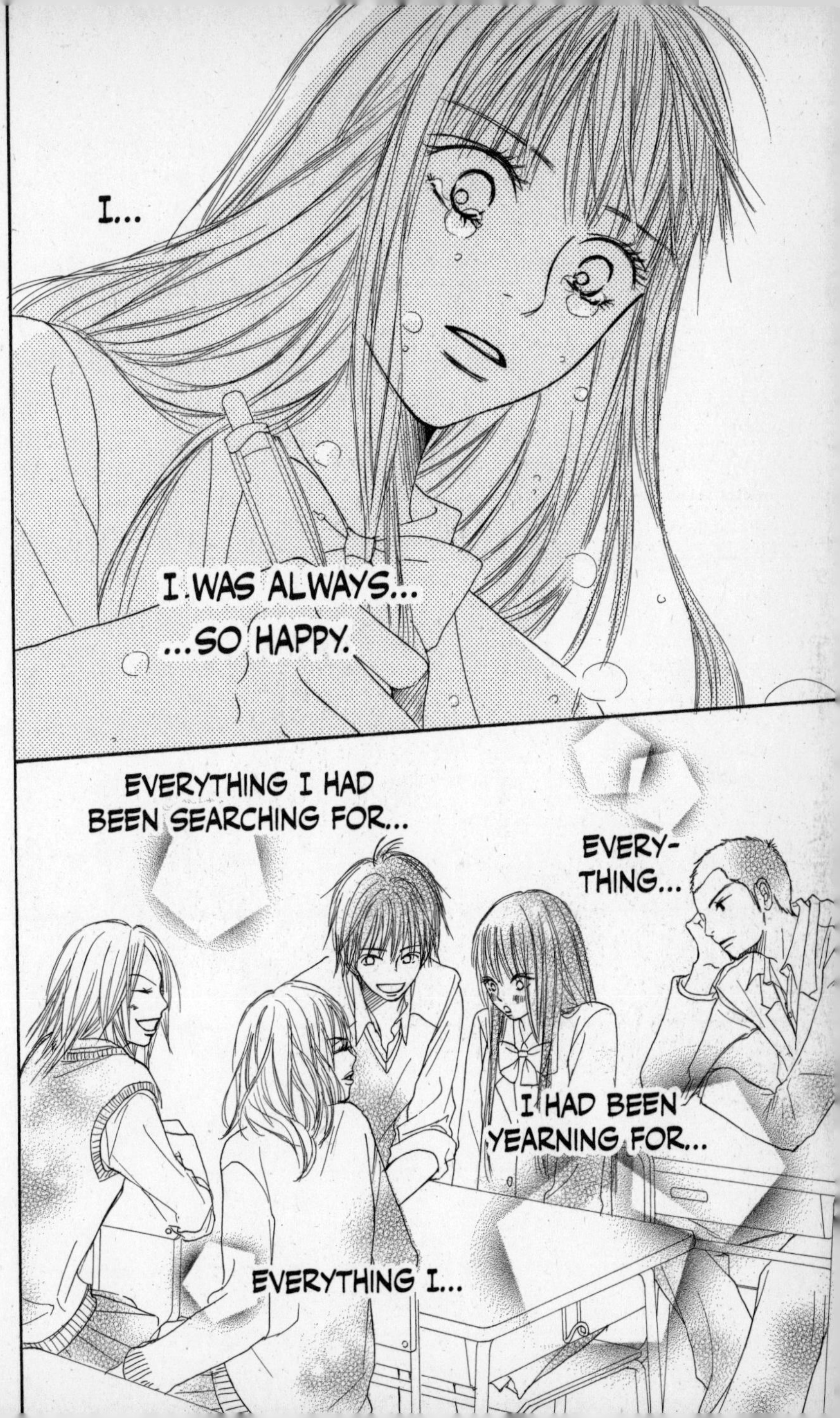
I...
I WAS ALWAYS...
...SO HAPPY.
EVERYTHING I HAD BEEN SEARCHING FOR...
EVERY-THING...
I HAD BEEN YEARNING FOR...
EVERYTHING I...

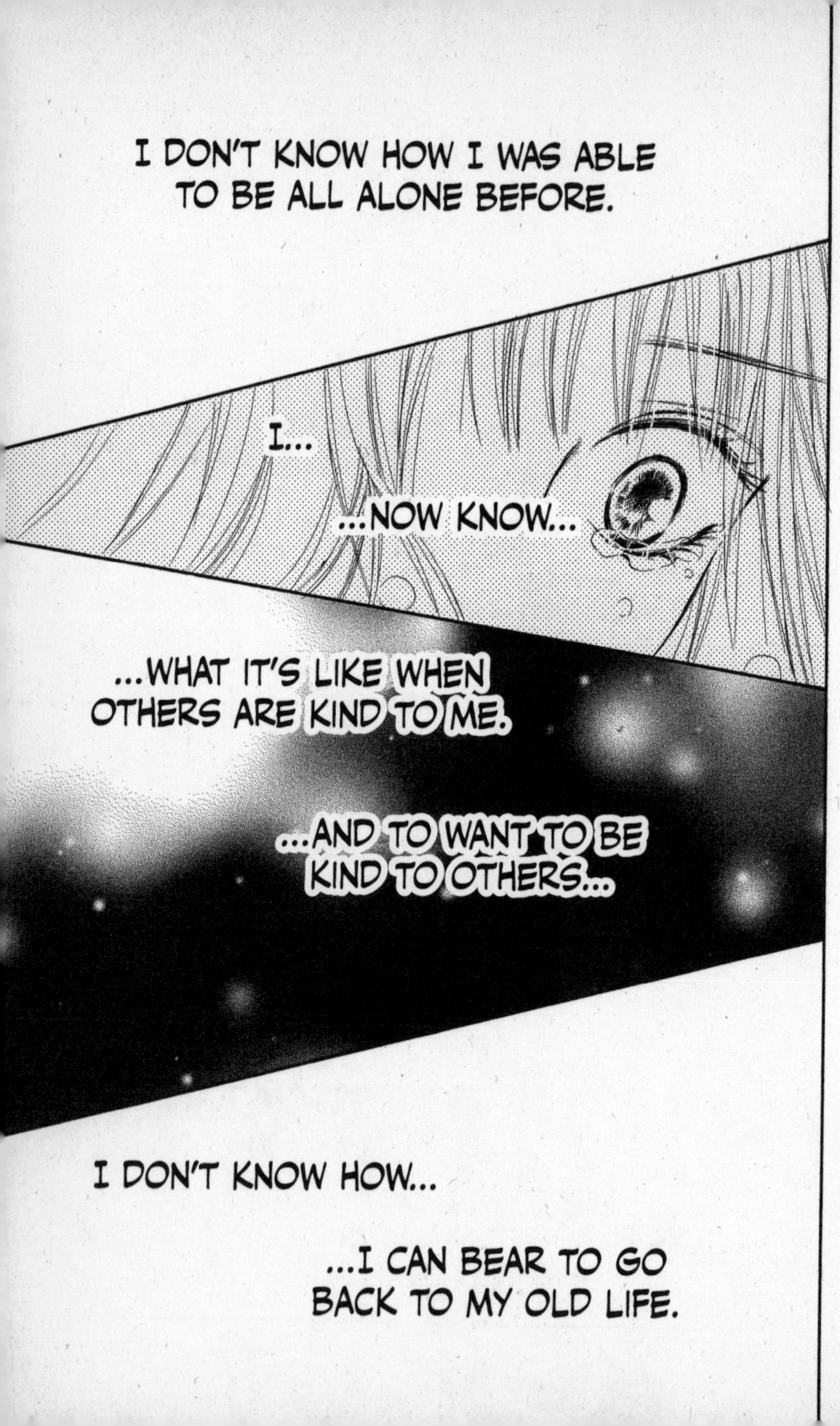
I DON'T KNOW HOW I WAS ABLE TO BE ALL ALONE BEFORE.
I...
...NOW KNOW...
...WHAT IT'S LIKE WHEN OTHERS ARE KIND TO ME.
...AND TO WANT TO BE KIND TO OTHERS...
I DON'T KNOW HOW...
...I CAN BEAR TO GO BACK TO MY OLD LIFE.

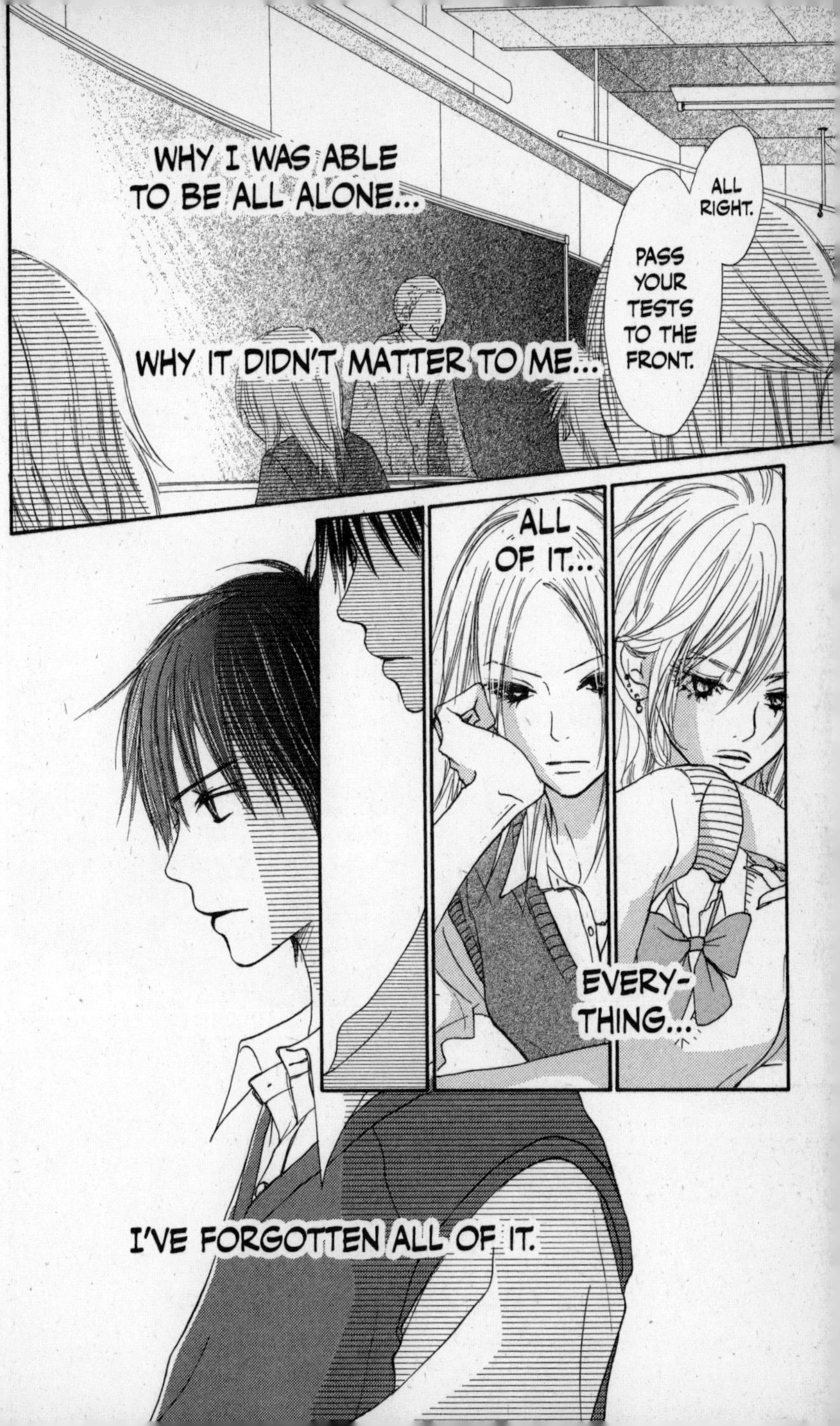

ALL RIGHT. PASS YOUR TESTS TO THE FRONT.
WHY I WAS ABLE TO BE ALL ALONE...
WHY IT DIDN'T MATTER TO ME...
EVERY-THING...
ALL OF IT...
I'VE FORGOTTEN ALL OF IT.

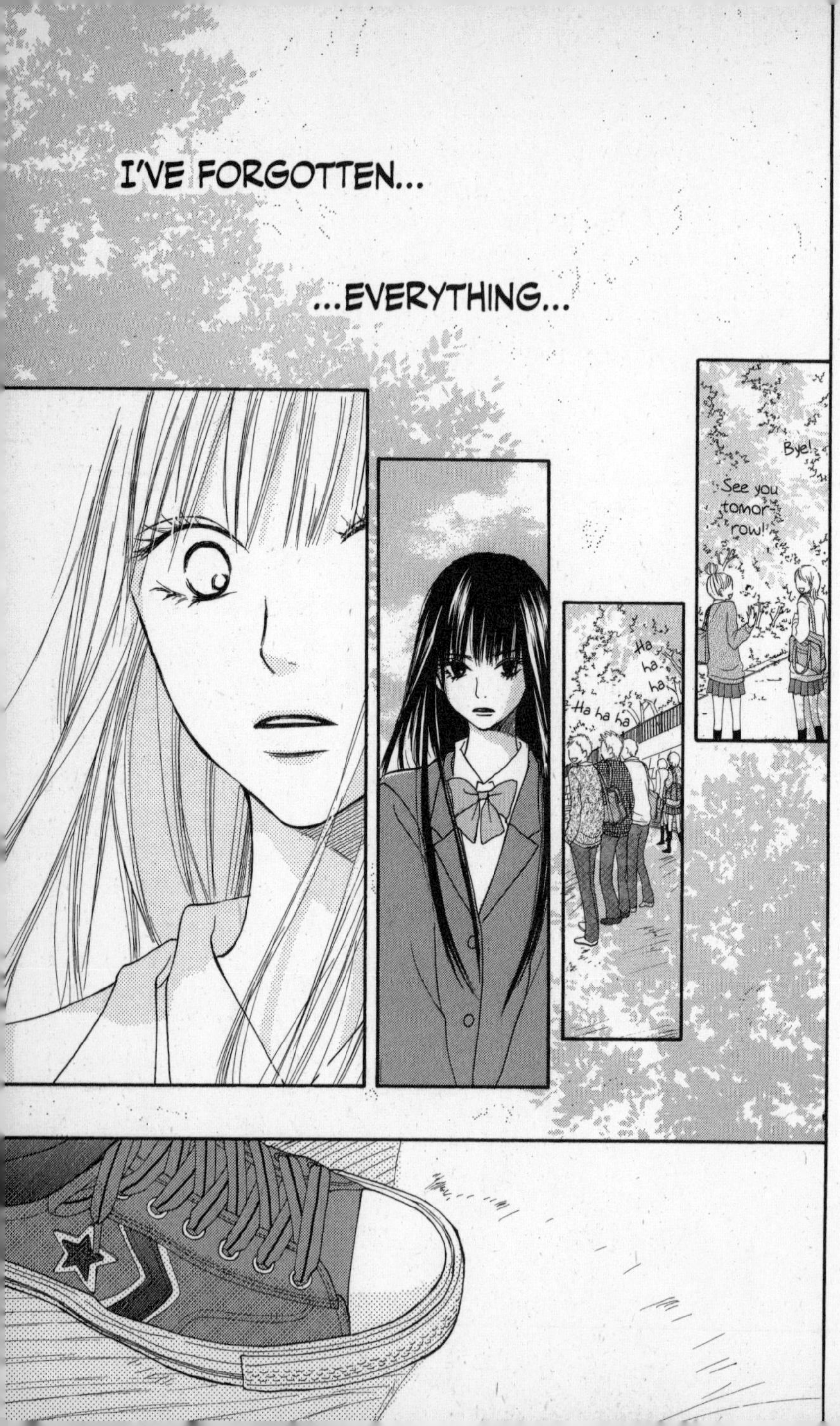
I'VE FORGOTTEN...
...EVERYTHING...
Bye!
See you tomor-row!
Ha ha ha
Ha ha ha

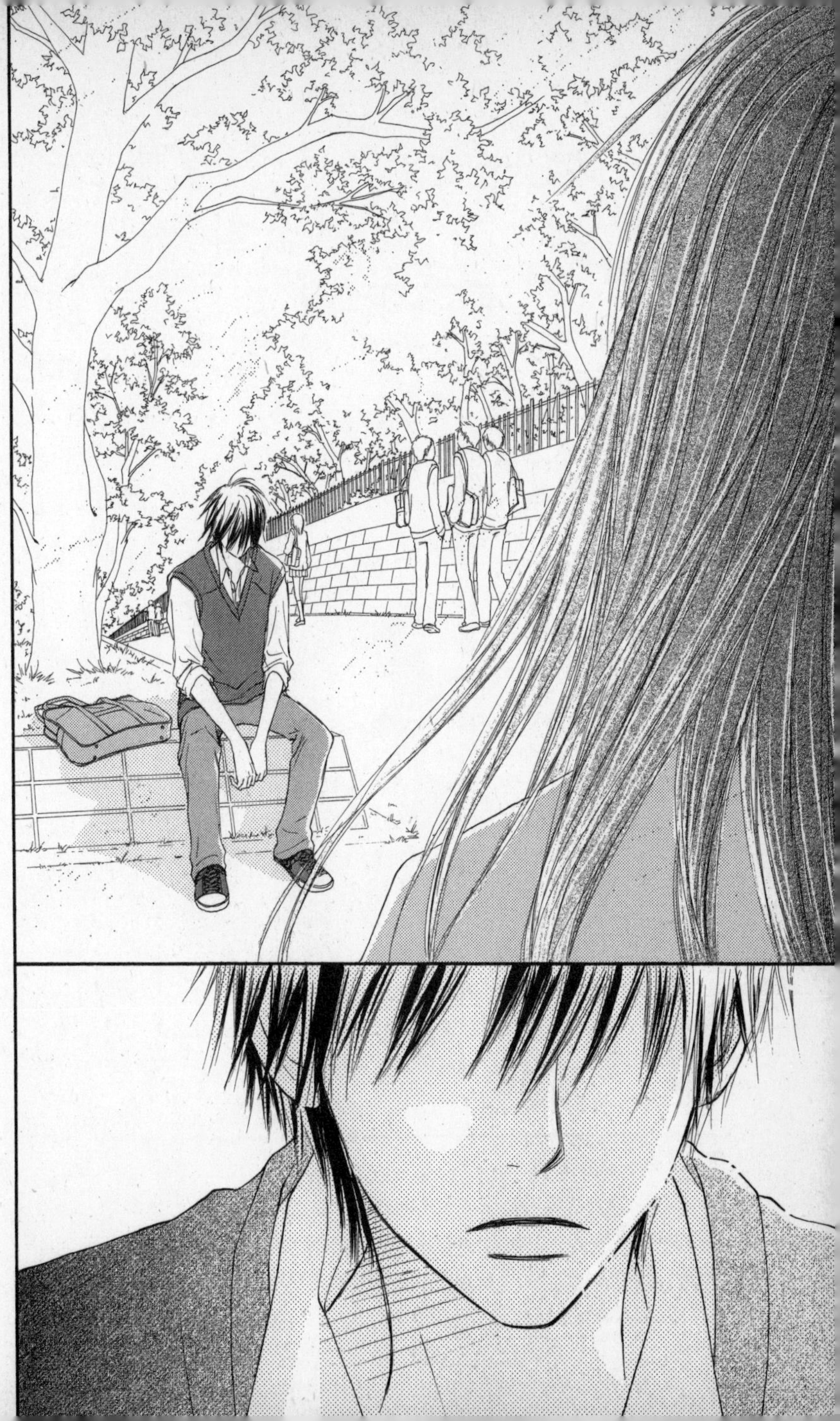

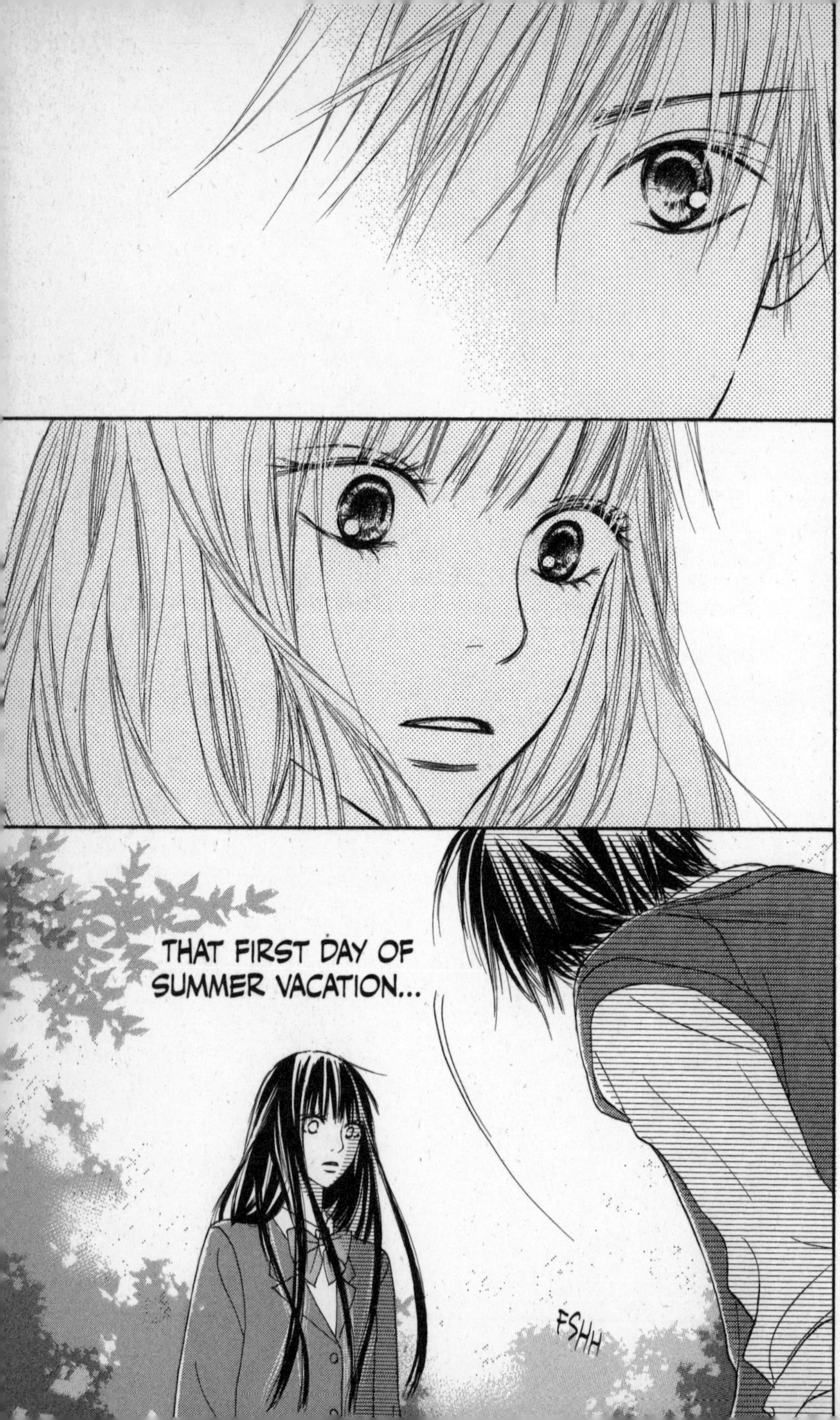
THAT FIRST DAY OF SUMMER VACATION...
FSHH

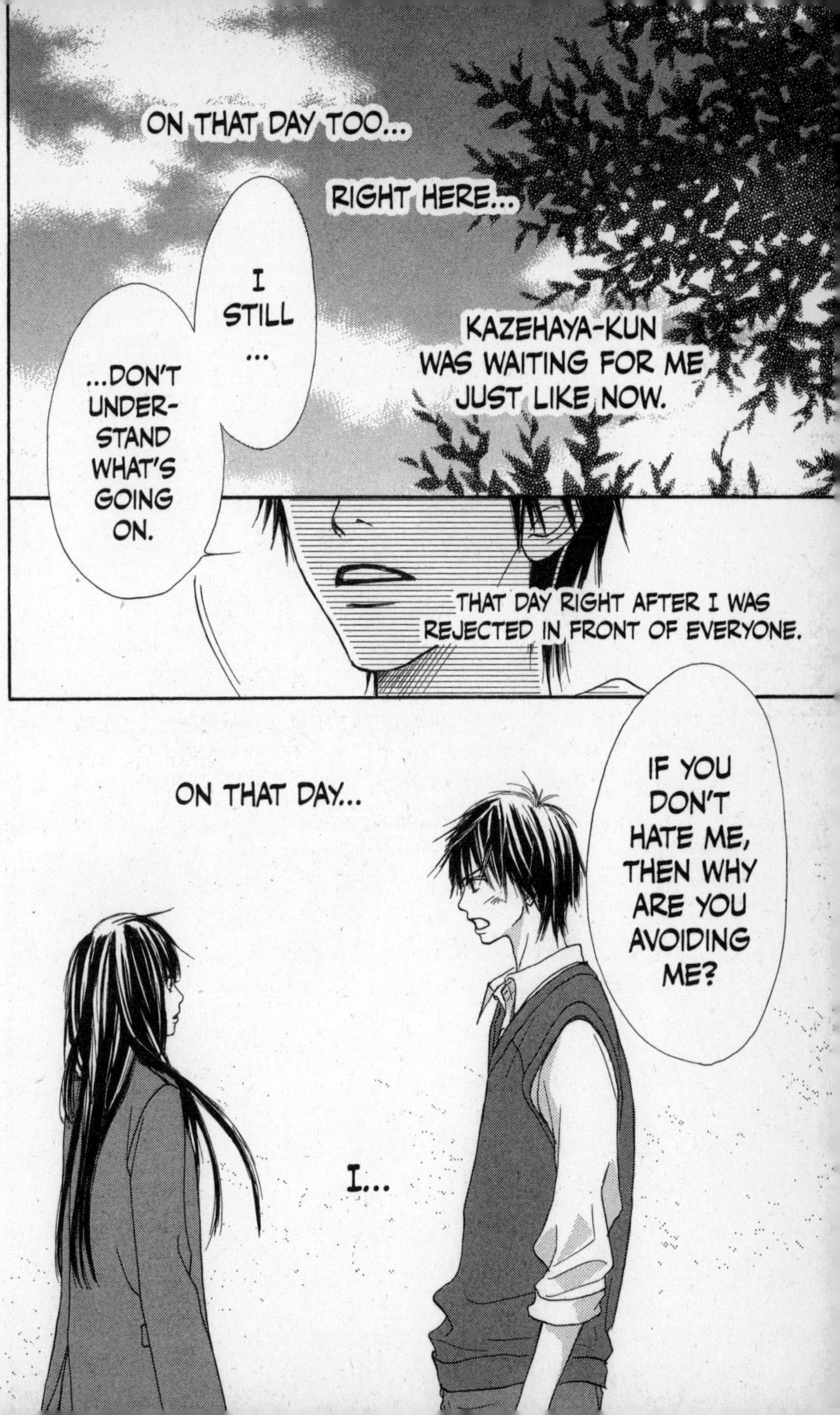
ON THAT DAY TOO...
RIGHT HERE...
KAZEHAYA-KUN WAS WAITING FOR ME JUST LIKE NOW.
I STILL ...
...DON'T UNDER-STAND WHAT'S GOING ON.
THAT DAY RIGHT AFTER I WAS REJECTED IN FRONT OF EVERYONE.
IF YOU DON'T HATE ME, THEN WHY ARE YOU AVOIDING ME?
ON THAT DAY...
I...

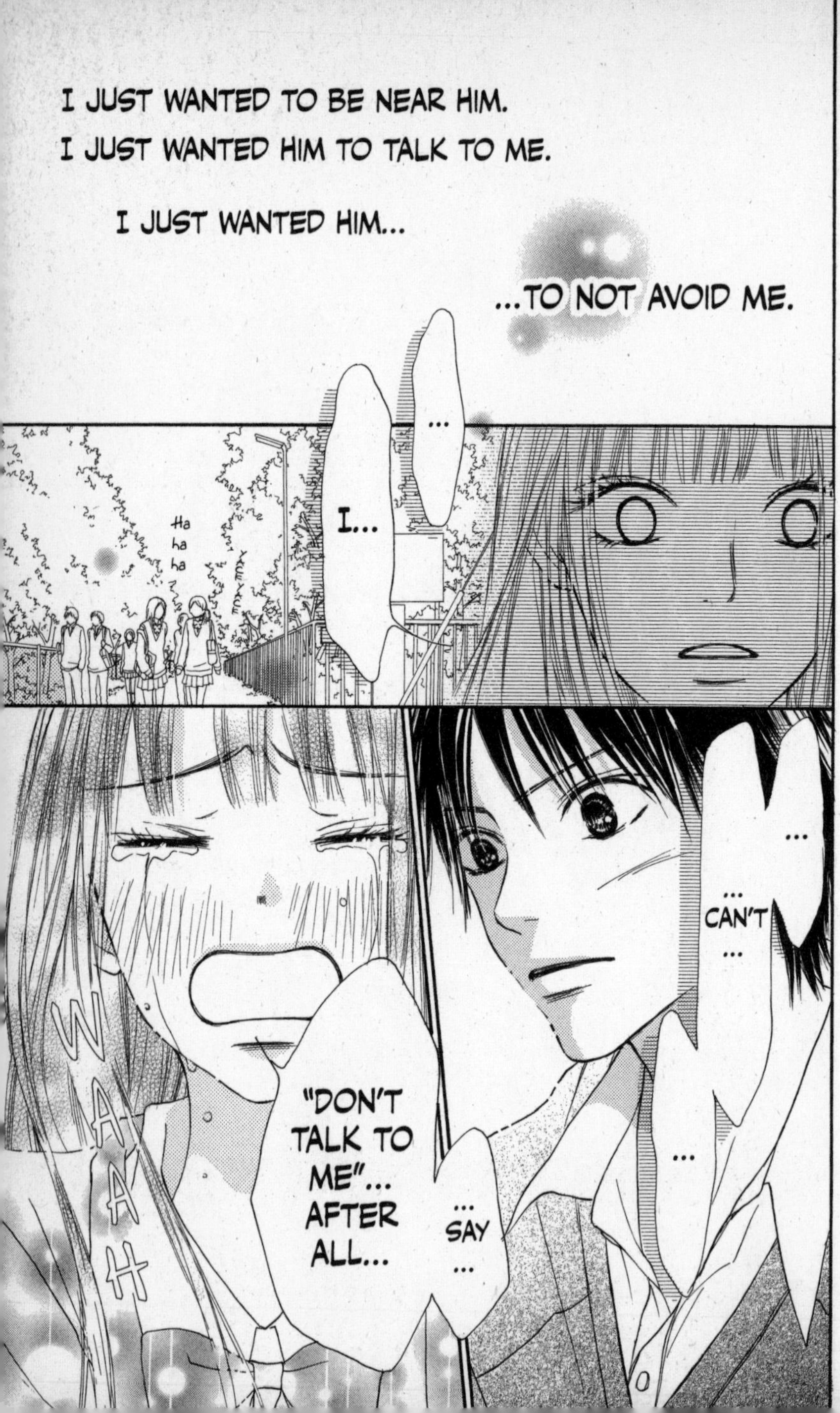

I JUST WANTED TO BE NEAR HIM.
I JUST WANTED HIM TO TALK TO ME.
I JUST WANTED HIM...
...TO NOT AVOID ME.
...
I...
YACK YACK
Ha ha ha
...
... CAN'T ...
...
... SAY ...
"DON'T TALK TO ME"... AFTER ALL...
WAAH

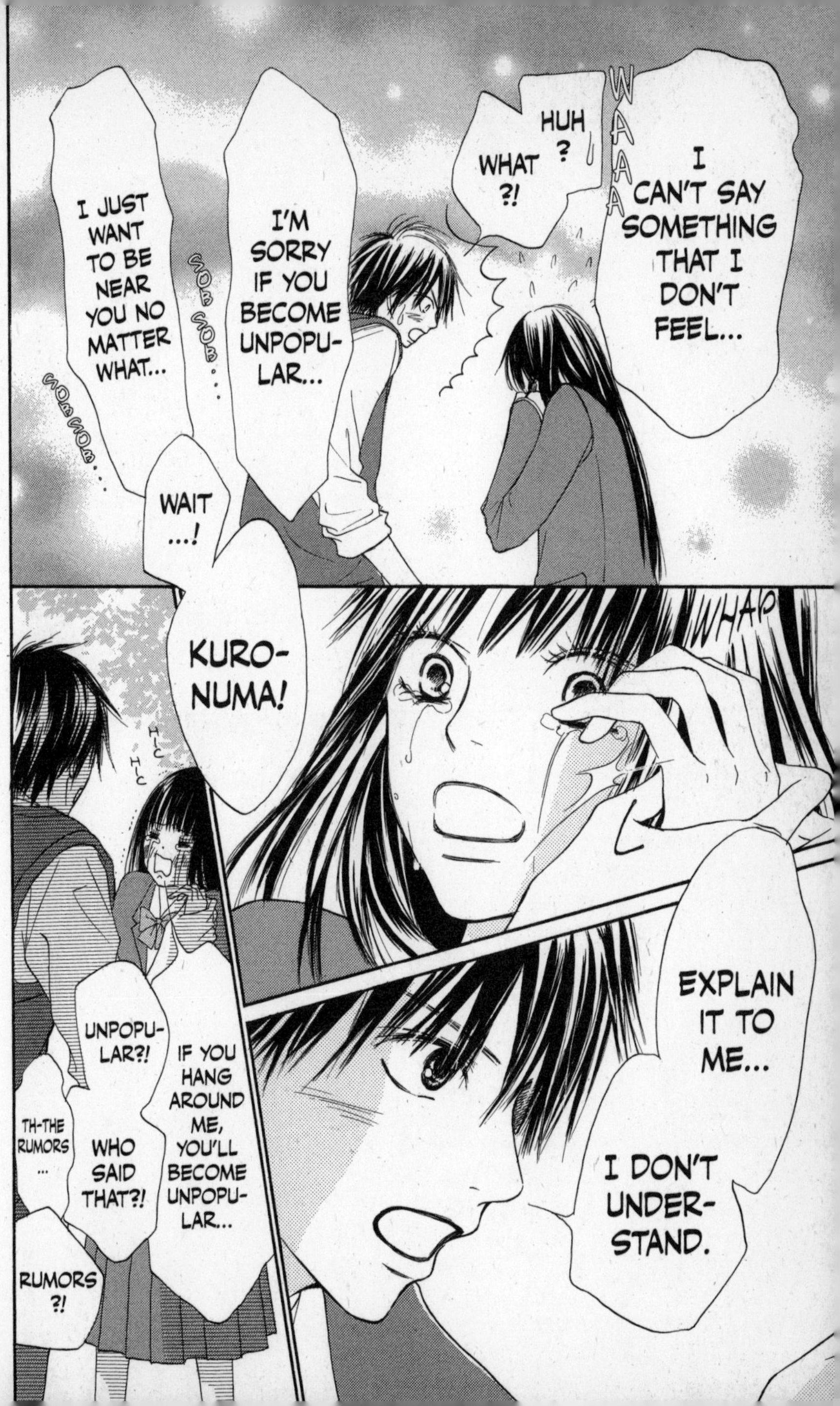
WAAAA
I CAN'T SAY SOMETHING THAT I DON'T FEEL...
HUH?
WHAT?!
I'M SORRY IF YOU BECOME UNPOPULAR...
SOB SOB...
I JUST WANT TO BE NEAR YOU NO MATTER WHAT...
SOB SOB...
WAIT...!
KURO-NUMA!
WHAP
EXPLAIN IT TO ME...
I DON'T UNDER-STAND.
HIC HIC
IF YOU HANG AROUND ME, YOU'LL BECOME UNPOPU-LAR...
UNPOPU-LAR?!
WHO SAID THAT?!
TH-THE RUMORS...
RUMORS?!

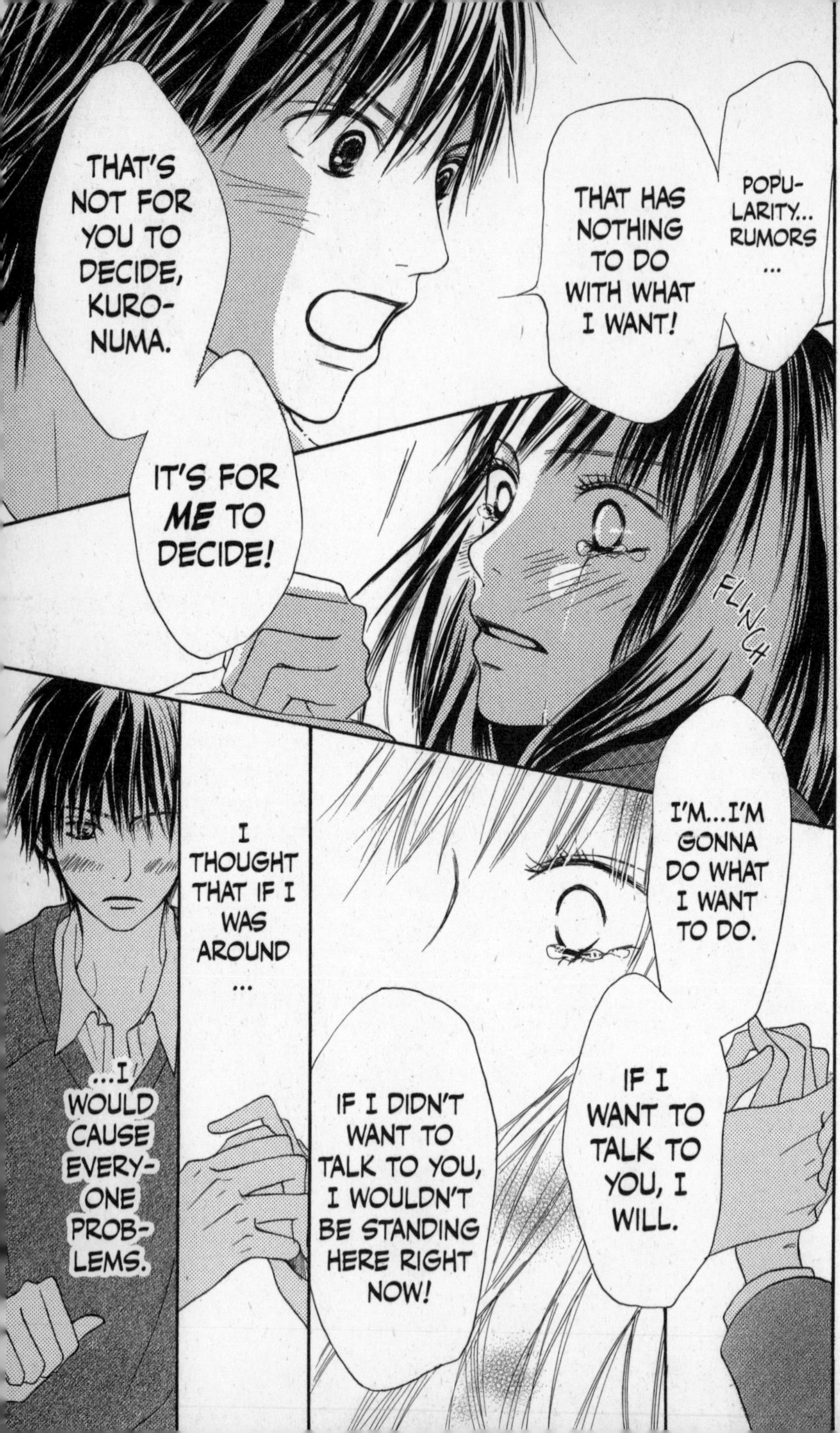
POPULARITY... RUMORS ...
THAT HAS NOTHING TO DO WITH WHAT I WANT!
THAT'S NOT FOR YOU TO DECIDE, KURONUMA.
IT'S FOR *ME* TO DECIDE!
FLINCH
I'M...I'M GONNA DO WHAT I WANT TO DO.
IF I WANT TO TALK TO YOU, I WILL.
IF I DIDN'T WANT TO TALK TO YOU, I WOULDN'T BE STANDING HERE RIGHT NOW!
I THOUGHT THAT IF I WAS AROUND ...
...I WOULD CAUSE EVERYONE PROBLEMS.

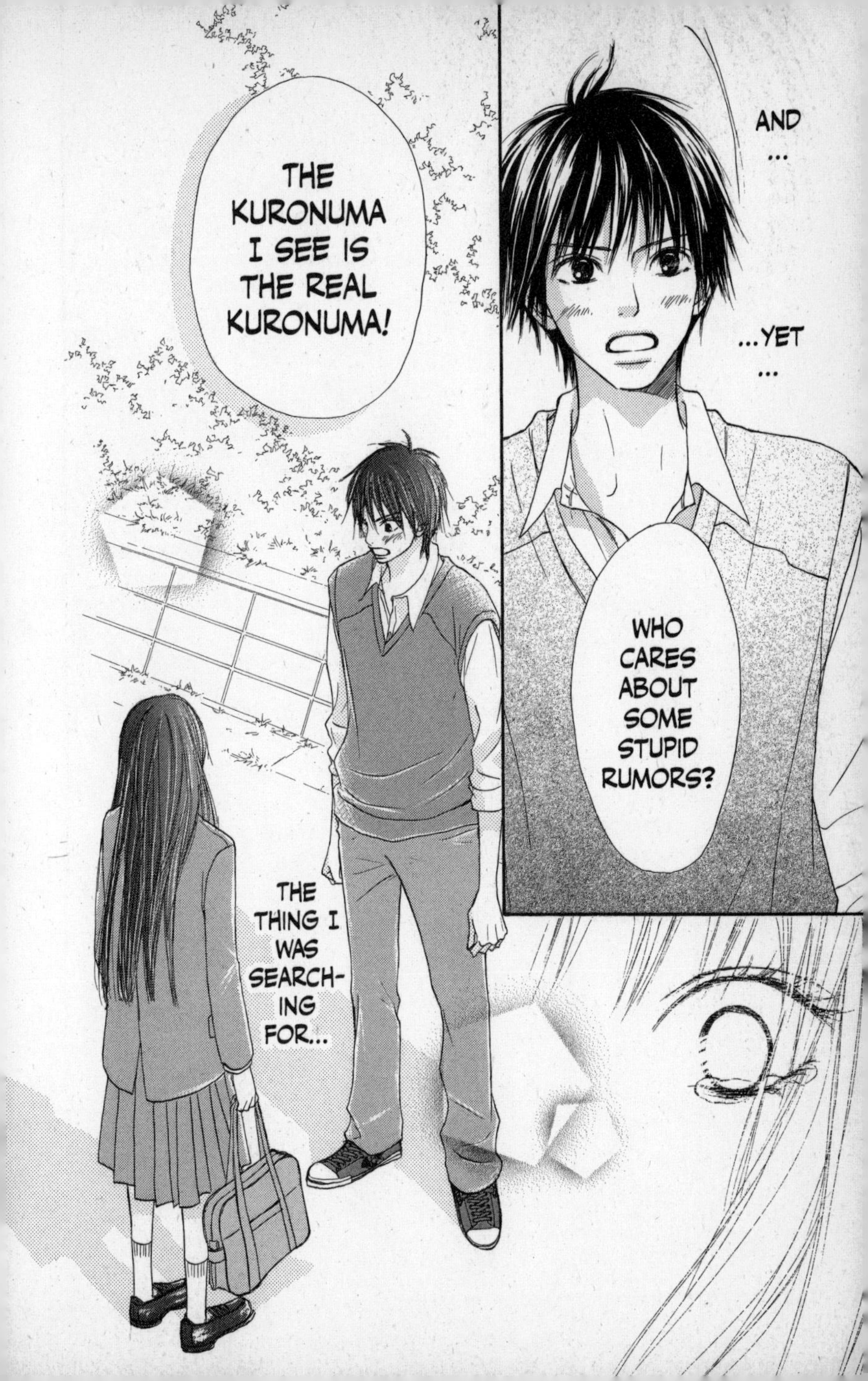
AND ...
...YET ...
WHO CARES ABOUT SOME STUPID RUMORS?
THE KURONUMA I SEE IS THE REAL KURONUMA!
THE THING I WAS SEARCH-ING FOR...

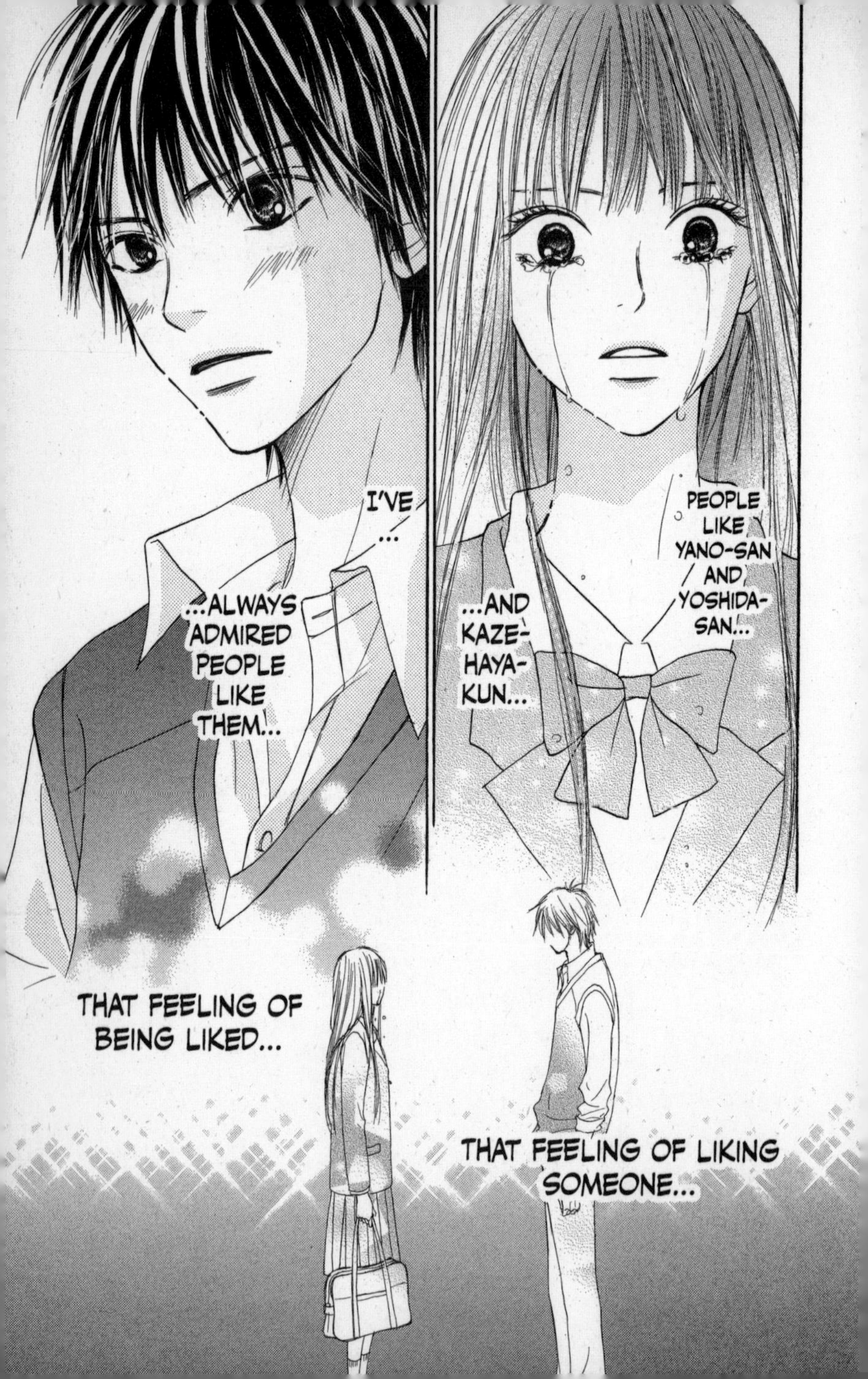
PEOPLE LIKE YANO-SAN AND YOSHIDA-SAN...
...AND KAZE-HAYA-KUN...
I'VE ...
...ALWAYS ADMIRED PEOPLE LIKE THEM...
THAT FEELING OF BEING LIKED...
THAT FEELING OF LIKING SOMEONE...

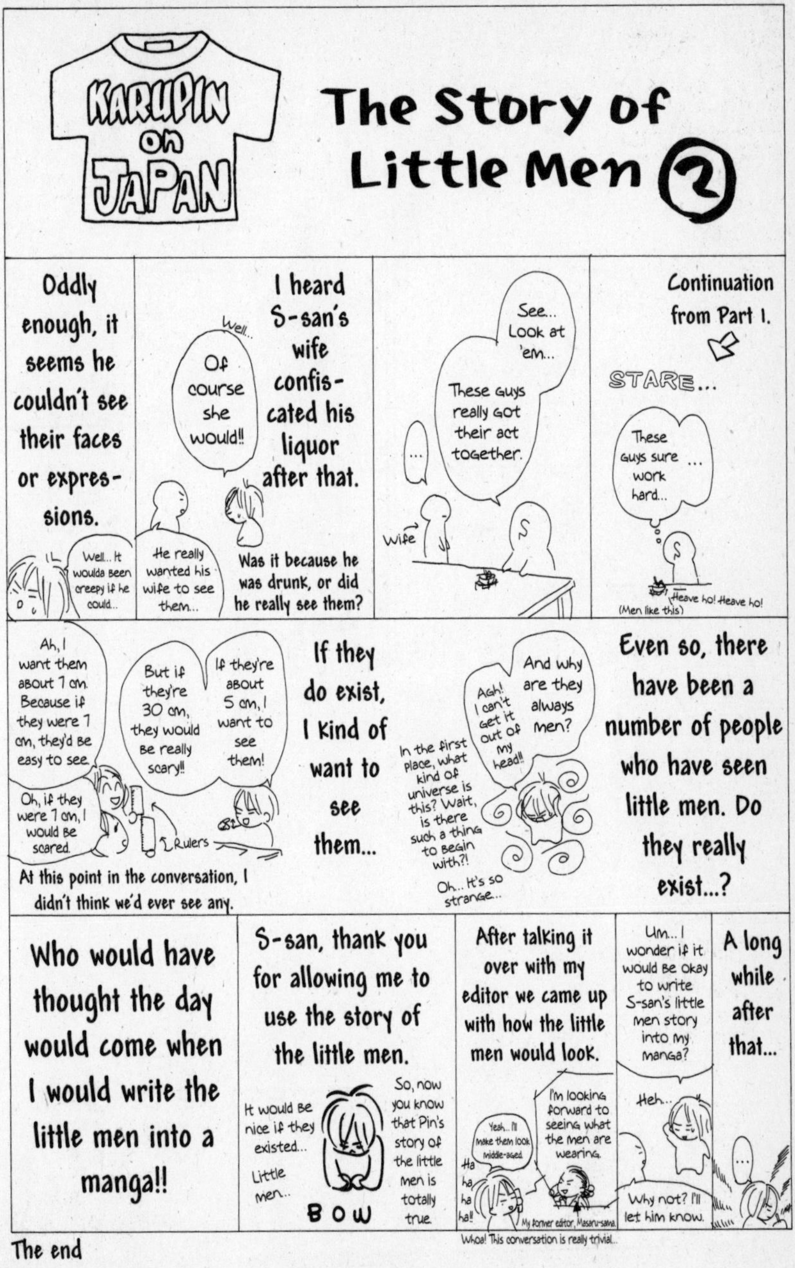

KARUPIN on JAPAN
The Story of Little Men 2
Continuation from Part 1.
STARE...
These guys sure work hard...
...
Heave ho! Heave ho!
(Men like this)
See... Look at 'em...
These guys really got their act together.
...
Wife
I heard S-san's wife confiscated his liquor after that.
Well...
Of course she would!!
He really wanted his wife to see them...
Was it because he was drunk, or did he really see them?
Oddly enough, it seems he couldn't see their faces or expressions.
Well... It woulda been creepy if he could...
Even so, there have been a number of people who have seen little men. Do they really exist...?
And why are they always men?
Agh! I can't get it out of my head!!
In the first place, what kind of universe is this? Wait, is there such a thing to begin with?!
Oh... It's so strange...
If they do exist, I kind of want to see them...
If they're about 5 cm, I want to see them!
But if they're 30 cm, they would be really scary!!
Ah, I want them about 7 cm. Because if they were 7 cm, they'd be easy to see.
Oh, if they were 7 cm, I would be scared.
Rulers
At this point in the conversation, I didn't think we'd ever see any.
A long while after that...
...
Um... I wonder if it would be okay to write S-san's little men story into my manga?
Heh...
Why not? I'll let him know.
After talking it over with my editor we came up with how the little men would look.
I'm looking forward to seeing what the men are wearing.
Yeah... I'll make them look middle-aged.
Ha ha ha ha!!
My former editor, Masaru-sama.
Whoa! This conversation is really trivial...
S-san, thank you for allowing me to use the story of the little men.
So, now you know that Pin's story of the little men is totally true.
It would be nice if they existed... Little men...
BOW
Who would have thought the day would come when I would write the little men into a manga!!
The end

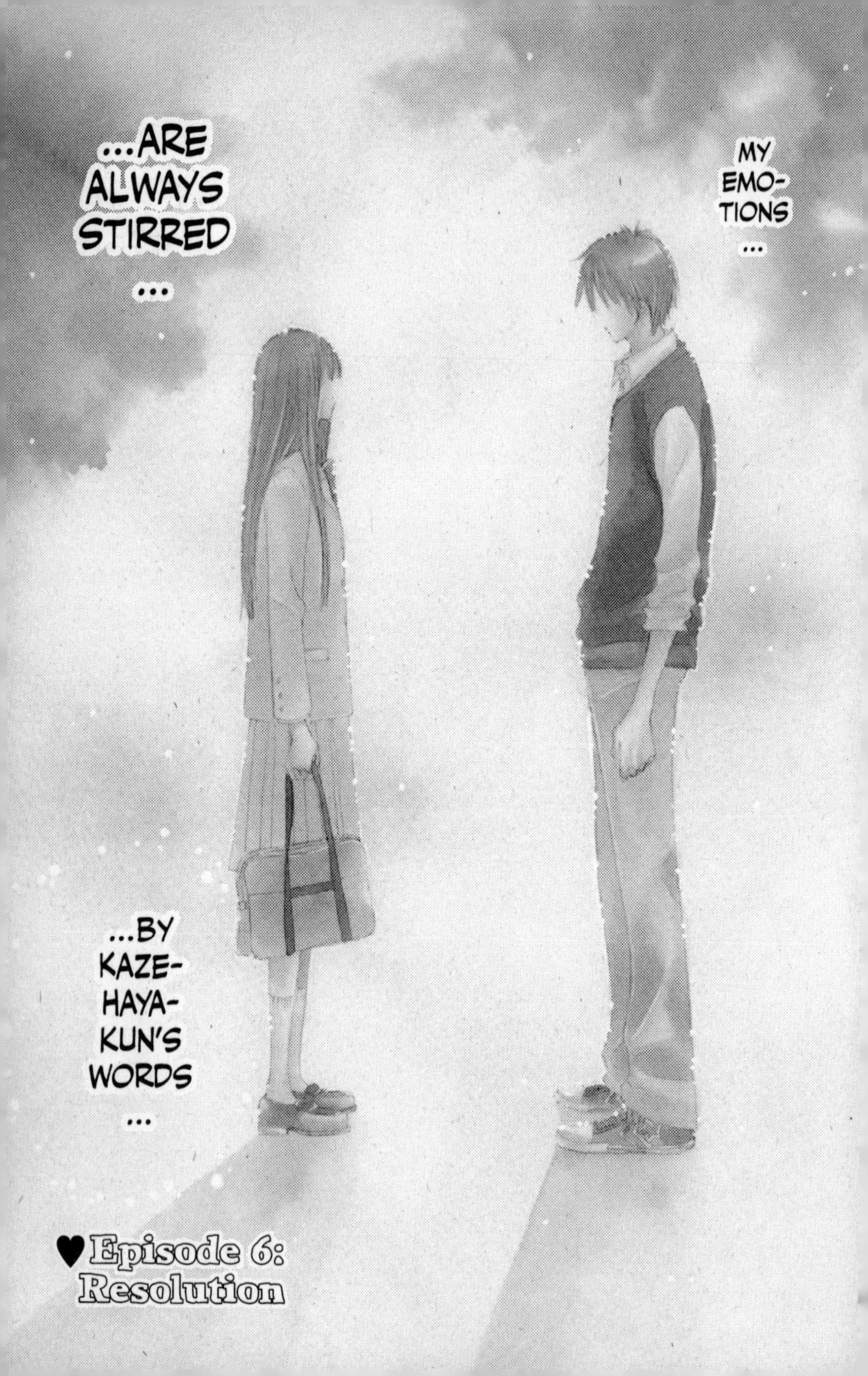
MY EMO-TIONS...
...ARE ALWAYS STIRRED...
...BY KAZE-HAYA-KUN'S WORDS...
♥Episode 6: Resolution

Episode 6: Resolution

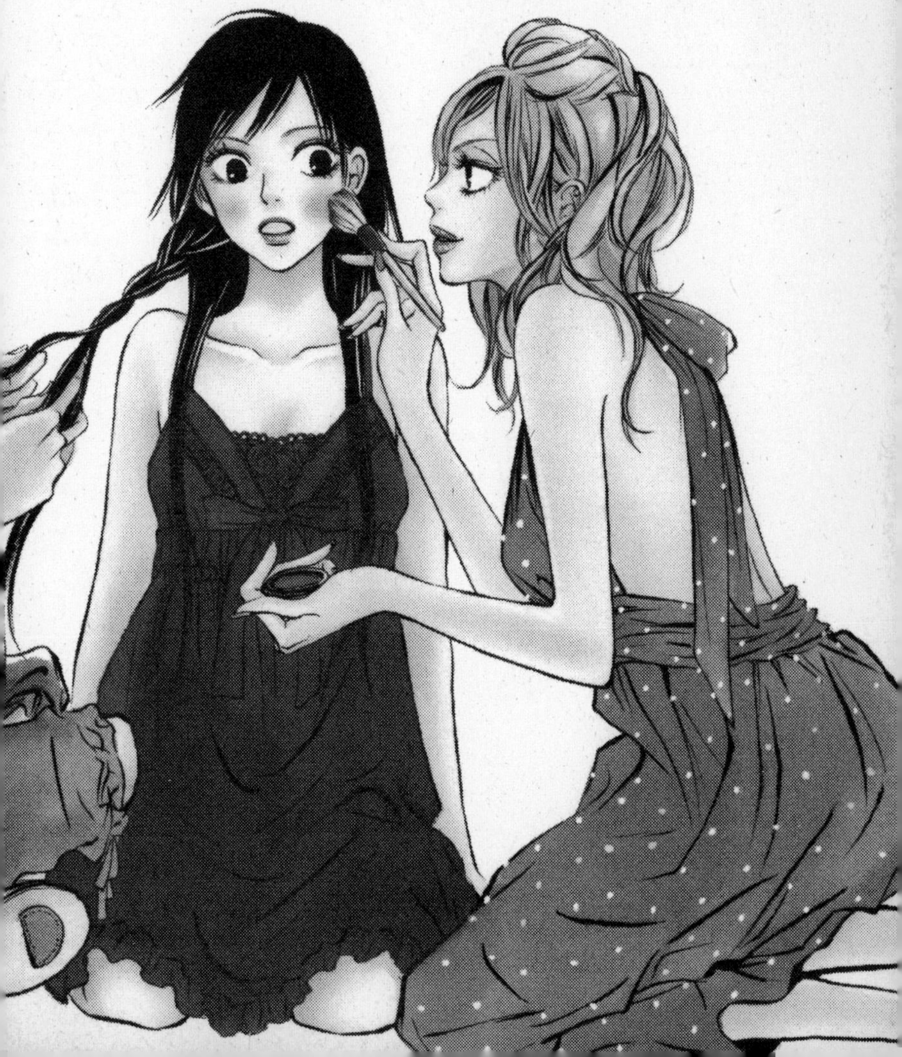

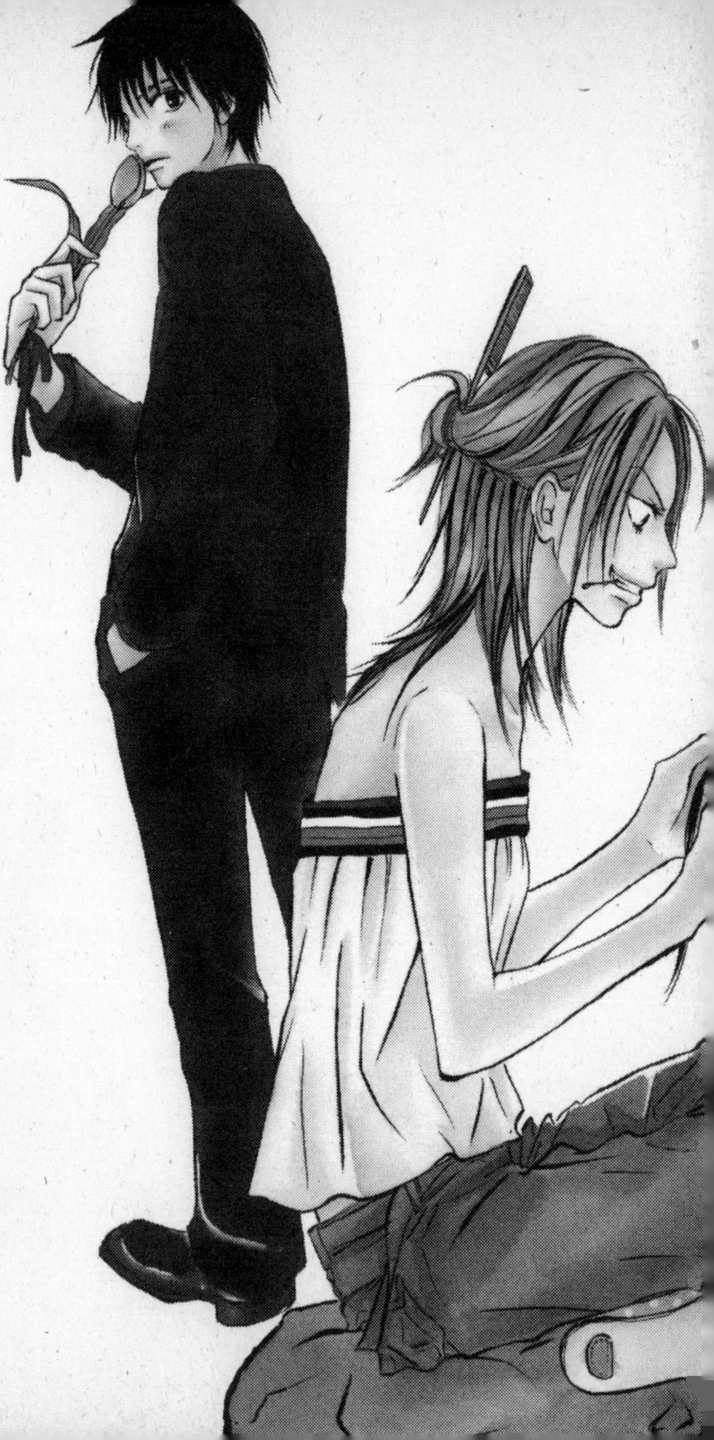

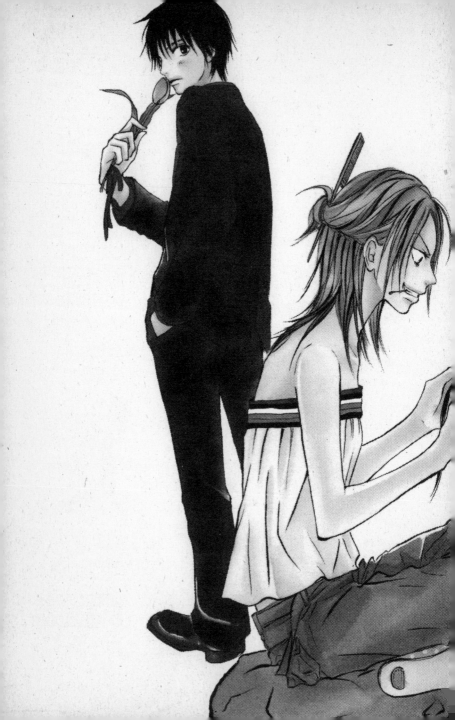

character #3

Chizuru Yoshida

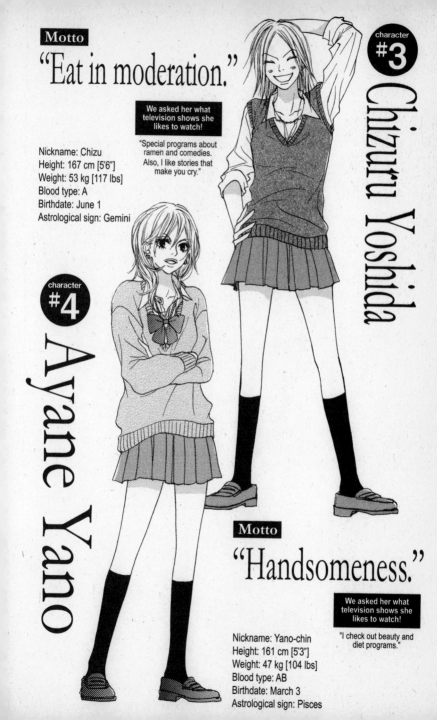

Motto

"Eat in moderation."

We asked her what television shows she likes to watch!

"Special programs about ramen and comedies. Also, I like stories that make you cry."

Nickname: Chizu
Height: 167 cm [5'6"]
Weight: 53 kg [117 lbs]
Blood type: A
Birthdate: June 1
Astrological sign: Gemini

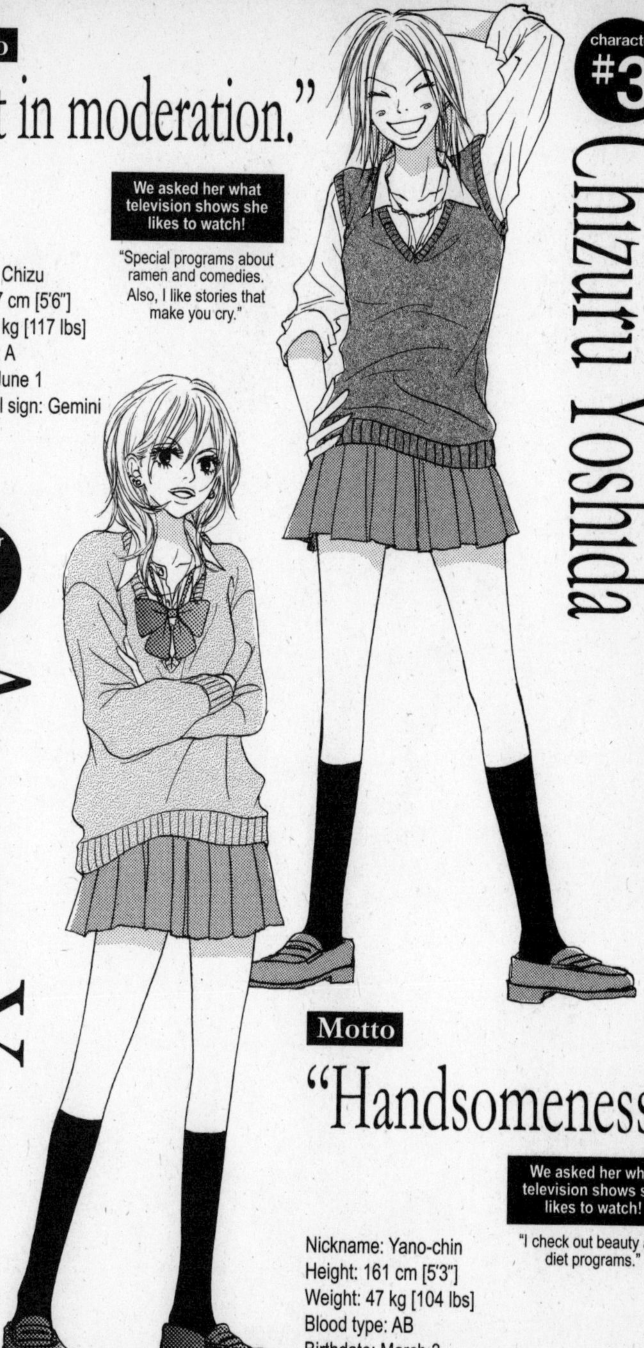

character #4

Ayane Yano

Motto

"Handsomeness."

We asked her what television shows she likes to watch!

"I check out beauty and diet programs."

Nickname: Yano-chin
Height: 161 cm [5'3"]
Weight: 47 kg [104 lbs]
Blood type: AB
Birthdate: March 3
Astrological sign: Pisces

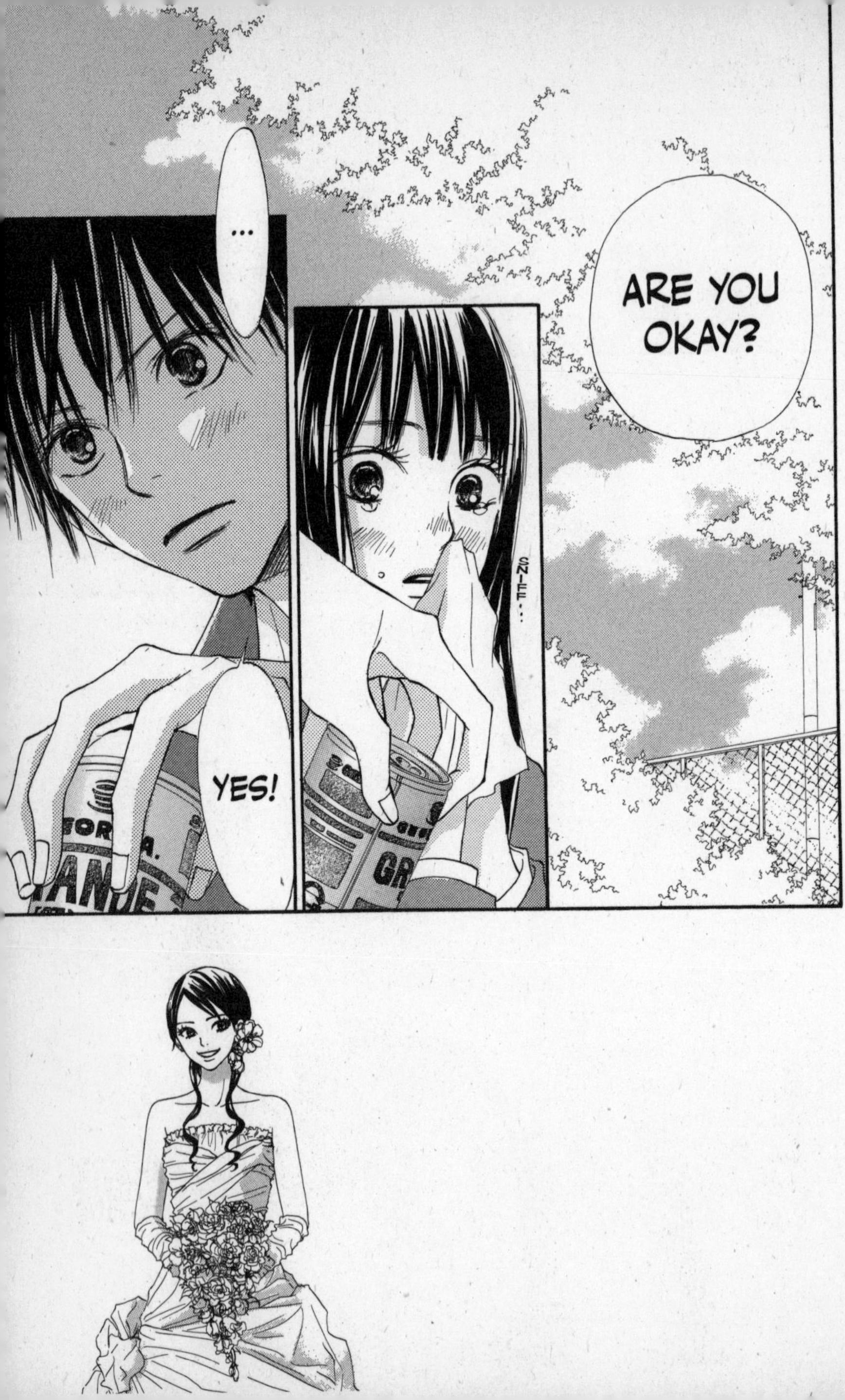
ARE YOU OKAY?
SNIFF..
...
YES!

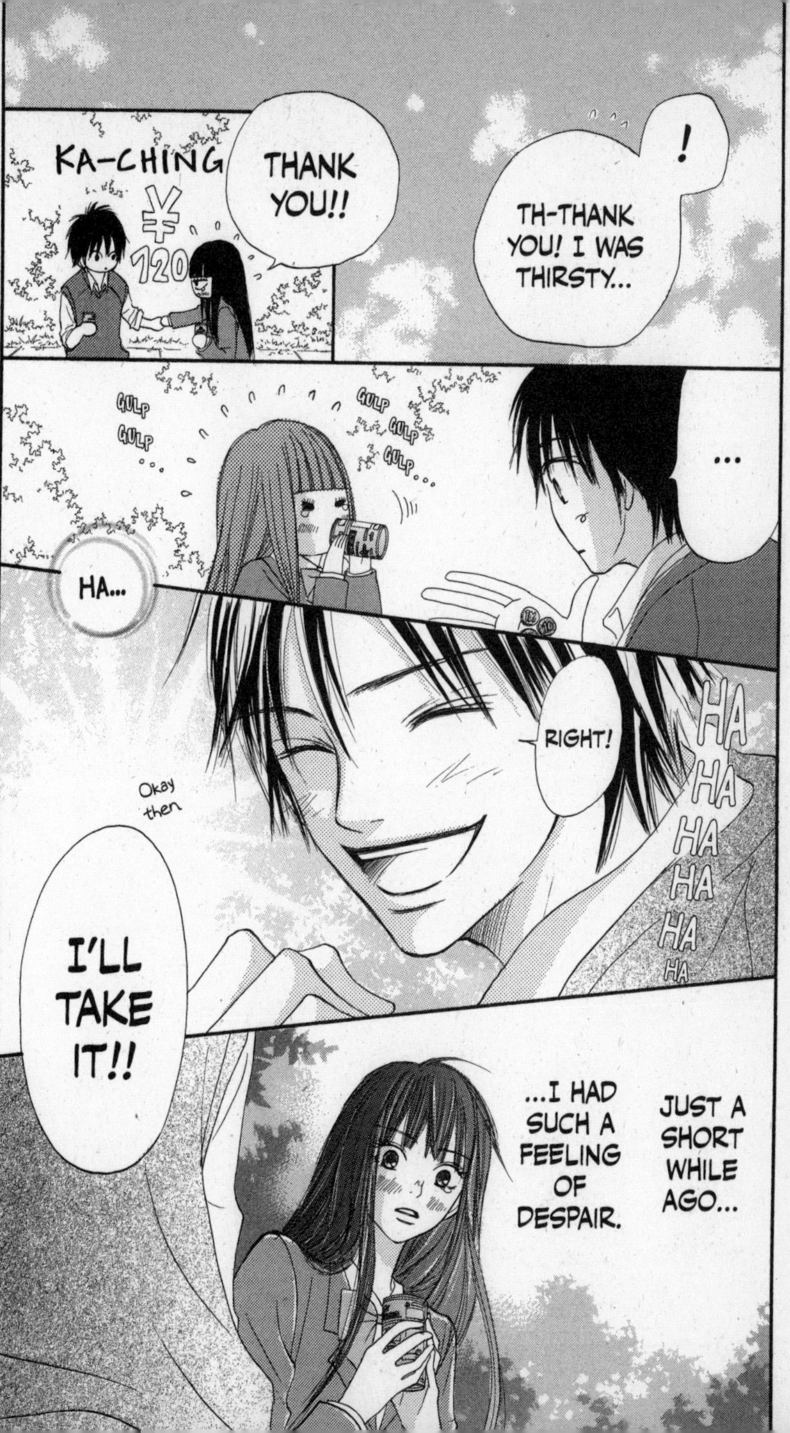
!
TH-THANK YOU! I WAS THIRSTY...
KA-CHING
¥120
THANK YOU!!
...
GULP GULP
GULP GULP...
HA...
RIGHT!
HA HA HA HA HA HA
Okay then
I'LL TAKE IT!!
JUST A SHORT WHILE AGO...
...I HAD SUCH A FEELING OF DESPAIR.

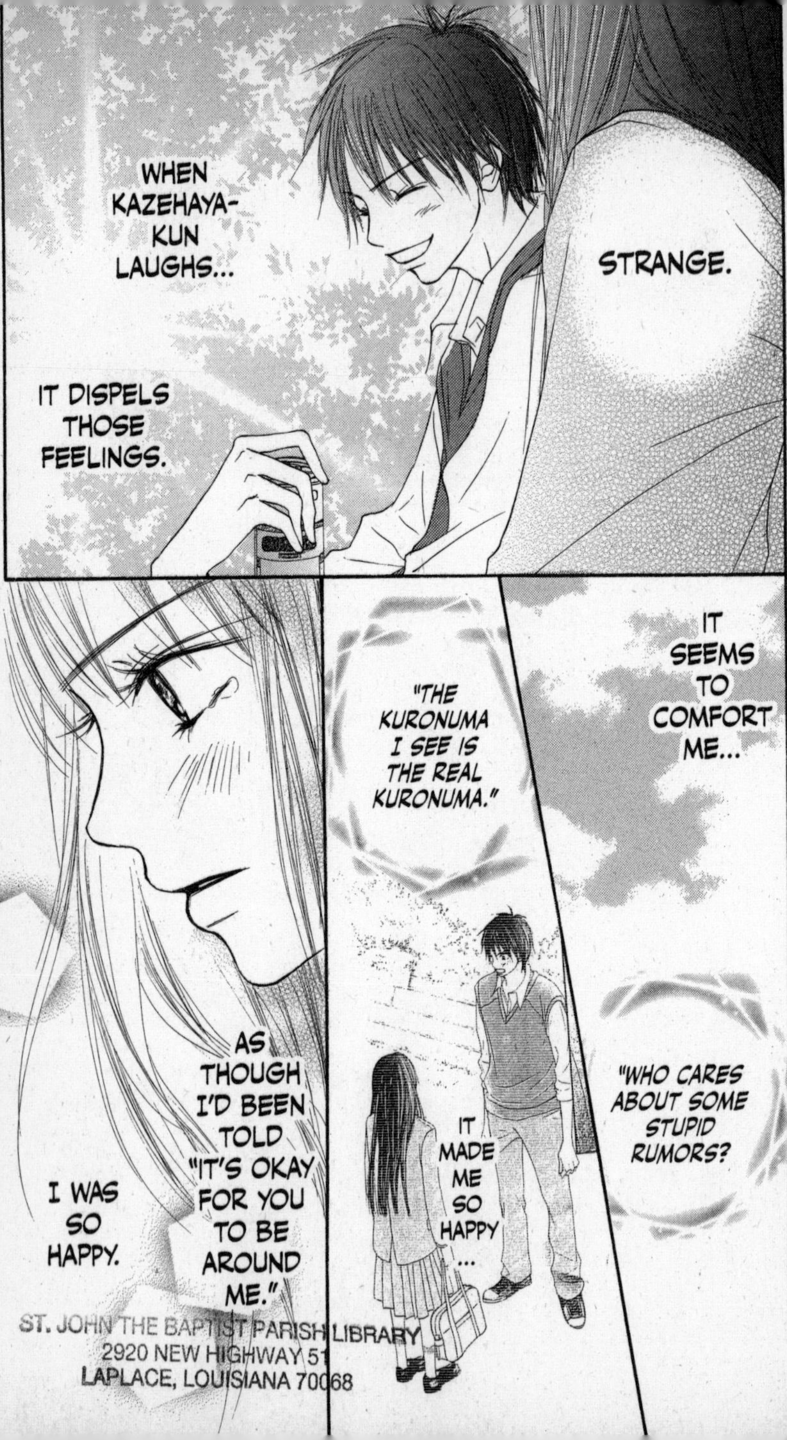
STRANGE.
WHEN KAZEHAYA-KUN LAUGHS...
IT DISPELS THOSE FEELINGS.
IT SEEMS TO COMFORT ME...
"WHO CARES ABOUT SOME STUPID RUMORS?
"THE KURONUMA I SEE IS THE REAL KURONUMA."
IT MADE ME SO HAPPY...
AS THOUGH I'D BEEN TOLD "IT'S OKAY FOR YOU TO BE AROUND ME."
I WAS SO HAPPY.

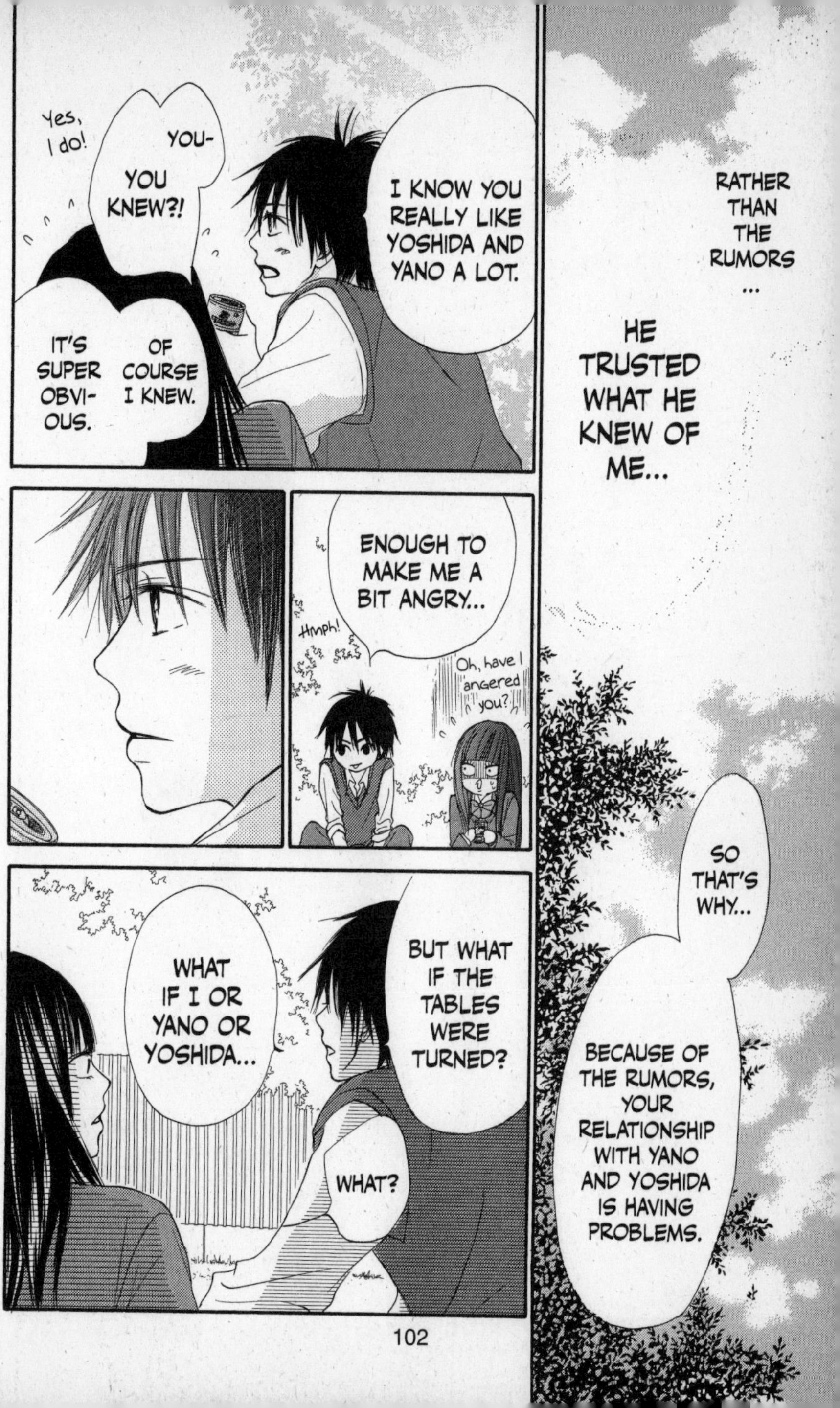
RATHER THAN THE RUMORS...
HE TRUSTED WHAT HE KNEW OF ME...
SO THAT'S WHY...
BECAUSE OF THE RUMORS, YOUR RELATIONSHIP WITH YANO AND YOSHIDA IS HAVING PROBLEMS.
I KNOW YOU REALLY LIKE YOSHIDA AND YANO A LOT.
YOU- YOU KNEW?!
Yes, I do!
OF COURSE I KNEW.
IT'S SUPER OBVI-OUS.
ENOUGH TO MAKE ME A BIT ANGRY...
Oh, have I angered you?
Hmph!
BUT WHAT IF THE TABLES WERE TURNED?
WHAT IF I OR YANO OR YOSHIDA...
WHAT?

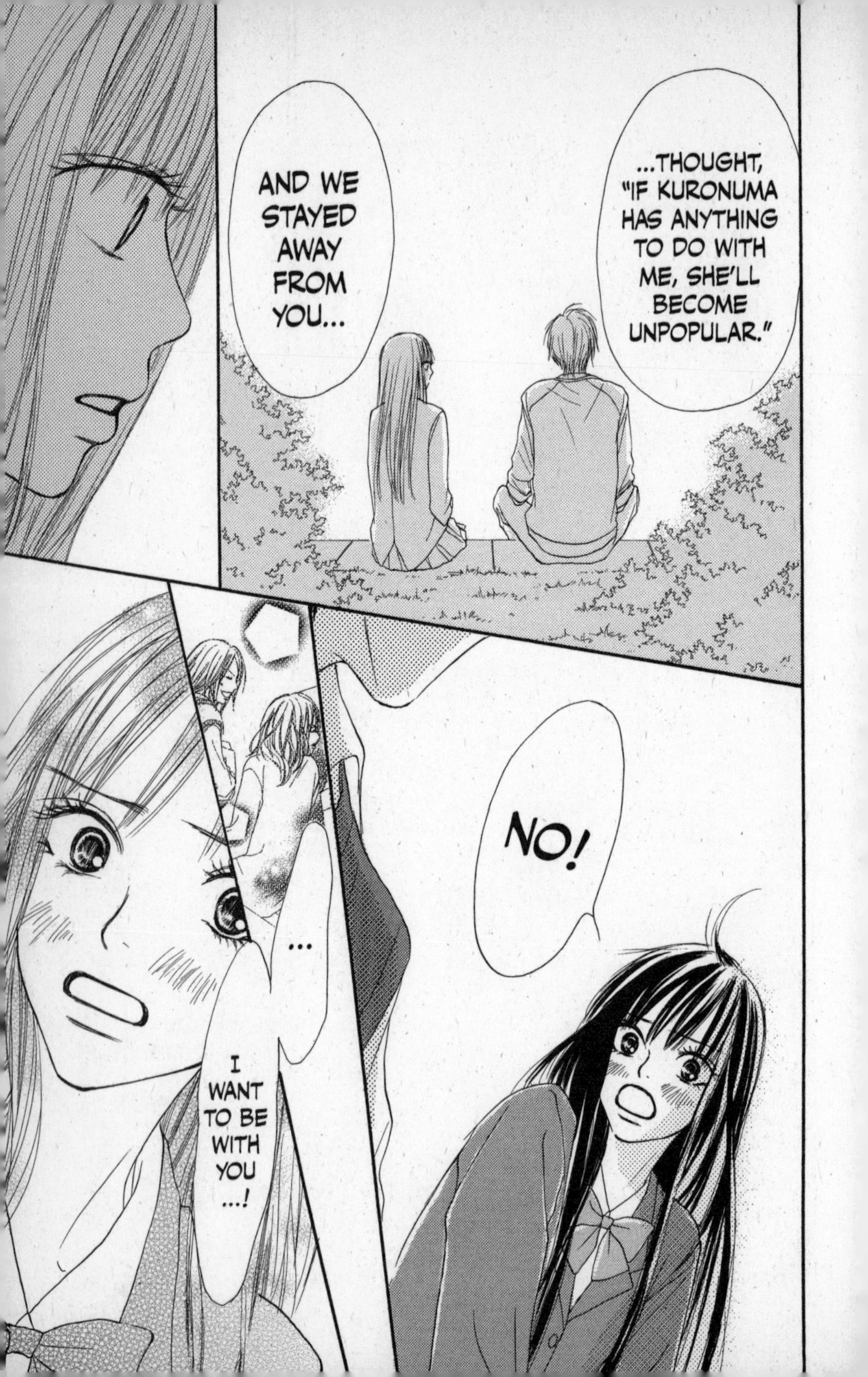
...THOUGHT, "IF KURONUMA HAS ANYTHING TO DO WITH ME, SHE'LL BECOME UNPOPULAR."
AND WE STAYED AWAY FROM YOU...
NO!
...
I WANT TO BE WITH YOU ...!

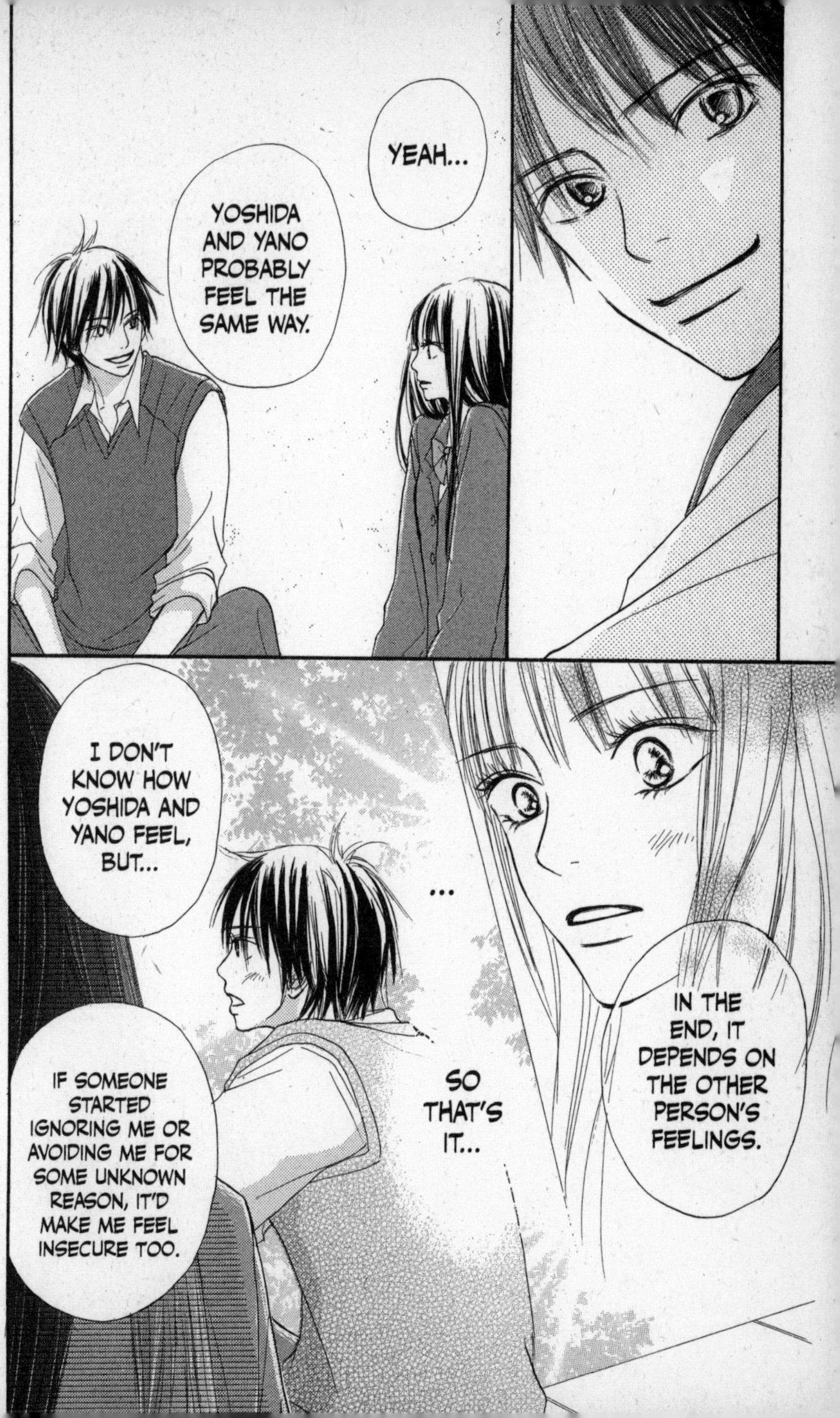
YEAH...
YOSHIDA AND YANO PROBABLY FEEL THE SAME WAY.
I DON'T KNOW HOW YOSHIDA AND YANO FEEL, BUT...
IF SOMEONE STARTED IGNORING ME OR AVOIDING ME FOR SOME UNKNOWN REASON, IT'D MAKE ME FEEL INSECURE TOO.
...
SO THAT'S IT...
IN THE END, IT DEPENDS ON THE OTHER PERSON'S FEELINGS.

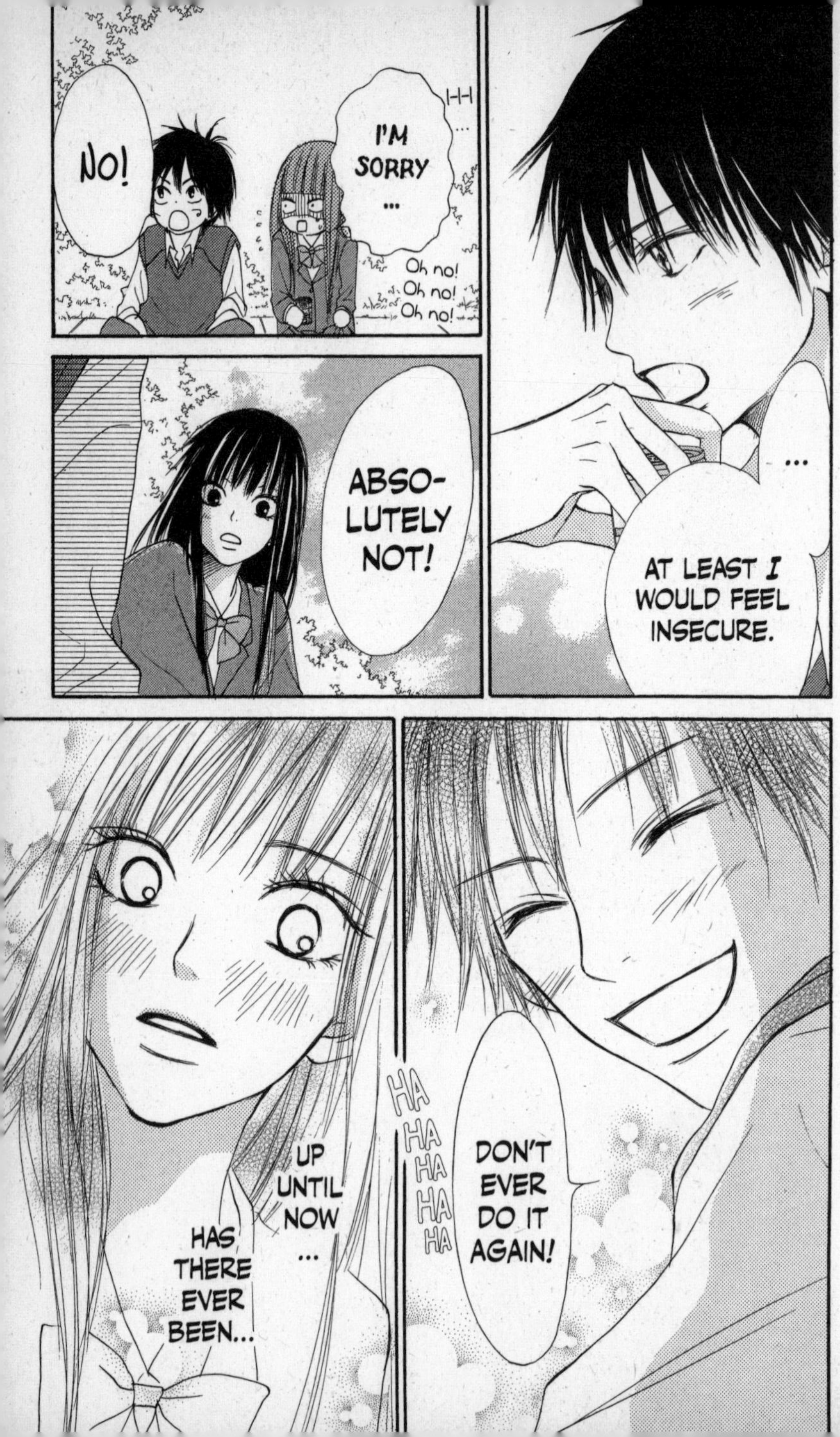
...
AT LEAST I WOULD FEEL INSECURE.
I-I ...
I'M SORRY ...
Oh no! Oh no! Oh no!
NO!
ABSO-LUTELY NOT!
HA HA HA HA HA HA
DON'T EVER DO IT AGAIN!
UP UNTIL NOW ...
HAS THERE EVER BEEN...

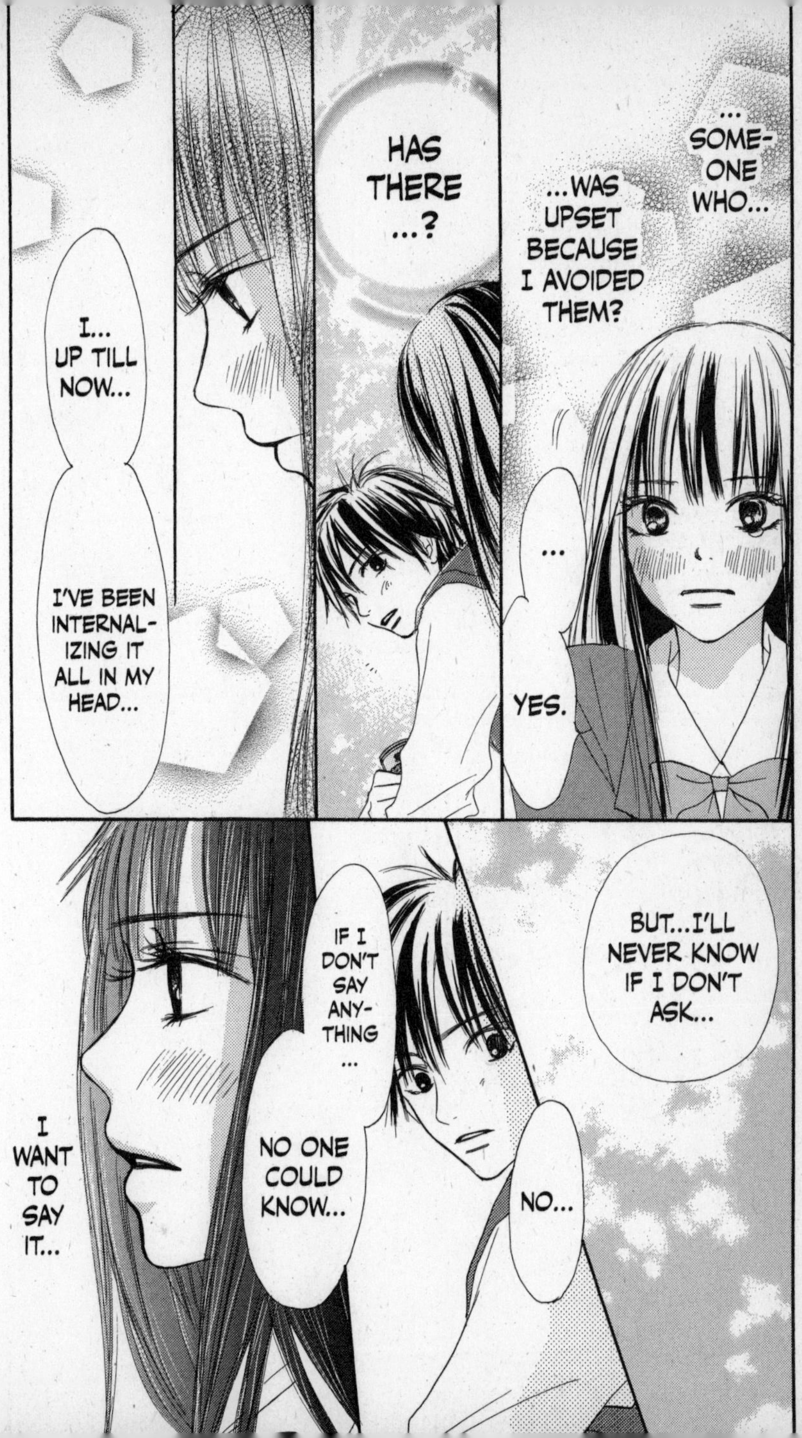
... SOME-ONE WHO...
...WAS UPSET BECAUSE I AVOIDED THEM?
...
YES.
HAS THERE ...?
I... UP TILL NOW...
I'VE BEEN INTERNAL-IZING IT ALL IN MY HEAD...
BUT...I'LL NEVER KNOW IF I DON'T ASK...
NO...
IF I DON'T SAY ANY-THING ...
NO ONE COULD KNOW...
I WANT TO SAY IT...

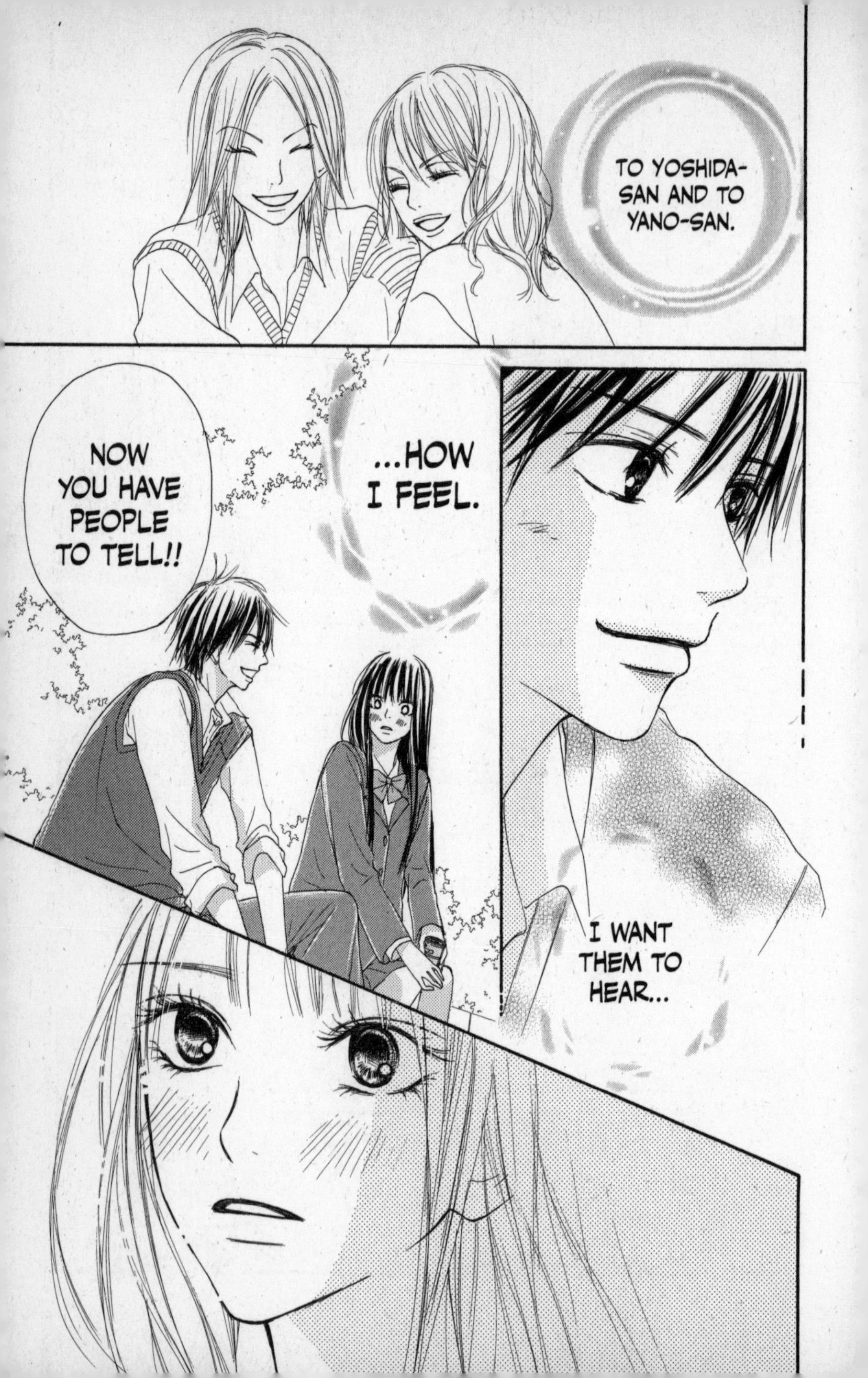
TO YOSHIDA-SAN AND TO YANO-SAN.
I WANT THEM TO HEAR...
...HOW I FEEL.
NOW YOU HAVE PEOPLE TO TELL!!

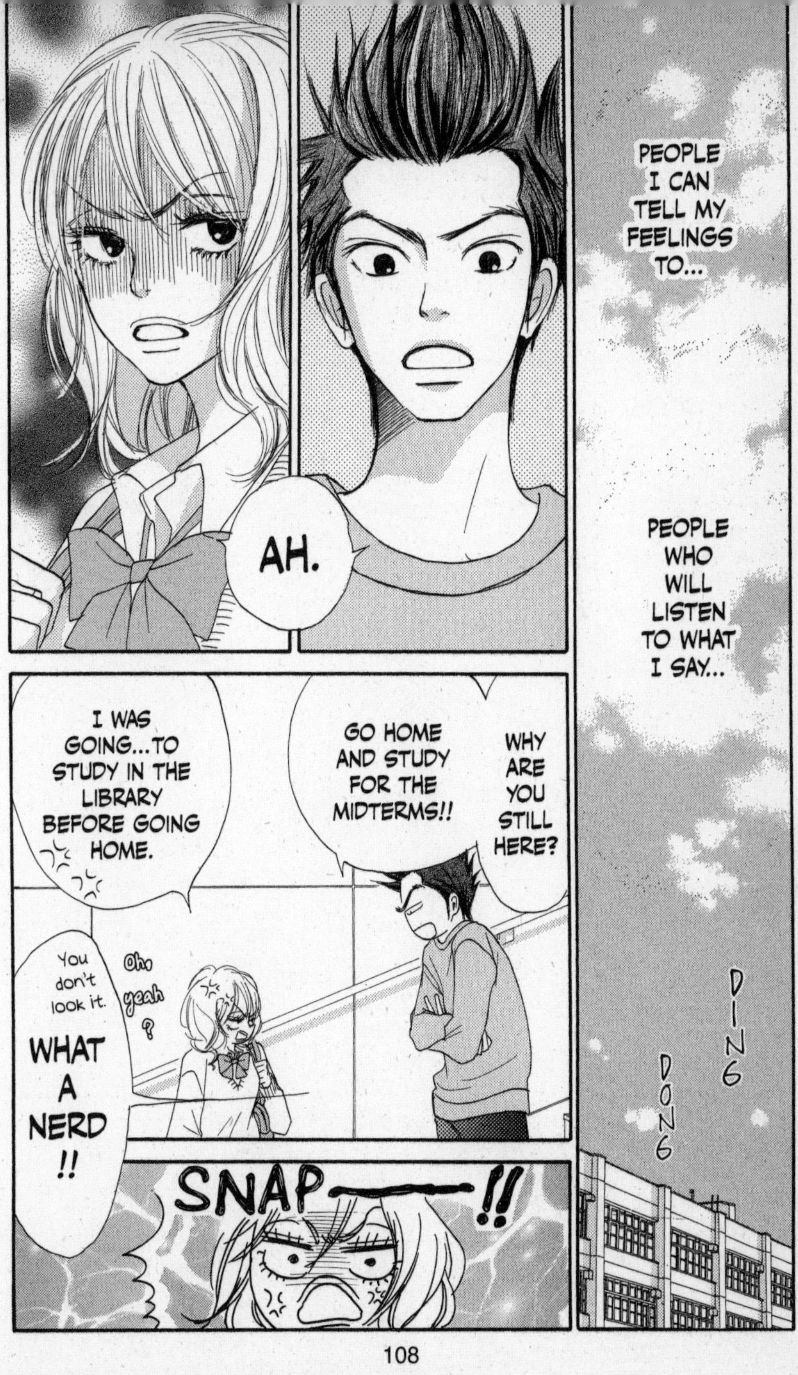
PEOPLE I CAN TELL MY FEELINGS TO...
PEOPLE WHO WILL LISTEN TO WHAT I SAY...
DING
DONG
AH.
WHY ARE YOU STILL HERE?
GO HOME AND STUDY FOR THE MIDTERMS!!
I WAS GOING...TO STUDY IN THE LIBRARY BEFORE GOING HOME.
Oh yeah?
You don't look it.
WHAT A NERD!!
SNAP——!!

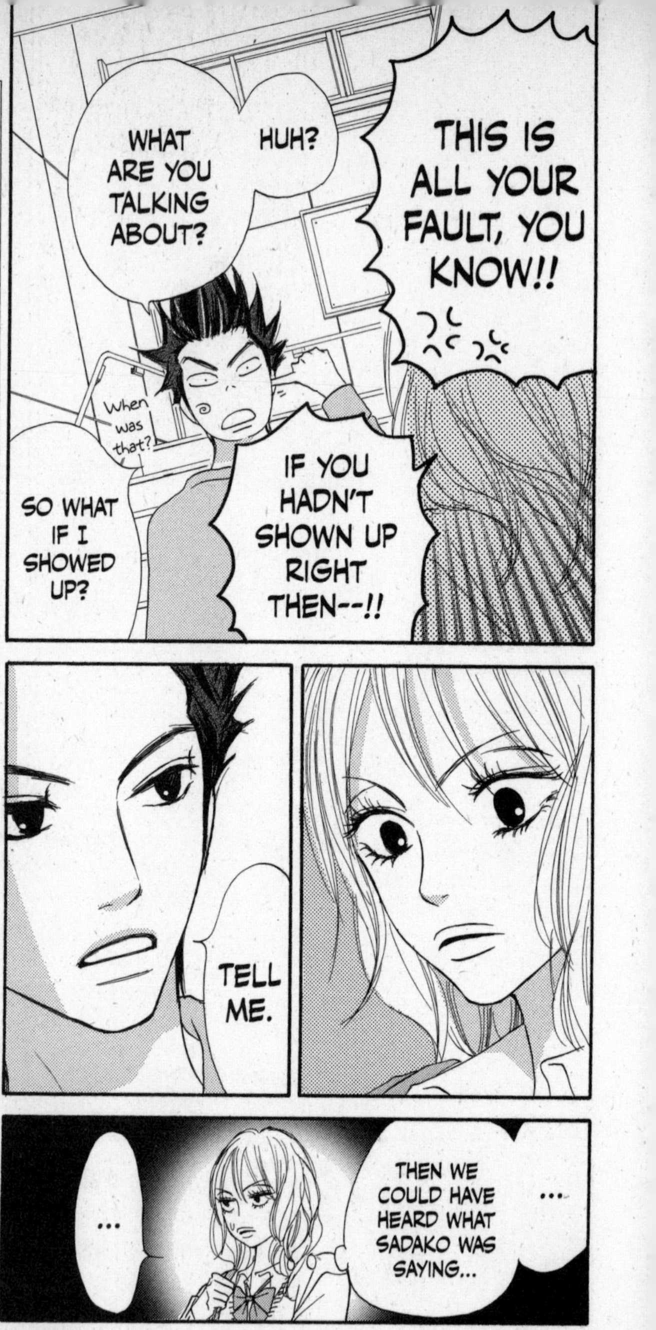
THIS IS ALL YOUR FAULT, YOU KNOW!!
HUH?
WHAT ARE YOU TALKING ABOUT?
IF YOU HADN'T SHOWN UP RIGHT THEN--!!
When was that?
SO WHAT IF I SHOWED UP?
TELL ME.
...
THEN WE COULD HAVE HEARD WHAT SADAKO WAS SAYING...
...

KARUPIN on JAPAN 3

When the first volume went on sale, Keibunsha's Banbio branch (a bookstore in Kyoto) created its own "Kimi ni Todoke" area with really lovely signs.

It was so great!

There was also a "Manpukuji" area right below which I was happy about!
(*I'm a fan!)

There was even a character relation chart. It was so nice!!

I only got to see a photo of it, but I wish I could have seen the real thing! If only Kyoto were closer! If only I could manage my time better so I'd have some free time...!!

To Miyagawa-sama and Ôtaki-sama of Keibunsha's Banbio branch, to Shueisha's Sales Department's Ichikawa-sama who took photos and to my editor Mariko-sama who quickly sent the photo to my cell phone... Thank you all so much!

I'll cherish the memory forever!

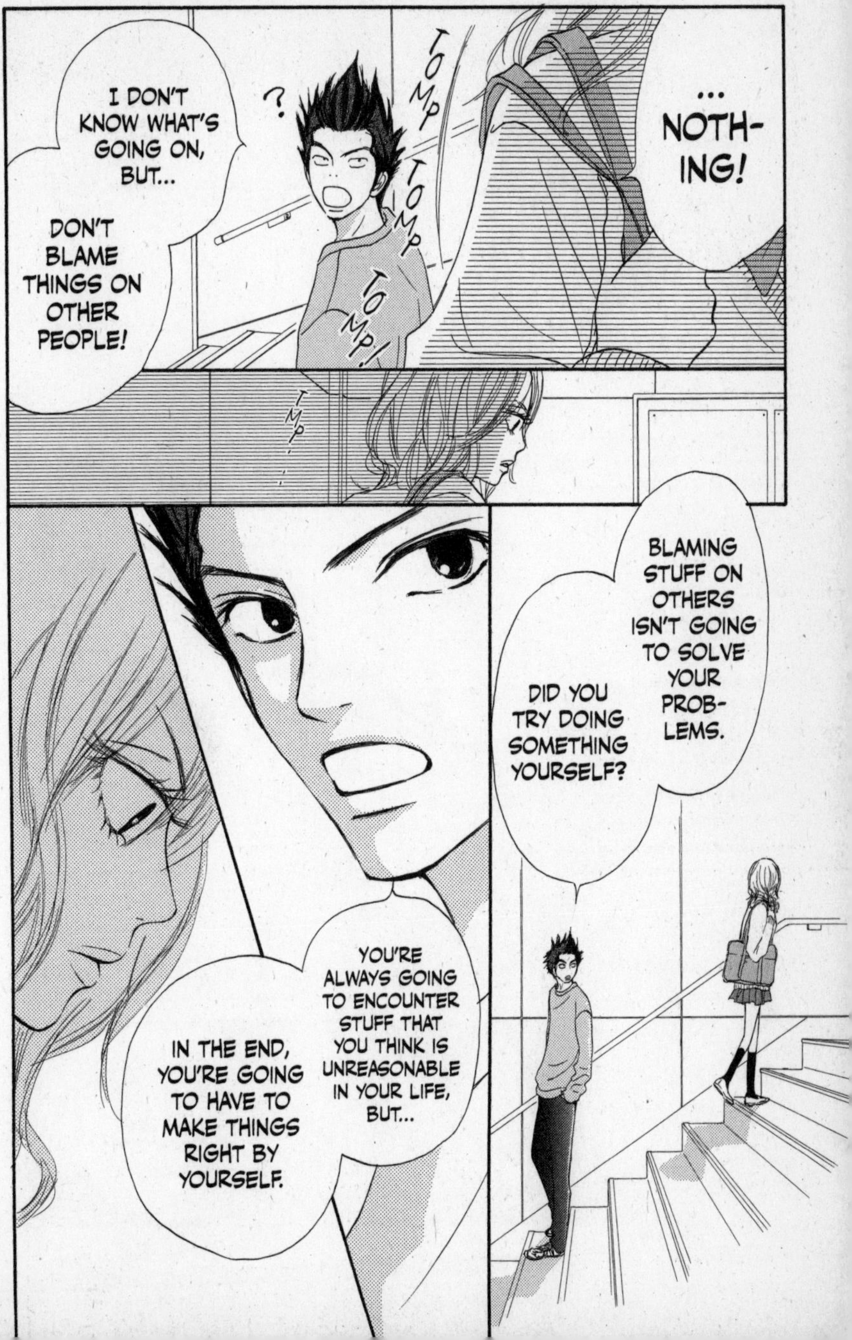
... NOTH-ING!
TOMP TOMP TOMP!
?
I DON'T KNOW WHAT'S GOING ON, BUT...
DON'T BLAME THINGS ON OTHER PEOPLE!
TMP...
BLAMING STUFF ON OTHERS ISN'T GOING TO SOLVE YOUR PROB-LEMS.
DID YOU TRY DOING SOMETHING YOURSELF?
YOU'RE ALWAYS GOING TO ENCOUNTER STUFF THAT YOU THINK IS UNREASONABLE IN YOUR LIFE, BUT...
IN THE END, YOU'RE GOING TO HAVE TO MAKE THINGS RIGHT BY YOURSELF.

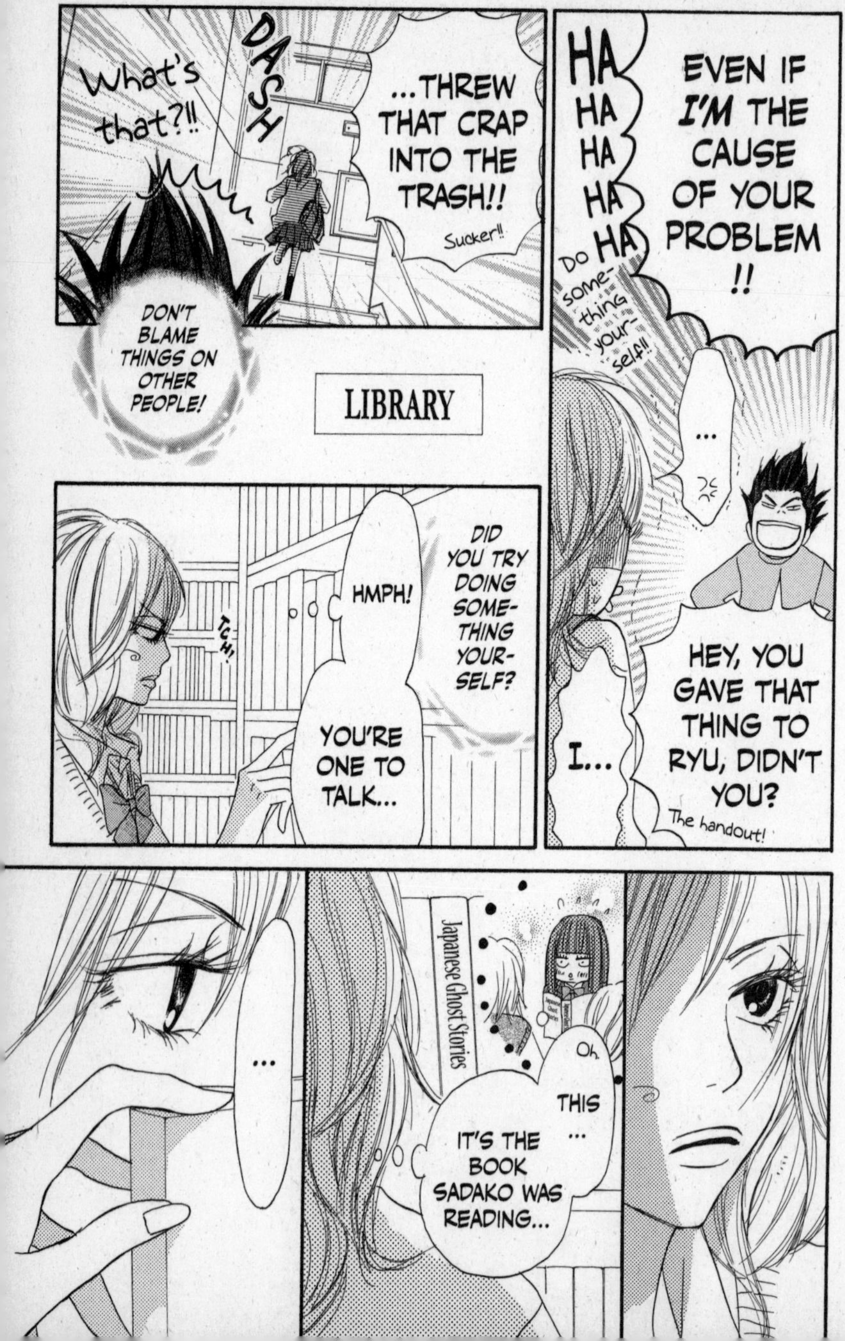
EVEN IF I'M THE CAUSE OF YOUR PROBLEM!!
HA HA HA HA HA
Do something yourself!!
...
HEY, YOU GAVE THAT THING TO RYU, DIDN'T YOU?
The handout!
I...
...THREW THAT CRAP INTO THE TRASH!!
Sucker!!
DASH
What's that?!!
DON'T BLAME THINGS ON OTHER PEOPLE!
LIBRARY
DID YOU TRY DOING SOMETHING YOURSELF?
HMPH!
TCH
YOU'RE ONE TO TALK...
Oh.
THIS ...
IT'S THE BOOK SADAKO WAS READING...
Japanese Ghost Stories
...

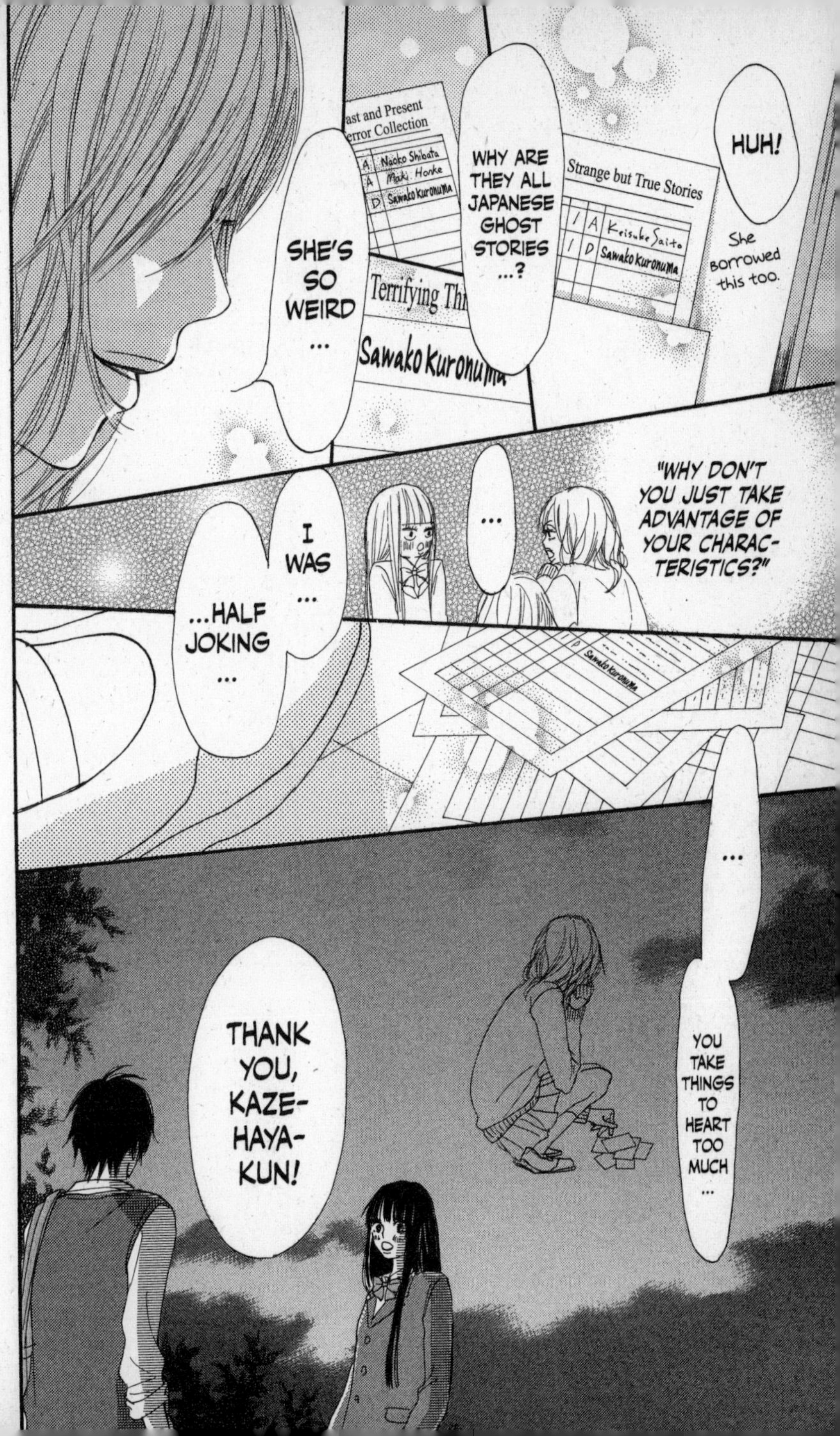
HUH!
She borrowed this too.
Strange but True Stories
Keisuke Saito
Sawako Kuronuma
WHY ARE THEY ALL JAPANESE GHOST STORIES ...?
Naoko Shibata
Maki Honke
Sawako Kuronuma
Sawako Kuronuma
SHE'S SO WEIRD ...
"WHY DON'T YOU JUST TAKE ADVANTAGE OF YOUR CHARAC-TERISTICS?"
...
I WAS ...
...HALF JOKING ...
Sawako Kuronuma
...
YOU TAKE THINGS TO HEART TOO MUCH ...
THANK YOU, KAZE-HAYA-KUN!

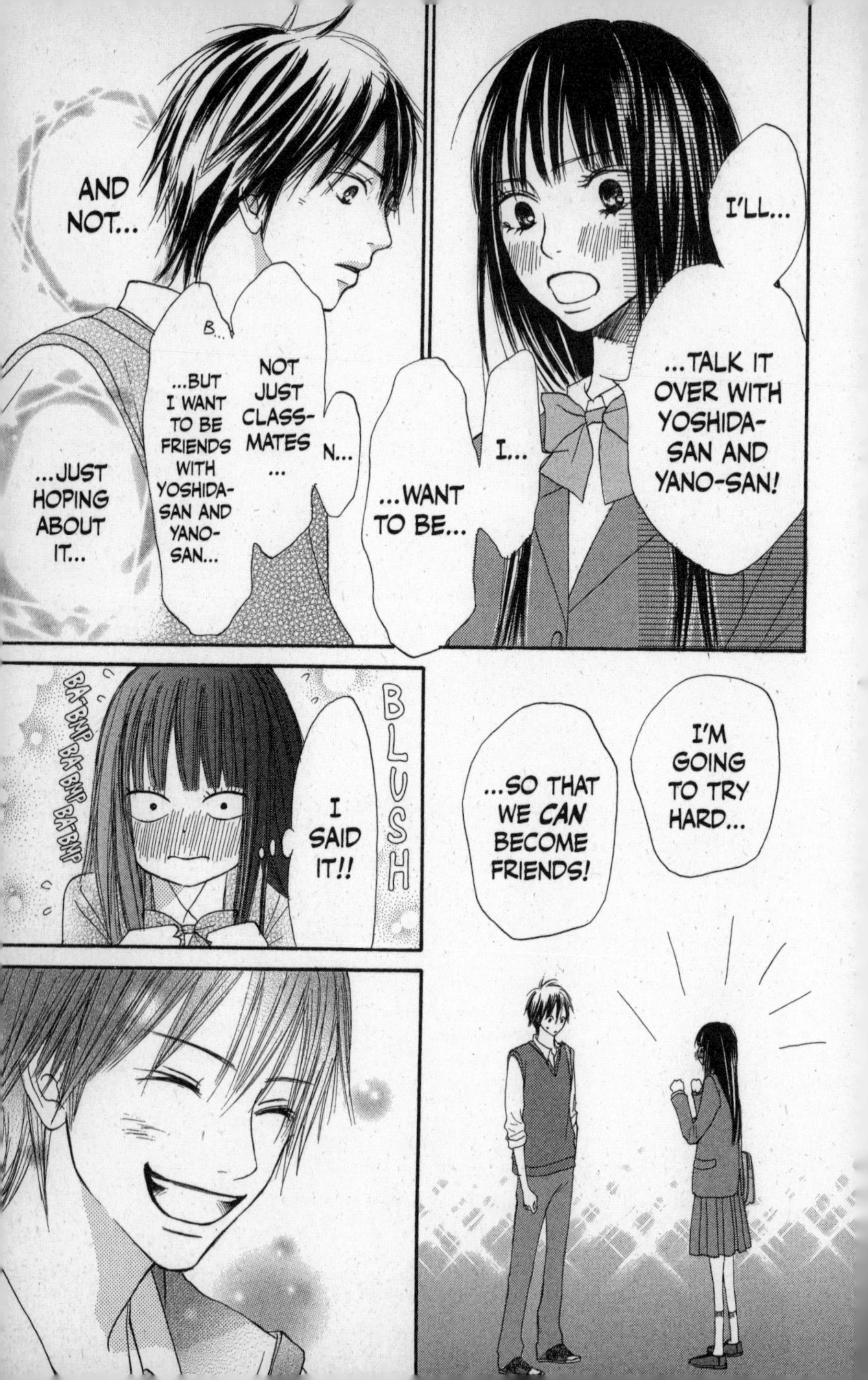
I'LL...
...TALK IT OVER WITH YOSHIDA-SAN AND YANO-SAN!
I...
...WANT TO BE...
N...
NOT JUST CLASSMATES...
B...
...BUT I WANT TO BE FRIENDS WITH YOSHIDA-SAN AND YANO-SAN...
AND NOT...
...JUST HOPING ABOUT IT...
I'M GOING TO TRY HARD...
...SO THAT WE *CAN* BECOME FRIENDS!
BLUSH
I SAID IT!!
BA-BMP BA-BMP BA-BMP

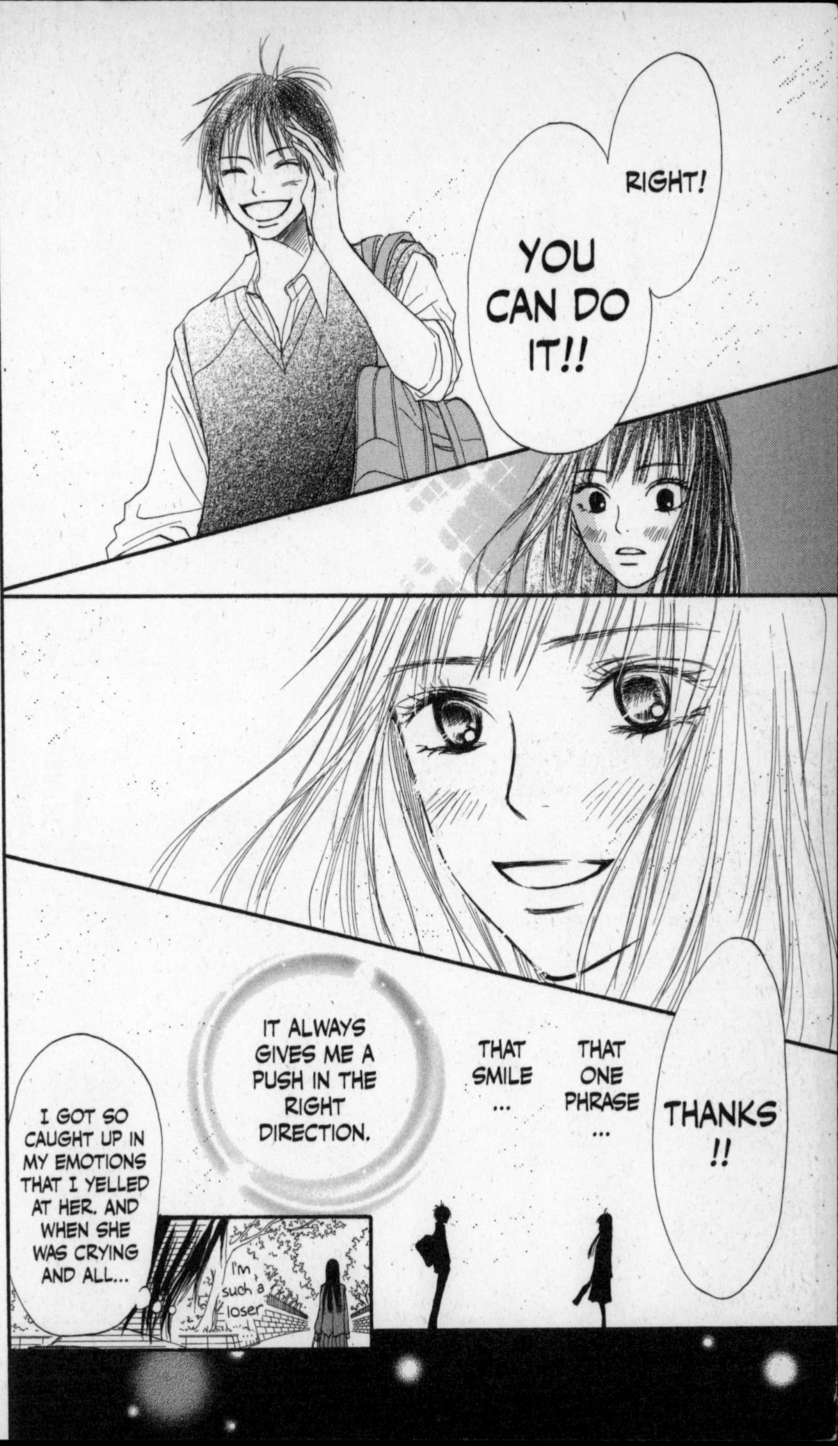
RIGHT! YOU CAN DO IT!!
THANKS!!
THAT ONE PHRASE...
THAT SMILE...
IT ALWAYS GIVES ME A PUSH IN THE RIGHT DIRECTION.
I GOT SO CAUGHT UP IN MY EMOTIONS THAT I YELLED AT HER. AND WHEN SHE WAS CRYING AND ALL...
I'm such a loser

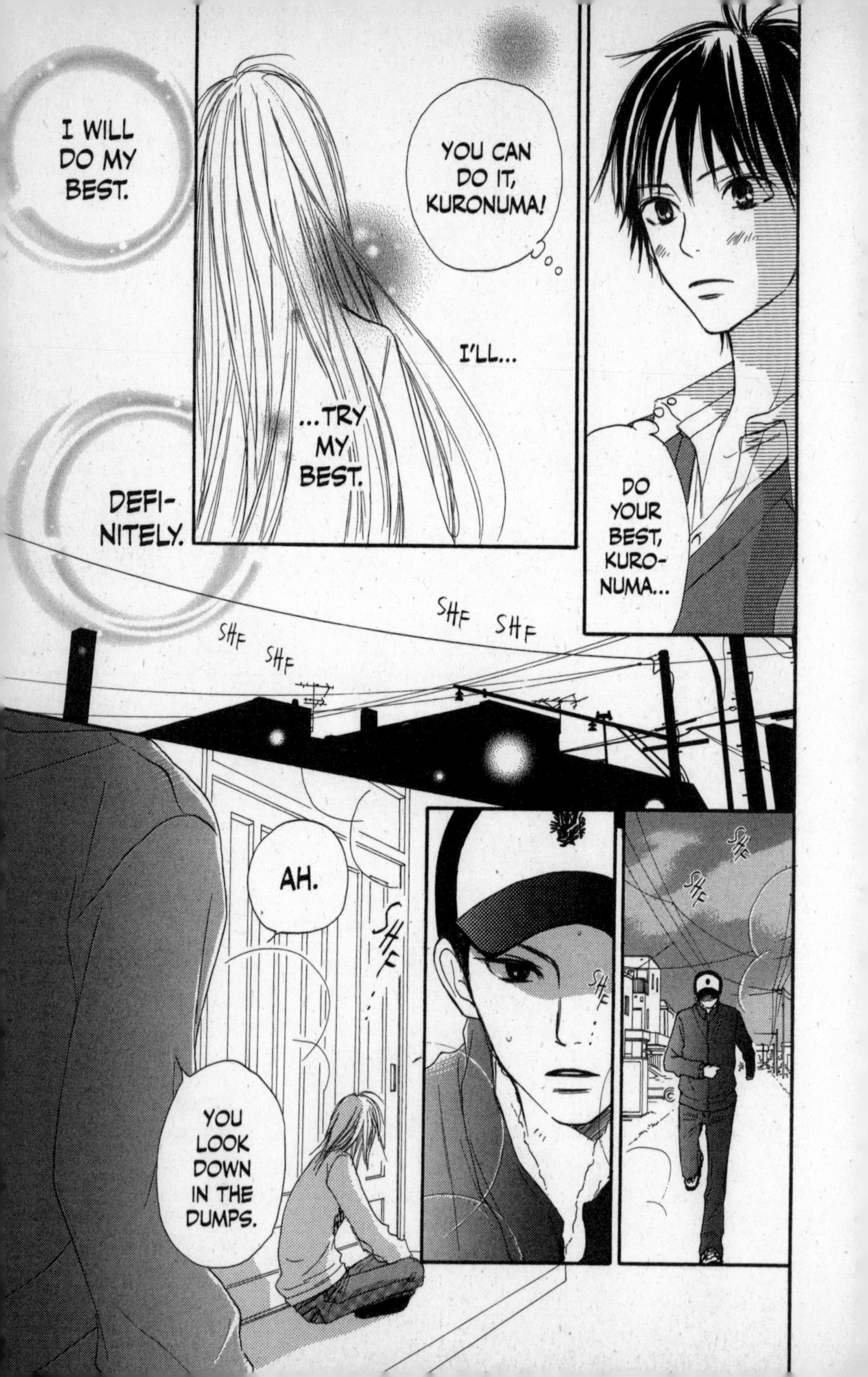
DO YOUR BEST, KURONUMA...
YOU CAN DO IT, KURONUMA!
I'LL...
...TRY MY BEST.
I WILL DO MY BEST.
DEFINITELY.
SHF SHF
SHF SHF
SHF
SHF
SHF
SHF
AH.
YOU LOOK DOWN IN THE DUMPS.

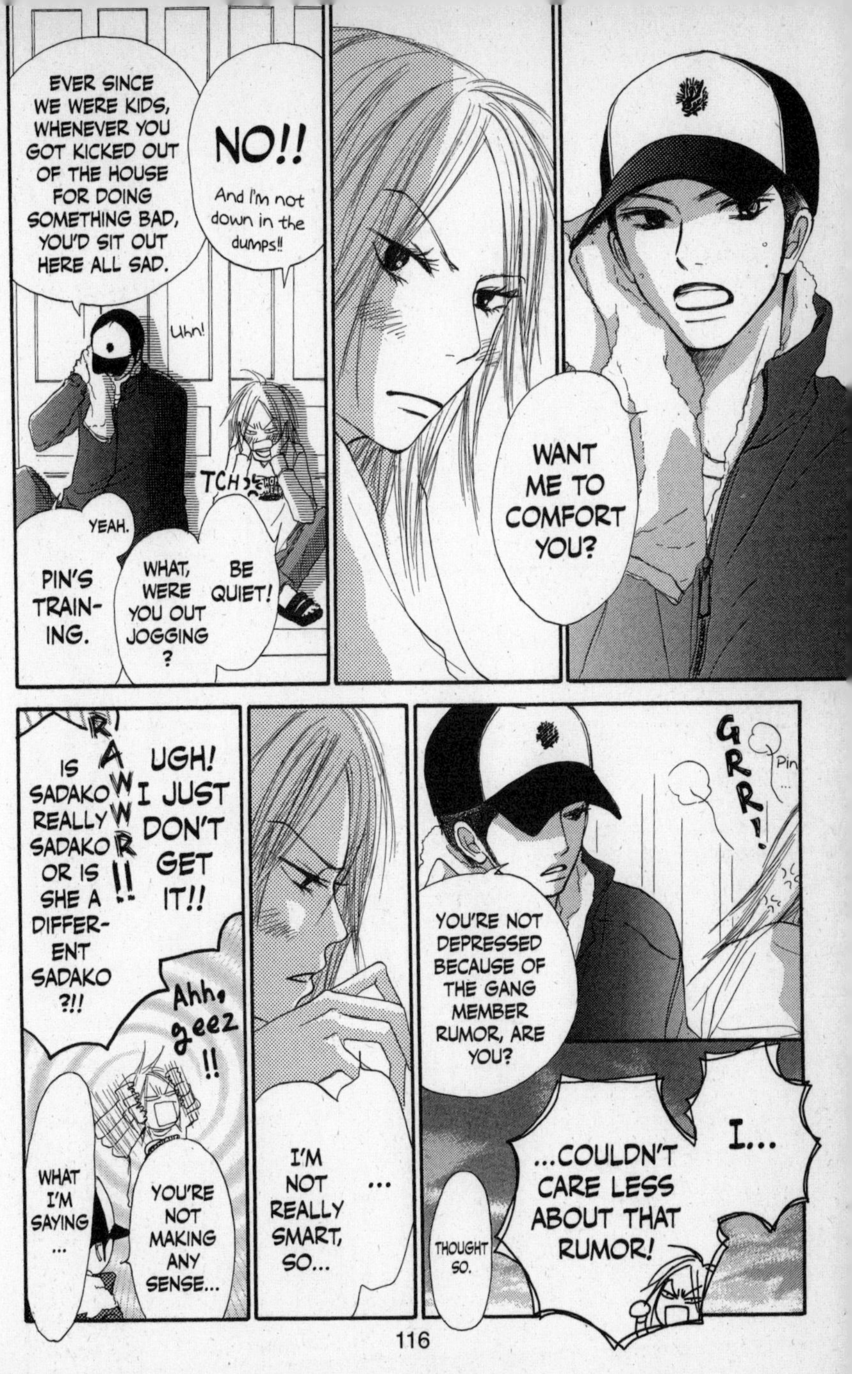
WANT ME TO COMFORT YOU?
NO!!
And I'm not down in the dumps!!
EVER SINCE WE WERE KIDS, WHENEVER YOU GOT KICKED OUT OF THE HOUSE FOR DOING SOMETHING BAD, YOU'D SIT OUT HERE ALL SAD.
Uhn!
TCH
BE QUIET!
WHAT, WERE YOU OUT JOGGING?
YEAH.
PIN'S TRAIN-ING.
GRR!
Pin...
YOU'RE NOT DEPRESSED BECAUSE OF THE GANG MEMBER RUMOR, ARE YOU?
I...
...COULDN'T CARE LESS ABOUT THAT RUMOR!
THOUGHT SO.
...
I'M NOT REALLY SMART, SO...
UGH! I JUST DON'T GET IT!!
RAWWR!!
IS SADAKO REALLY SADAKO OR IS SHE A DIFFER-ENT SADAKO?!!
Ahh, geez!!
YOU'RE NOT MAKING ANY SENSE...
WHAT I'M SAYING...

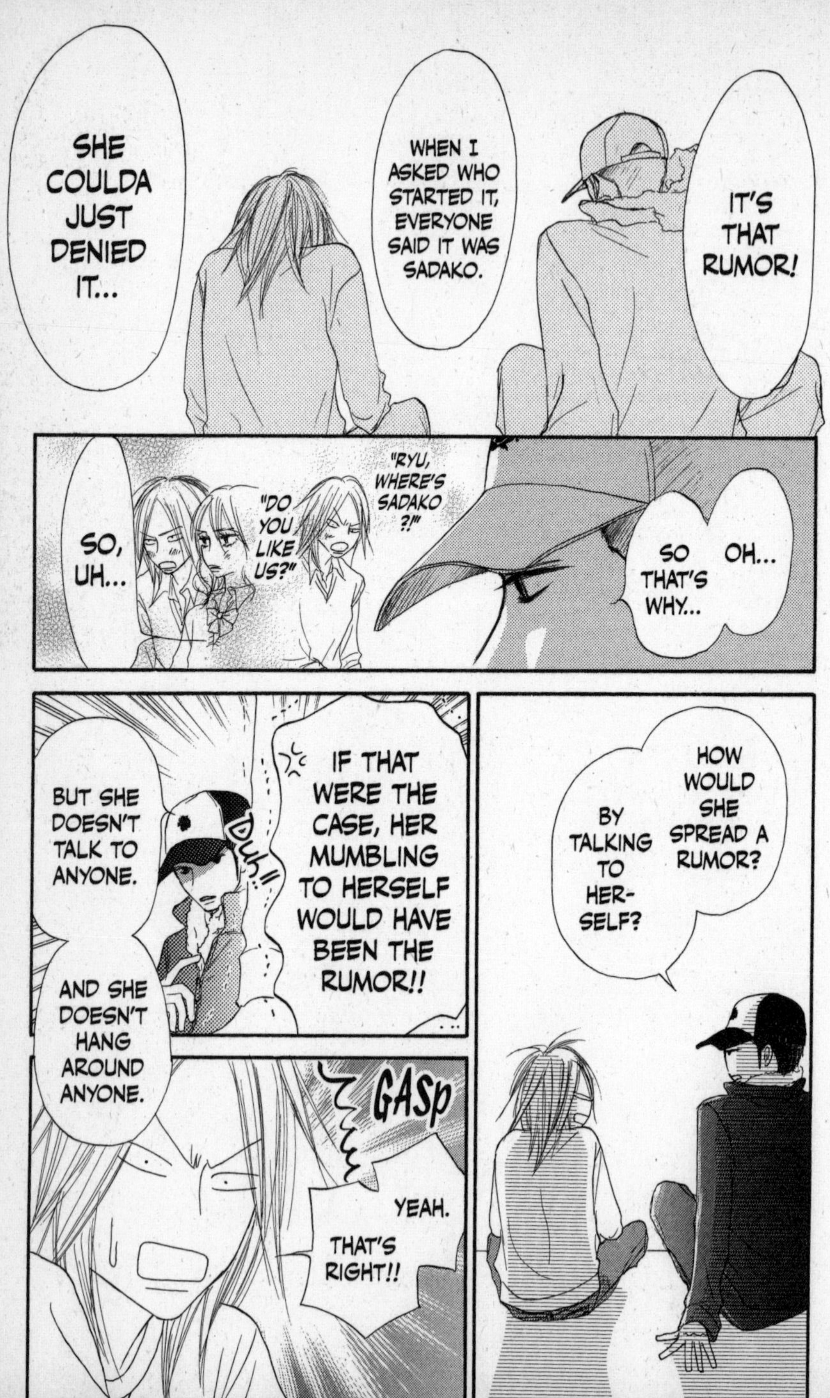
IT'S THAT RUMOR!
WHEN I ASKED WHO STARTED IT, EVERYONE SAID IT WAS SADAKO.
SHE COULDA JUST DENIED IT...
OH... SO THAT'S WHY...
"RYU, WHERE'S SADAKO?!"
"DO YOU LIKE US?"
SO, UH...
HOW WOULD SHE SPREAD A RUMOR?
BY TALKING TO HER-SELF?
IF THAT WERE THE CASE, HER MUMBLING TO HERSELF WOULD HAVE BEEN THE RUMOR!!
DUH!!
BUT SHE DOESN'T TALK TO ANYONE.
AND SHE DOESN'T HANG AROUND ANYONE.
GASP
YEAH.
THAT'S RIGHT!!

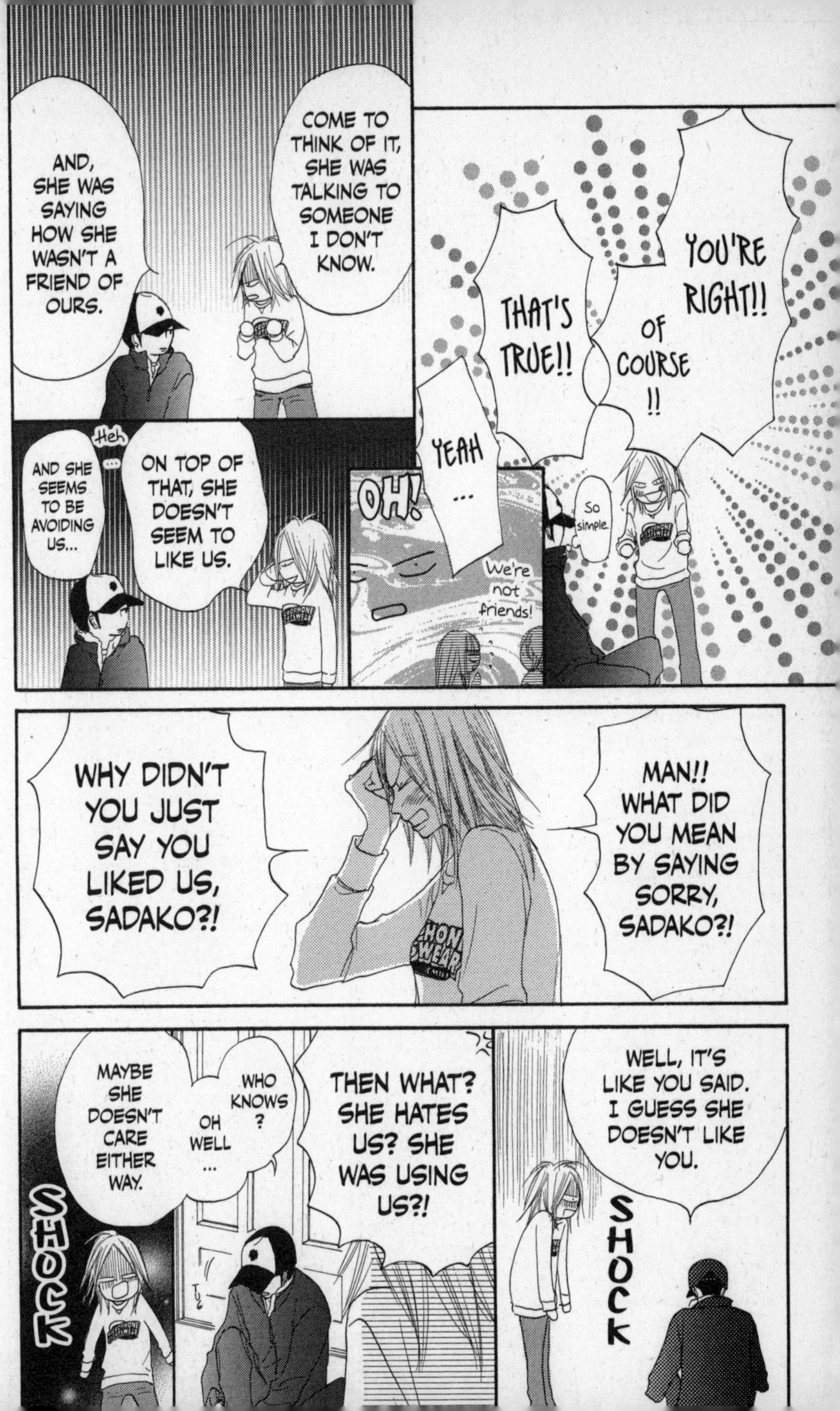
COME TO THINK OF IT, SHE WAS TALKING TO SOMEONE I DON'T KNOW.
AND, SHE WAS SAYING HOW SHE WASN'T A FRIEND OF OURS.
ON TOP OF THAT, SHE DOESN'T SEEM TO LIKE US.
Heh ...
AND SHE SEEMS TO BE AVOIDING US...
OH!
We're not friends!
YEAH ...
YOU'RE RIGHT!!
OF COURSE !!
THAT'S TRUE!!
So simple.
MAN!! WHAT DID YOU MEAN BY SAYING SORRY, SADAKO?!
WHY DIDN'T YOU JUST SAY YOU LIKED US, SADAKO?!
WELL, IT'S LIKE YOU SAID. I GUESS SHE DOESN'T LIKE YOU.
SHOCK
THEN WHAT? SHE HATES US? SHE WAS USING US?!
WHO KNOWS ?
OH WELL ...
MAYBE SHE DOESN'T CARE EITHER WAY.
SHOCK

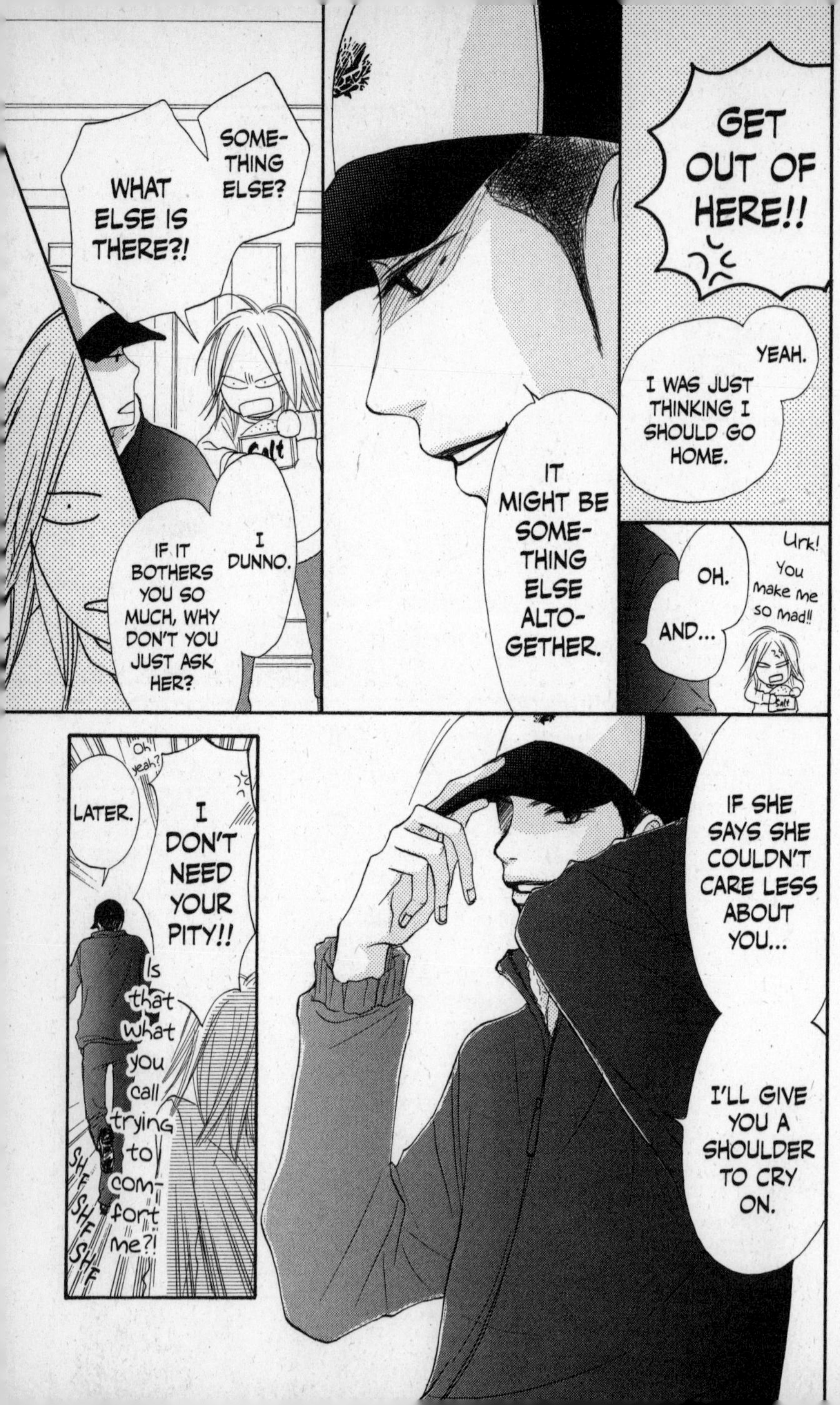
GET OUT OF HERE!!
YEAH.
I WAS JUST THINKING I SHOULD GO HOME.
OH.
AND...
Urk! You make me so mad!!
IT MIGHT BE SOMETHING ELSE ALTOGETHER.
SOME-THING ELSE?
WHAT ELSE IS THERE?!
I DUNNO.
IF IT BOTHERS YOU SO MUCH, WHY DON'T YOU JUST ASK HER?
IF SHE SAYS SHE COULDN'T CARE LESS ABOUT YOU...
I'LL GIVE YOU A SHOULDER TO CRY ON.
I DON'T NEED YOUR PITY!!
Oh yeah?
LATER.
Is that what you call trying to com-fort me?!
SHF SHF SHF

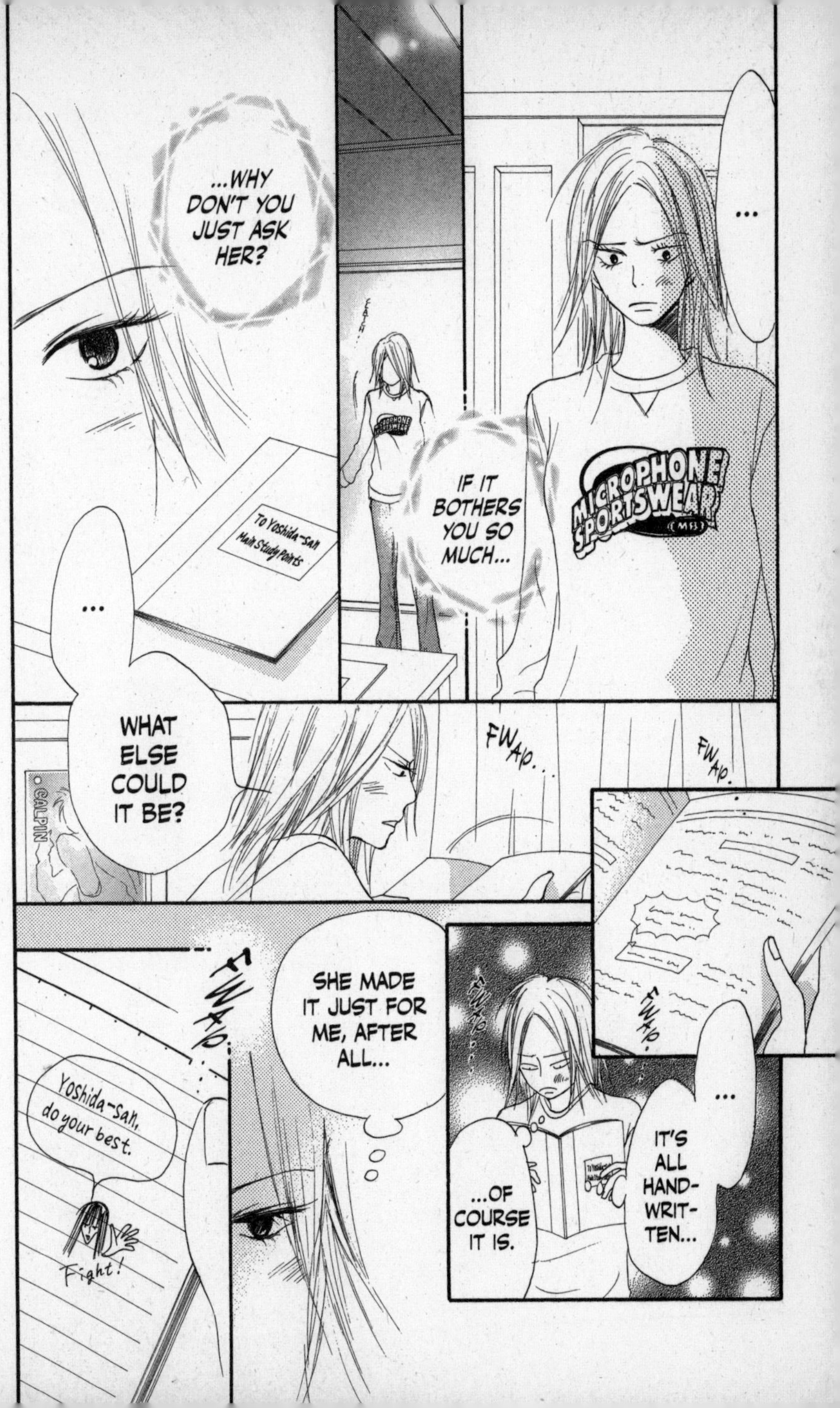
...
CATCH...
IF IT BOTHERS YOU SO MUCH...
...WHY DON'T YOU JUST ASK HER?
To Yoshida-san Main Study Points
...
WHAT ELSE COULD IT BE?
FWAP.
FWAP...
CALPIN
FWAP.
...
IT'S ALL HAND-WRIT-TEN...
...OF COURSE IT IS.
FWAP...
SHE MADE IT JUST FOR ME, AFTER ALL...
FWAP...
Yoshida-san, do your best.
Fight!

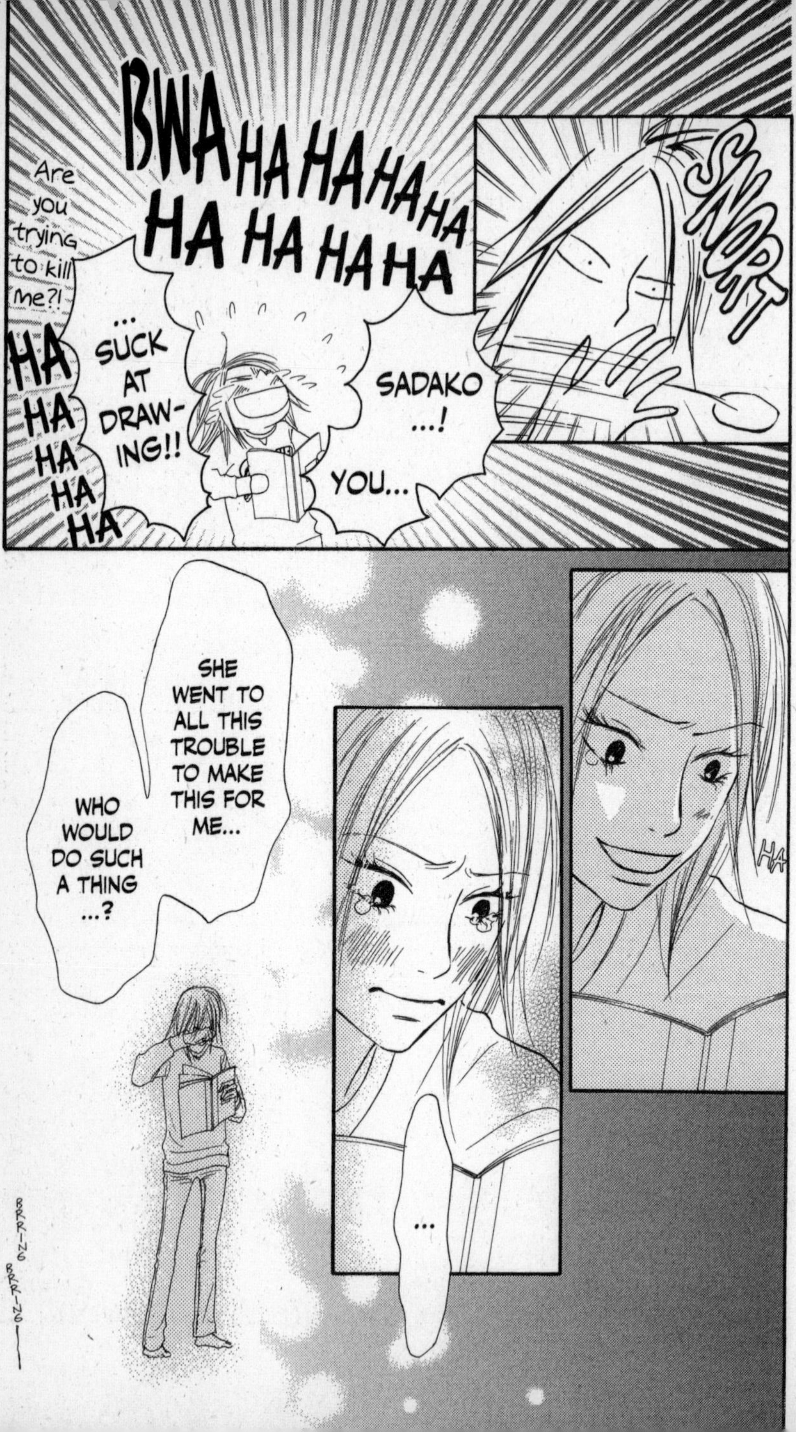
SNORT
BWAHAHAHAHAHA HA HA HA HA
SADAKO ...!
YOU...
... SUCK AT DRAWING!!
Are you trying to kill me?!
HA HA HA HA HA
HA
...
SHE WENT TO ALL THIS TROUBLE TO MAKE THIS FOR ME...
WHO WOULD DO SUCH A THING ...?
BRRRING BRRRING

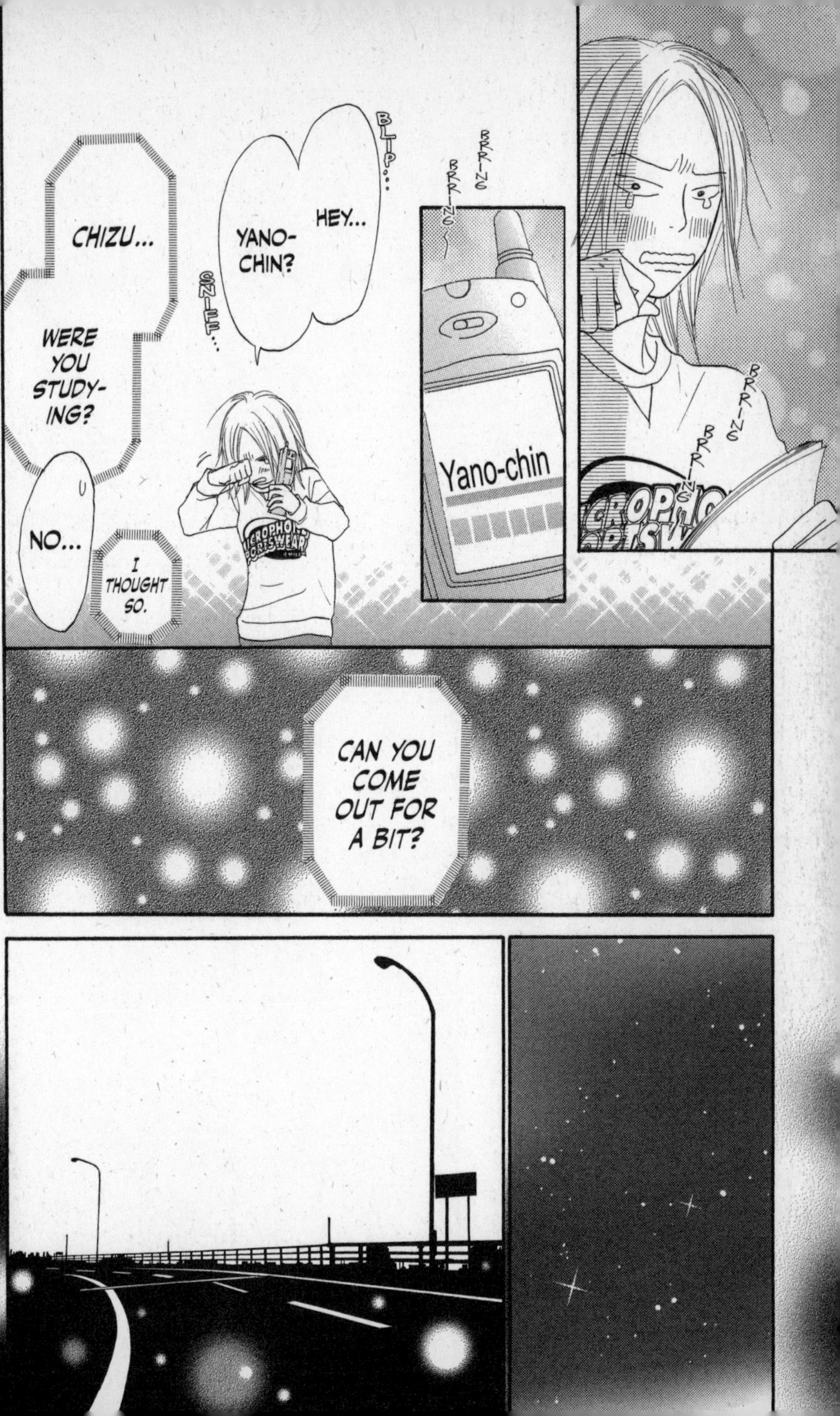
BRRING
BRRING
BRRING
BRRING
Yano-chin
BLIP...
HEY...
YANO-CHIN?
SNIFF...
CHIZU...
WERE YOU STUDYING?
NO...
I THOUGHT SO.
CAN YOU COME OUT FOR A BIT?

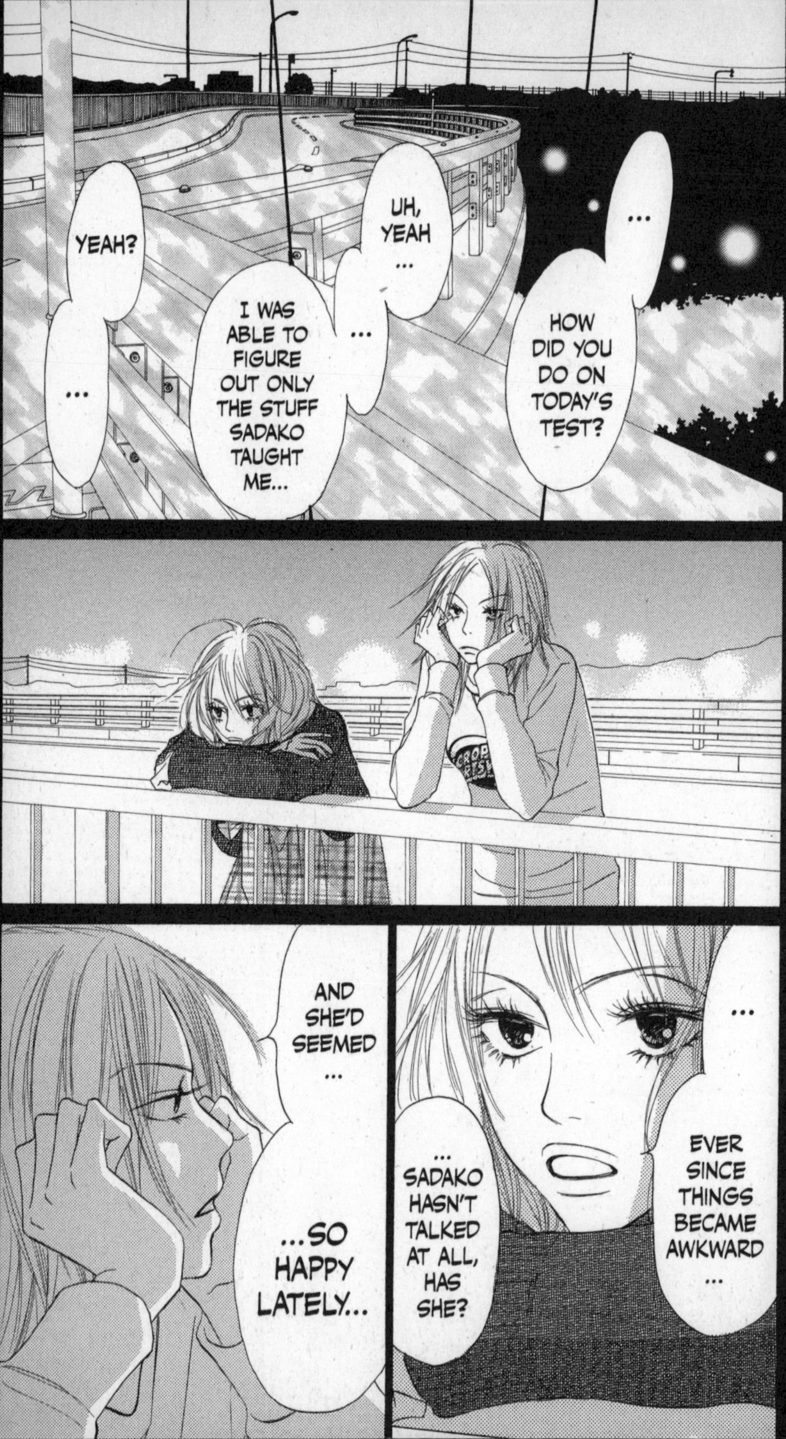
...
HOW DID YOU DO ON TODAY'S TEST?
UH, YEAH ...
...
I WAS ABLE TO FIGURE OUT ONLY THE STUFF SADAKO TAUGHT ME...
YEAH?
...
...
EVER SINCE THINGS BECAME AWKWARD ...
... SADAKO HASN'T TALKED AT ALL, HAS SHE?
AND SHE'D SEEMED ...
...SO HAPPY LATELY...

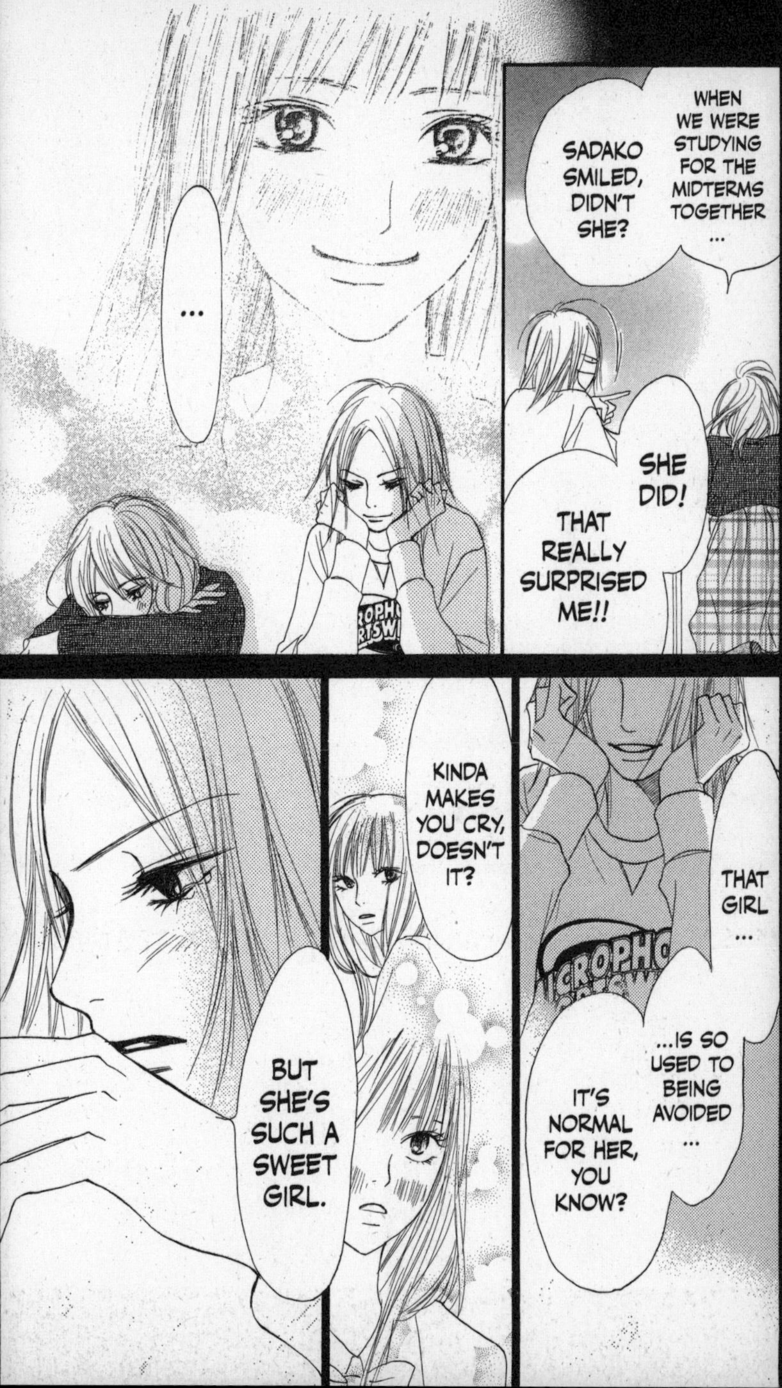
WHEN WE WERE STUDYING FOR THE MIDTERMS TOGETHER ...
SADAKO SMILED, DIDN'T SHE?
SHE DID!
THAT REALLY SURPRISED ME!!
...
THAT GIRL ...
...IS SO USED TO BEING AVOIDED ...
IT'S NORMAL FOR HER, YOU KNOW?
KINDA MAKES YOU CRY, DOESN'T IT?
BUT SHE'S SUCH A SWEET GIRL.

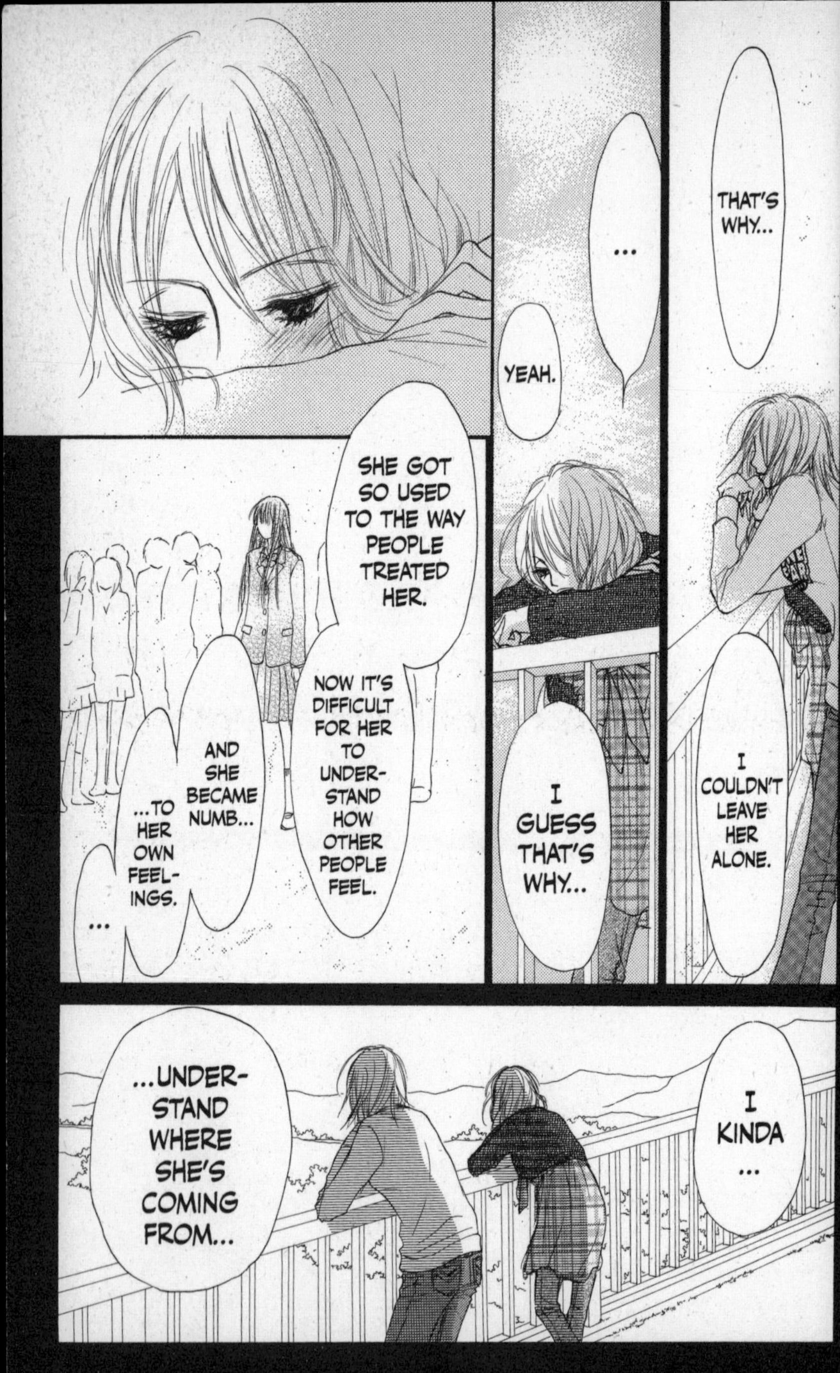
THAT'S WHY...
I COULDN'T LEAVE HER ALONE.
...
YEAH.
I GUESS THAT'S WHY...
SHE GOT SO USED TO THE WAY PEOPLE TREATED HER.
NOW IT'S DIFFICULT FOR HER TO UNDER-STAND HOW OTHER PEOPLE FEEL.
AND SHE BECAME NUMB...
...TO HER OWN FEEL-INGS.
...
I KINDA ...
...UNDER-STAND WHERE SHE'S COMING FROM...

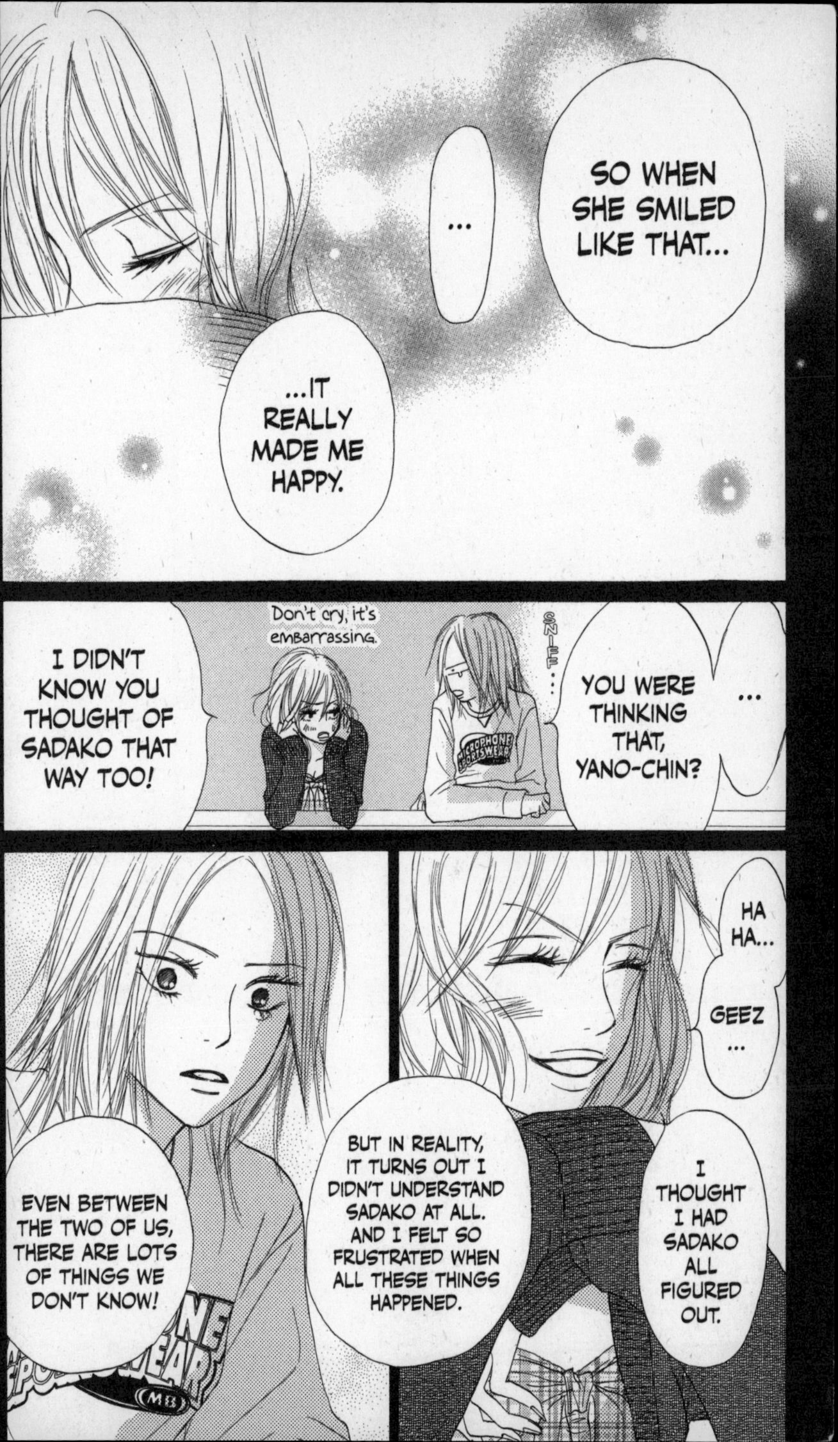
SO WHEN SHE SMILED LIKE THAT...
...
...IT REALLY MADE ME HAPPY.
...
YOU WERE THINKING THAT, YANO-CHIN?
SNIFF...
Don't cry, it's embarrassing.
I DIDN'T KNOW YOU THOUGHT OF SADAKO THAT WAY TOO!
HA HA...
GEEZ...
I THOUGHT I HAD SADAKO ALL FIGURED OUT.
BUT IN REALITY, IT TURNS OUT I DIDN'T UNDERSTAND SADAKO AT ALL. AND I FELT SO FRUSTRATED WHEN ALL THESE THINGS HAPPENED.
EVEN BETWEEN THE TWO OF US, THERE ARE LOTS OF THINGS WE DON'T KNOW!

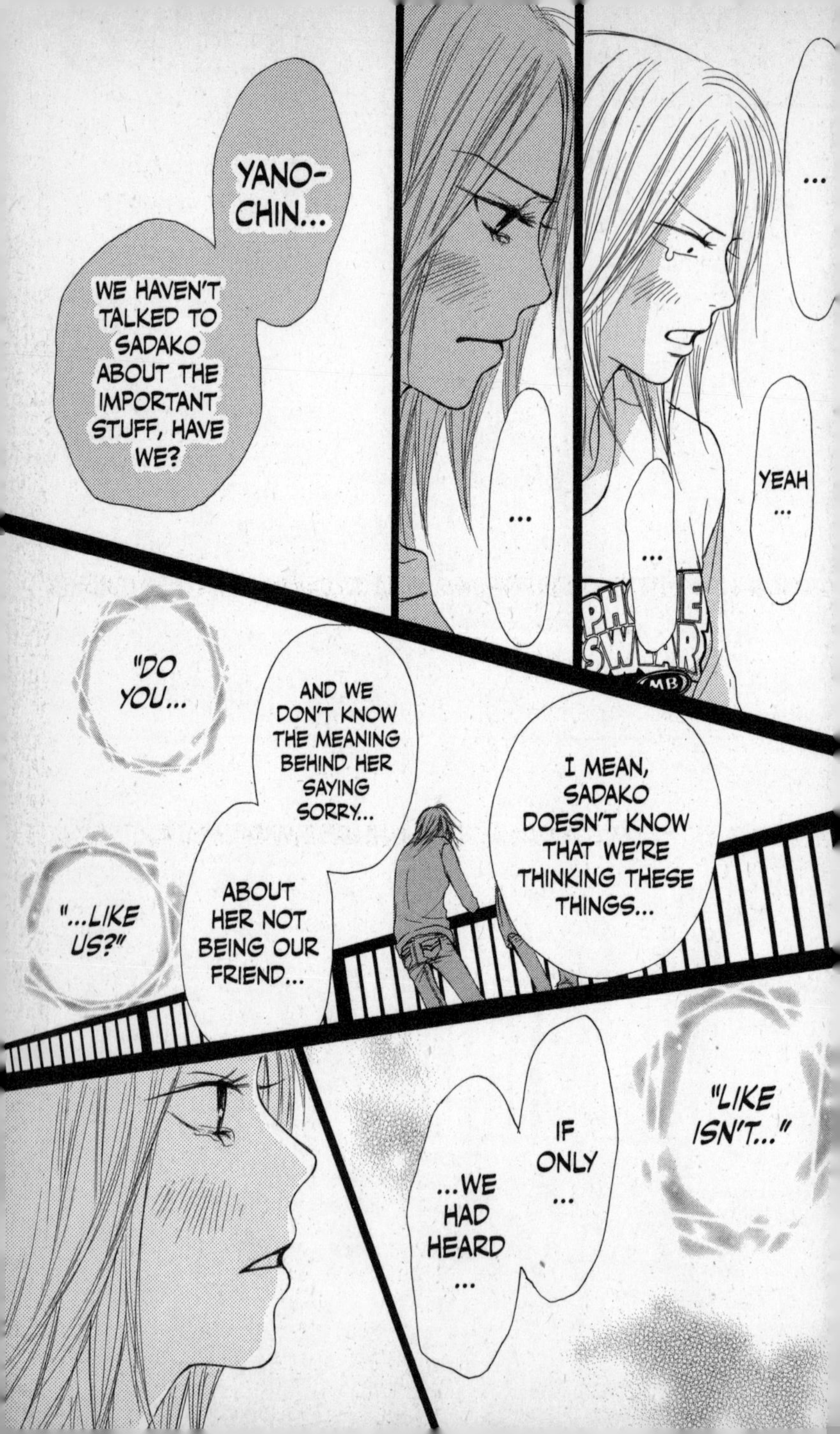
...
YEAH ...
...
...
YANO-CHIN...
WE HAVEN'T TALKED TO SADAKO ABOUT THE IMPORTANT STUFF, HAVE WE?
I MEAN, SADAKO DOESN'T KNOW THAT WE'RE THINKING THESE THINGS...
AND WE DON'T KNOW THE MEANING BEHIND HER SAYING SORRY...
ABOUT HER NOT BEING OUR FRIEND...
"DO YOU...
"...LIKE US?"
"LIKE ISN'T..."
IF ONLY ...
...WE HAD HEARD ...

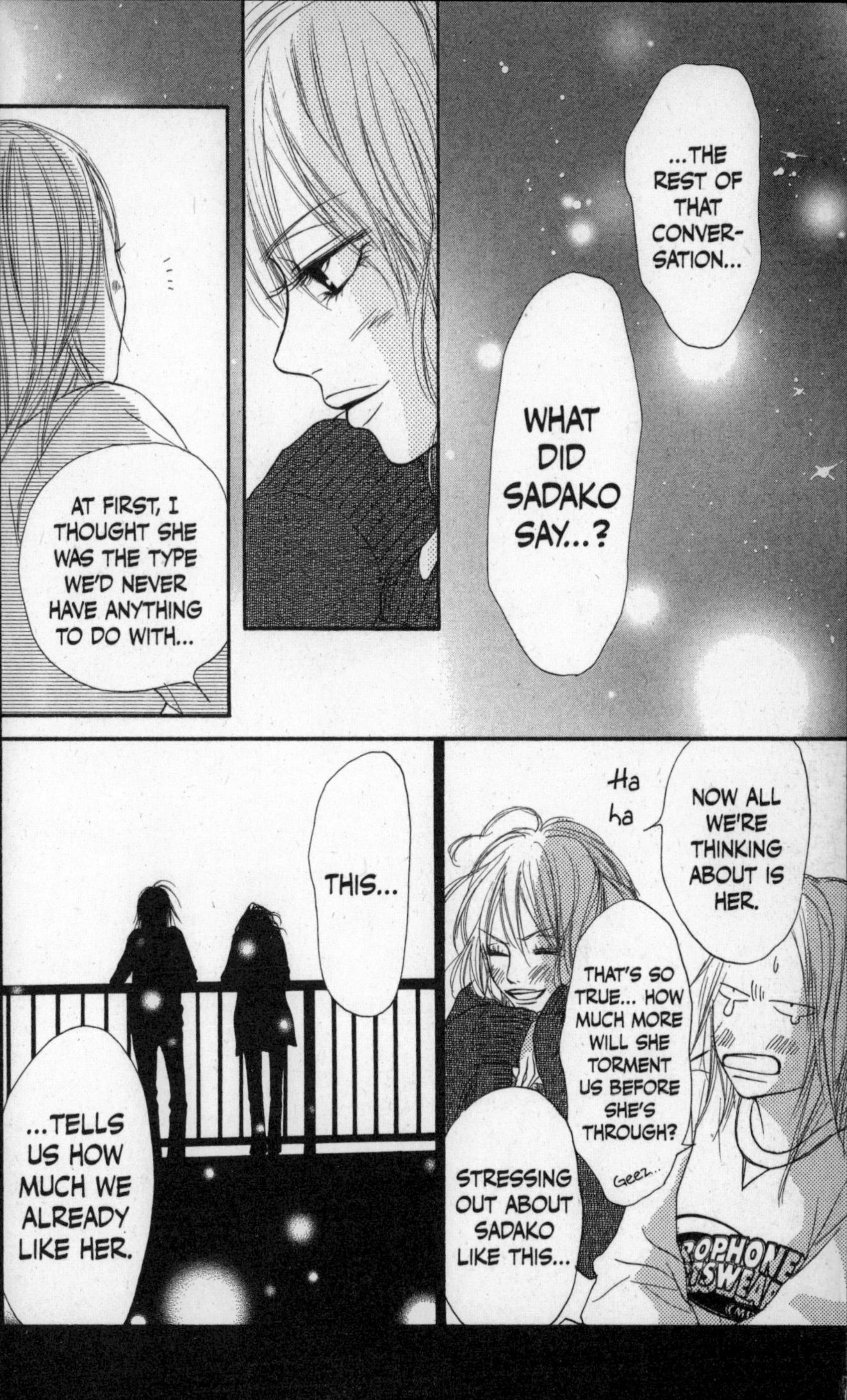
...THE REST OF THAT CONVERSATION...
WHAT DID SADAKO SAY...?
AT FIRST, I THOUGHT SHE WAS THE TYPE WE'D NEVER HAVE ANYTHING TO DO WITH...
Ha ha
NOW ALL WE'RE THINKING ABOUT IS HER.
THAT'S SO TRUE... HOW MUCH MORE WILL SHE TORMENT US BEFORE SHE'S THROUGH?
Geez...
STRESSING OUT ABOUT SADAKO LIKE THIS...
THIS...
...TELLS US HOW MUCH WE ALREADY LIKE HER.

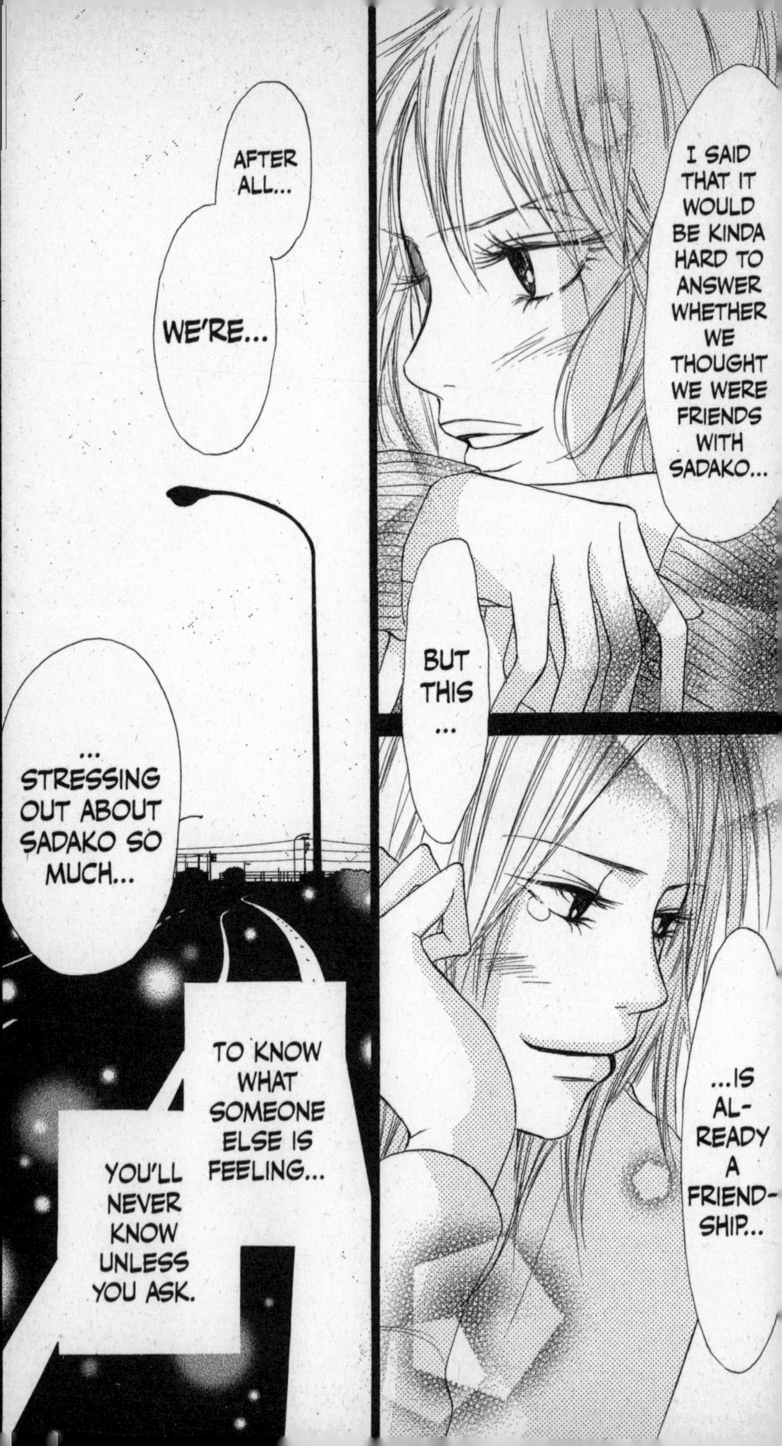
I SAID THAT IT WOULD BE KINDA HARD TO ANSWER WHETHER WE THOUGHT WE WERE FRIENDS WITH SADAKO...
BUT THIS...
...IS AL-READY A FRIEND-SHIP...
AFTER ALL...
WE'RE...
...STRESSING OUT ABOUT SADAKO SO MUCH...
TO KNOW WHAT SOMEONE ELSE IS FEELING...
YOU'LL NEVER KNOW UNLESS YOU ASK.

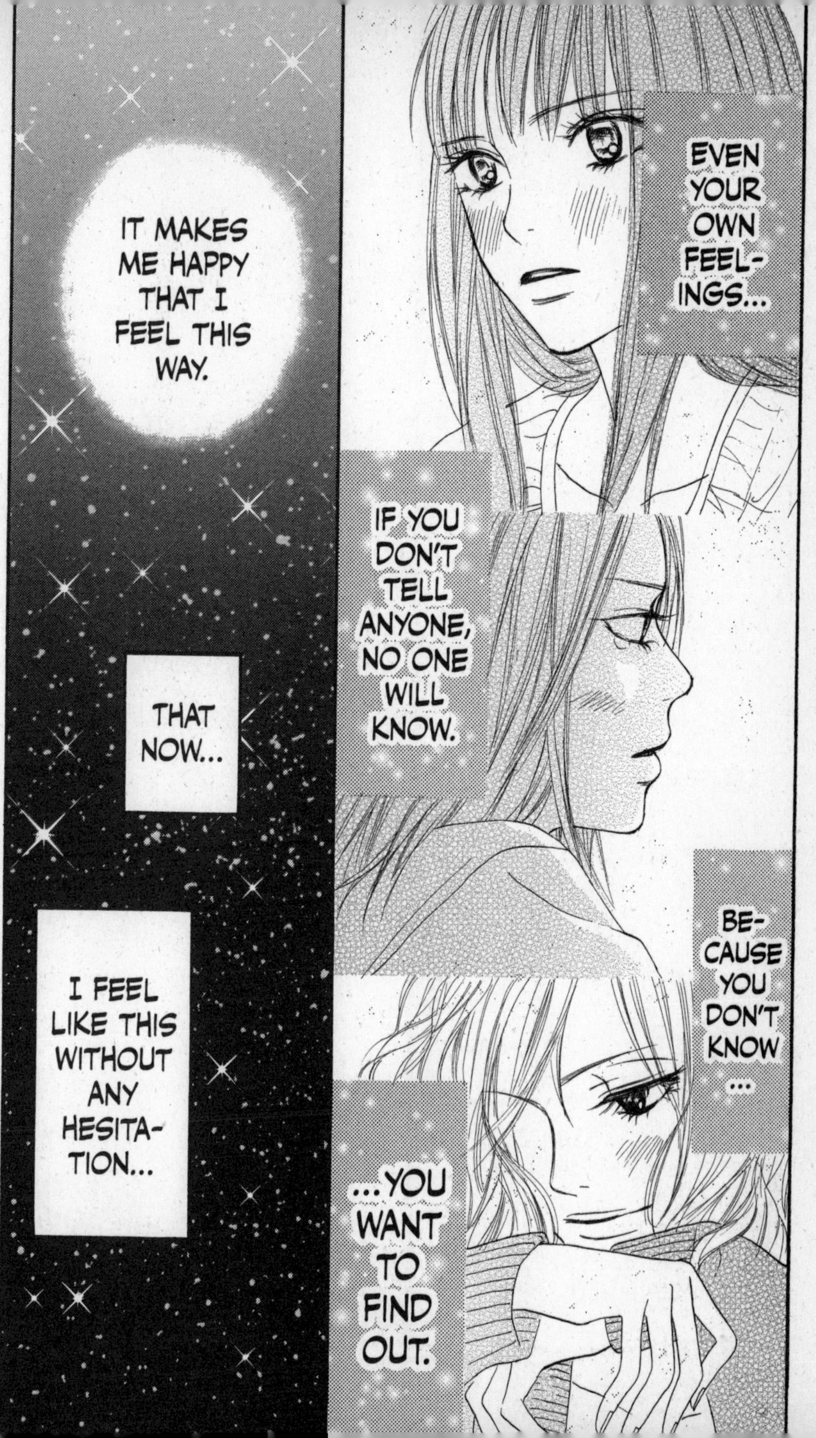
EVEN YOUR OWN FEEL-INGS...
IF YOU DON'T TELL ANYONE, NO ONE WILL KNOW.
BE-CAUSE YOU DON'T KNOW...
...YOU WANT TO FIND OUT.
IT MAKES ME HAPPY THAT I FEEL THIS WAY.
THAT NOW...
I FEEL LIKE THIS WITHOUT ANY HESITA-TION...

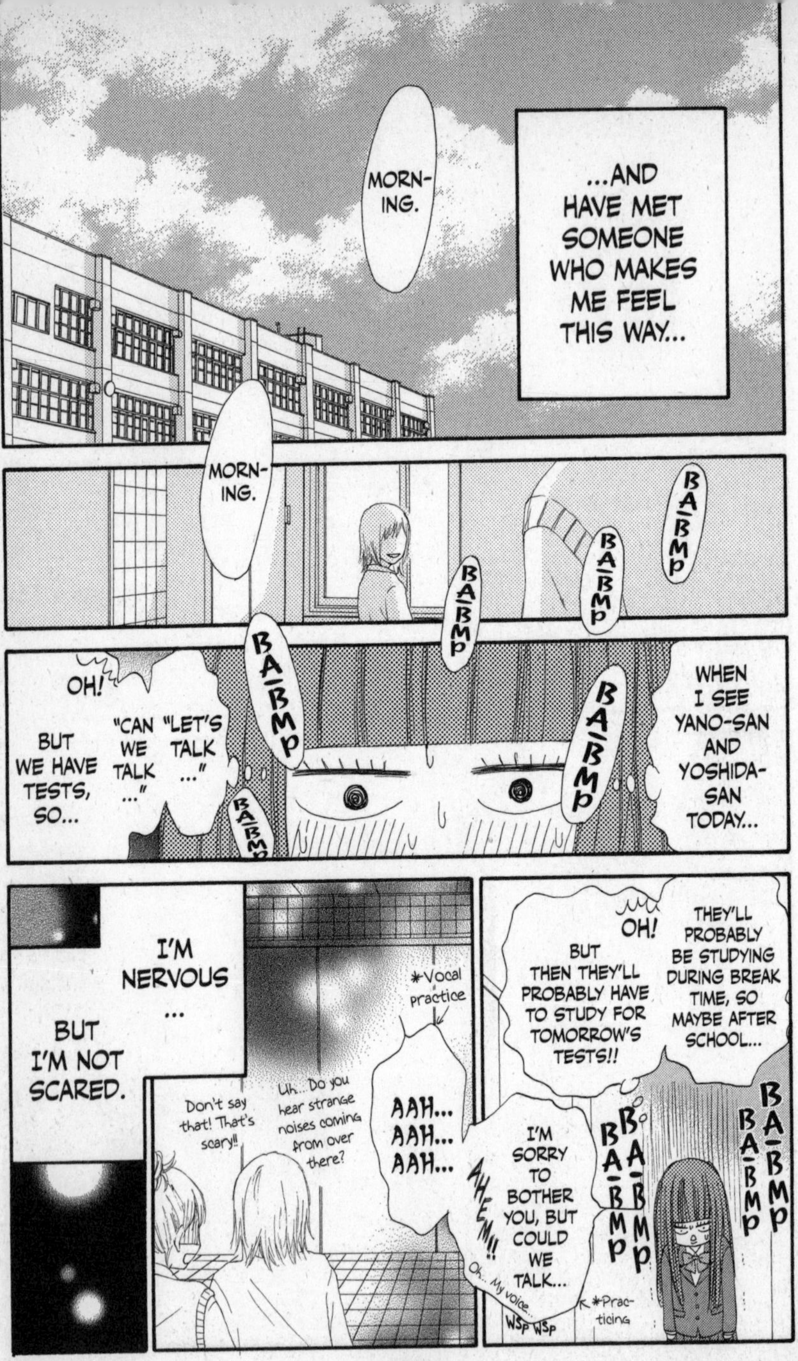
...AND HAVE MET SOMEONE WHO MAKES ME FEEL THIS WAY...
MORNING.
MORNING.
BA-BMP
BA-BMP
BA-BMP
WHEN I SEE YANO-SAN AND YOSHIDA-SAN TODAY...
BA-BMP
BA-BMP
"LET'S TALK..."
"CAN WE TALK..."
OH!
BUT WE HAVE TESTS, SO...
BA-BMP
THEY'LL PROBABLY BE STUDYING DURING BREAK TIME, SO MAYBE AFTER SCHOOL...
OH! BUT THEN THEY'LL PROBABLY HAVE TO STUDY FOR TOMORROW'S TESTS!!
BA-BMP BA-BMP
BA-BMP BA-BMP
I'M SORRY TO BOTHER YOU, BUT COULD WE TALK...
*Prac-ticing
AHEM!!
Oh... My voice...
WSP WSP
AAH... AAH... AAH...
*Vocal practice
Uh... Do you hear strange noises coming from over there?
Don't say that! That's scary!!
I'M NERVOUS...
BUT I'M NOT SCARED.

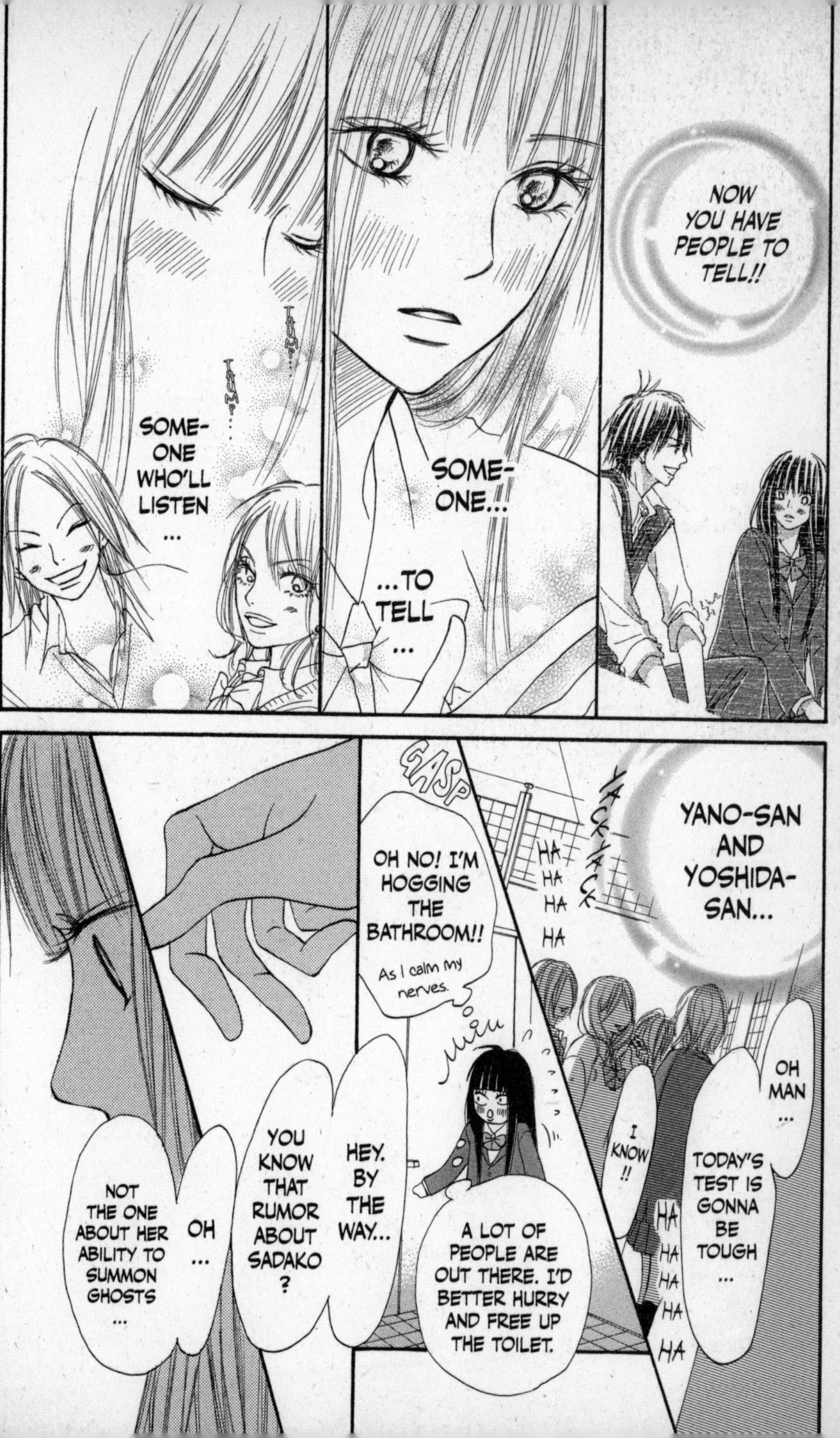
NOW YOU HAVE PEOPLE TO TELL!!
SOME-ONE...
...TO TELL ...
THUMP...
THUMP...
SOME-ONE WHO'LL LISTEN ...
YANO-SAN AND YOSHIDA-SAN...
YACK YACK
HA HA HA HA
OH MAN ...
TODAY'S TEST IS GONNA BE TOUGH ...
I KNOW !!
HA HA HA HA HA
GASP
OH NO! I'M HOGGING THE BATHROOM!!
As I calm my nerves.
A LOT OF PEOPLE ARE OUT THERE. I'D BETTER HURRY AND FREE UP THE TOILET.
HEY. BY THE WAY...
YOU KNOW THAT RUMOR ABOUT SADAKO ?
OH ...
NOT THE ONE ABOUT HER ABILITY TO SUMMON GHOSTS ...

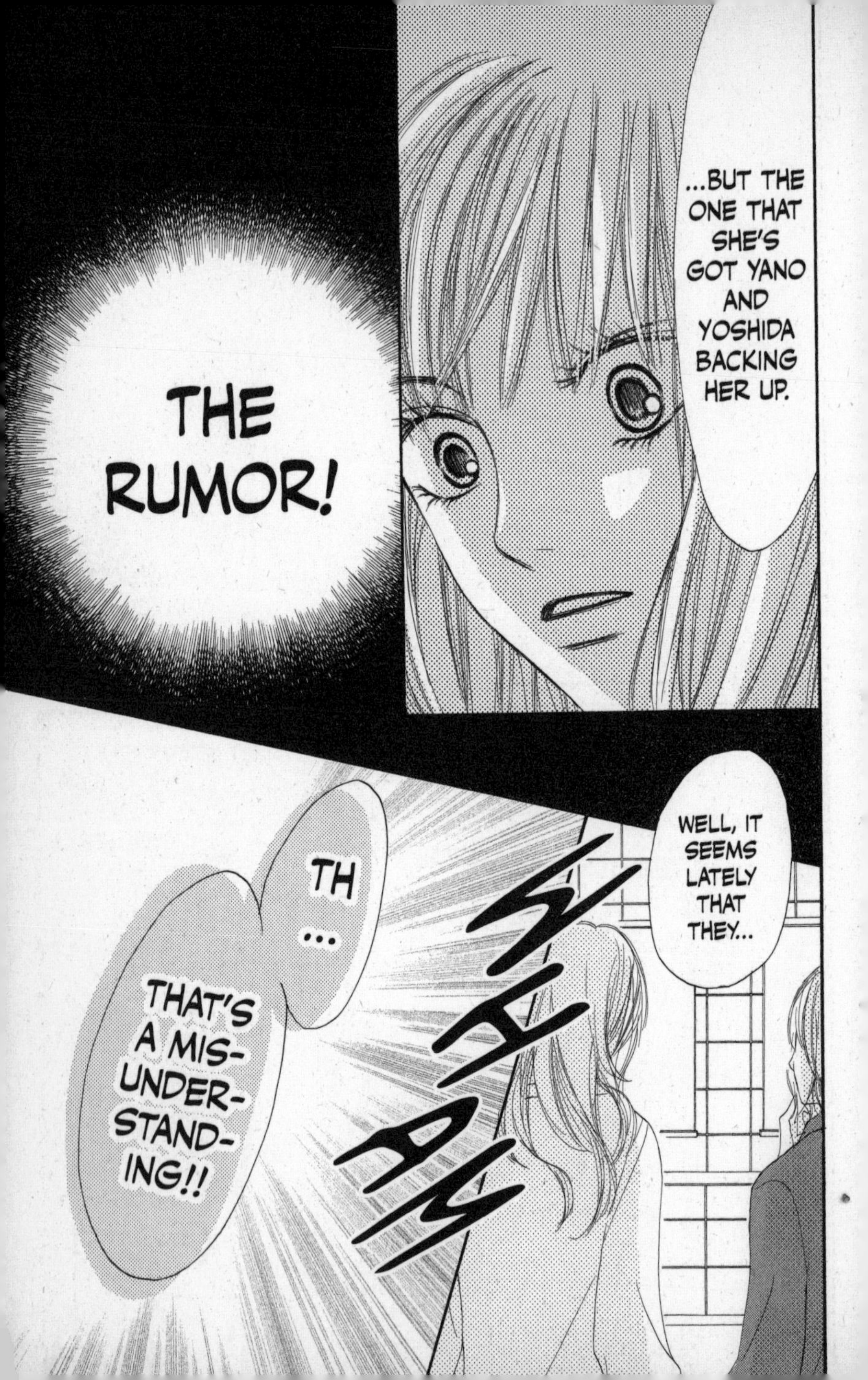
...BUT THE ONE THAT SHE'S GOT YANO AND YOSHIDA BACKING HER UP.
THE RUMOR!
WELL, IT SEEMS LATELY THAT THEY...
WHAM
TH...
THAT'S A MIS-UNDER-STAND-ING!!

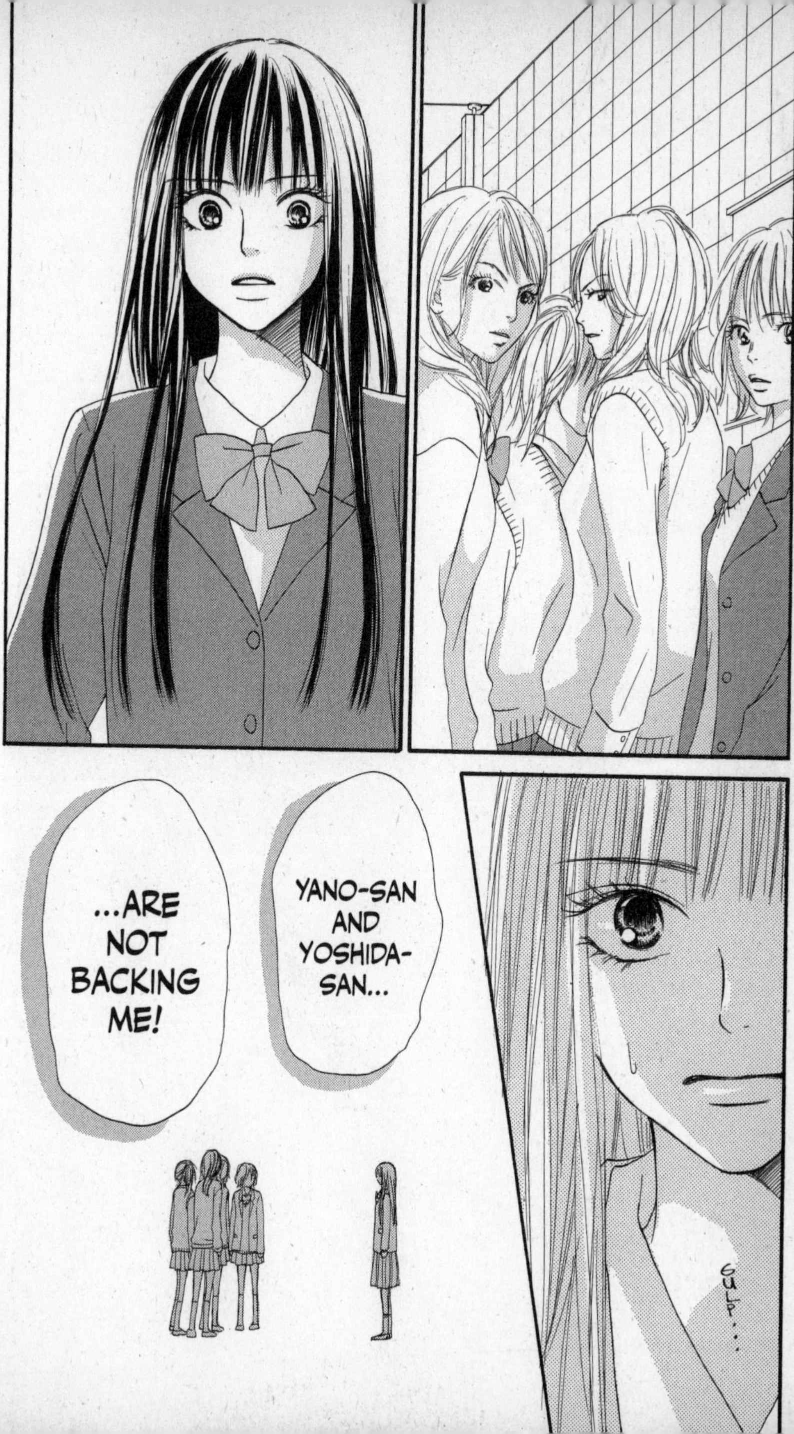
GULP...
YANO-SAN AND YOSHIDA-SAN...
...ARE NOT BACKING ME!

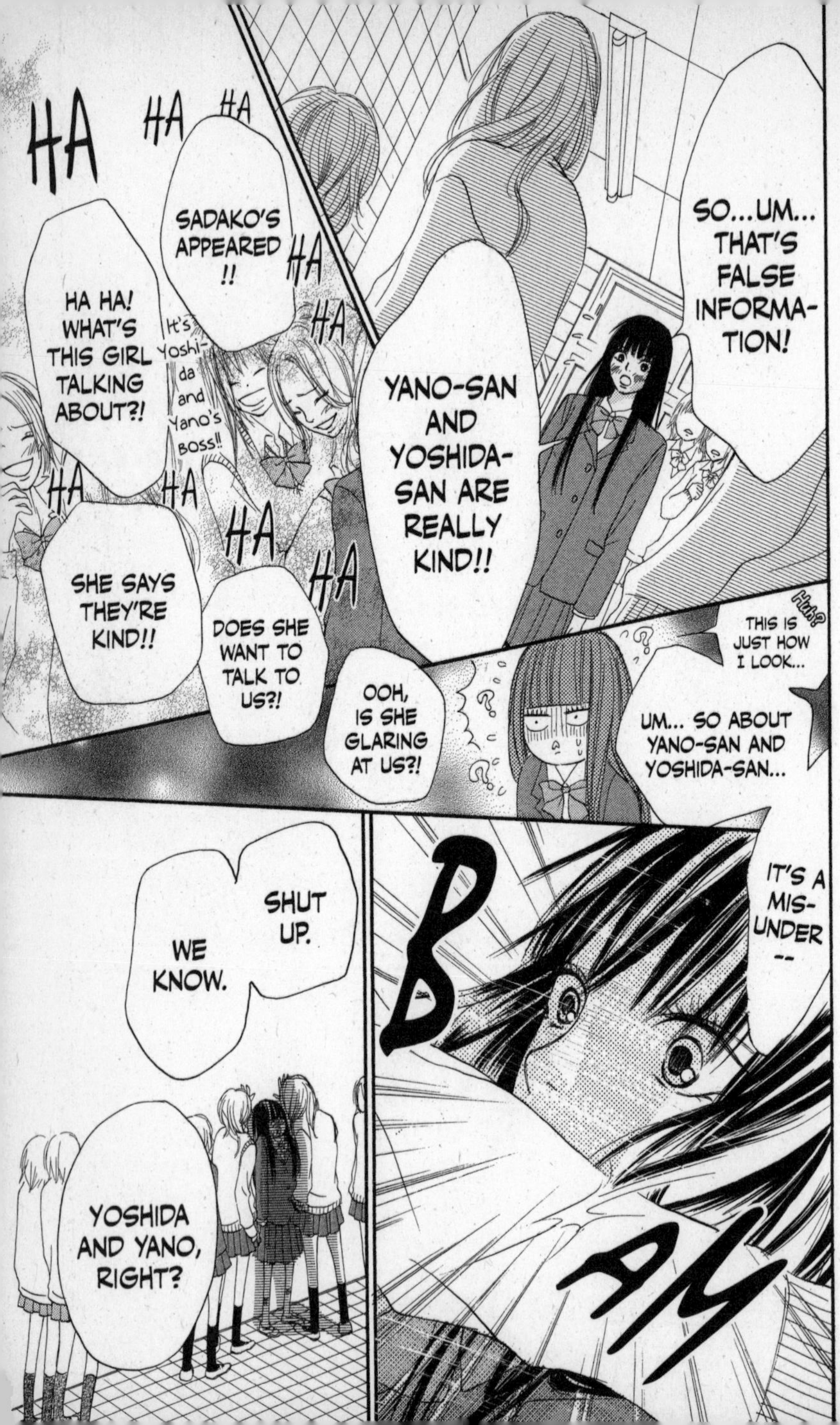
SO...UM... THAT'S FALSE INFORMATION!
YANO-SAN AND YOSHIDA-SAN ARE REALLY KIND!!
HA HA HA
SADAKO'S APPEARED!!
HA HA HA
HA HA! WHAT'S THIS GIRL TALKING ABOUT?!
It's Yoshida and Yano's boss!!
HA HA HA HA
SHE SAYS THEY'RE KIND!!
DOES SHE WANT TO TALK TO US?!
OOH, IS SHE GLARING AT US?!
Huh?
THIS IS JUST HOW I LOOK...
UM... SO ABOUT YANO-SAN AND YOSHIDA-SAN...
IT'S A MIS-UNDER --
BAM
SHUT UP.
WE KNOW.
YOSHIDA AND YANO, RIGHT?

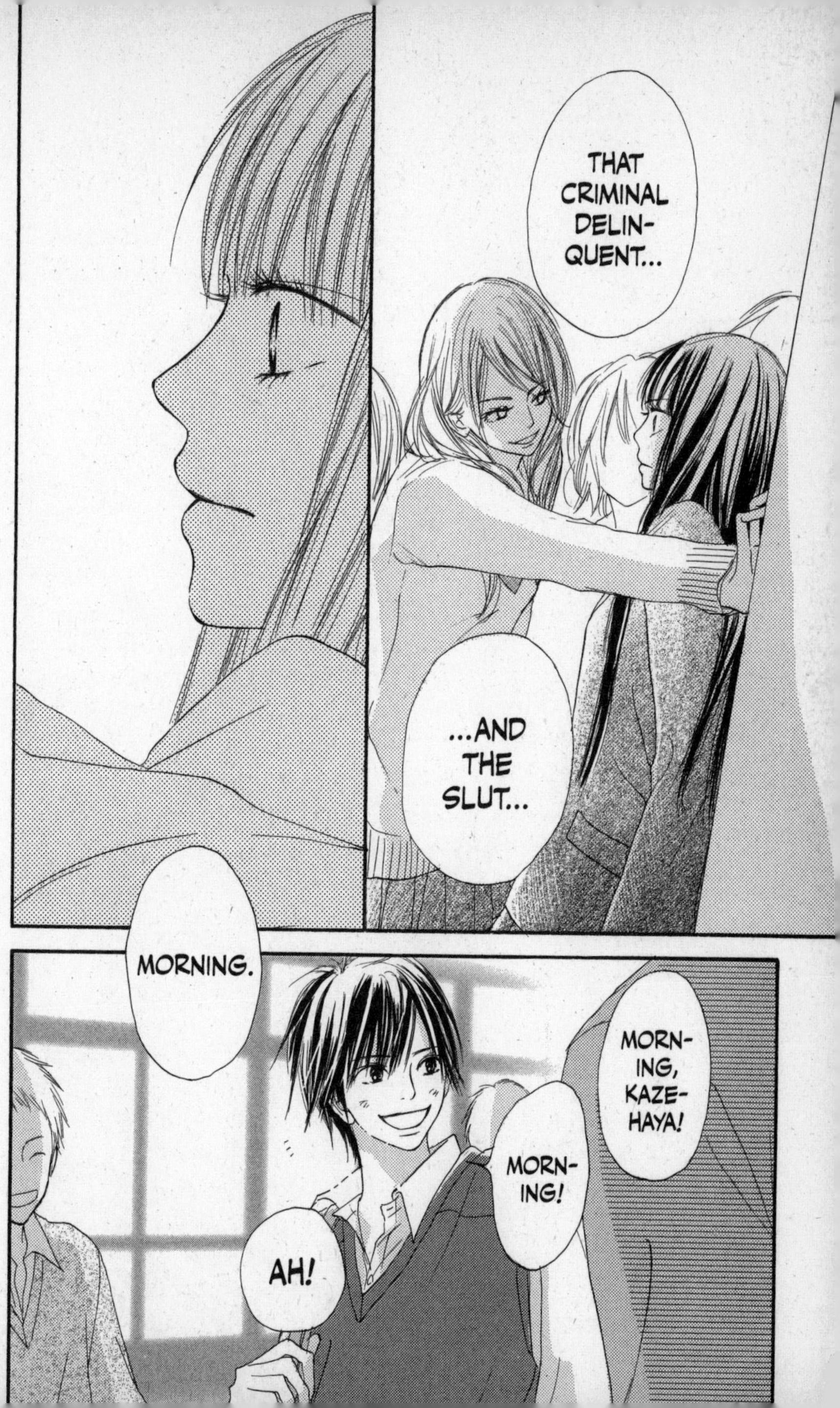
THAT CRIMINAL DELIN-QUENT...
...AND THE SLUT...
MORN-ING, KAZE-HAYA!
MORN-ING!
MORNING.
AH!

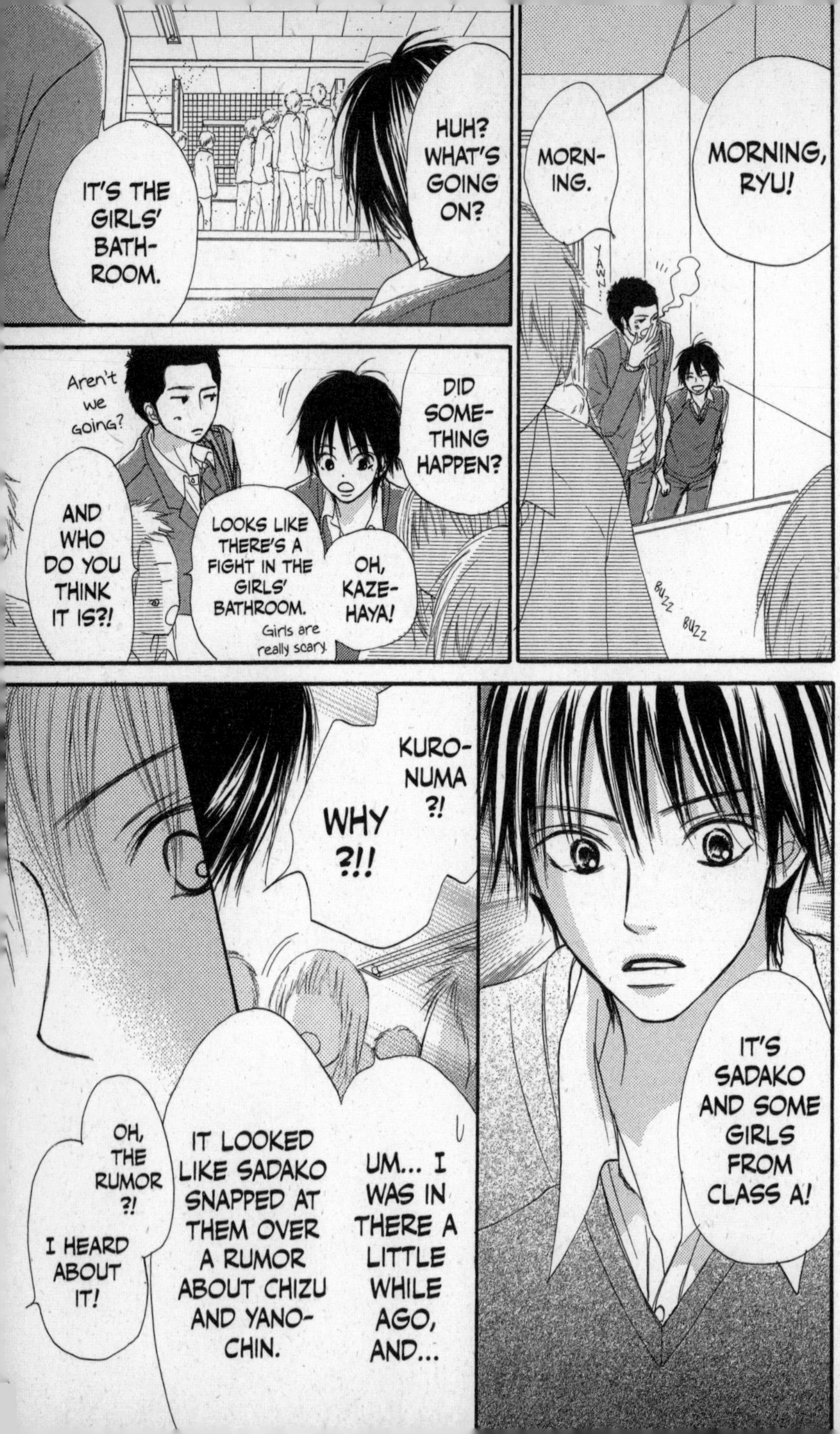
MORNING, RYU!
MORN-ING.
YAWN...
BUZZ
BUZZ
HUH? WHAT'S GOING ON?
IT'S THE GIRLS' BATH-ROOM.
DID SOME-THING HAPPEN?
OH, KAZE-HAYA!
LOOKS LIKE THERE'S A FIGHT IN THE GIRLS' BATHROOM.
Girls are really scary.
Aren't we going?
AND WHO DO YOU THINK IT IS?!
IT'S SADAKO AND SOME GIRLS FROM CLASS A!
KURO-NUMA?!
WHY?!!
UM... I WAS IN THERE A LITTLE WHILE AGO, AND...
IT LOOKED LIKE SADAKO SNAPPED AT THEM OVER A RUMOR ABOUT CHIZU AND YANO-CHIN.
OH, THE RUMOR?!
I HEARD ABOUT IT!

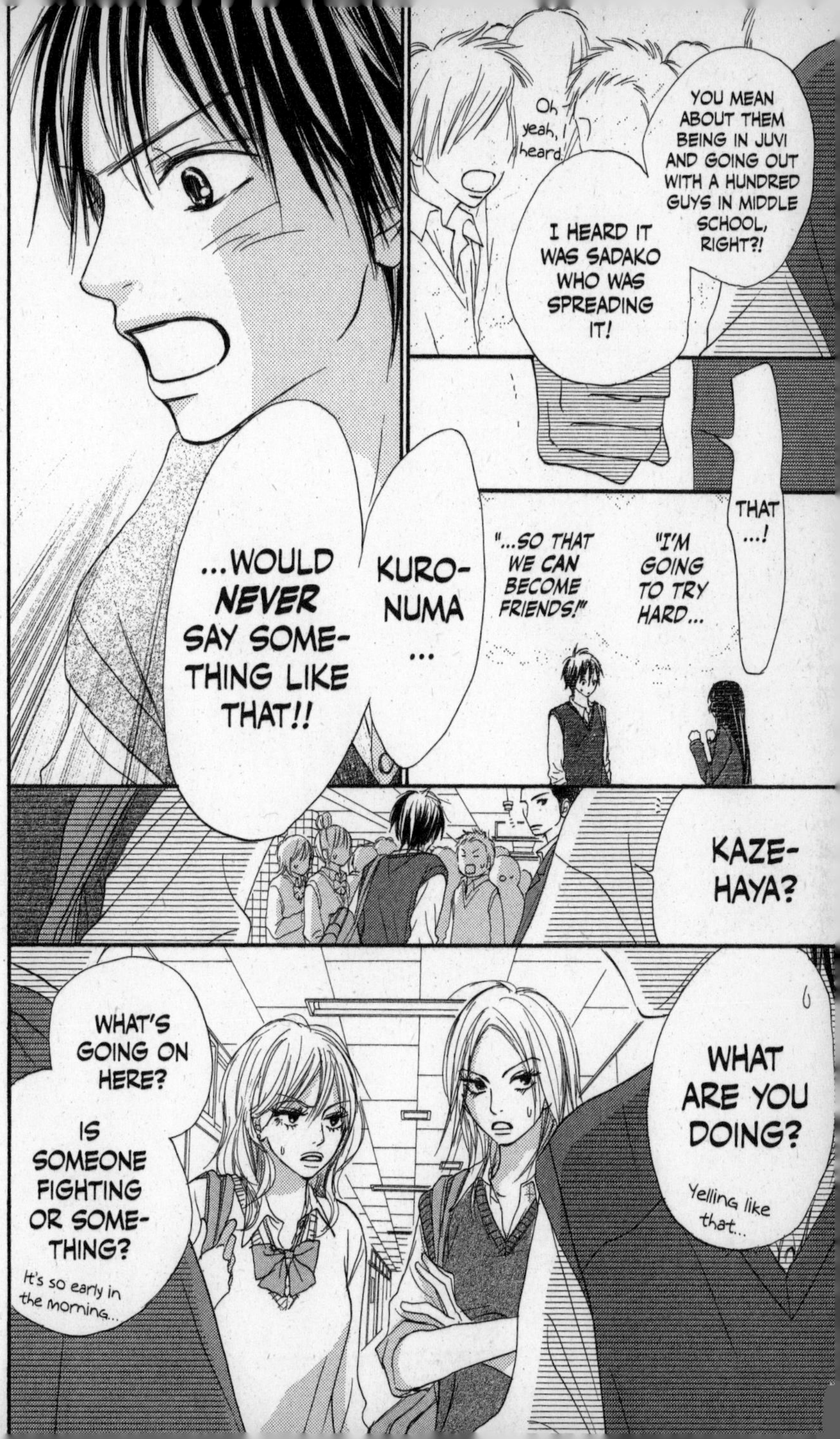
YOU MEAN ABOUT THEM BEING IN JUVI AND GOING OUT WITH A HUNDRED GUYS IN MIDDLE SCHOOL, RIGHT?!
Oh yeah, I heard.
I HEARD IT WAS SADAKO WHO WAS SPREADING IT!
THAT ...!
"I'M GOING TO TRY HARD...
"...SO THAT WE CAN BECOME FRIENDS!"
KURO-NUMA ...
...WOULD NEVER SAY SOME-THING LIKE THAT!!
KAZE-HAYA?
WHAT ARE YOU DOING?
Yelling like that...
WHAT'S GOING ON HERE?
IS SOMEONE FIGHTING OR SOME-THING?
It's so early in the morning...

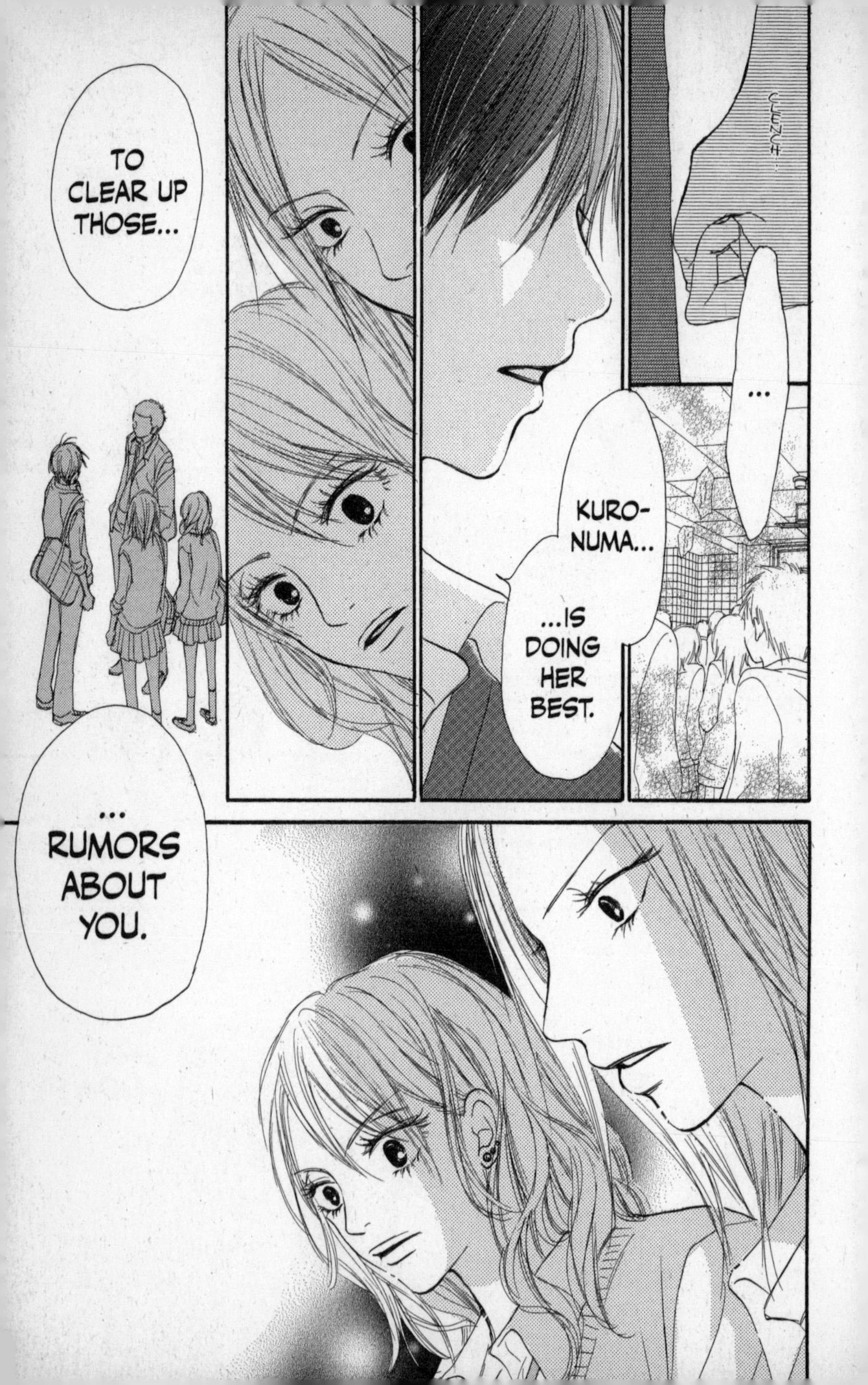
CLENCH...
...
KURO-NUMA...
...IS DOING HER BEST.
TO CLEAR UP THOSE...
...RUMORS ABOUT YOU.

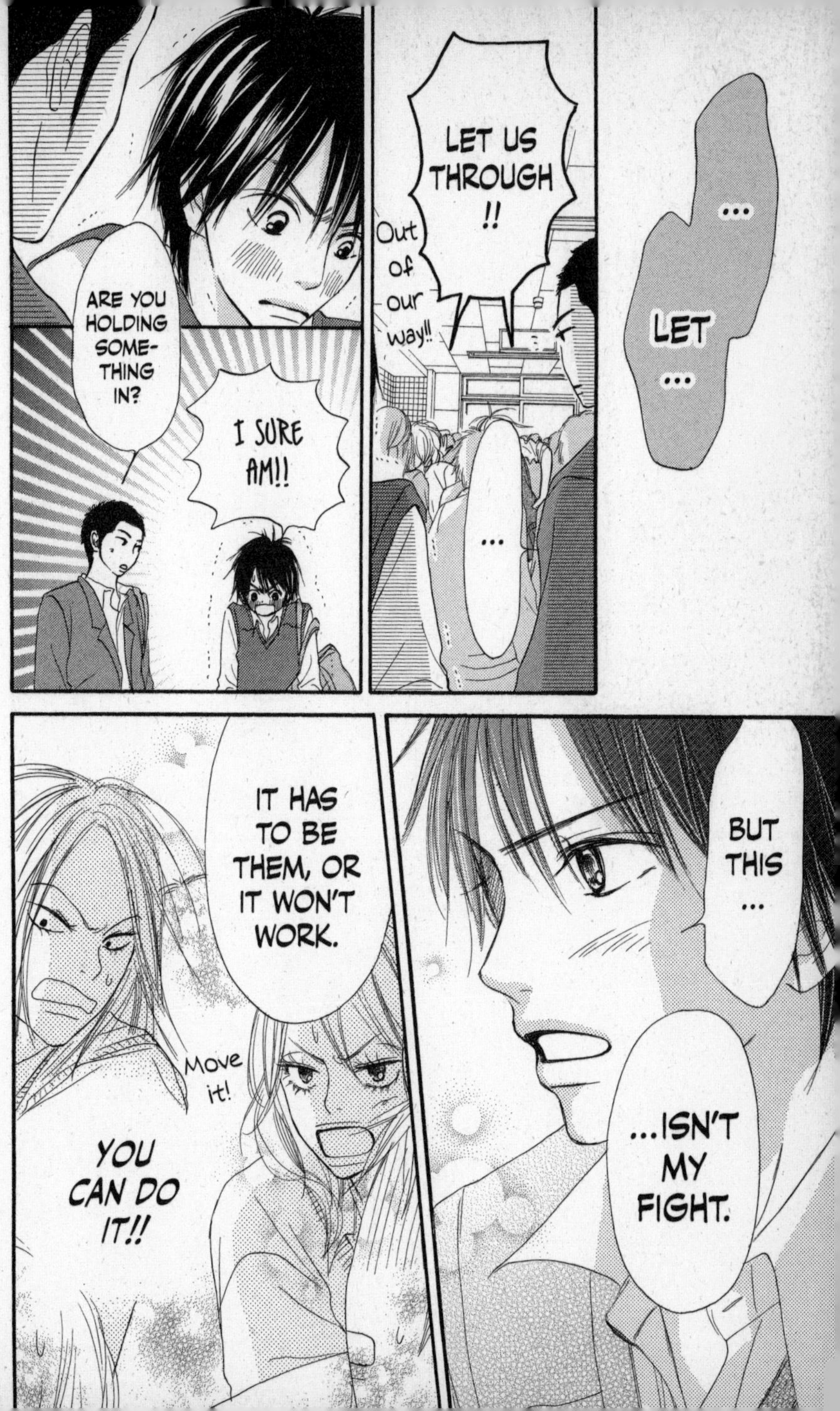
... LET ...
LET US THROUGH!!
Out of our way!!
...
ARE YOU HOLDING SOME-THING IN?
I SURE AM!!
BUT THIS ...
...ISN'T MY FIGHT.
IT HAS TO BE THEM, OR IT WON'T WORK.
Move it!
YOU CAN DO IT!!

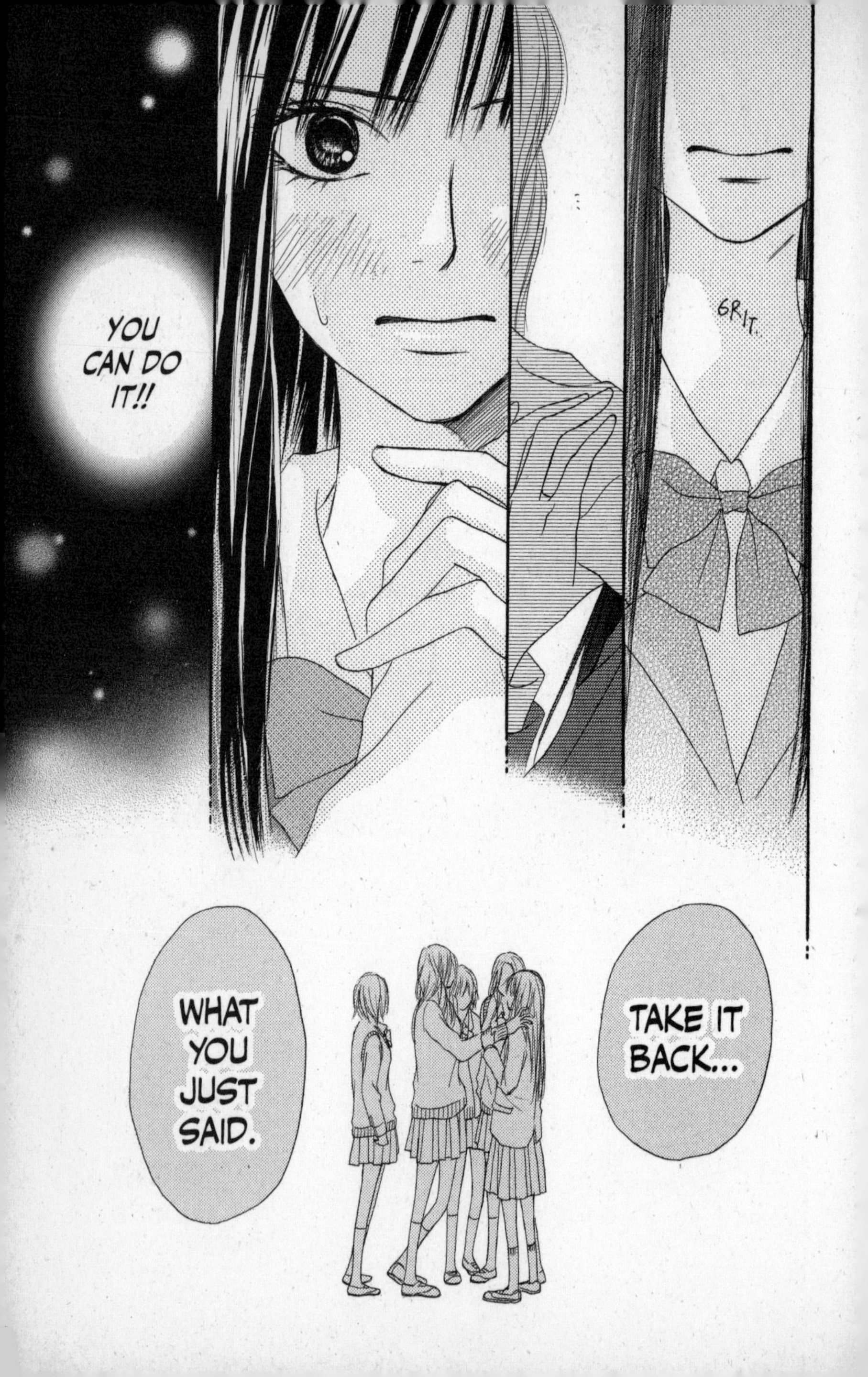
GRIT.
YOU CAN DO IT!!
TAKE IT BACK...
WHAT YOU JUST SAID.

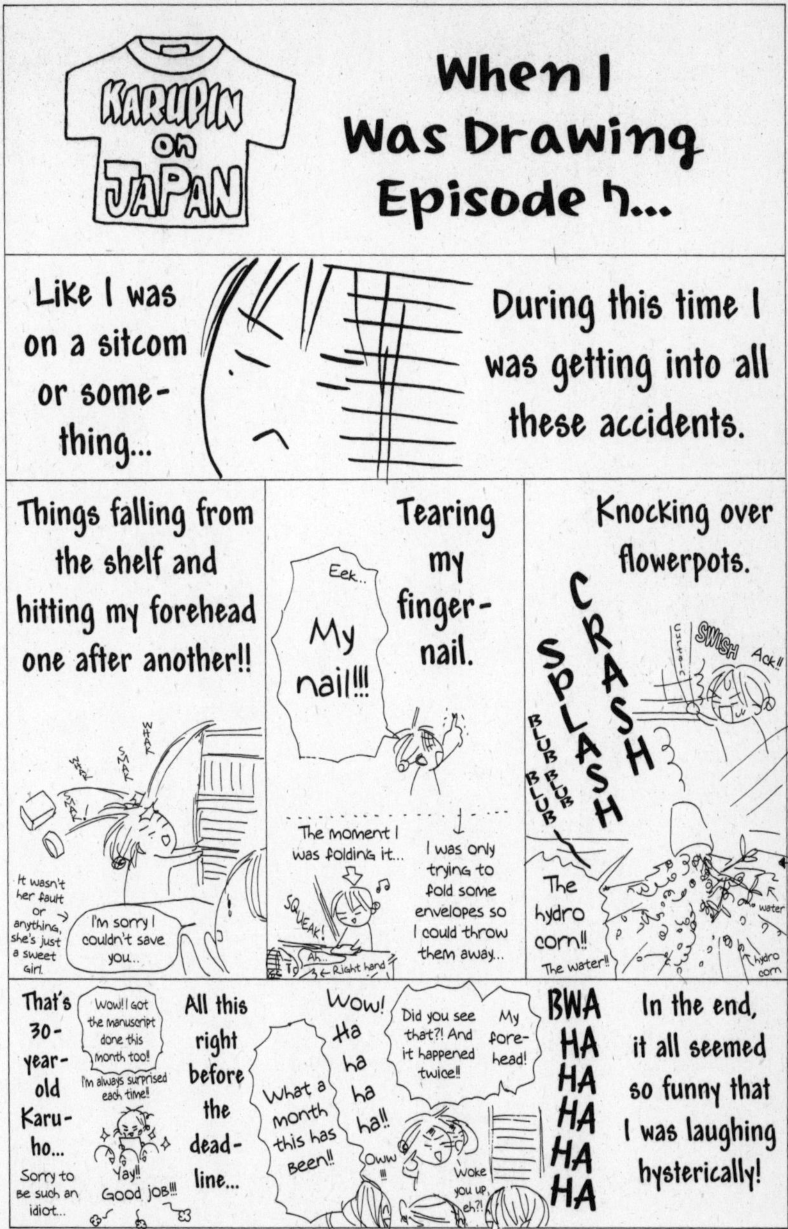
When I Was Drawing Episode 7...
KARUPIN on JAPAN
During this time I was getting into all these accidents.
Like I was on a sitcom or something...
Knocking over flowerpots.
CRASH
SPLASH
BLUB BLUB BLUB
SWISH
Curtain
Ack!!
The hydro corn!!
The water!!
water
hydro corn
Tearing my finger-nail.
Eek...
My nail!!!
I was only trying to fold some envelopes so I could throw them away...
The moment I was folding it...
SQUEAK!
Ah...
Right hand
Things falling from the shelf and hitting my forehead one after another!!
WHAK
SMAK
WHAK
SMAK!
It wasn't her fault or anything, she's just a sweet girl.
I'm sorry I couldn't save you...
In the end, it all seemed so funny that I was laughing hysterically!
BWA HA HA HA HA HA
My fore-head!
Did you see that?! And it happened twice!!
Wow! Ha ha ha ha!!
What a month this has been!!
Oww!!!
Woke you up, eh?!
All this right before the dead-line...
That's 30-year-old Karu-ho...
Wow!! Got the manuscript done this month too!!
I'm always surprised each time!!
Yay!! Good job!!!
Sorry to be such an idiot...

I had to pick up each kernel piece by piece and then wipe the floor.

There's no punch line, but the situation was a bit funny...

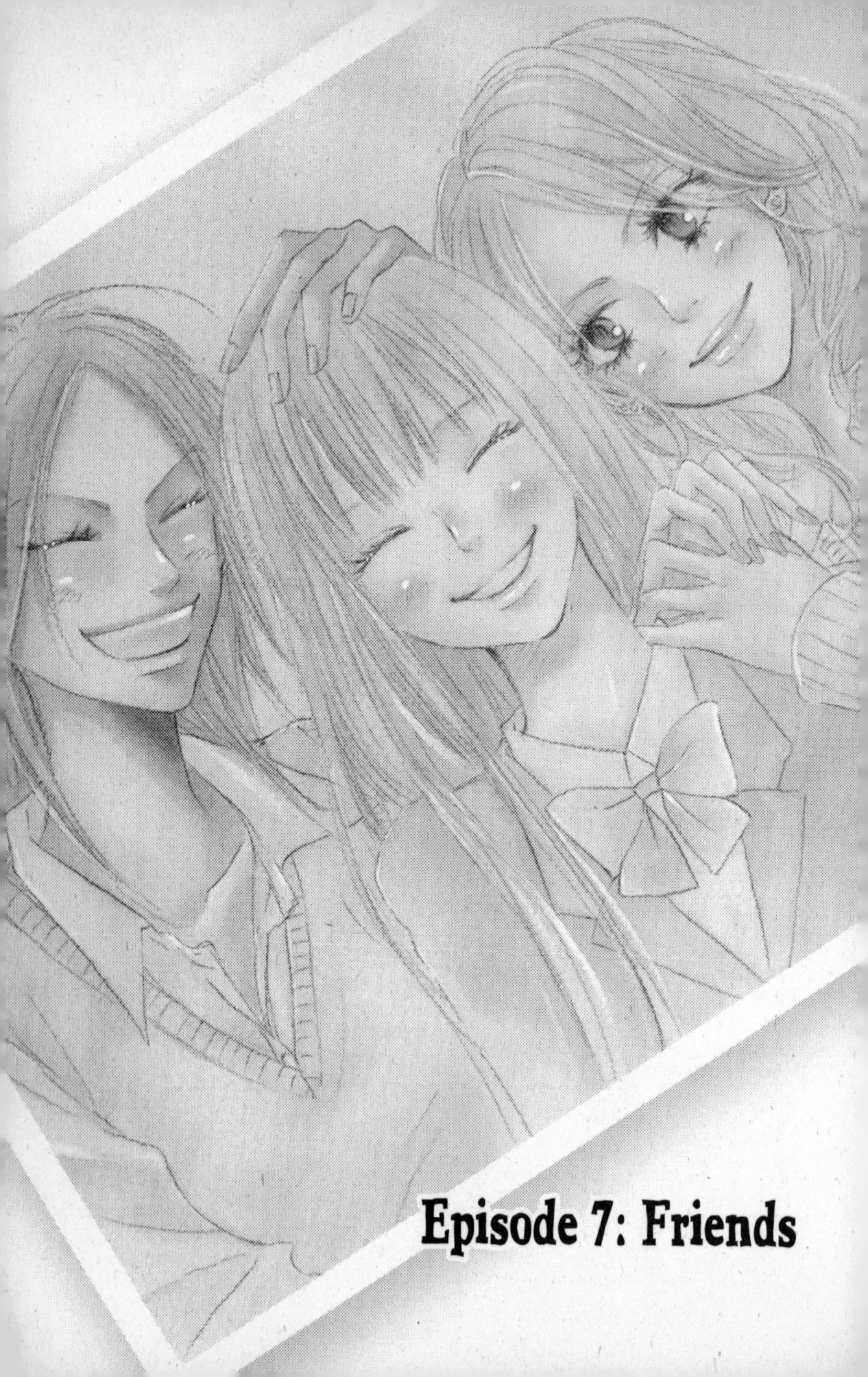

Episode 7: Friends

character

#5

Ryu Sanada

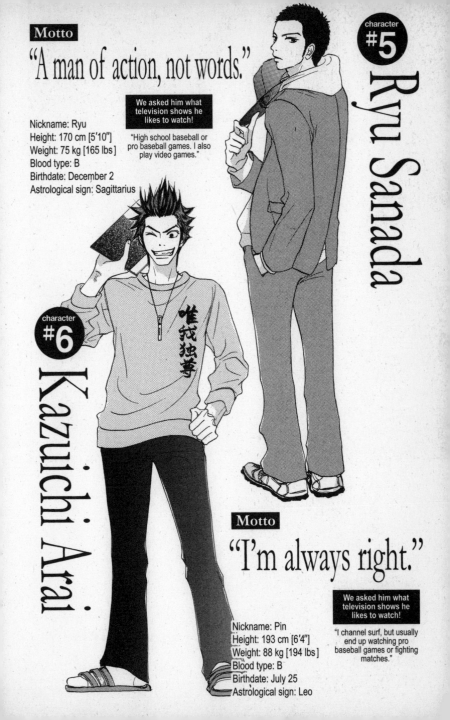

Motto

"A man of action, not words."

Nickname: Ryu
Height: 170 cm [5′10″]
Weight: 75 kg [165 lbs]
Blood type: B
Birthdate: December 2
Astrological sign: Sagittarius

We asked him what television shows he likes to watch!

"High school baseball or pro baseball games. I also play video games."

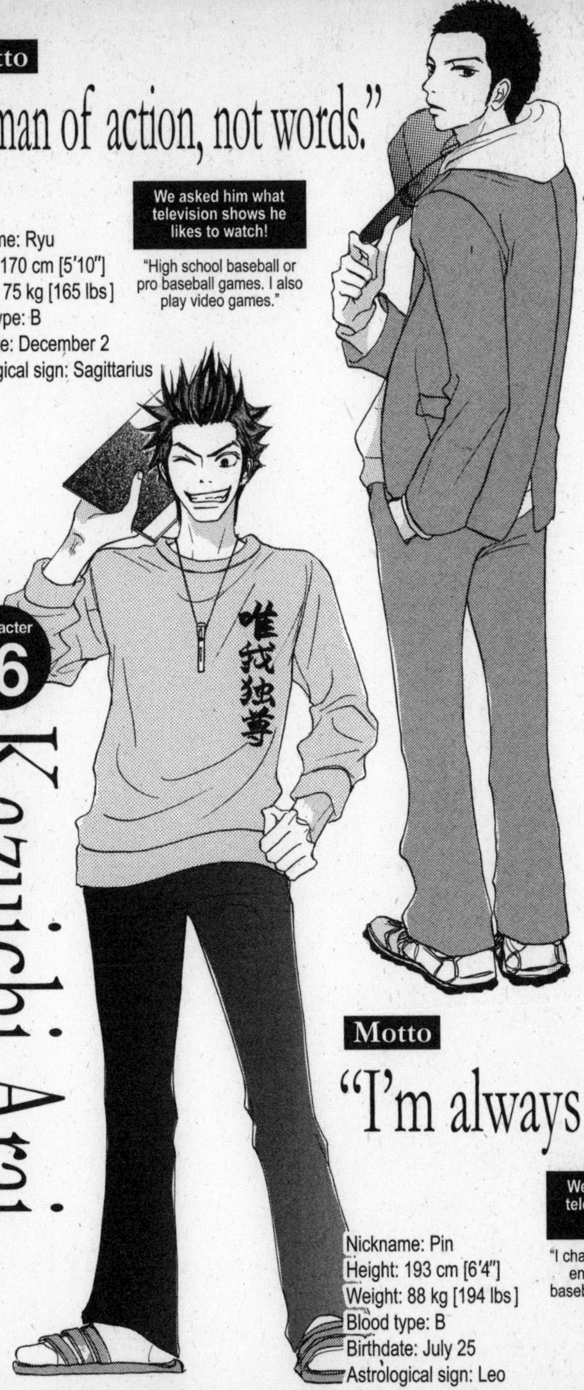
唯我独尊

character

#6

Kazuichi Arai

Motto

"I'm always right."

Nickname: Pin
Height: 193 cm [6′4″]
Weight: 88 kg [194 lbs]
Blood type: B
Birthdate: July 25
Astrological sign: Leo

We asked him what television shows he likes to watch!

"I channel surf, but usually end up watching pro baseball games or fighting matches."

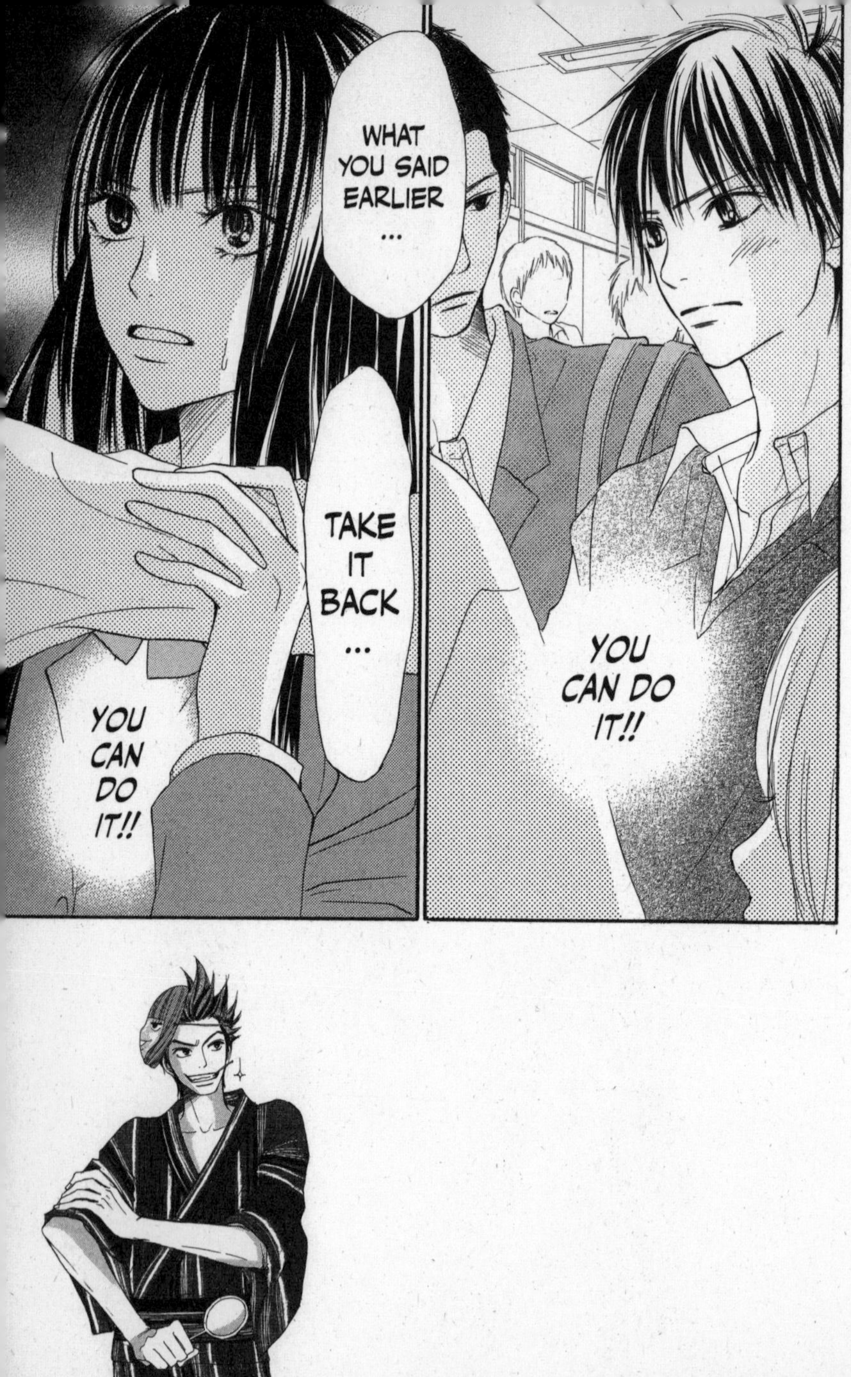
WHAT YOU SAID EARLIER ...
TAKE IT BACK ...
YOU CAN DO IT!!
YOU CAN DO IT!!

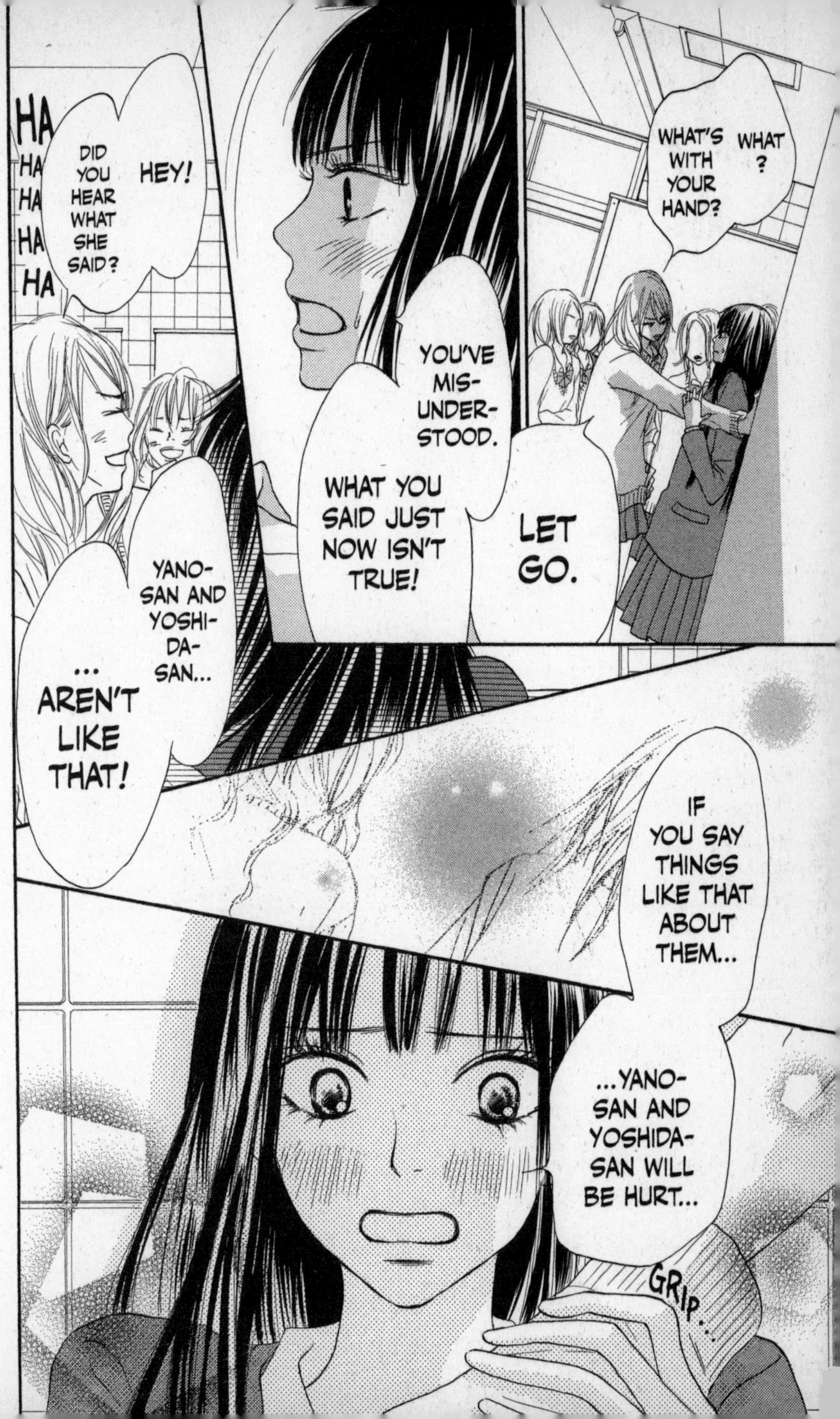
WHAT ?
WHAT'S WITH YOUR HAND?
LET GO.
YOU'VE MISUNDERSTOOD.
WHAT YOU SAID JUST NOW ISN'T TRUE!
HEY!
DID YOU HEAR WHAT SHE SAID?
HA HA HA HA HA
YANO-SAN AND YOSHIDA-SAN...
...AREN'T LIKE THAT!
IF YOU SAY THINGS LIKE THAT ABOUT THEM...
...YANO-SAN AND YOSHIDA-SAN WILL BE HURT...
GRIP...

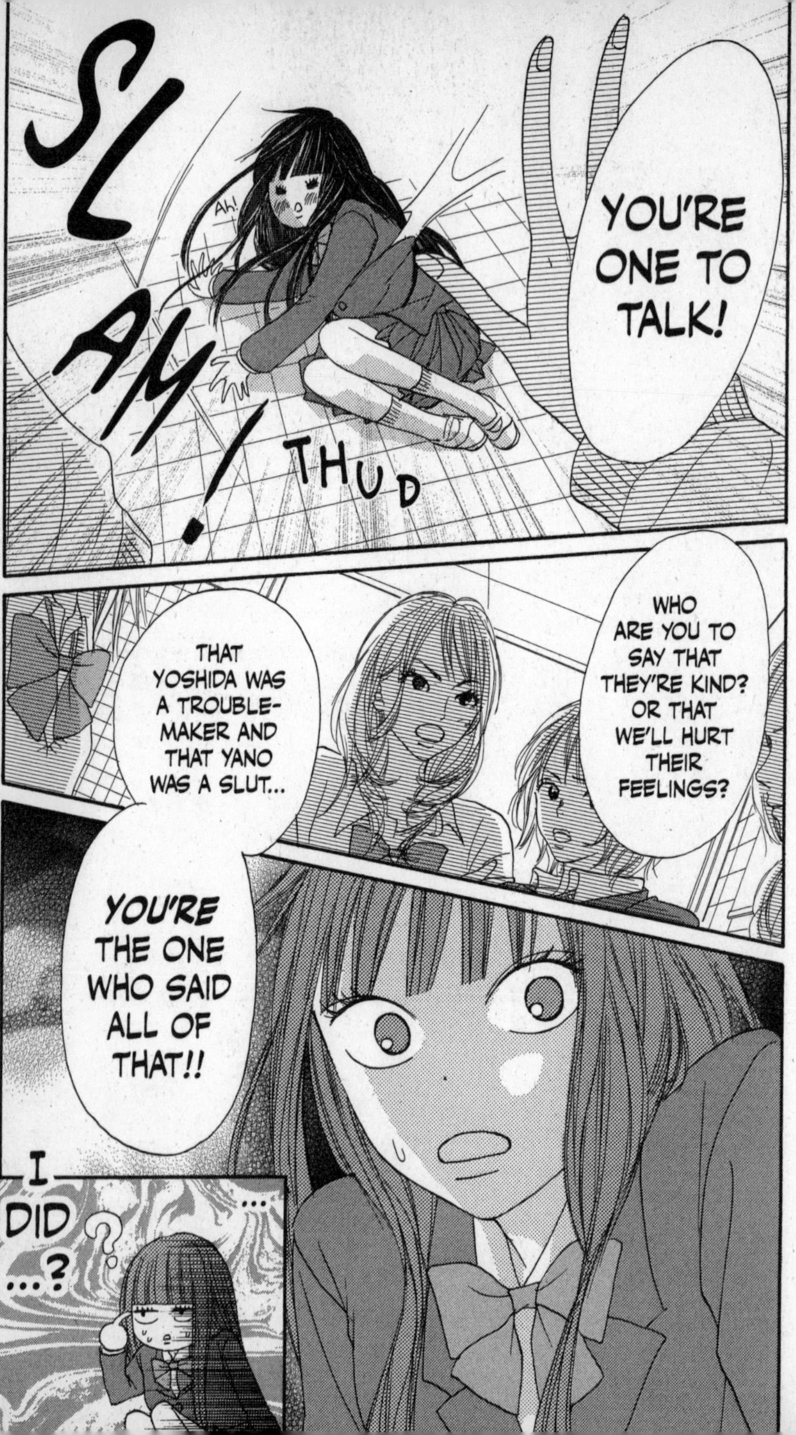
YOU'RE ONE TO TALK!
SLAM!
Ah!
THUD
WHO ARE YOU TO SAY THAT THEY'RE KIND? OR THAT WE'LL HURT THEIR FEELINGS?
THAT YOSHIDA WAS A TROUBLE-MAKER AND THAT YANO WAS A SLUT...
YOU'RE THE ONE WHO SAID ALL OF THAT!!
I DID ...?
...

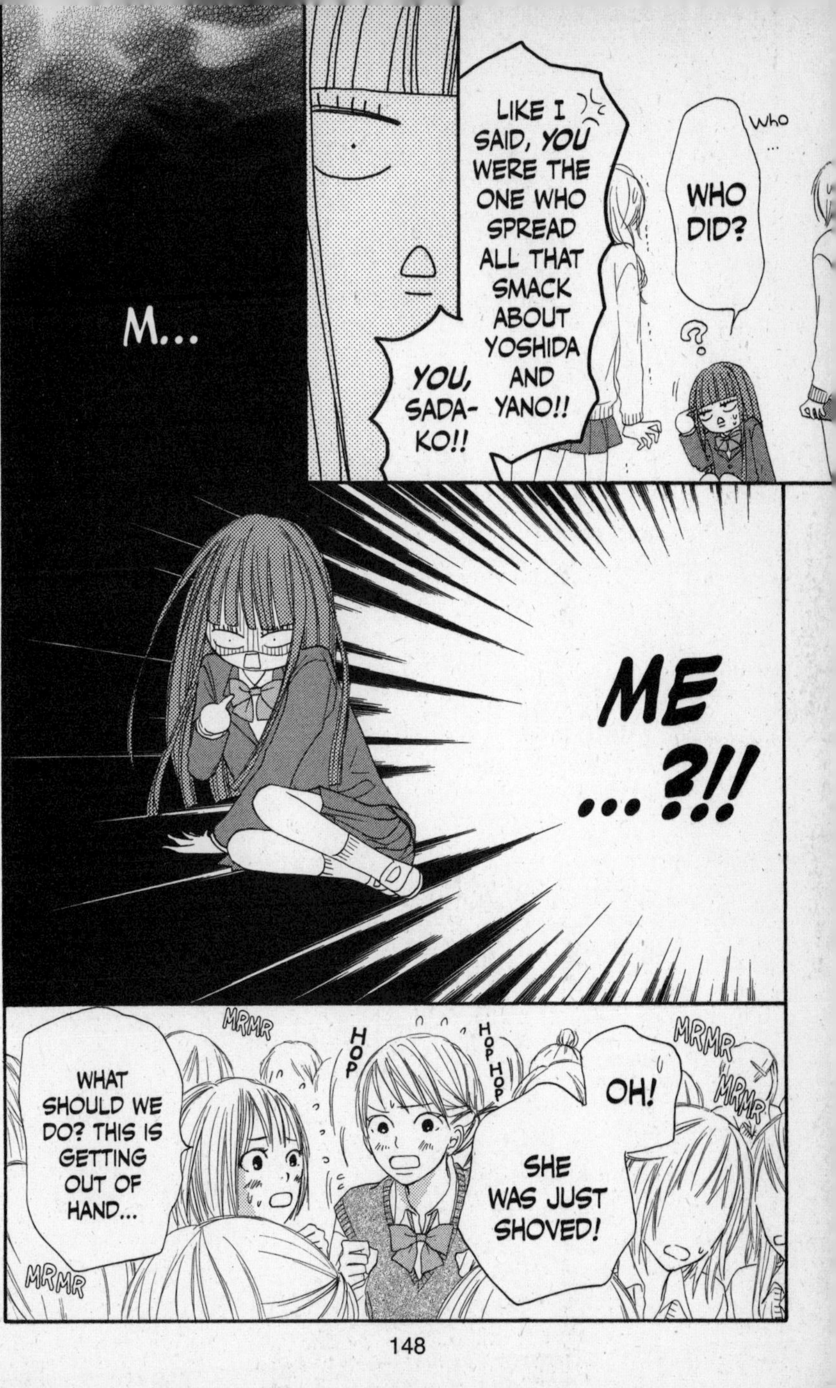
Who...
WHO DID?
LIKE I SAID, YOU WERE THE ONE WHO SPREAD ALL THAT SMACK ABOUT YOSHIDA AND YANO!!
YOU, SADA-KO!!
M...
ME...?!!
MRMR
MRMR
OH!
SHE WAS JUST SHOVED!
HOP HOP
HOP
MRMR
WHAT SHOULD WE DO? THIS IS GETTING OUT OF HAND...
MRMR

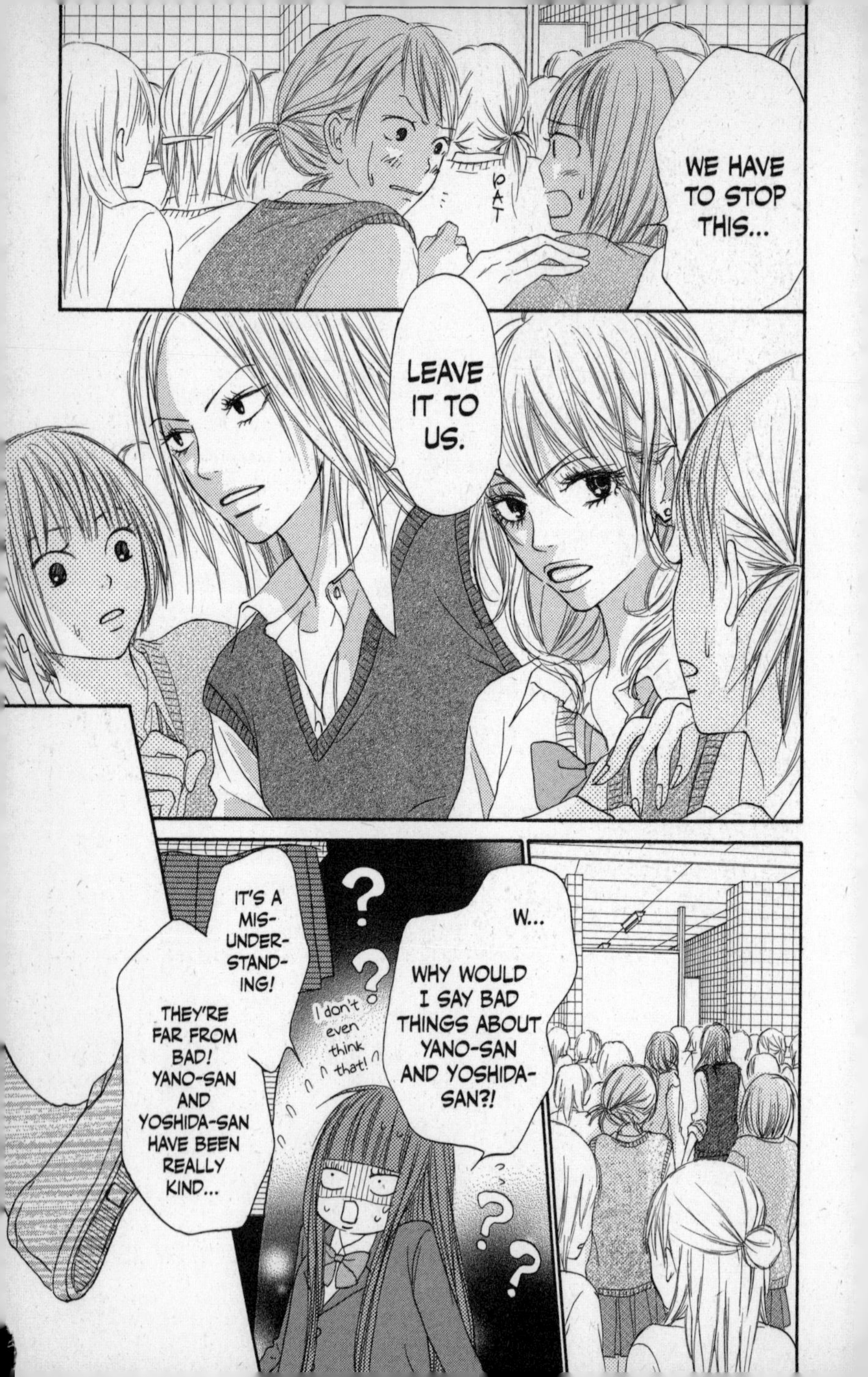
PAT
WE HAVE TO STOP THIS...
LEAVE IT TO US.
W...
WHY WOULD I SAY BAD THINGS ABOUT YANO-SAN AND YOSHIDA-SAN?!
I don't even think that!
IT'S A MIS-UNDER-STAND-ING!
THEY'RE FAR FROM BAD! YANO-SAN AND YOSHIDA-SAN HAVE BEEN REALLY KIND...

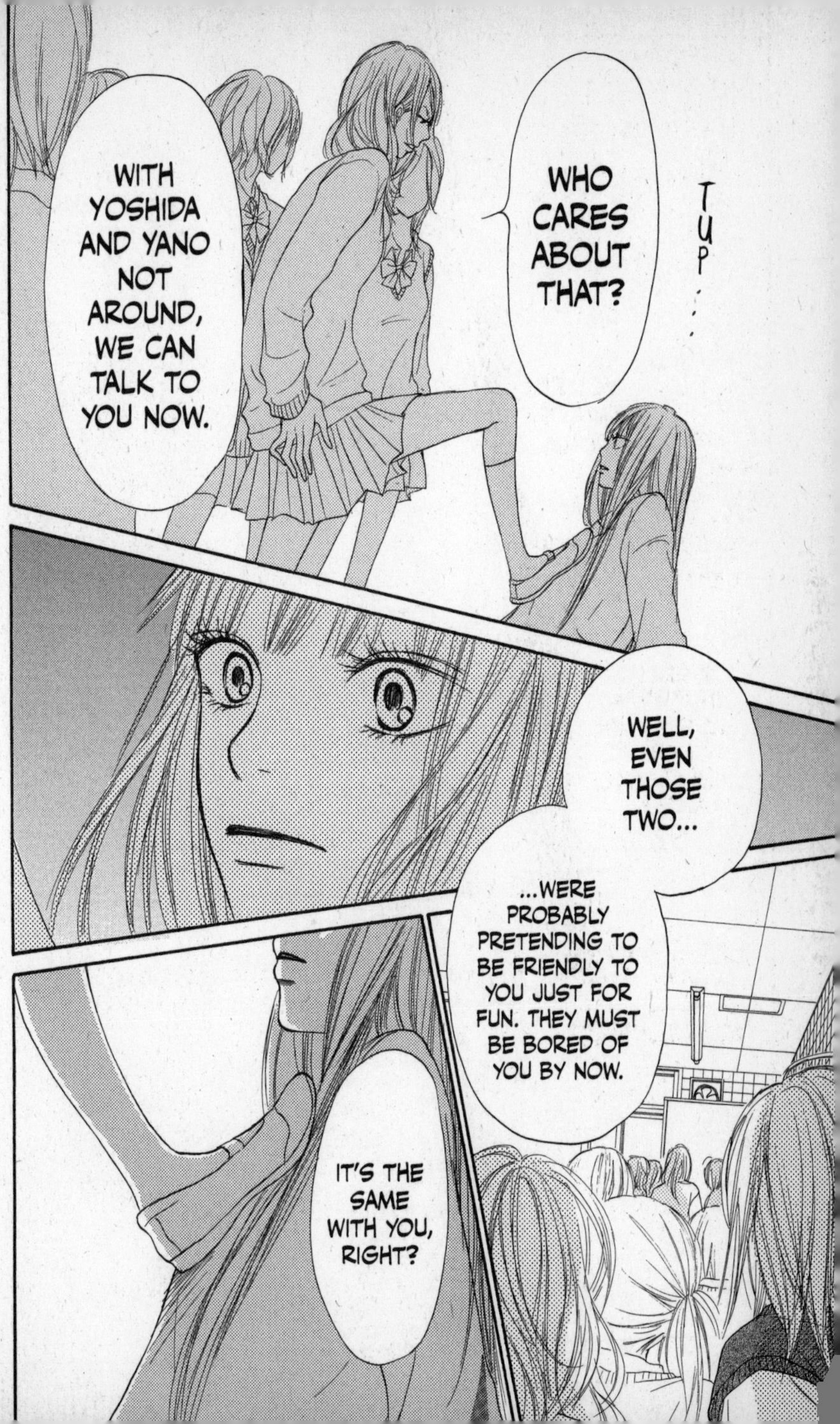
TUP...
WHO CARES ABOUT THAT?
WITH YOSHIDA AND YANO NOT AROUND, WE CAN TALK TO YOU NOW.
WELL, EVEN THOSE TWO...
...WERE PROBABLY PRETENDING TO BE FRIENDLY TO YOU JUST FOR FUN. THEY MUST BE BORED OF YOU BY NOW.
IT'S THE SAME WITH YOU, RIGHT?

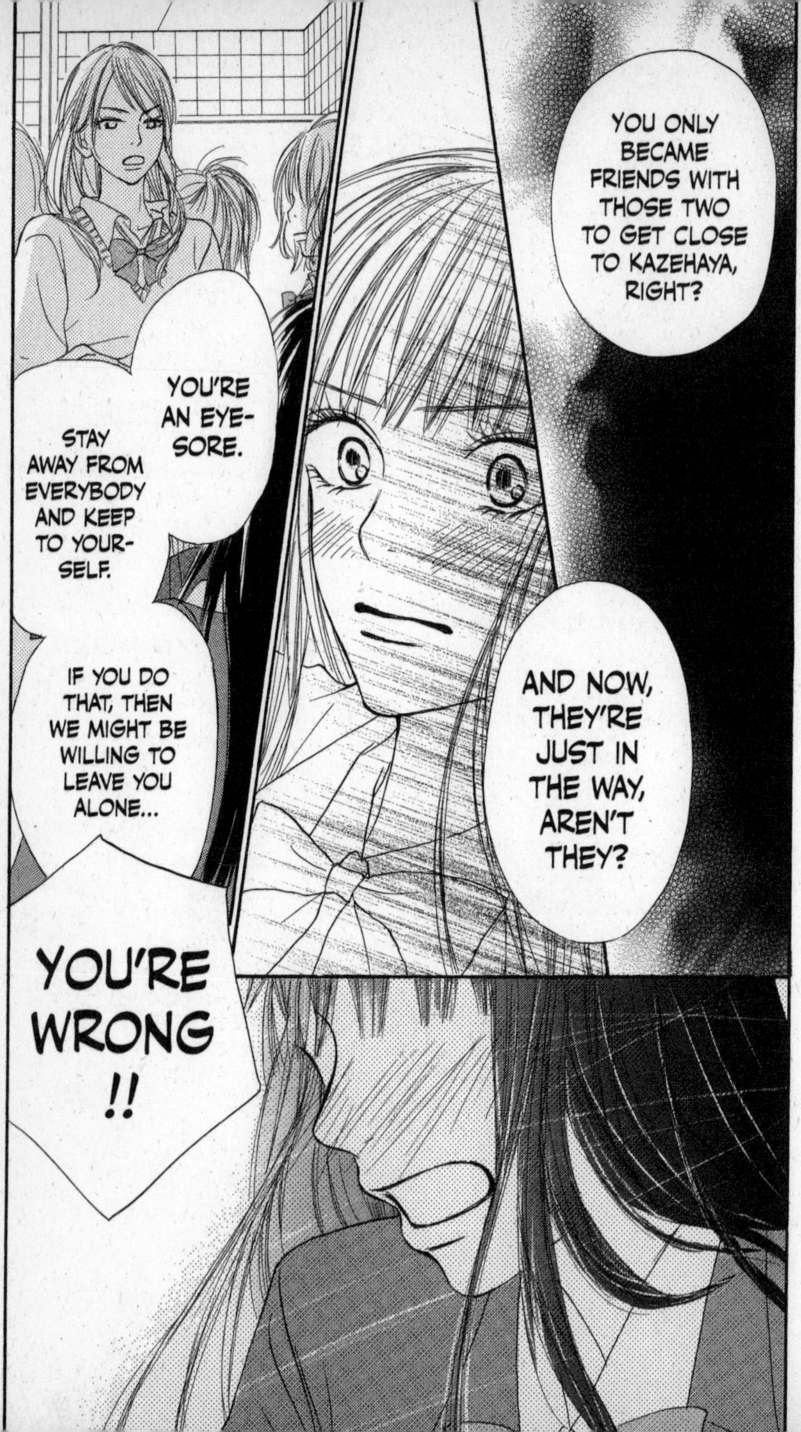
YOU ONLY BECAME FRIENDS WITH THOSE TWO TO GET CLOSE TO KAZEHAYA, RIGHT?
AND NOW, THEY'RE JUST IN THE WAY, AREN'T THEY?
YOU'RE AN EYE-SORE.
STAY AWAY FROM EVERYBODY AND KEEP TO YOUR-SELF.
IF YOU DO THAT, THEN WE MIGHT BE WILLING TO LEAVE YOU ALONE...
YOU'RE WRONG!!

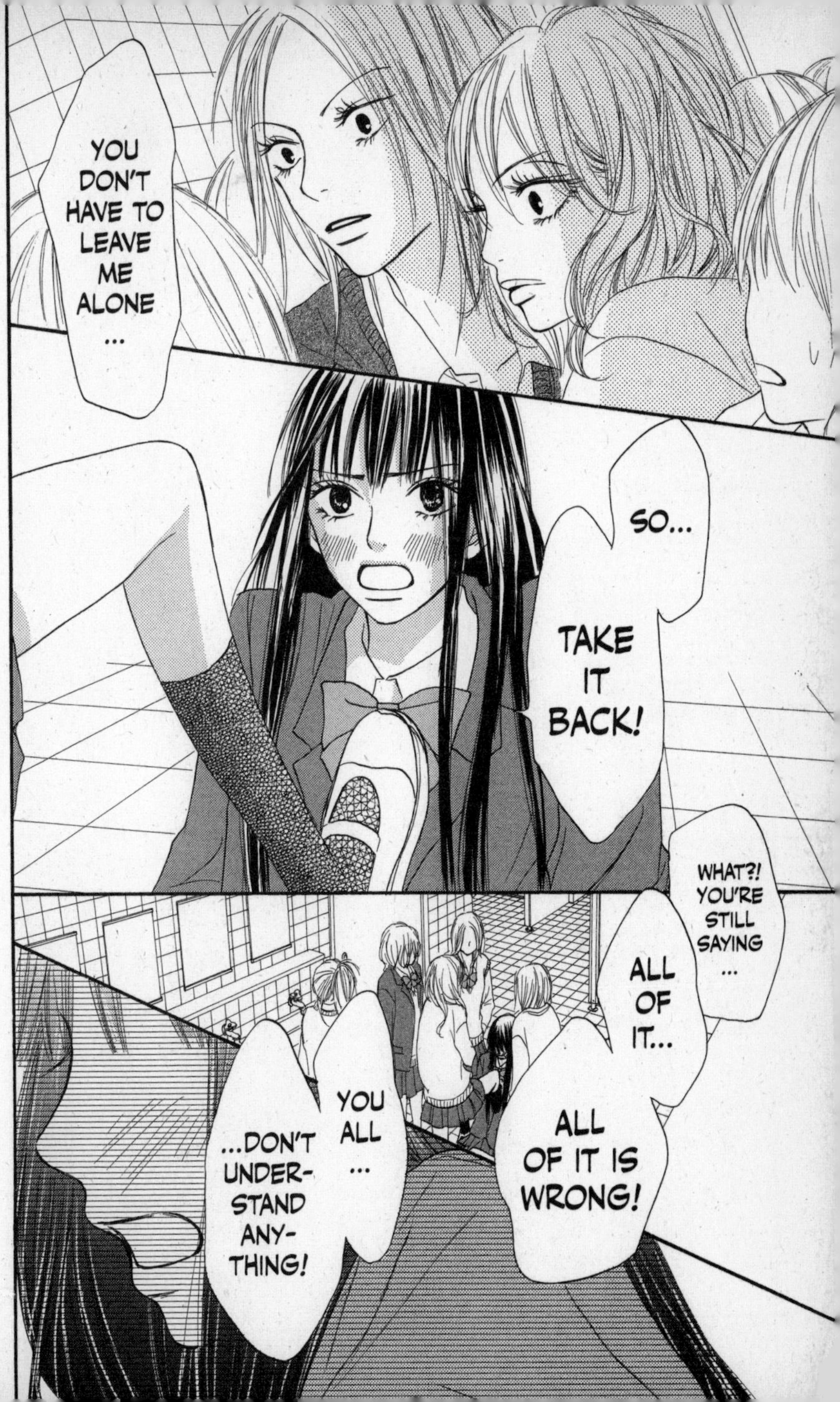
YOU DON'T HAVE TO LEAVE ME ALONE ...
SO...
TAKE IT BACK!
WHAT?! YOU'RE STILL SAYING ...
ALL OF IT...
ALL OF IT IS WRONG!
YOU ALL ...
...DON'T UNDER-STAND ANY-THING!

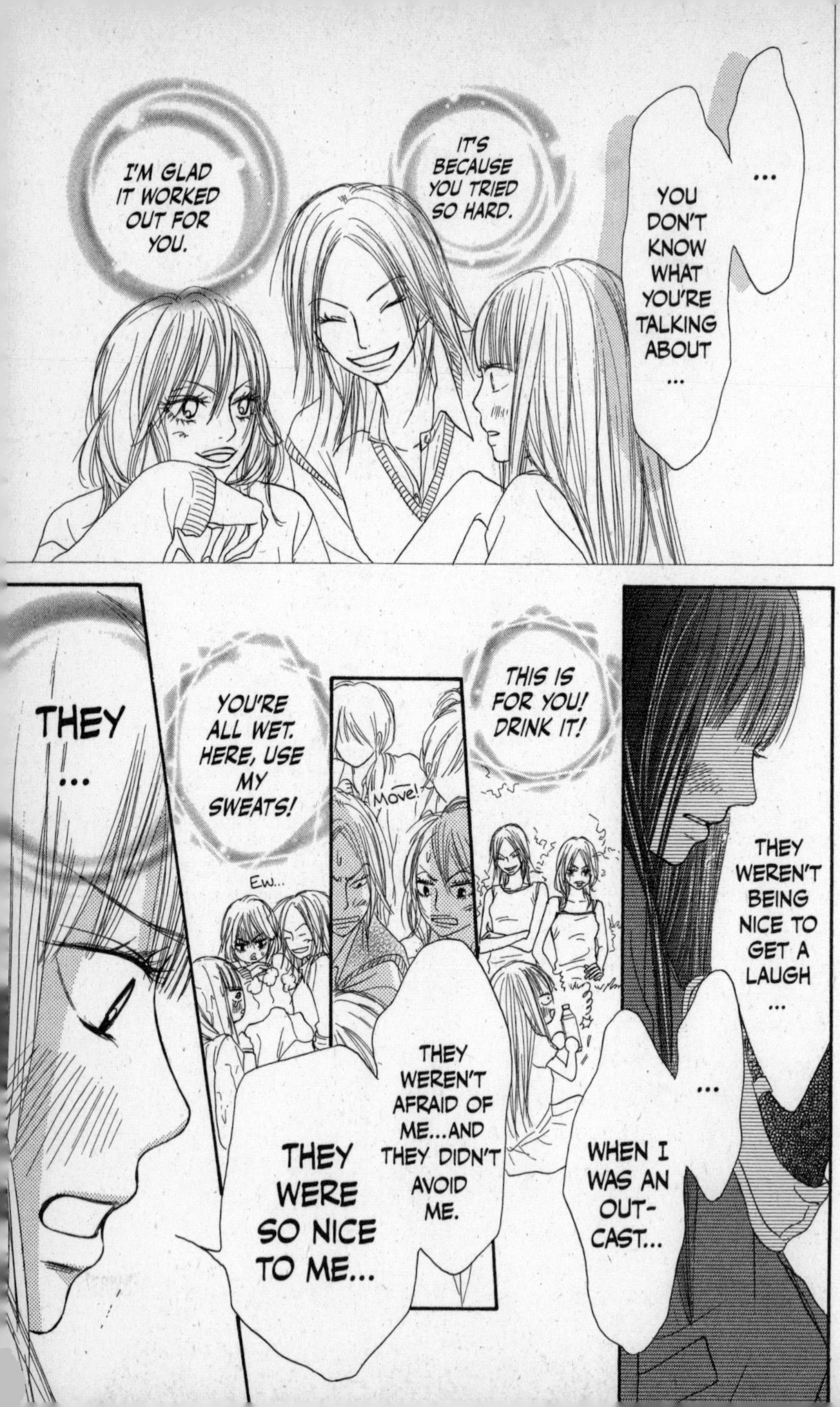
...
YOU DON'T KNOW WHAT YOU'RE TALKING ABOUT...
IT'S BECAUSE YOU TRIED SO HARD.
I'M GLAD IT WORKED OUT FOR YOU.
THEY WEREN'T BEING NICE TO GET A LAUGH...
...
WHEN I WAS AN OUT-CAST...
THIS IS FOR YOU! DRINK IT!
YOU'RE ALL WET. HERE, USE MY SWEATS!
Move!
Ew...
THEY WEREN'T AFRAID OF ME...AND THEY DIDN'T AVOID ME.
THEY WERE SO NICE TO ME...
THEY...

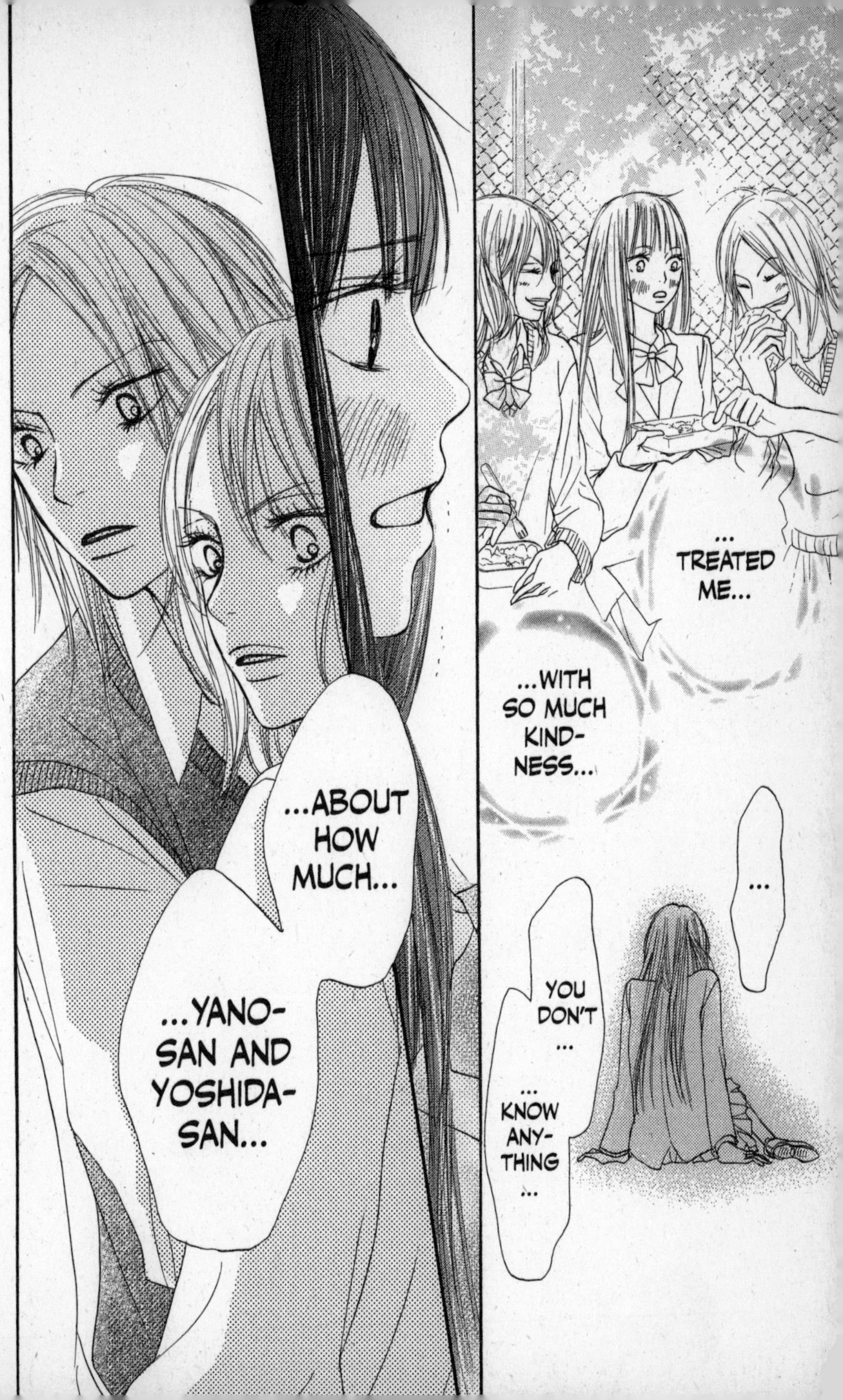
... TREATED ME...
...WITH SO MUCH KIND- NESS...
...
YOU DON'T ...
... KNOW ANY- THING ...
...ABOUT HOW MUCH...
...YANO- SAN AND YOSHIDA- SAN...

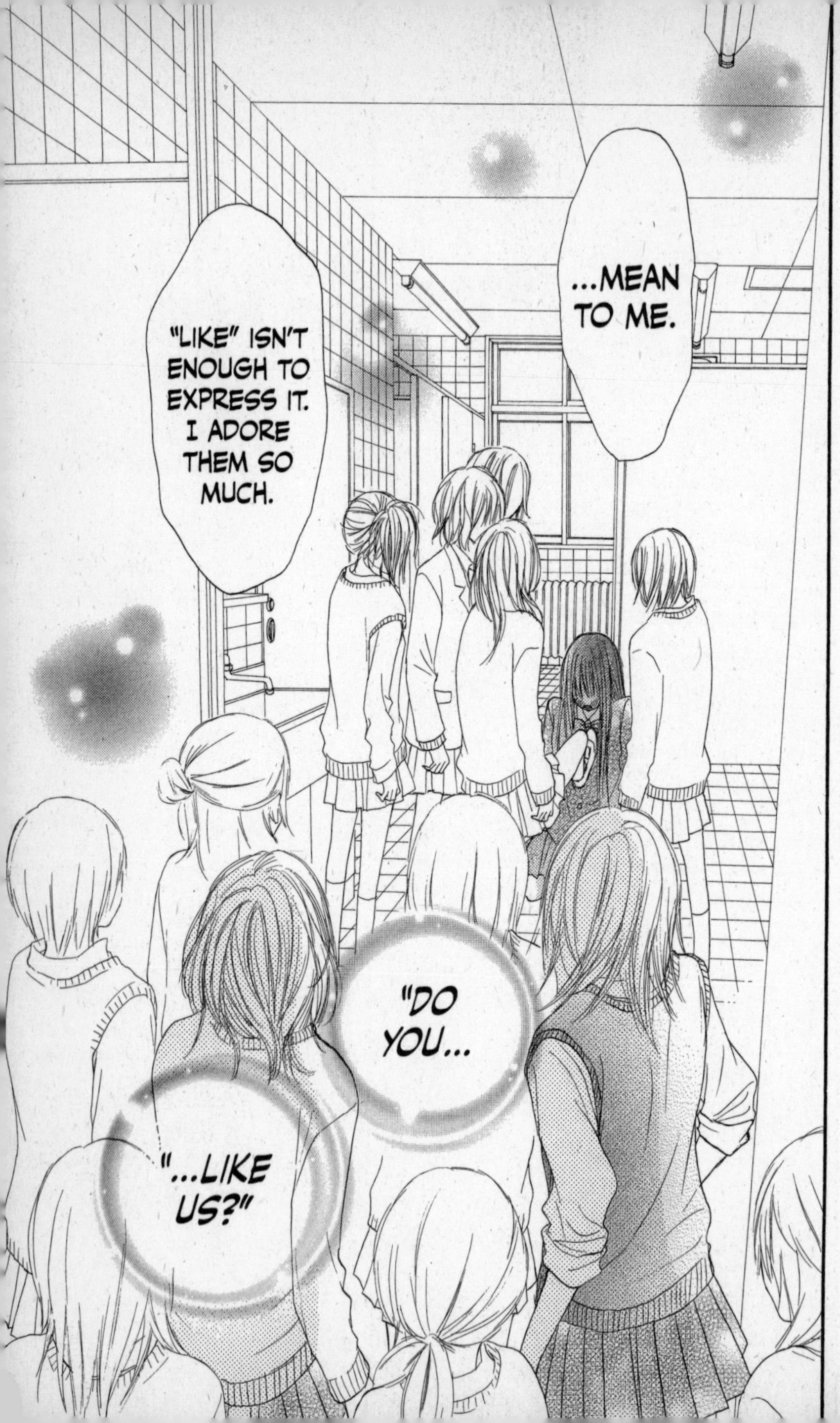
...MEAN TO ME.
"LIKE" ISN'T ENOUGH TO EXPRESS IT. I ADORE THEM SO MUCH.
"DO YOU...
"...LIKE US?"

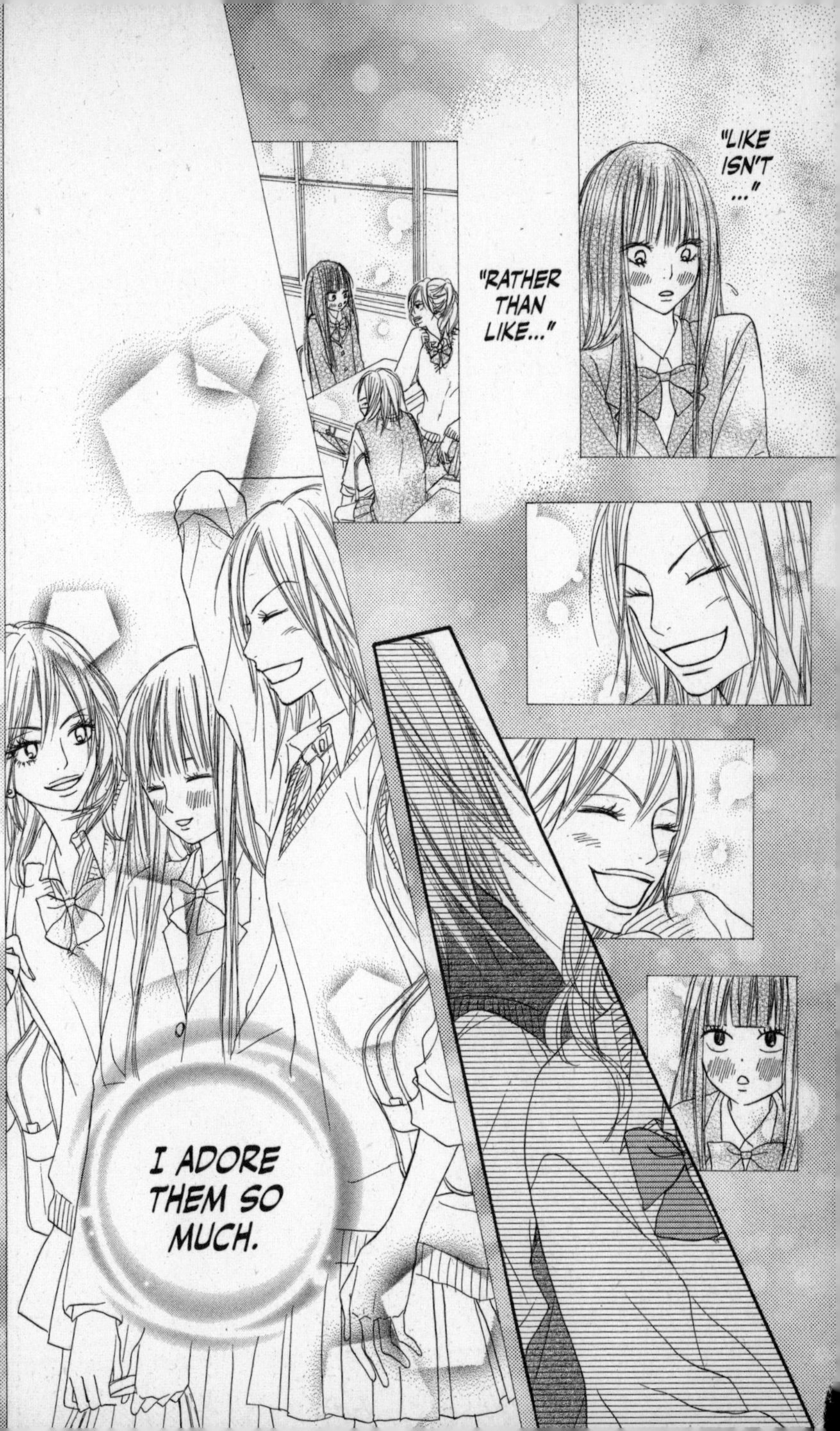
"LIKE ISN'T ..."
"RATHER THAN LIKE..."
I ADORE THEM SO MUCH.

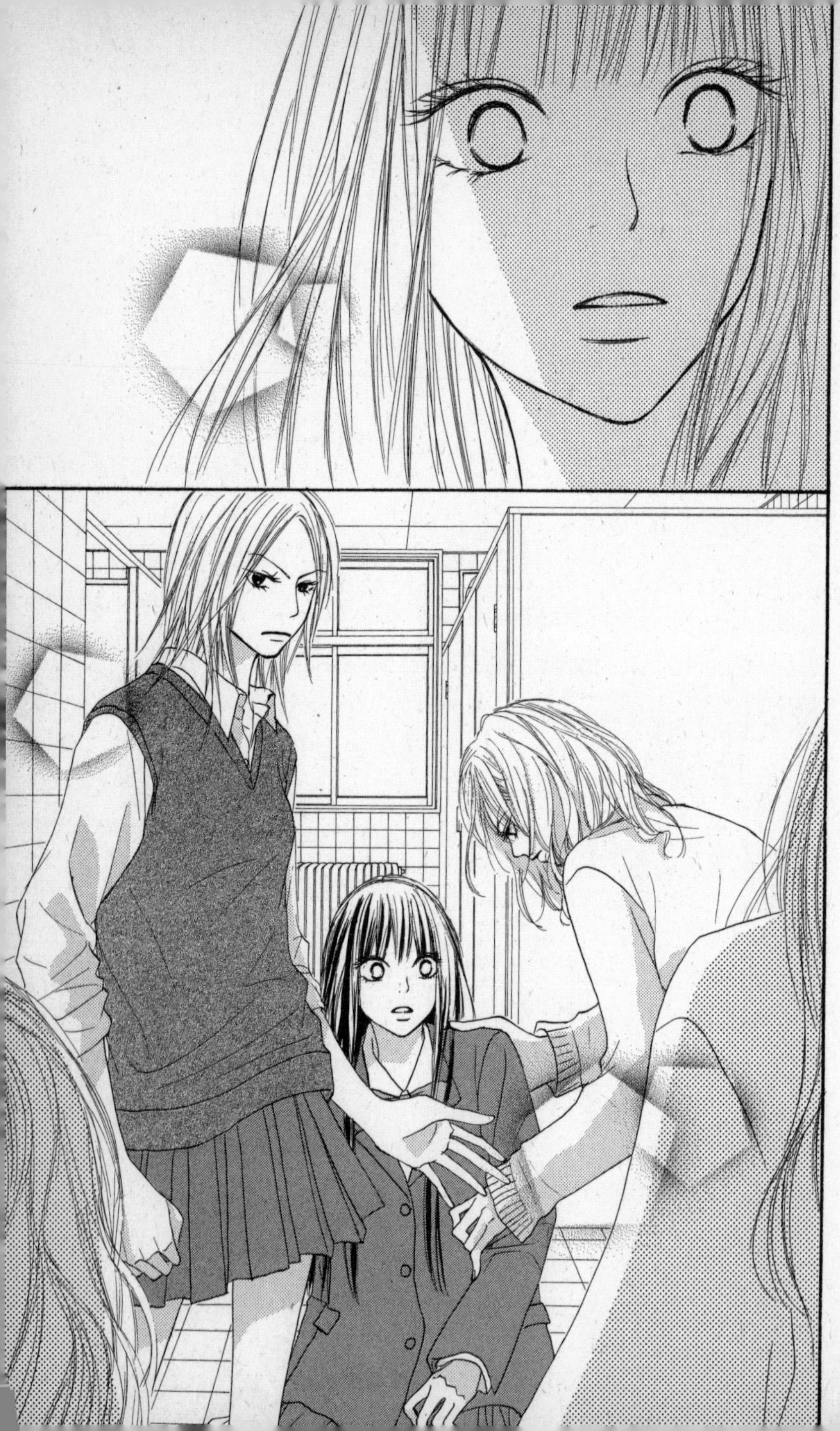

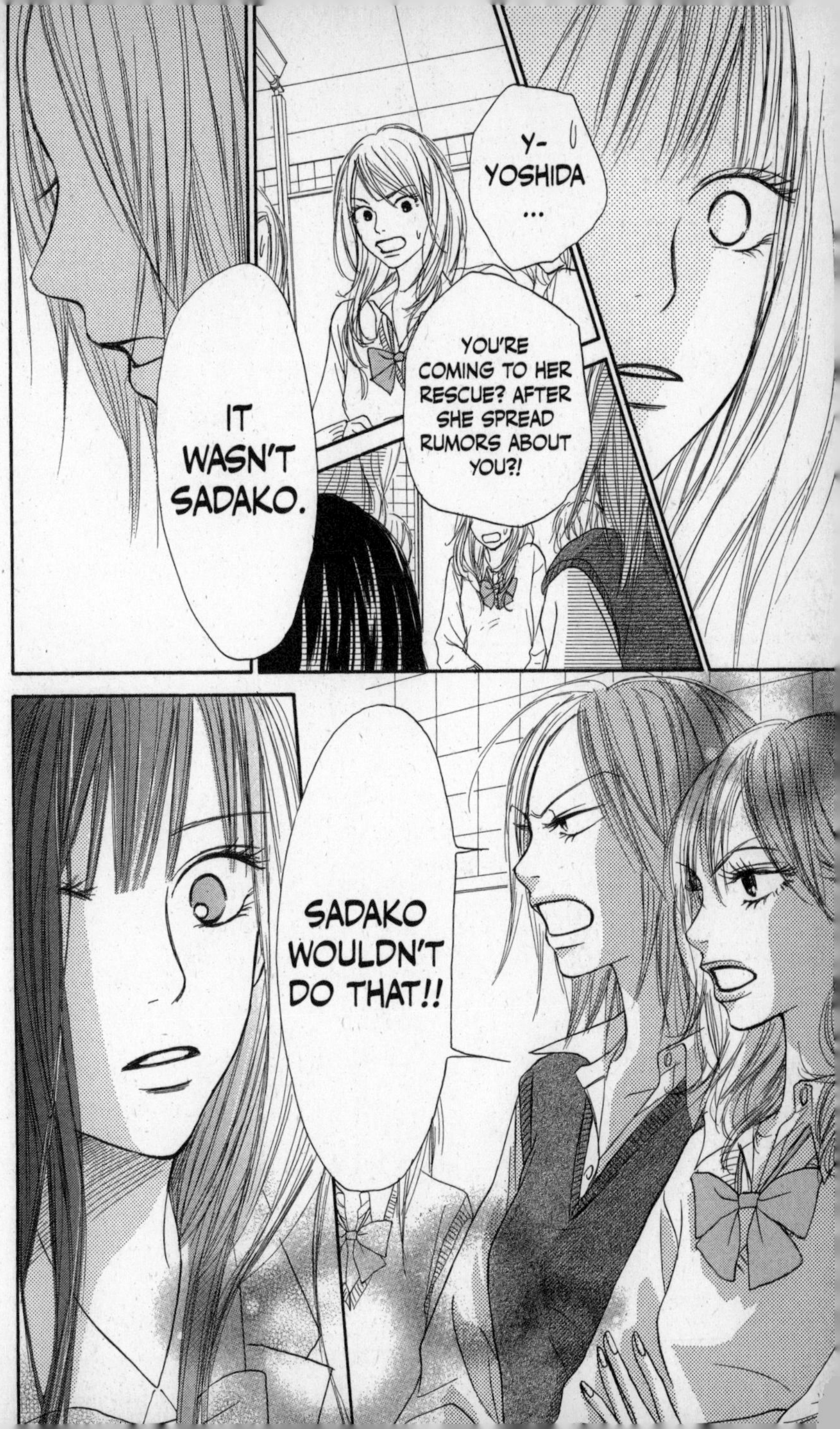
Y-YOSHIDA ...
YOU'RE COMING TO HER RESCUE? AFTER SHE SPREAD RUMORS ABOUT YOU?!
IT WASN'T SADAKO.
SADAKO WOULDN'T DO THAT!!

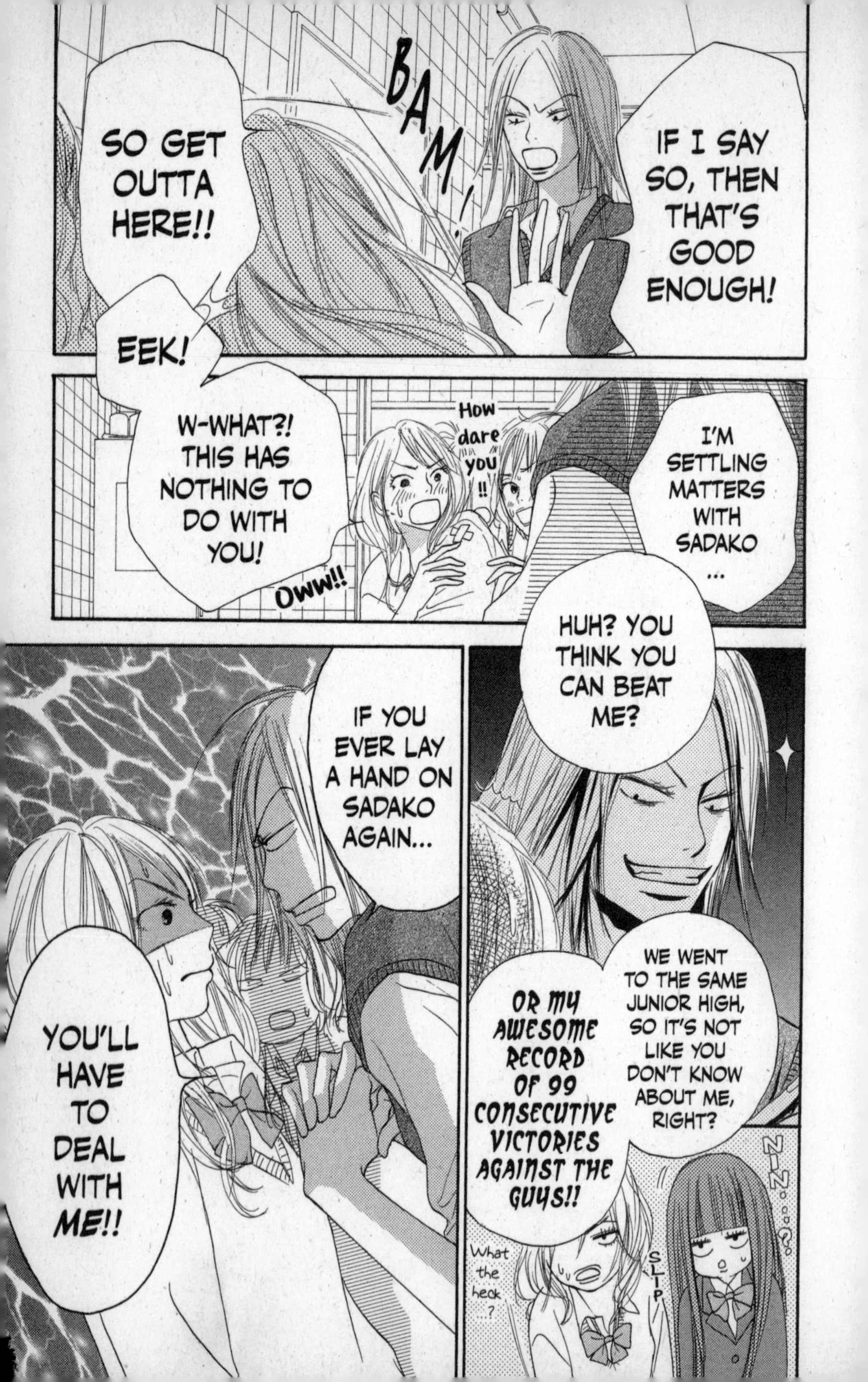
IF I SAY SO, THEN THAT'S GOOD ENOUGH!
BAM!
SO GET OUTTA HERE!!
EEK!
I'M SETTLING MATTERS WITH SADAKO ...
How dare you!!
W-WHAT?! THIS HAS NOTHING TO DO WITH YOU!
OWW!!
HUH? YOU THINK YOU CAN BEAT ME?
WE WENT TO THE SAME JUNIOR HIGH, SO IT'S NOT LIKE YOU DON'T KNOW ABOUT ME, RIGHT?
OR MY AWESOME RECORD OF 99 CONSECUTIVE VICTORIES AGAINST THE GUYS!!
NIN...?
SLIP
What the heck...?
IF YOU EVER LAY A HAND ON SADAKO AGAIN...
YOU'LL HAVE TO DEAL WITH ME!!

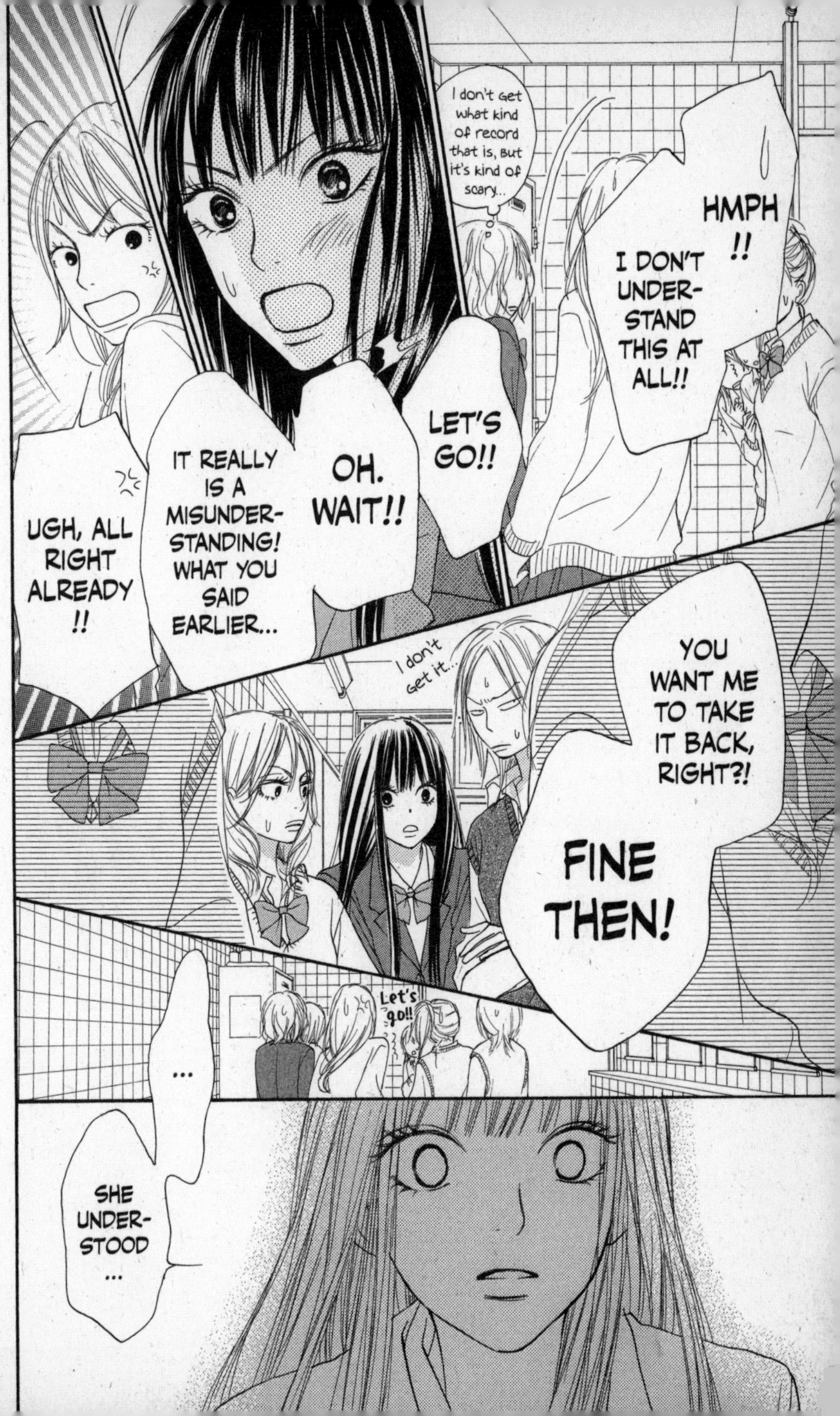
HMPH!!
I DON'T UNDERSTAND THIS AT ALL!!
I don't get what kind of record that is, but it's kind of scary...
LET'S GO!!
OH. WAIT!!
IT REALLY IS A MISUNDERSTANDING! WHAT YOU SAID EARLIER...
UGH, ALL RIGHT ALREADY!!
YOU WANT ME TO TAKE IT BACK, RIGHT?!
FINE THEN!
I don't get it...
Let's go!!
...
SHE UNDERSTOOD...

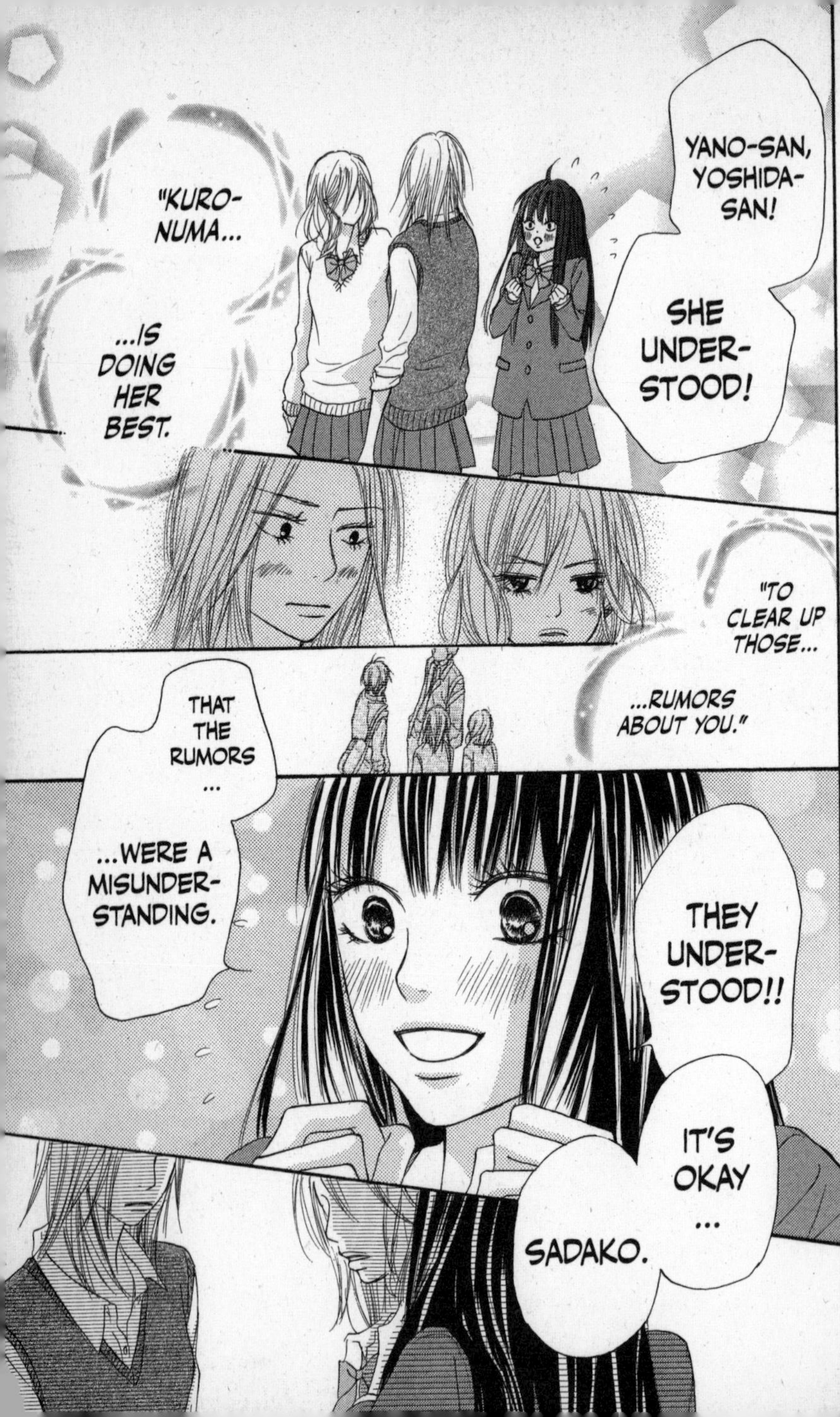
YANO-SAN, YOSHIDA-SAN!
SHE UNDERSTOOD!
"KURO-NUMA...
...IS DOING HER BEST.
"TO CLEAR UP THOSE...
...RUMORS ABOUT YOU."
THAT THE RUMORS...
...WERE A MISUNDERSTANDING.
THEY UNDERSTOOD!!
IT'S OKAY... SADAKO.

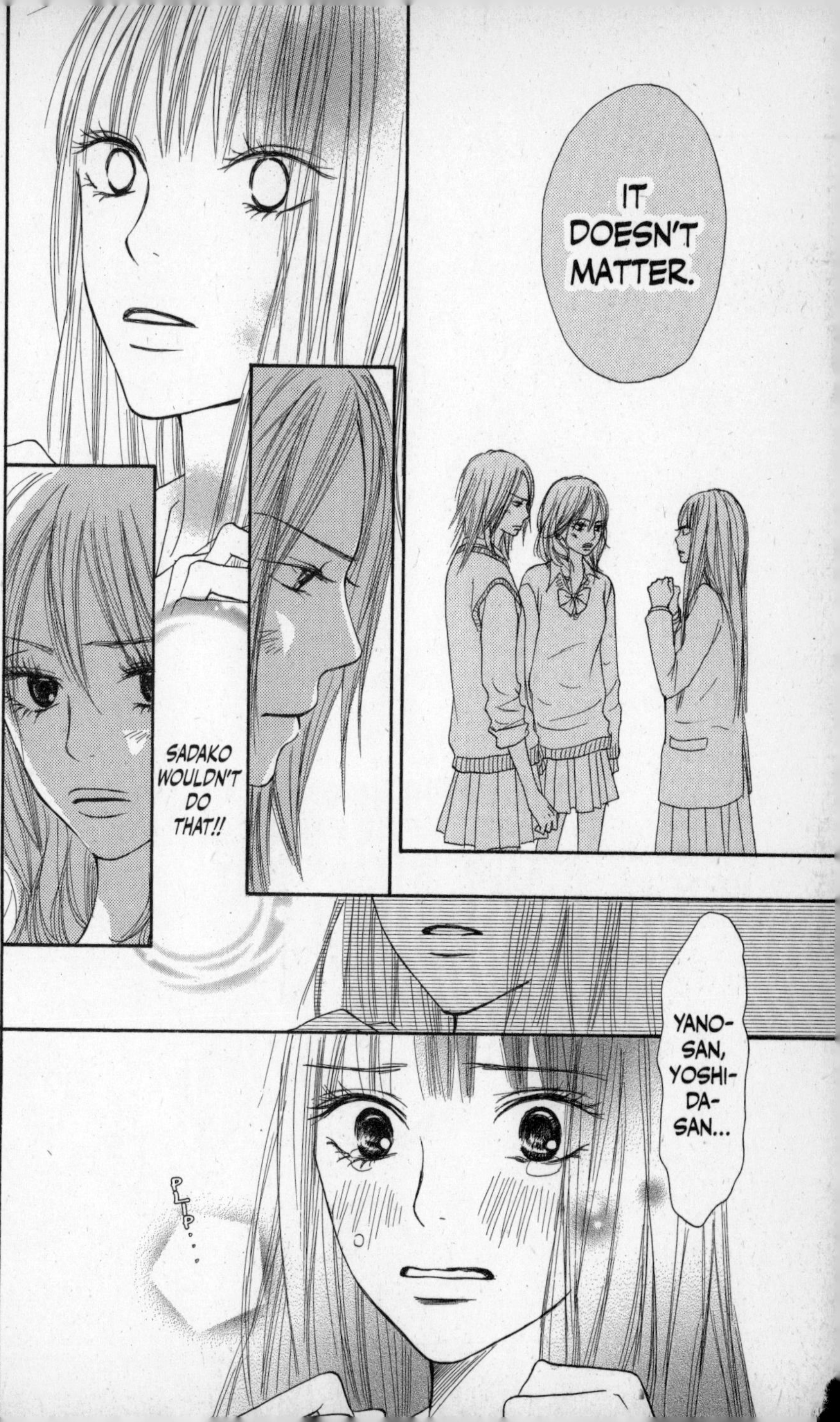
IT DOESN'T MATTER.
SADAKO WOULDN'T DO THAT!!
YANO-SAN, YOSHIDA-SAN...
PLIP...

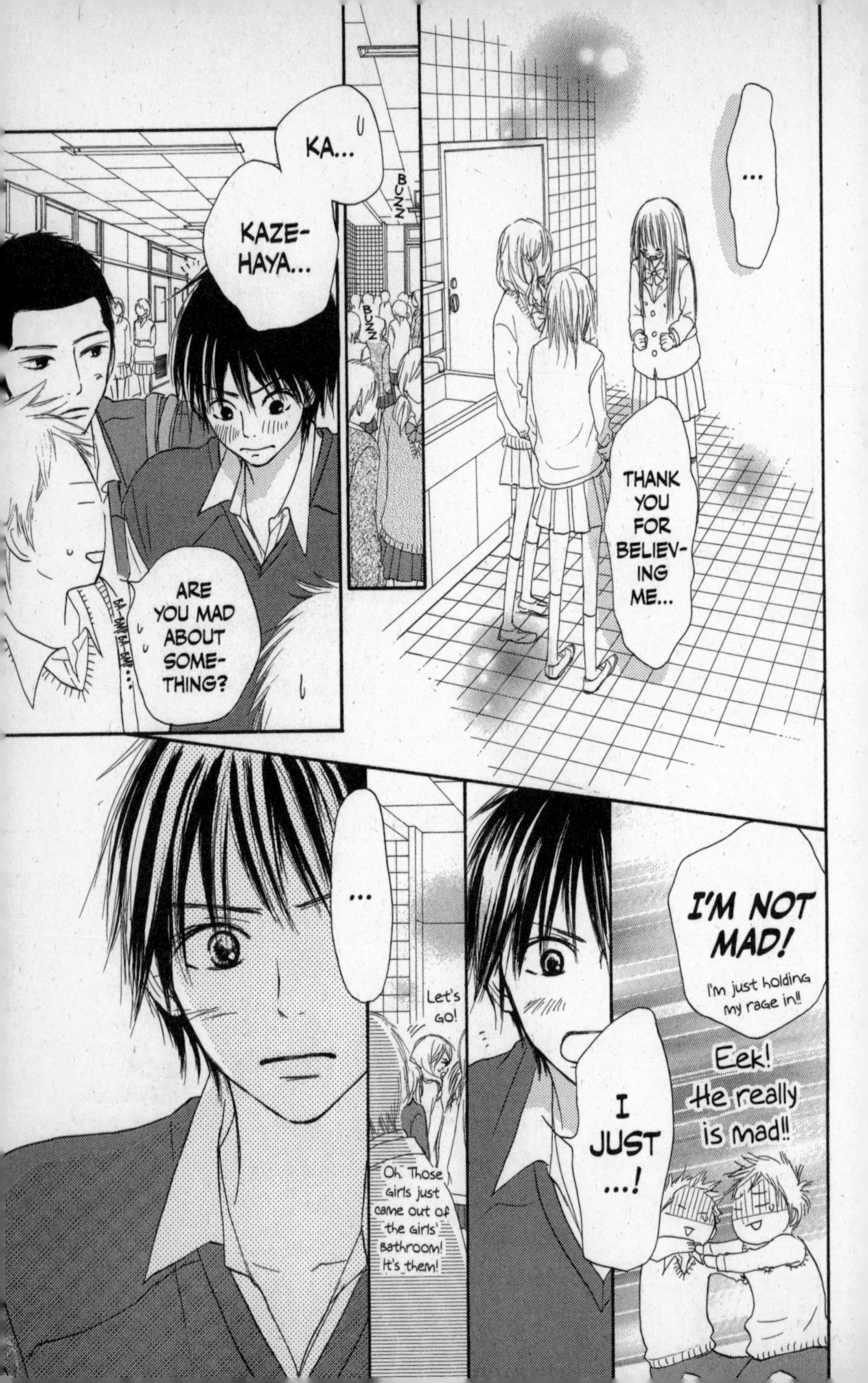
...
THANK YOU FOR BELIEVING ME...
BUZZ
BUZZ
KA...
KAZE-HAYA...
ARE YOU MAD ABOUT SOMETHING?
BA-DMP BA-DMP...
I'M NOT MAD!
I'm just holding my rage in!!
Eek! He really is mad!!
I JUST ...!
...
Let's go!
Oh. Those girls just came out of the girls' bathroom! It's them!

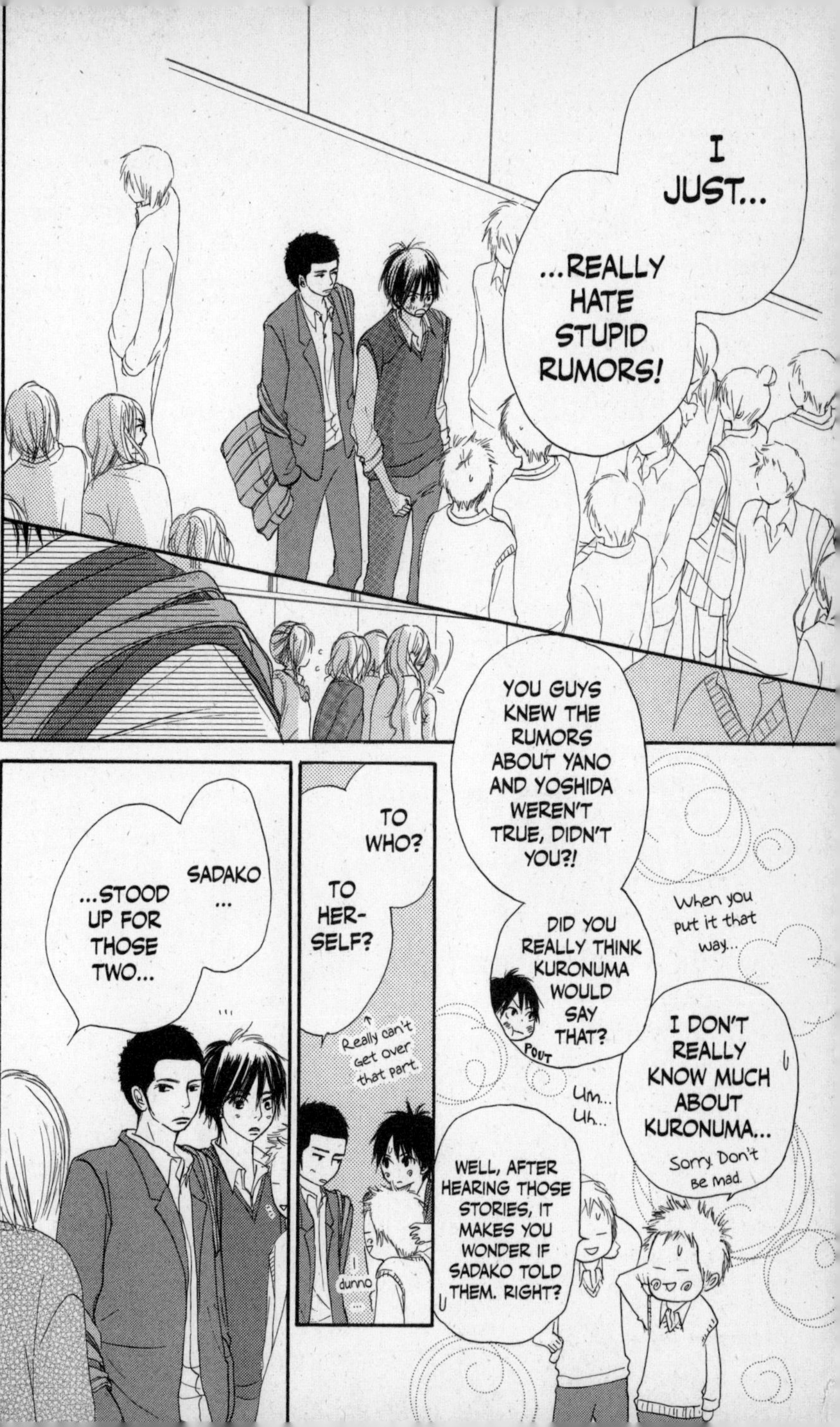
I JUST...
...REALLY HATE STUPID RUMORS!
YOU GUYS KNEW THE RUMORS ABOUT YANO AND YOSHIDA WEREN'T TRUE, DIDN'T YOU?!
When you put it that way...
DID YOU REALLY THINK KURONUMA WOULD SAY THAT?
POUT
I DON'T REALLY KNOW MUCH ABOUT KURONUMA...
Sorry. Don't be mad.
Um... Uh...
WELL, AFTER HEARING THOSE STORIES, IT MAKES YOU WONDER IF SADAKO TOLD THEM. RIGHT?
TO WHO?
TO HER-SELF?
Really can't get over that part.
I dunno...
SADAKO...
...STOOD UP FOR THOSE TWO...

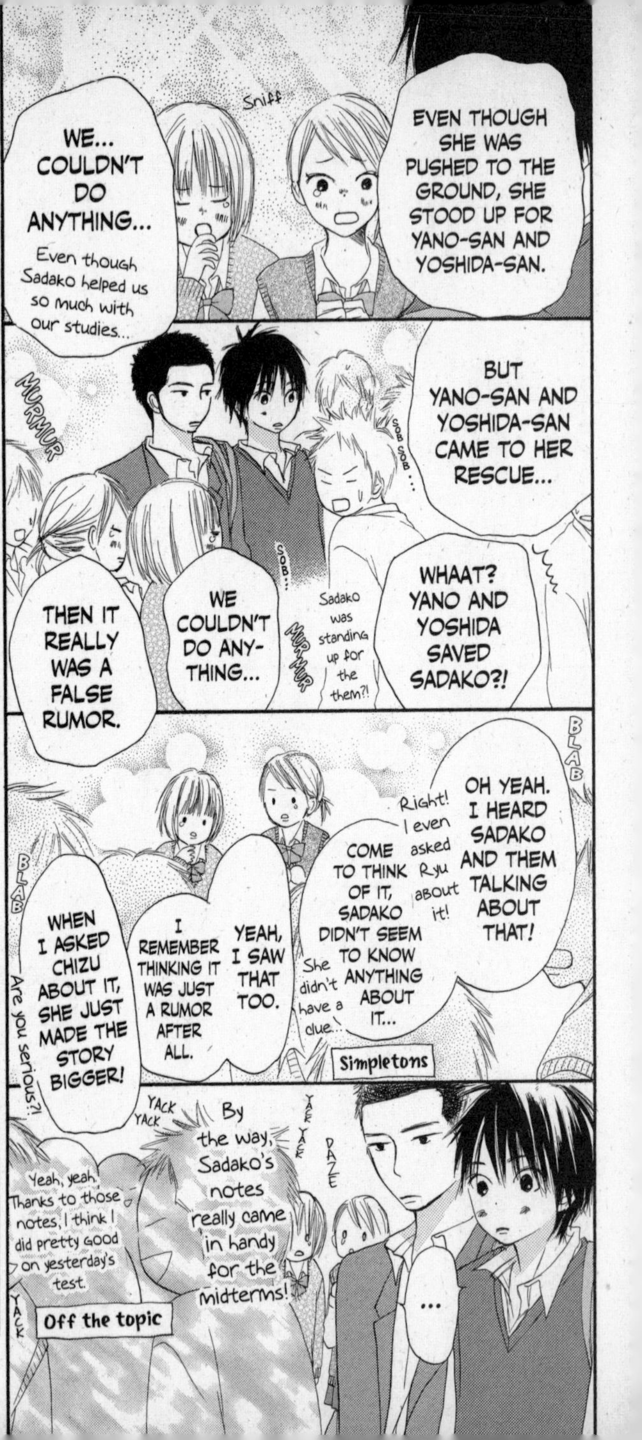
EVEN THOUGH SHE WAS PUSHED TO THE GROUND, SHE STOOD UP FOR YANO-SAN AND YOSHIDA-SAN.
Sniff
WE... COULDN'T DO ANYTHING...
Even though Sadako helped us so much with our studies...
BUT YANO-SAN AND YOSHIDA-SAN CAME TO HER RESCUE...
SOB SOB...
WHAAT? YANO AND YOSHIDA SAVED SADAKO?!
Sadako was standing up for the them?!
MUR-MUR
WE COULDN'T DO ANY-THING...
SOB...
THEN IT REALLY WAS A FALSE RUMOR.
MURMUR
BLAB
OH YEAH. I HEARD SADAKO AND THEM TALKING ABOUT THAT!
Right! I even asked Ryu about it!
COME TO THINK OF IT, SADAKO DIDN'T SEEM TO KNOW ANYTHING ABOUT IT...
She didn't have a clue...
Simpletons
YEAH, I SAW THAT TOO.
I REMEMBER THINKING IT WAS JUST A RUMOR AFTER ALL.
WHEN I ASKED CHIZU ABOUT IT, SHE JUST MADE THE STORY BIGGER!
BLAB
Are you serious?!
...
DAZE
YAK YAK
By the way, Sadako's notes really came in handy for the midterms!
YACK YACK
Yeah, yeah. Thanks to those notes, I think I did pretty good on yesterday's test.
YACK
Off the topic

KARUPIN on JAPAN 4

I'd like to talk about the exclusives that were made for when this series started in the magazine and when it got top billing.

① The Sawako Towel

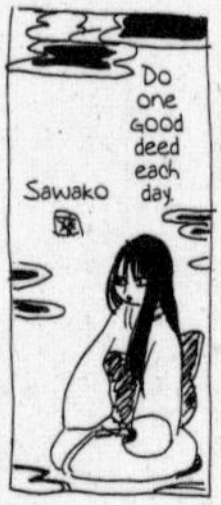
Do one good deed each day.
Sawako

(This image was also used for the bookmark that was included in the first printing of volume 1.)

It was indigo on a beige background. It was really cute. It came out beautiful!

② The Sawako Teacup "Sawa Cha"

*My editor named it.

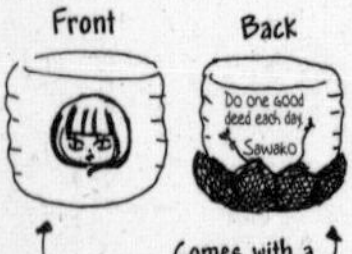
Front
Back
Do one good deed each day.
Sawako

I like the cute plump shape.

Comes with a very cute magenta coaster.

Ah... You might not be able to tell what it looks like from my drawings. Sorry, it didn't come out well! The real thing is very cute.

Maybe one of you won one! I hope you use it a lot!

Well, that's it for now.

Hope to see you again! Karu

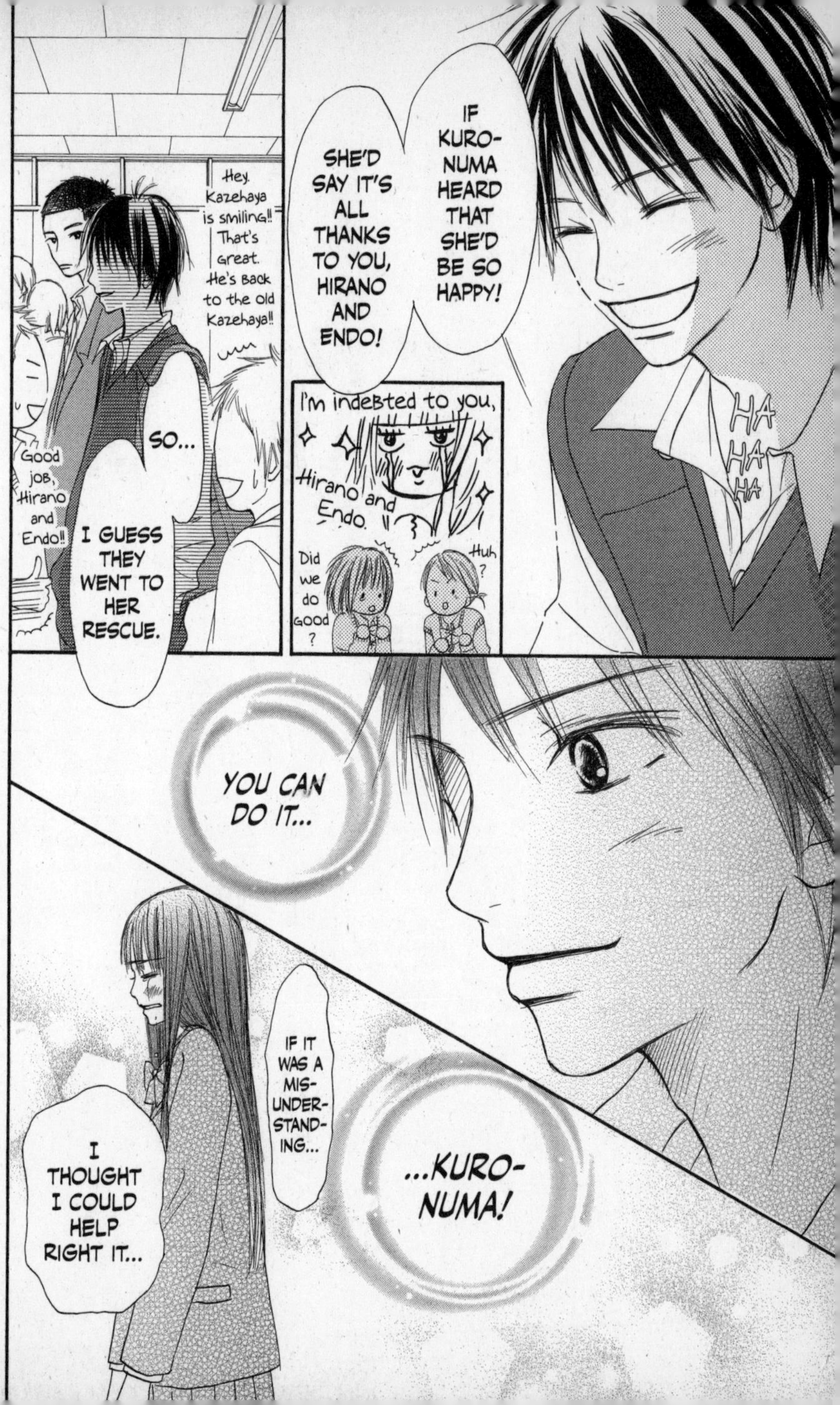
IF KURO-NUMA HEARD THAT SHE'D BE SO HAPPY!
SHE'D SAY IT'S ALL THANKS TO YOU, HIRANO AND ENDO!
HA HA HA
I'm indebted to you, Hirano and Endo.
Huh?
Did we do good?
Hey. Kazehaya is smiling!! That's great. He's back to the old Kazehaya!!
SO...
I GUESS THEY WENT TO HER RESCUE.
Good job, Hirano and Endo!!
YOU CAN DO IT...
...KURO-NUMA!
IF IT WAS A MIS-UNDER-STAND-ING...
I THOUGHT I COULD HELP RIGHT IT...

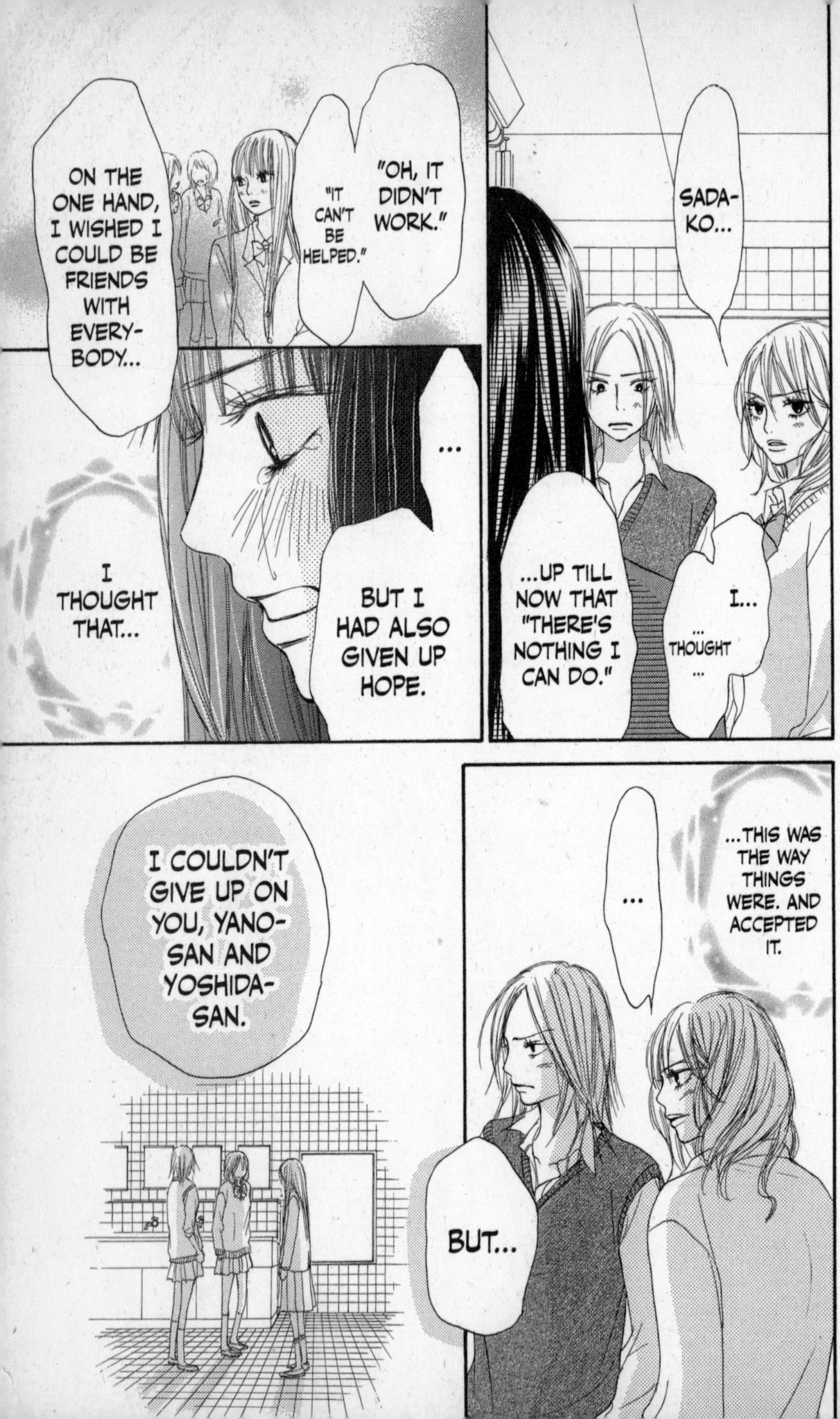
SADA-KO...
I... ...THOUGHT...
...UP TILL NOW THAT "THERE'S NOTHING I CAN DO."
"OH, IT DIDN'T WORK."
"IT CAN'T BE HELPED."
ON THE ONE HAND, I WISHED I COULD BE FRIENDS WITH EVERY-BODY...
...
BUT I HAD ALSO GIVEN UP HOPE.
I THOUGHT THAT...
...
...THIS WAS THE WAY THINGS WERE. AND ACCEPTED IT.
BUT...
I COULDN'T GIVE UP ON YOU, YANO-SAN AND YOSHIDA-SAN.

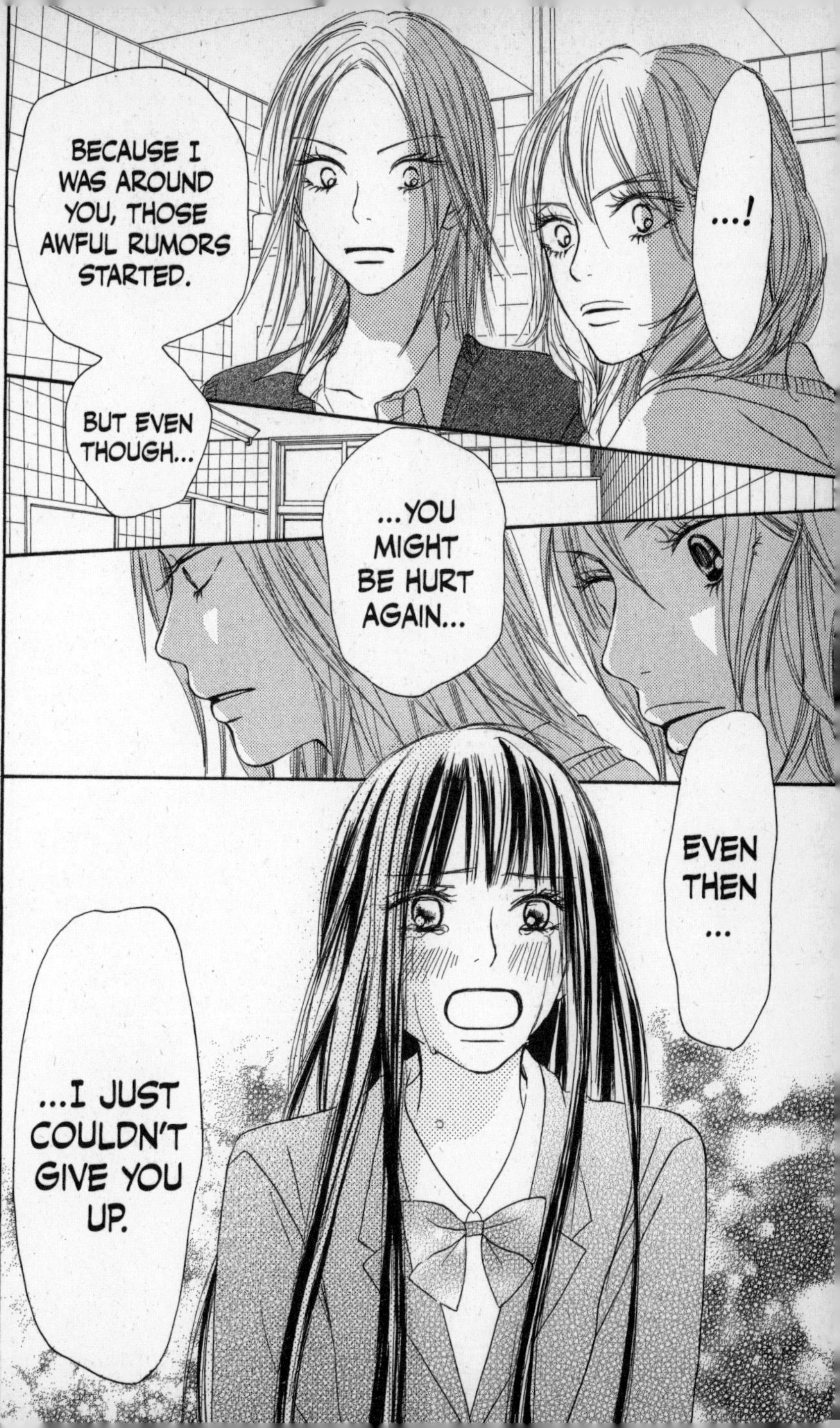
...!
BECAUSE I WAS AROUND YOU, THOSE AWFUL RUMORS STARTED.
BUT EVEN THOUGH...
...YOU MIGHT BE HURT AGAIN...
EVEN THEN ...
...I JUST COULDN'T GIVE YOU UP.

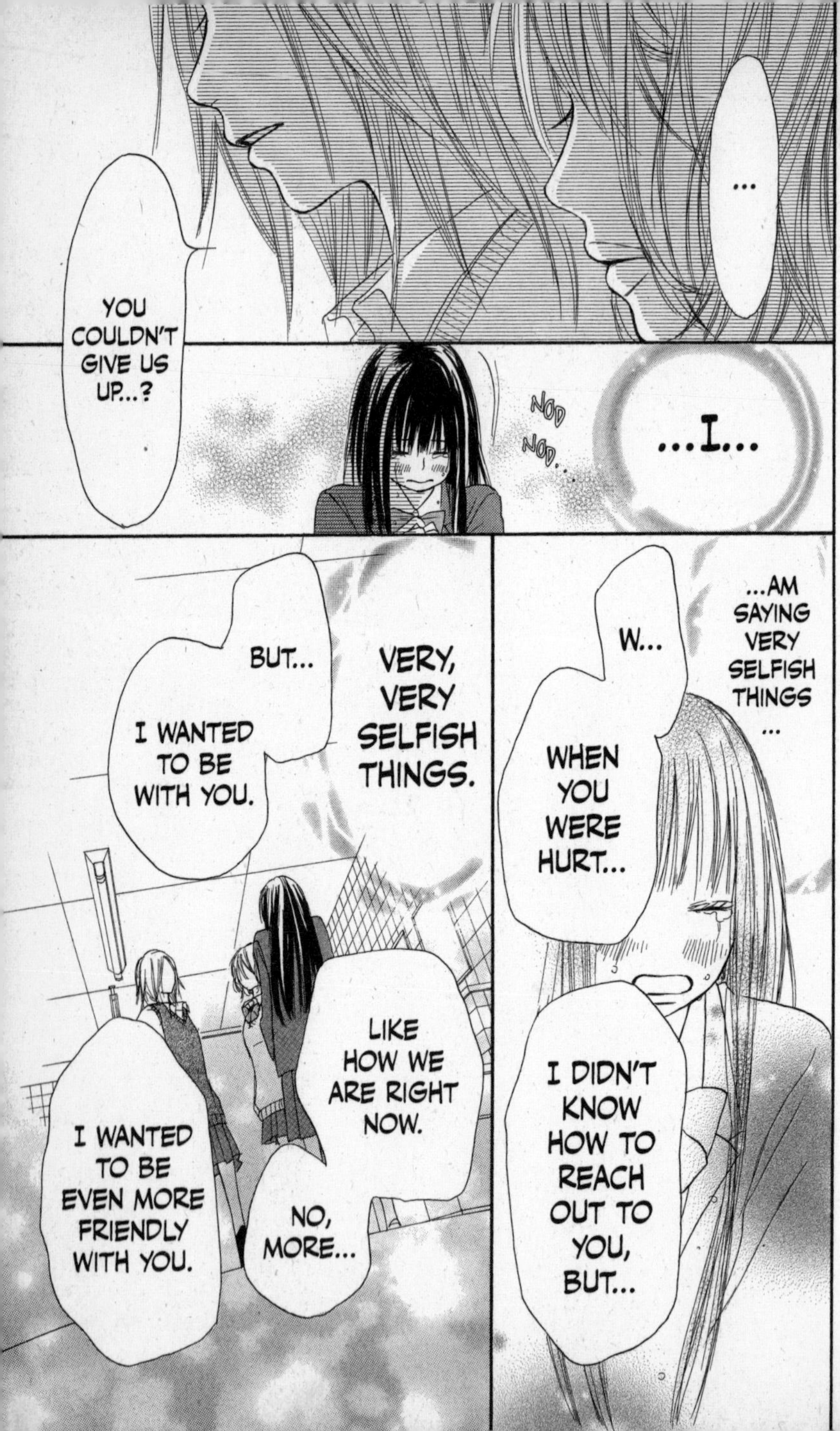
...
YOU COULDN'T GIVE US UP...?
...I...
NOD NOD...
...AM SAYING VERY SELFISH THINGS...
W...
WHEN YOU WERE HURT...
I DIDN'T KNOW HOW TO REACH OUT TO YOU, BUT...
VERY, VERY SELFISH THINGS.
BUT...
I WANTED TO BE WITH YOU.
LIKE HOW WE ARE RIGHT NOW.
NO, MORE...
I WANTED TO BE EVEN MORE FRIENDLY WITH YOU.

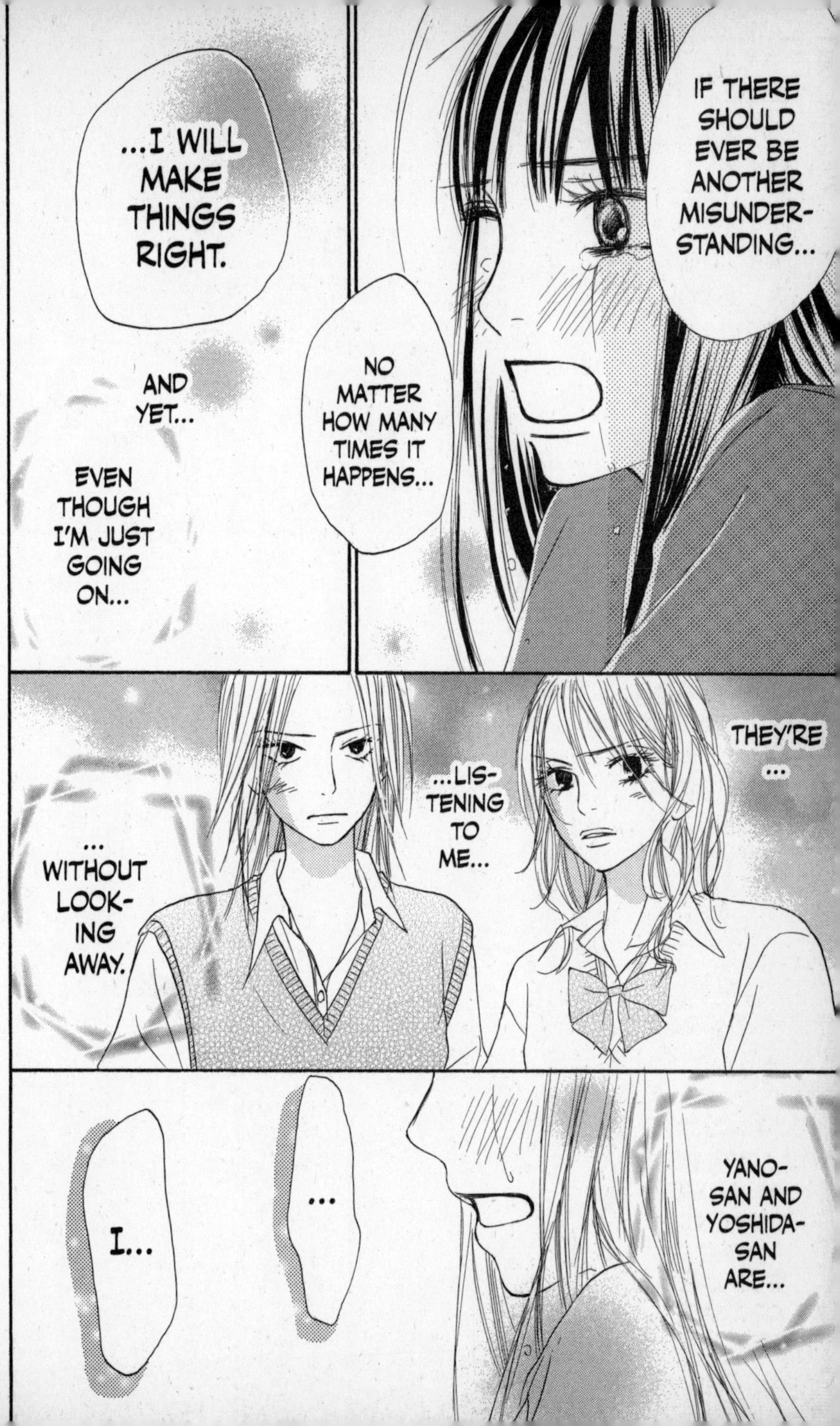
IF THERE SHOULD EVER BE ANOTHER MISUNDER-STANDING...
NO MATTER HOW MANY TIMES IT HAPPENS...
...I WILL MAKE THINGS RIGHT.
AND YET...
EVEN THOUGH I'M JUST GOING ON...
THEY'RE ...
...LIS-TENING TO ME...
... WITHOUT LOOK-ING AWAY.
YANO-SAN AND YOSHIDA-SAN ARE...
...
I...

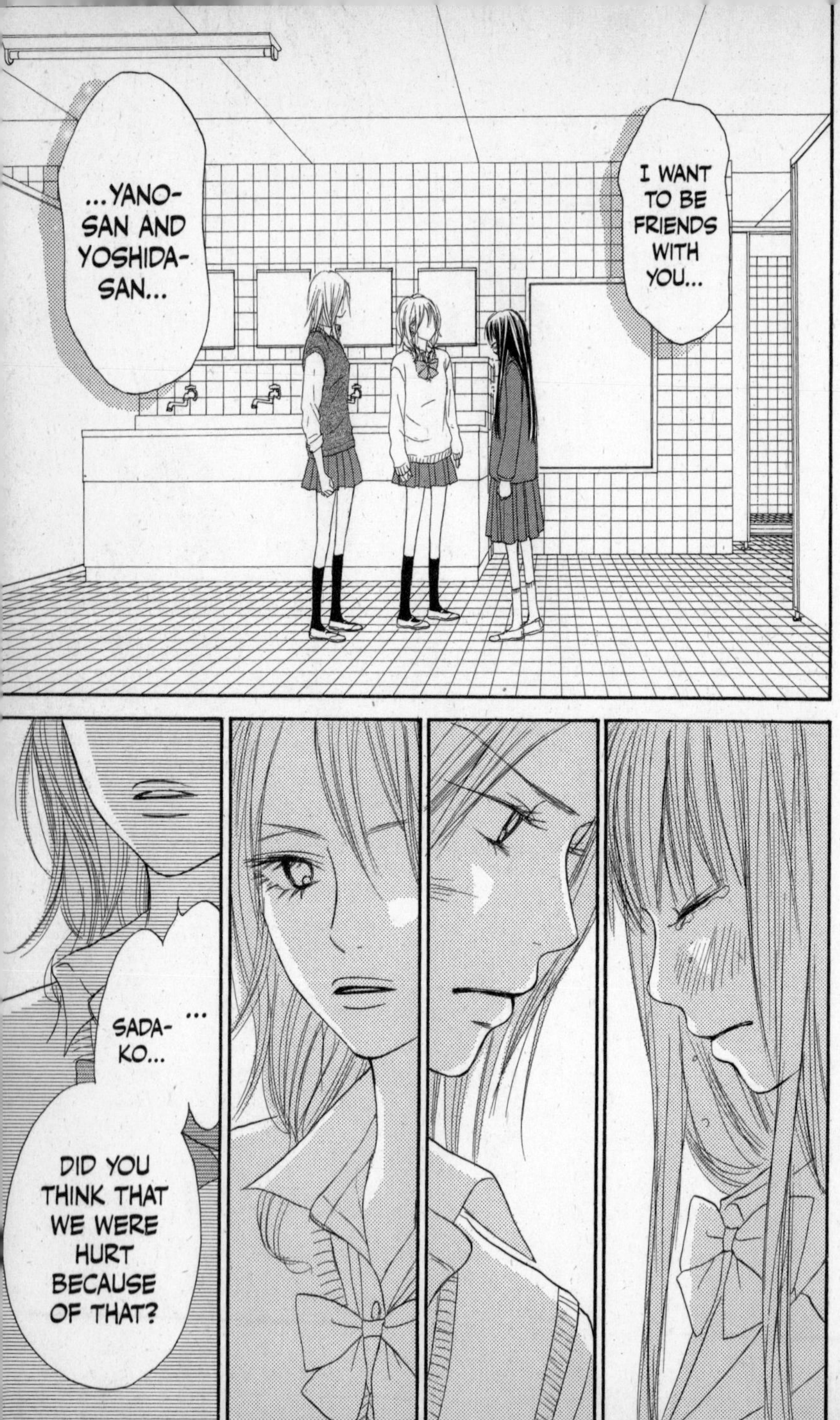
I WANT TO BE FRIENDS WITH YOU...
...YANO-SAN AND YOSHIDA-SAN...
...
SADA-KO...
DID YOU THINK THAT WE WERE HURT BECAUSE OF THAT?

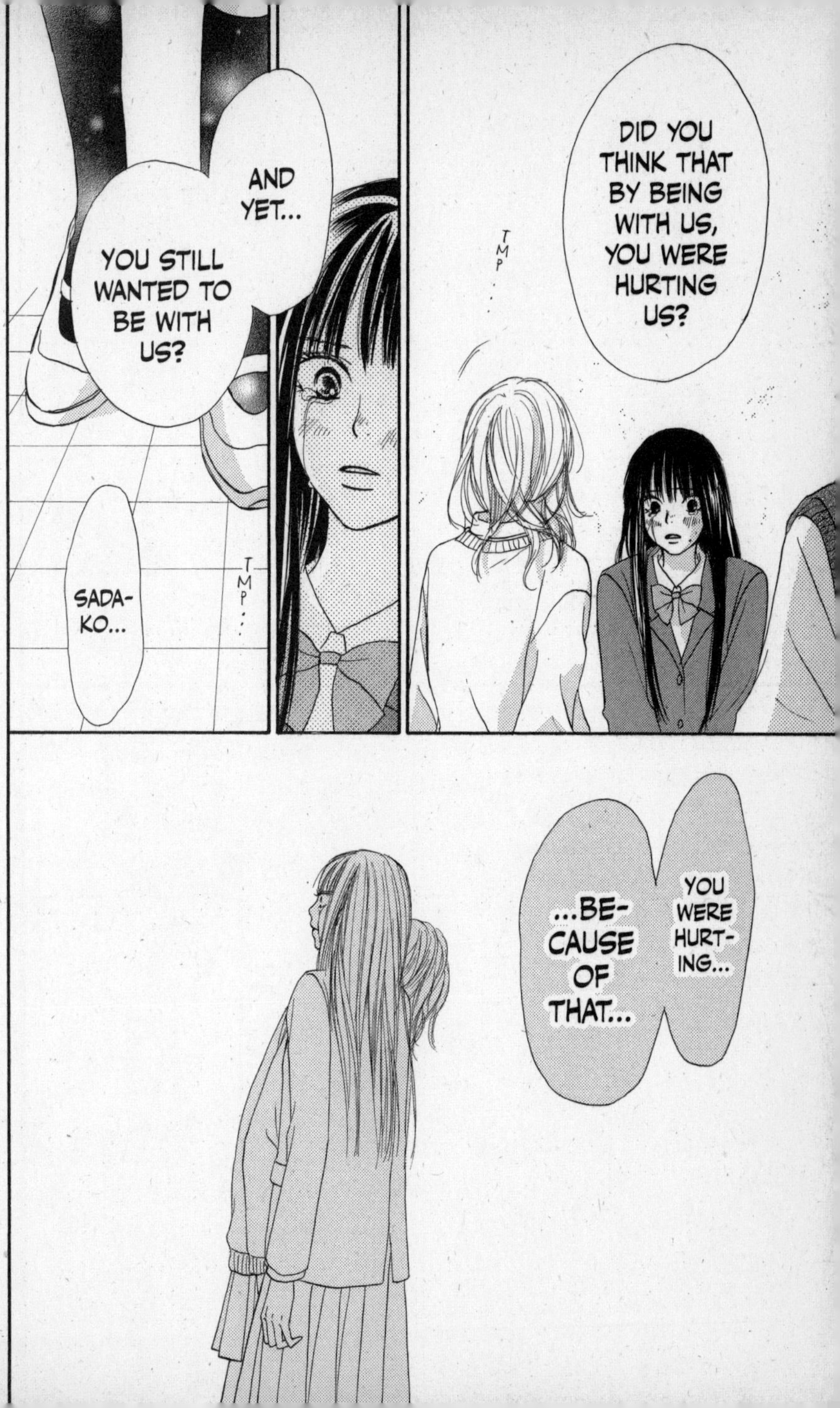
DID YOU THINK THAT BY BEING WITH US, YOU WERE HURTING US?
TMP
AND YET...
YOU STILL WANTED TO BE WITH US?
SADA-KO...
TMP...
YOU WERE HURT-ING...
...BE-CAUSE OF THAT...

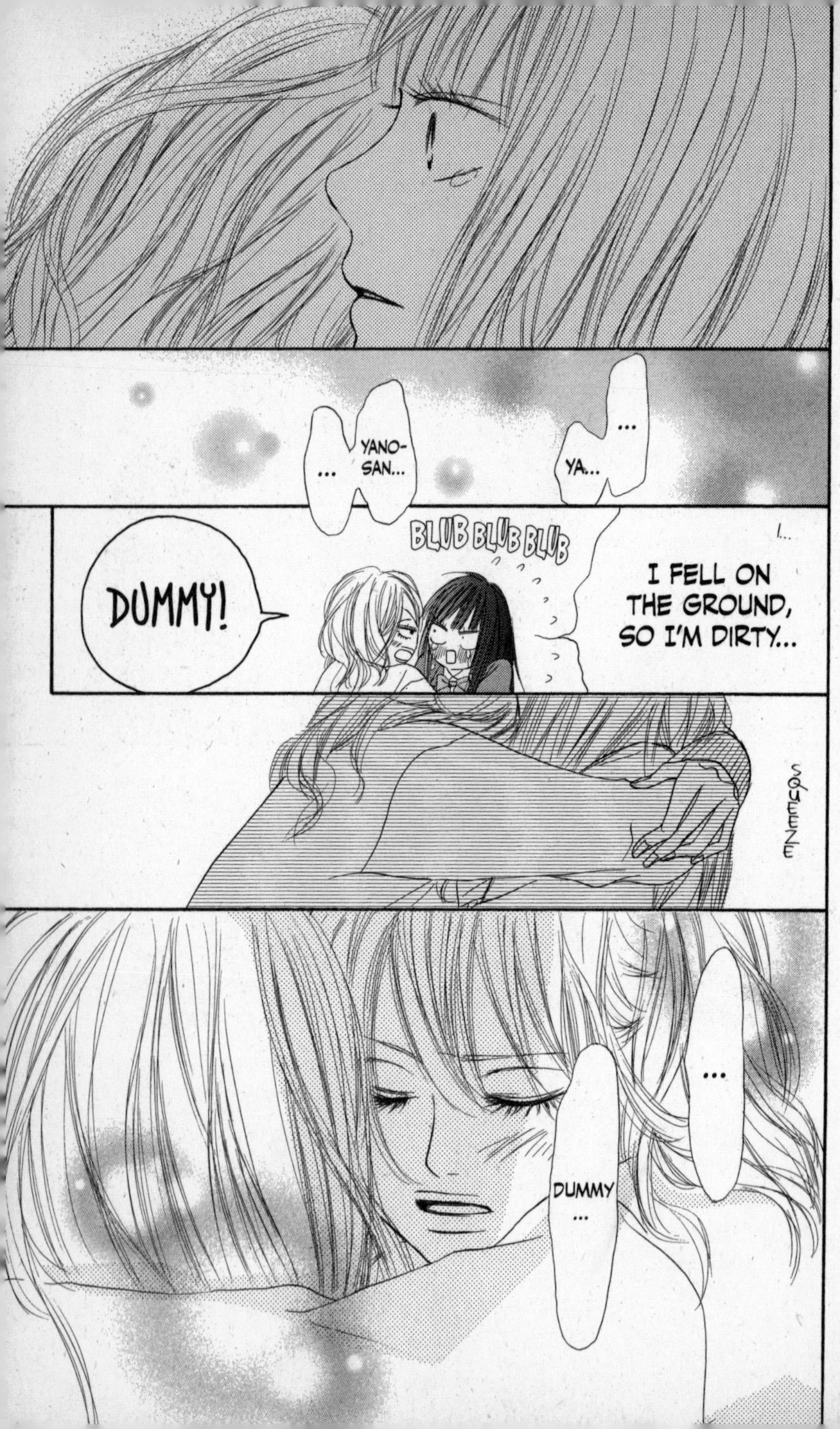
...
YA...
YANO-SAN...
...
I...
I FELL ON THE GROUND, SO I'M DIRTY...
BLUB BLUB BLUB
DUMMY!
SQUEEZE
...
DUMMY ...

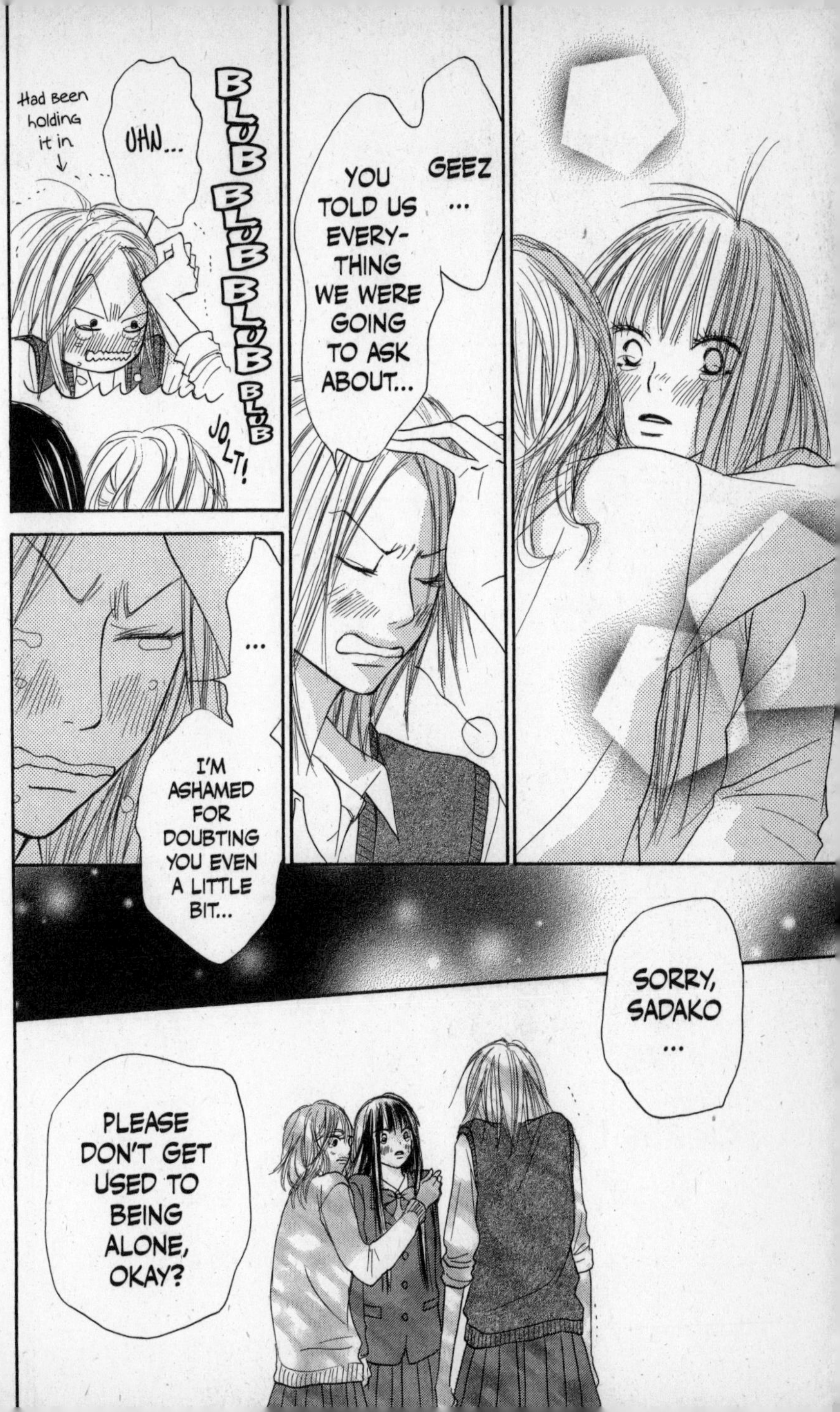
GEEZ ...
YOU TOLD US EVERYTHING WE WERE GOING TO ASK ABOUT...
UHN...
Had been holding it in
BLUB BLUB BLUB BLUB
JOLT!
...
I'M ASHAMED FOR DOUBTING YOU EVEN A LITTLE BIT...
SORRY, SADAKO ...
PLEASE DON'T GET USED TO BEING ALONE, OKAY?

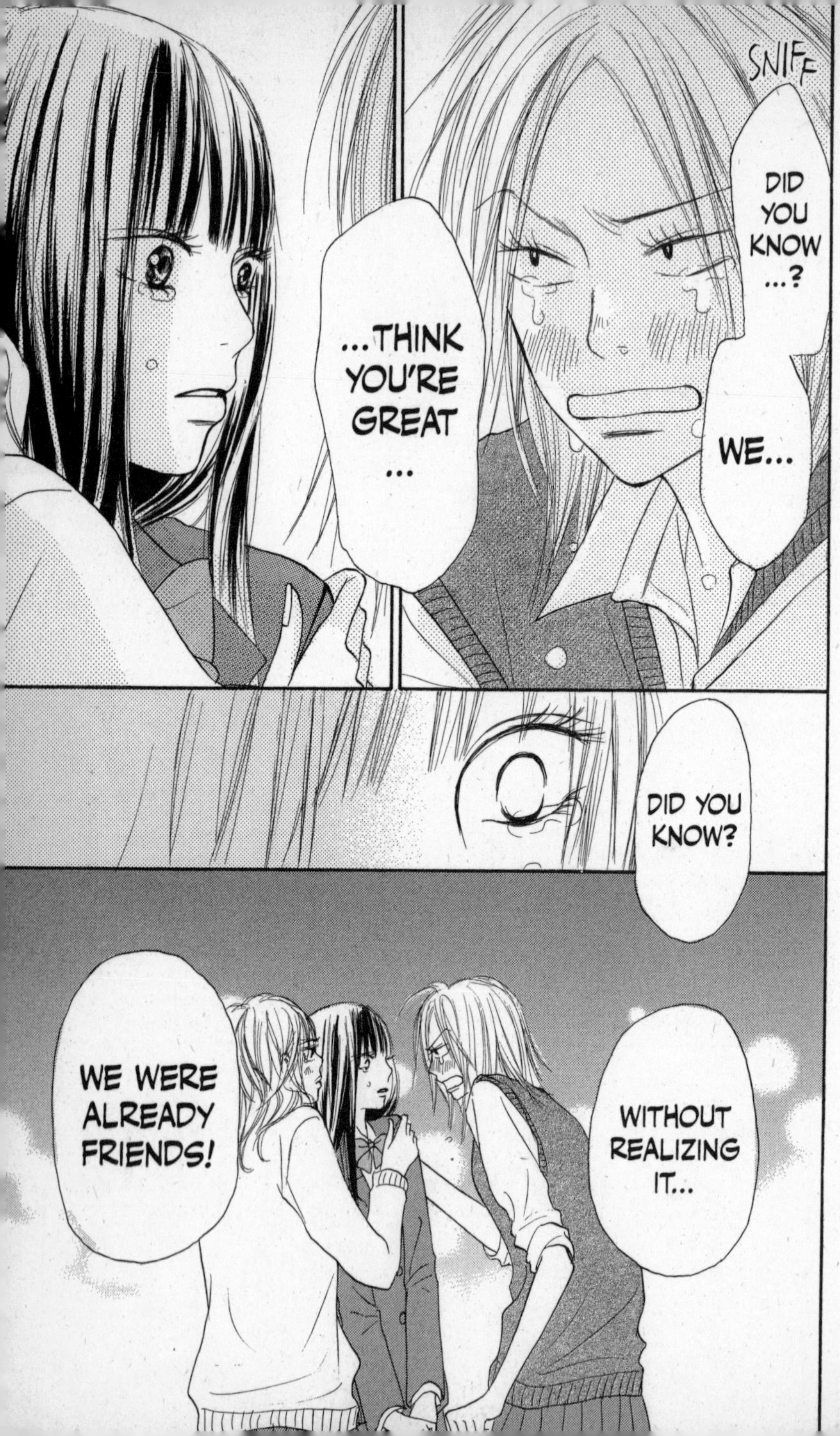
SNIFF
DID YOU KNOW ...?
WE...
...THINK YOU'RE GREAT ...
DID YOU KNOW?
WITHOUT REALIZING IT...
WE WERE ALREADY FRIENDS!

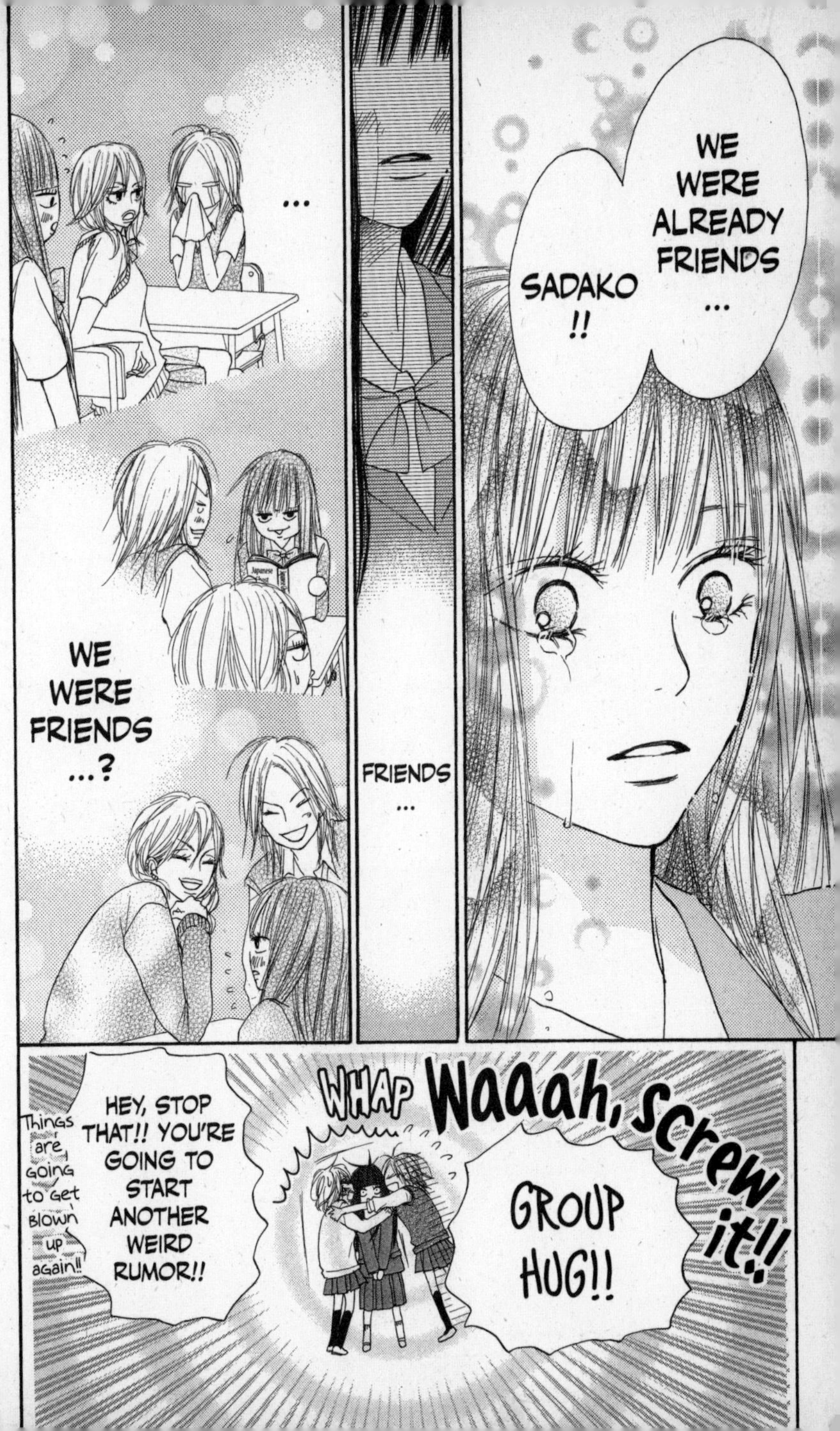
WE WERE ALREADY FRIENDS ...
SADAKO !!
FRIENDS ...
...
WE WERE FRIENDS ...?
Waaah, screw it!!
GROUP HUG!!
WHAP
HEY, STOP THAT!! YOU'RE GOING TO START ANOTHER WEIRD RUMOR!!
Things are going to get blown up again!!

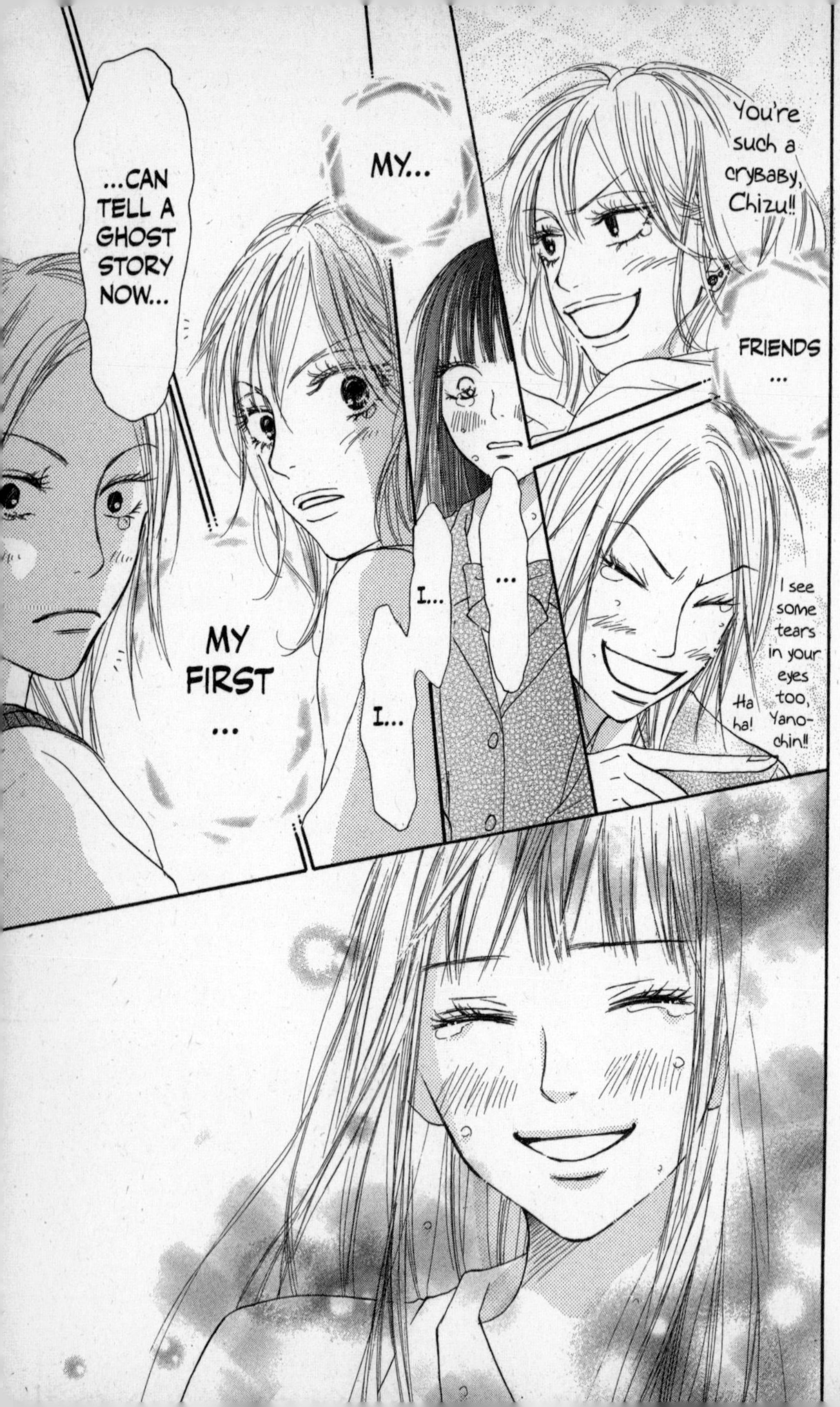
You're such a crybaby, Chizu!!
FRIENDS ...
I see some tears in your eyes too, Yano-chin!!
Ha ha!
MY...
...
I...
I...
MY FIRST ...
...CAN TELL A GHOST STORY NOW...

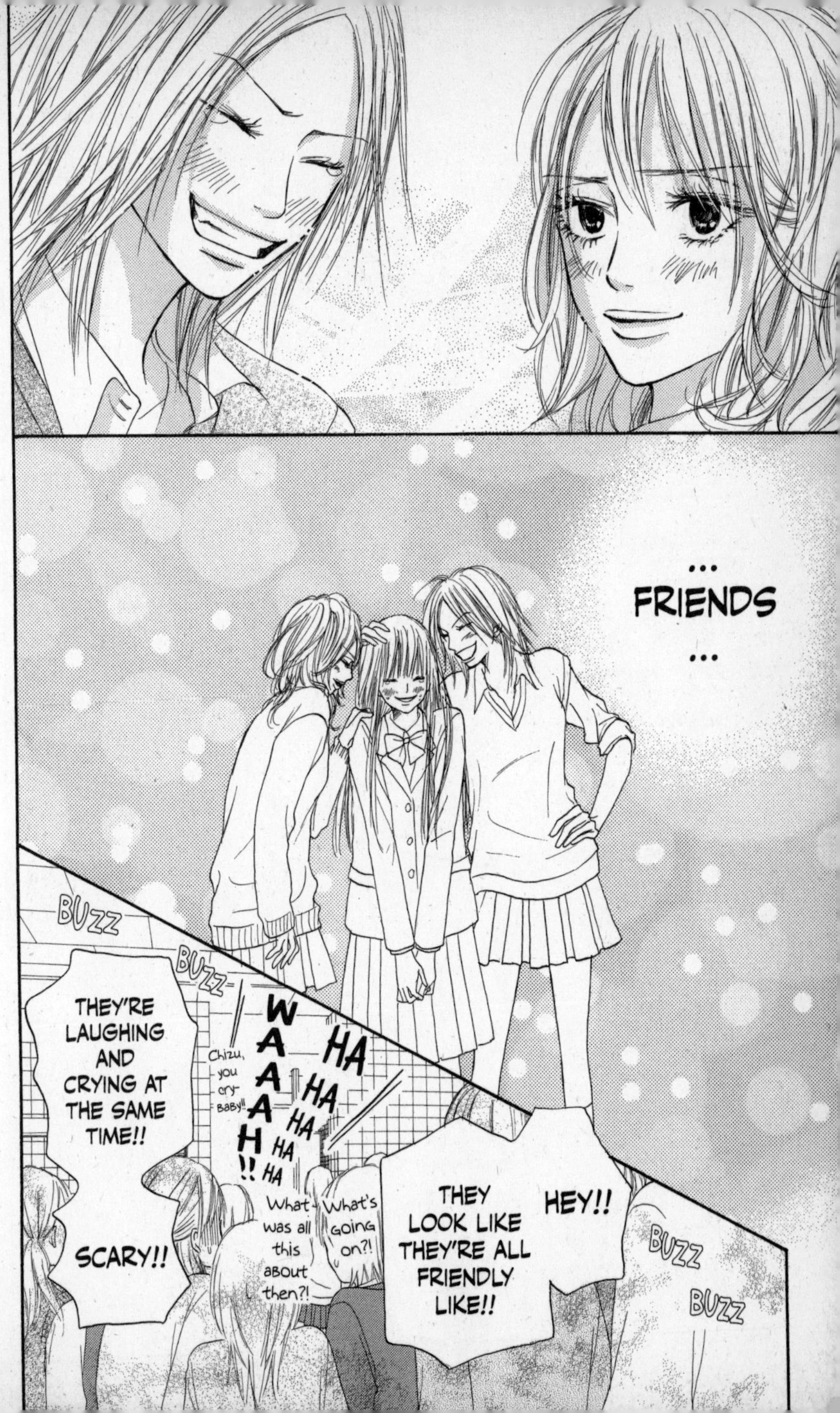
... FRIENDS ...
HEY!!
BUZZ
BUZZ
THEY LOOK LIKE THEY'RE ALL FRIENDLY LIKE!!
What's going on?!
What was all this about then?!
HA HA HA HA HA HA
WAAAAH!!
Chizu, you cry-baby!!
BUZZ
BUZZ
THEY'RE LAUGHING AND CRYING AT THE SAME TIME!!
SCARY!!

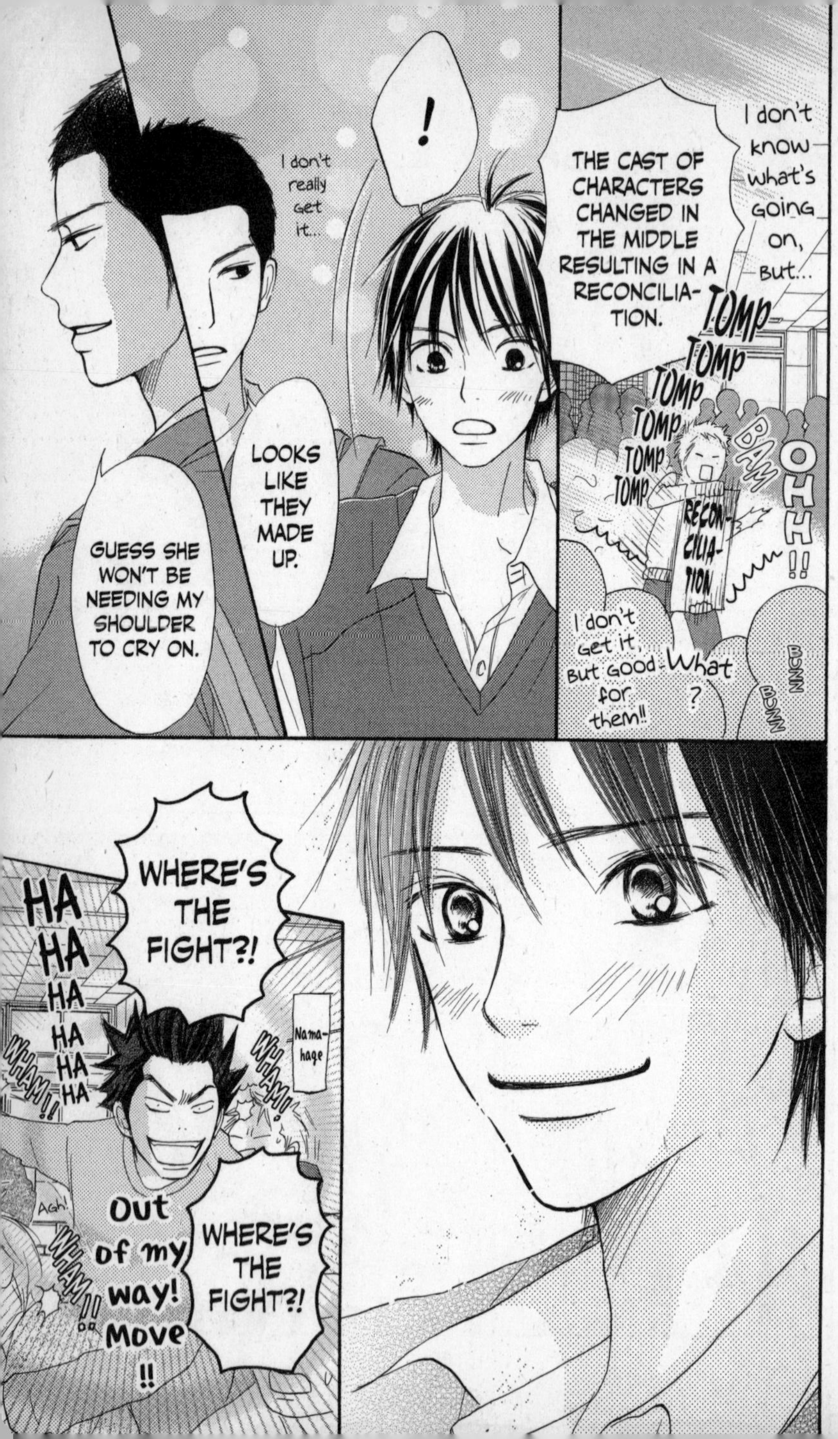
I don't know what's going on, but...
THE CAST OF CHARACTERS CHANGED IN THE MIDDLE RESULTING IN A RECONCILIA-TION.
TOMP TOMP TOMP TOMP TOMP TOMP
BAM
OHHH!!
RECON-CILIA-TION
I don't get it, but good for them!!
What?
BUNN BUNN
!
I don't really get it...
LOOKS LIKE THEY MADE UP.
GUESS SHE WON'T BE NEEDING MY SHOULDER TO CRY ON.
WHERE'S THE FIGHT?!
HA HA HA HA HA HA
Namahage
WHAM!
WHAM!!
WHERE'S THE FIGHT?!
Out of my way! Move!!
Agh!
WHAM!!

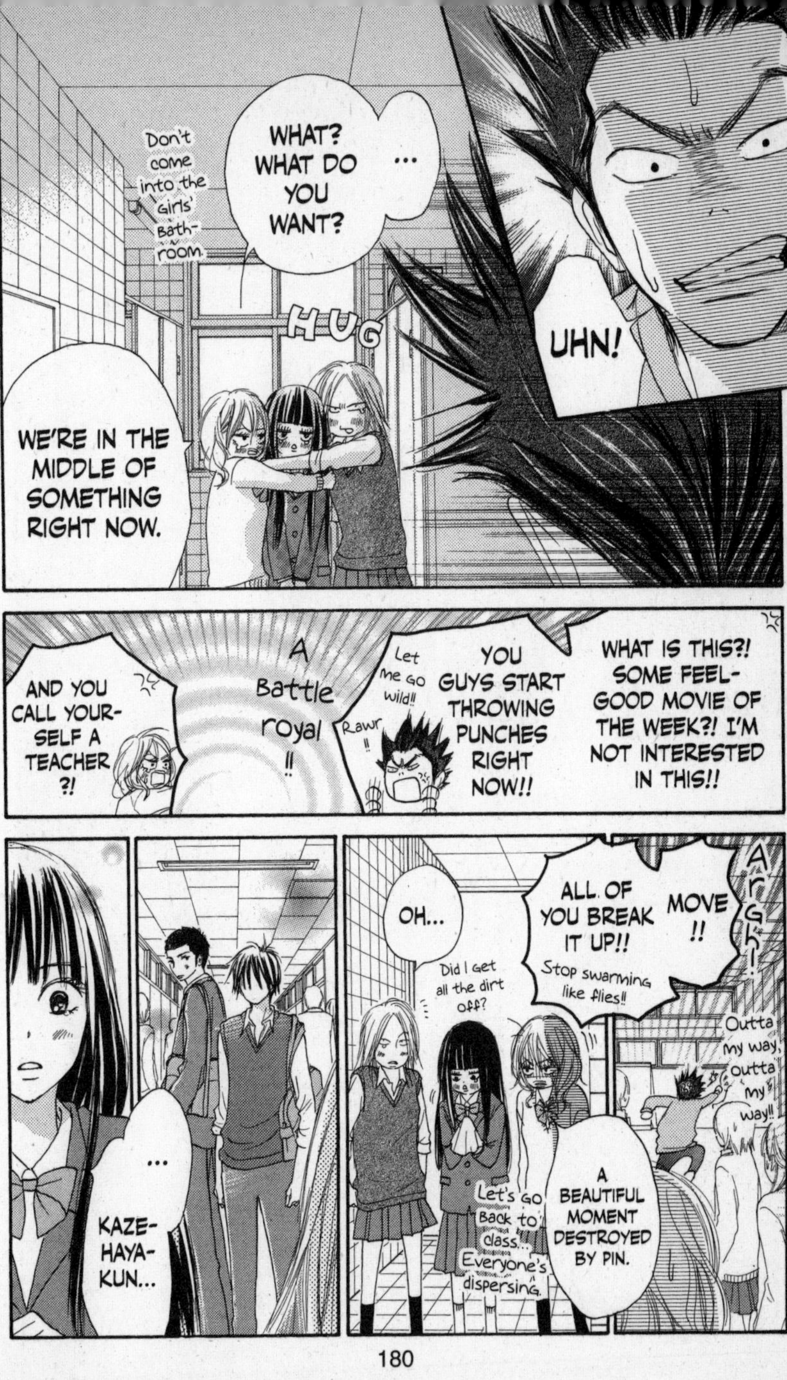
UHN!
...
WHAT? WHAT DO YOU WANT?
Don't come into the Girls' Bath-room.
HUG
WE'RE IN THE MIDDLE OF SOMETHING RIGHT NOW.
WHAT IS THIS?! SOME FEEL-GOOD MOVIE OF THE WEEK?! I'M NOT INTERESTED IN THIS!!
YOU GUYS START THROWING PUNCHES RIGHT NOW!!
Let me go wild!!
Rawr!!
A Battle royal!!
AND YOU CALL YOUR-SELF A TEACHER?!
Arghh!!
MOVE!!
ALL OF YOU BREAK IT UP!!
Stop swarming like flies!!
Outta my way, outta my way!!
OH...
Did I get all the dirt off?
A BEAUTIFUL MOMENT DESTROYED BY PIN.
Let's go back to class... Everyone's dispersing.
...
KAZE-HAYA-KUN...

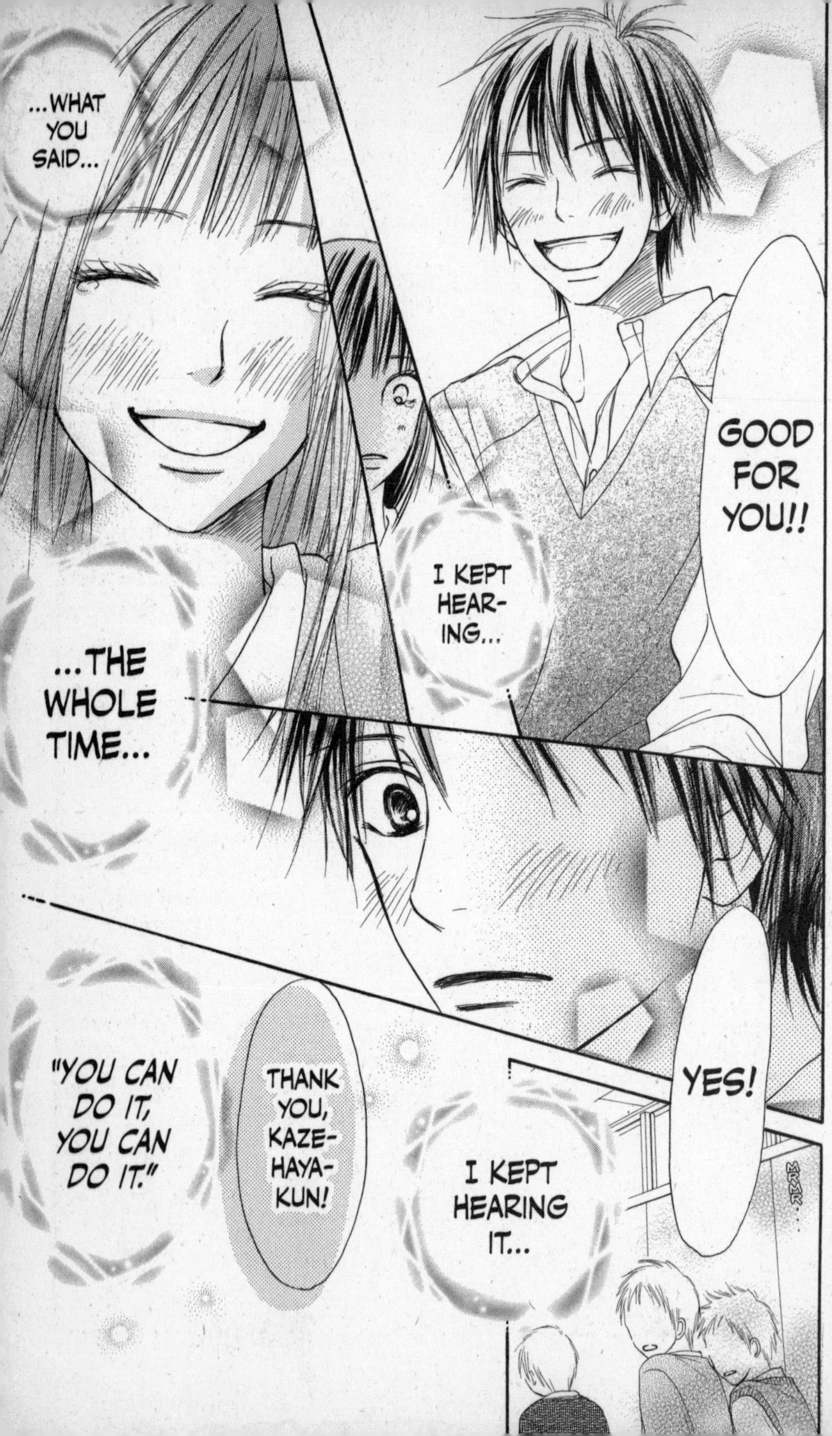
GOOD FOR YOU!!
I KEPT HEARING...
...WHAT YOU SAID...
...THE WHOLE TIME...
YES!
MRMR...
I KEPT HEARING IT...
THANK YOU, KAZEHAYA-KUN!
"YOU CAN DO IT, YOU CAN DO IT."

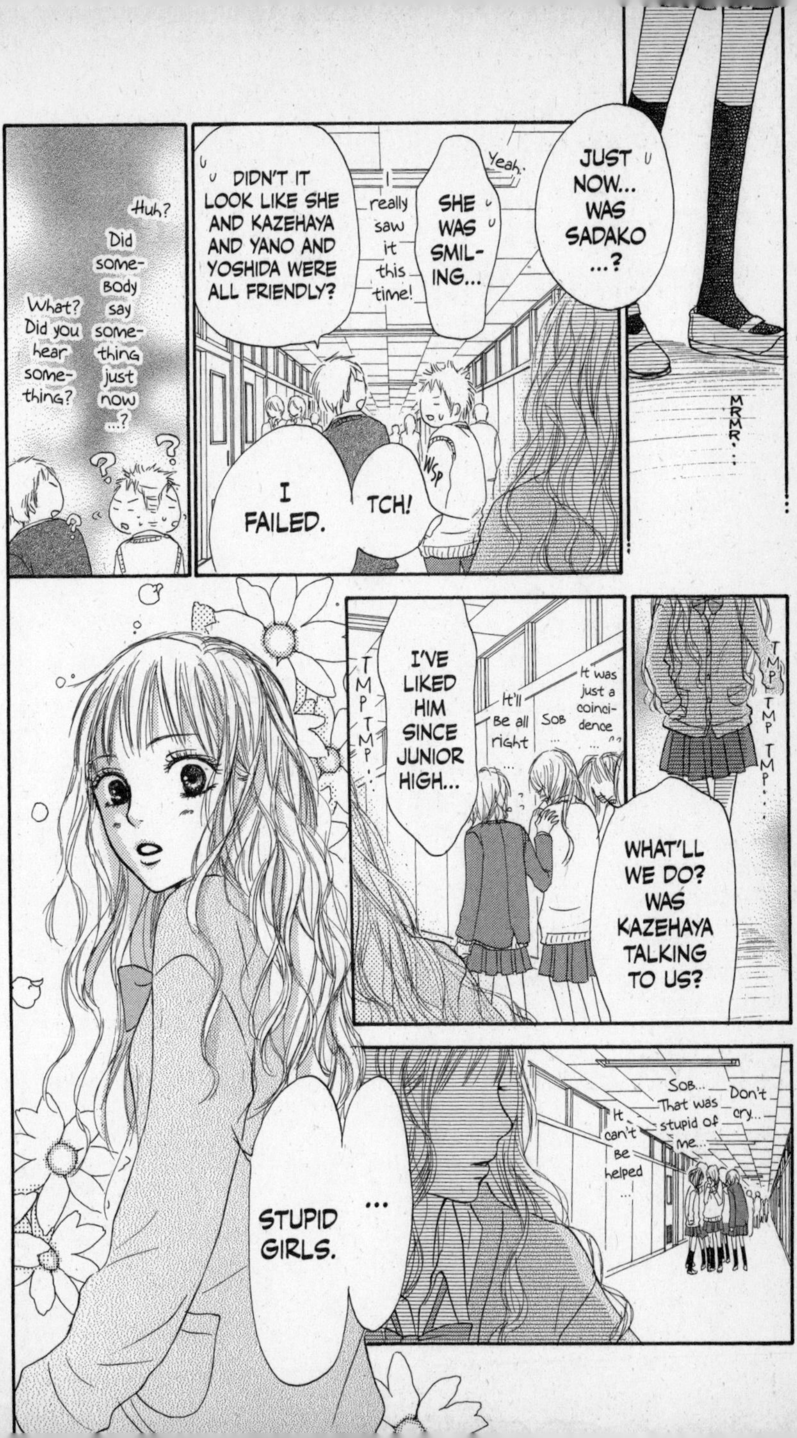
JUST NOW... WAS SADAKO ...?
MRMR...
Yeah.
SHE WAS SMIL-ING...
I really saw it this time!
DIDN'T IT LOOK LIKE SHE AND KAZEHAYA AND YANO AND YOSHIDA WERE ALL FRIENDLY?
TCH!
WSP
I FAILED.
Huh?
Did some-body say some-thing just now ...?
What? Did you hear some-thing?
TMP TMP TMP...
WHAT'LL WE DO? WAS KAZEHAYA TALKING TO US?
It was just a coinci-dence ...
SOB ...
It'll Be all right ...
I'VE LIKED HIM SINCE JUNIOR HIGH...
TMP TMP...
Don't cry...
SOB... That was stupid of me...
It can't Be helped ...
...
STUPID GIRLS.

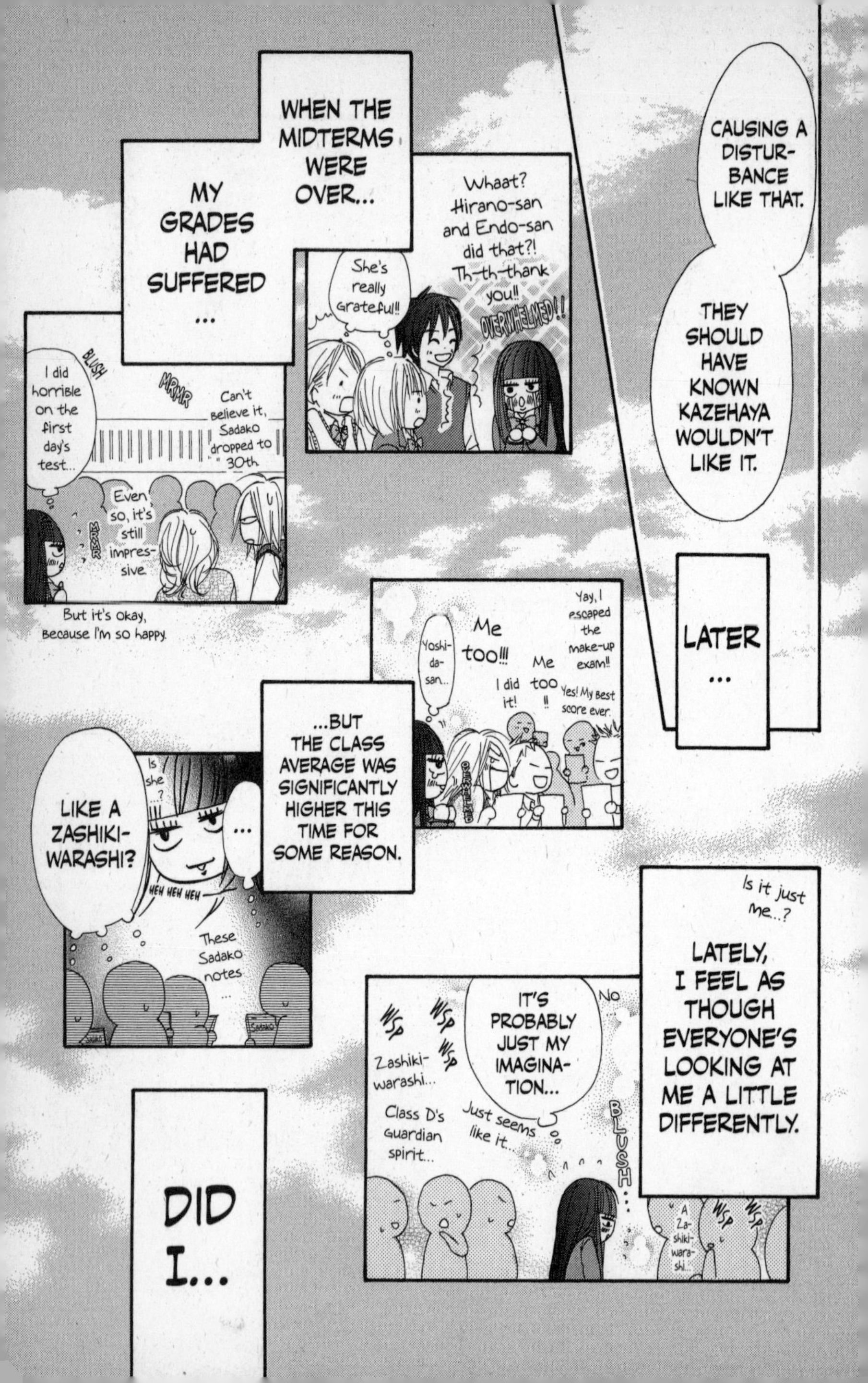
CAUSING A DISTUR-BANCE LIKE THAT.
THEY SHOULD HAVE KNOWN KAZEHAYA WOULDN'T LIKE IT.
LATER...
WHEN THE MIDTERMS WERE OVER...
Whaat? Hirano-san and Endo-san did that?! Th-th-thank you!!
OVERWHELMED!!
She's really grateful!!
MY GRADES HAD SUFFERED ...
MRMR
Can't believe it, Sadako dropped to 30th.
BLUSH
I did horrible on the first day's test...
Even so, it's still impres-sive.
MRMR
But it's okay, because I'm so happy.
Yay, I escaped the make-up exam!!
Yes! My best score ever.
Me too!!!
Me too !!
I did it!
Yoshi-da-san...
...BUT THE CLASS AVERAGE WAS SIGNIFICANTLY HIGHER THIS TIME FOR SOME REASON.
Is she ...?
...
LIKE A ZASHIKI-WARASHI?
HEH HEH HEH
These Sadako notes ...
Is it just me...?
LATELY, I FEEL AS THOUGH EVERYONE'S LOOKING AT ME A LITTLE DIFFERENTLY.
No ...
IT'S PROBABLY JUST MY IMAGINA-TION...
Just seems like it...
WSP WSP
Zashiki-warashi...
Class D's Guardian spirit...
WSP
BLUSH...
WSP WSP
A Za-shiki-wara-shi...
DID I...

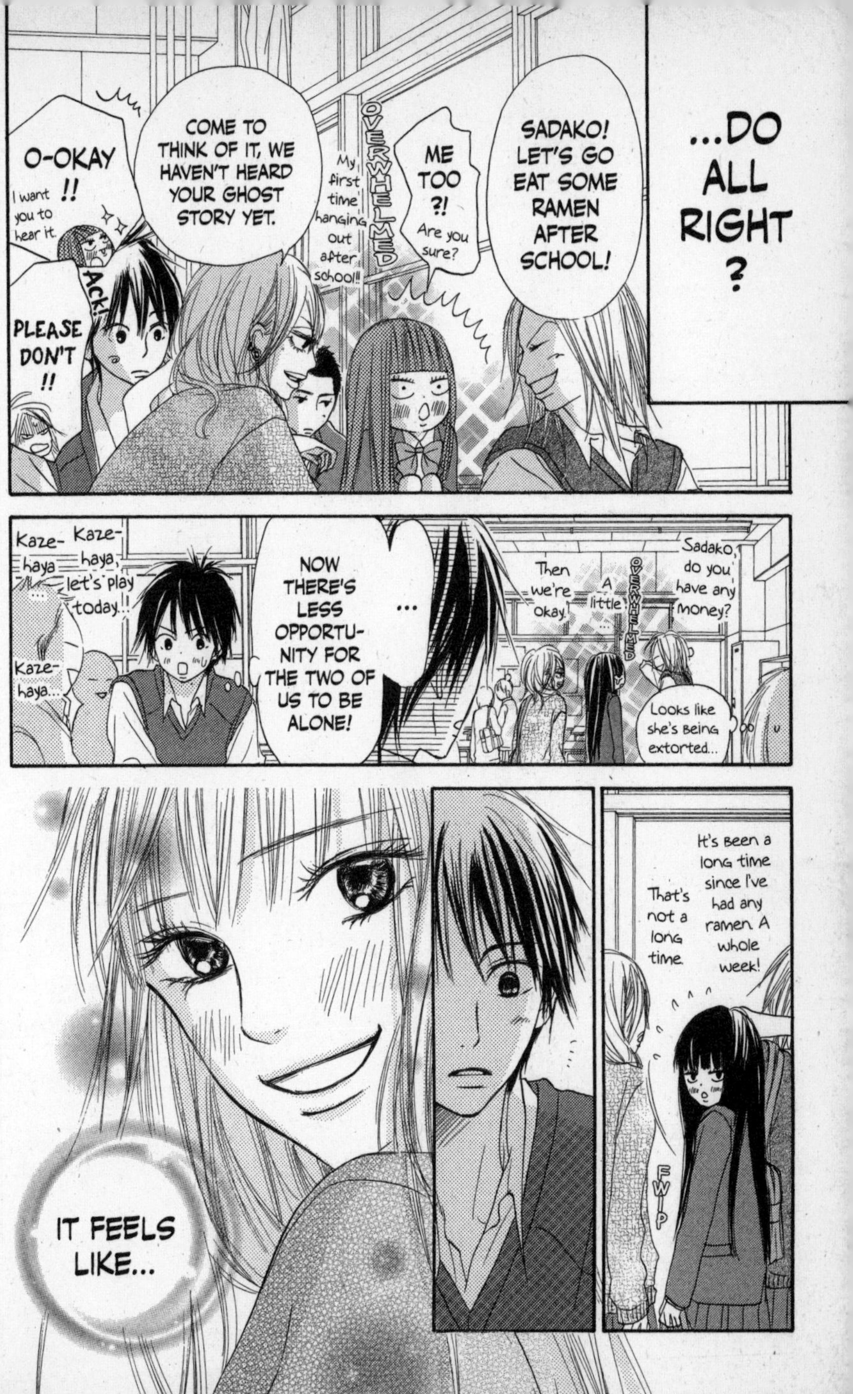
...DO ALL RIGHT?
SADAKO! LET'S GO EAT SOME RAMEN AFTER SCHOOL!
ME TOO?!
Are you sure?
OVERWHELMED
My first time hanging out after school!!
COME TO THINK OF IT, WE HAVEN'T HEARD YOUR GHOST STORY YET.
O-OKAY!!
I want you to hear it.
ACK!
PLEASE DON'T!!
Sadako, do you have any money?
Looks like she's being extorted...
Then we're okay.
A little...
OVERWHELMED
...
NOW THERE'S LESS OPPORTUNITY FOR THE TWO OF US TO BE ALONE!
Kaze-haya, let's play today...
Kaze-haya
...
Kaze-haya...
It's been a long time since I've had any ramen. A whole week!
That's not a long time.
FWIP
IT FEELS LIKE...

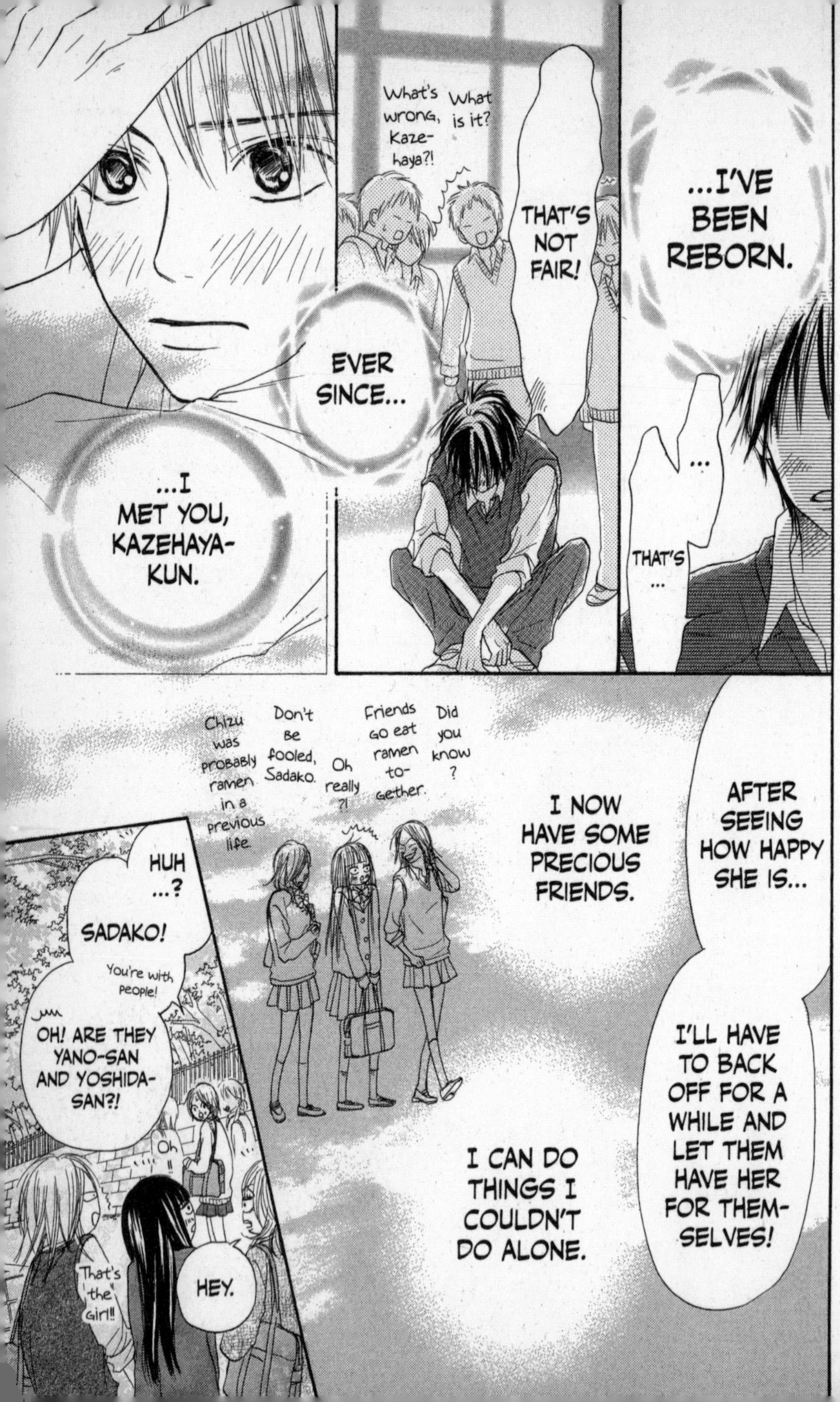
...I'VE BEEN REBORN.
...THAT'S...
THAT'S NOT FAIR!
What is it?
What's wrong, Kaze-haya?!
EVER SINCE...
...I MET YOU, KAZEHAYA-KUN.
AFTER SEEING HOW HAPPY SHE IS...
I'LL HAVE TO BACK OFF FOR A WHILE AND LET THEM HAVE HER FOR THEM-SELVES!
I NOW HAVE SOME PRECIOUS FRIENDS.
I CAN DO THINGS I COULDN'T DO ALONE.
Did you know?
Friends go eat ramen to-gether.
Oh really?!
Don't be fooled, Sadako.
Chizu was probably ramen in a previous life.
HUH ...?
SADAKO!
You're with people!
OH! ARE THEY YANO-SAN AND YOSHIDA-SAN?!
Oh !!
HEY.
That's the girl!!

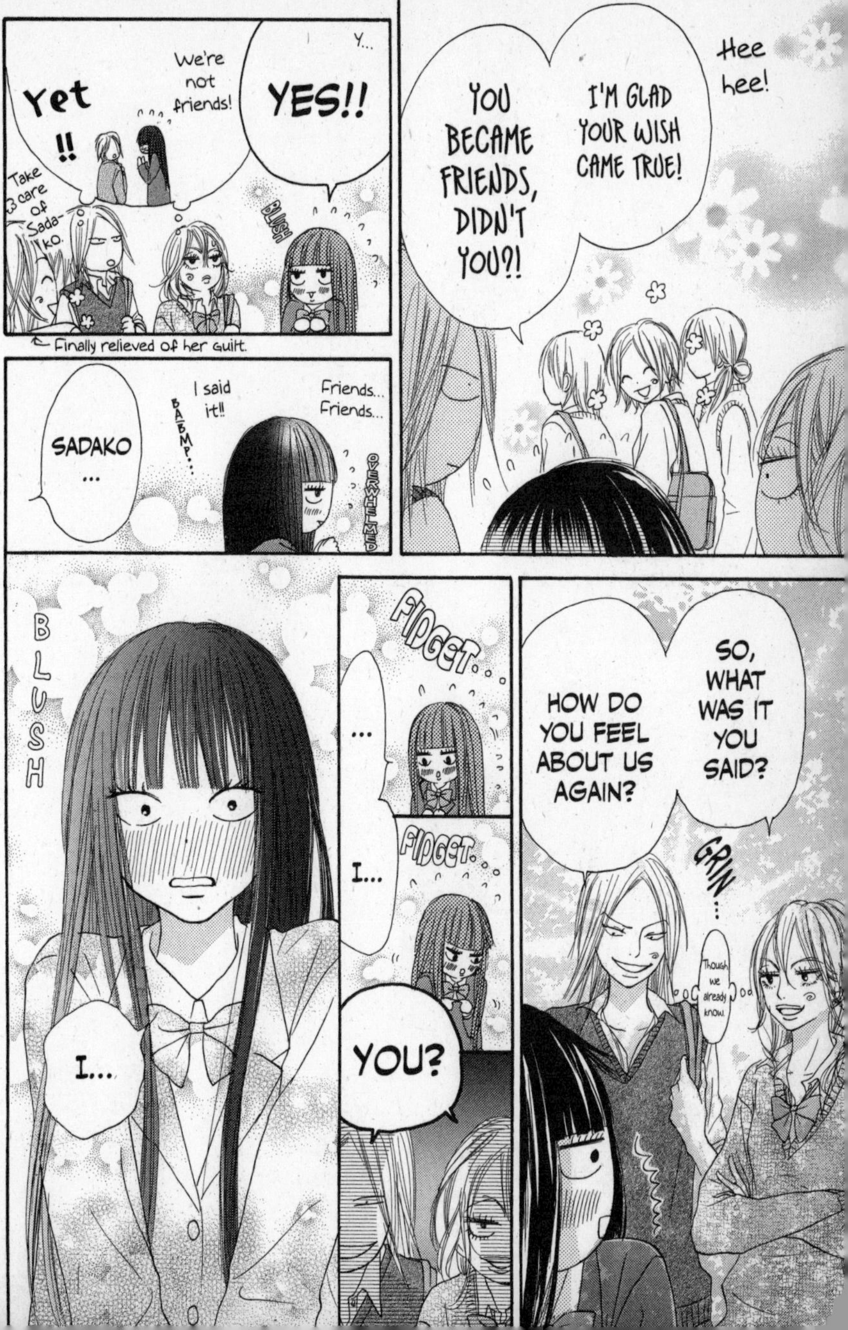
Hee hee!
I'M GLAD YOUR WISH CAME TRUE!
YOU BECAME FRIENDS, DIDN'T YOU?!
Y...
YES!!
BLUSH
We're not friends!
Yet!!
Take care of Sada-ko.
Finally relieved of her guilt.
Friends... Friends...
OVERWHELMED
I said it!!
BA-BMP...
SADAKO...
SO, WHAT WAS IT YOU SAID?
HOW DO YOU FEEL ABOUT US AGAIN?
GRIN...
Though we already know.
FIDGET...
...
FIDGET...
I...
YOU?
BLUSH
I...

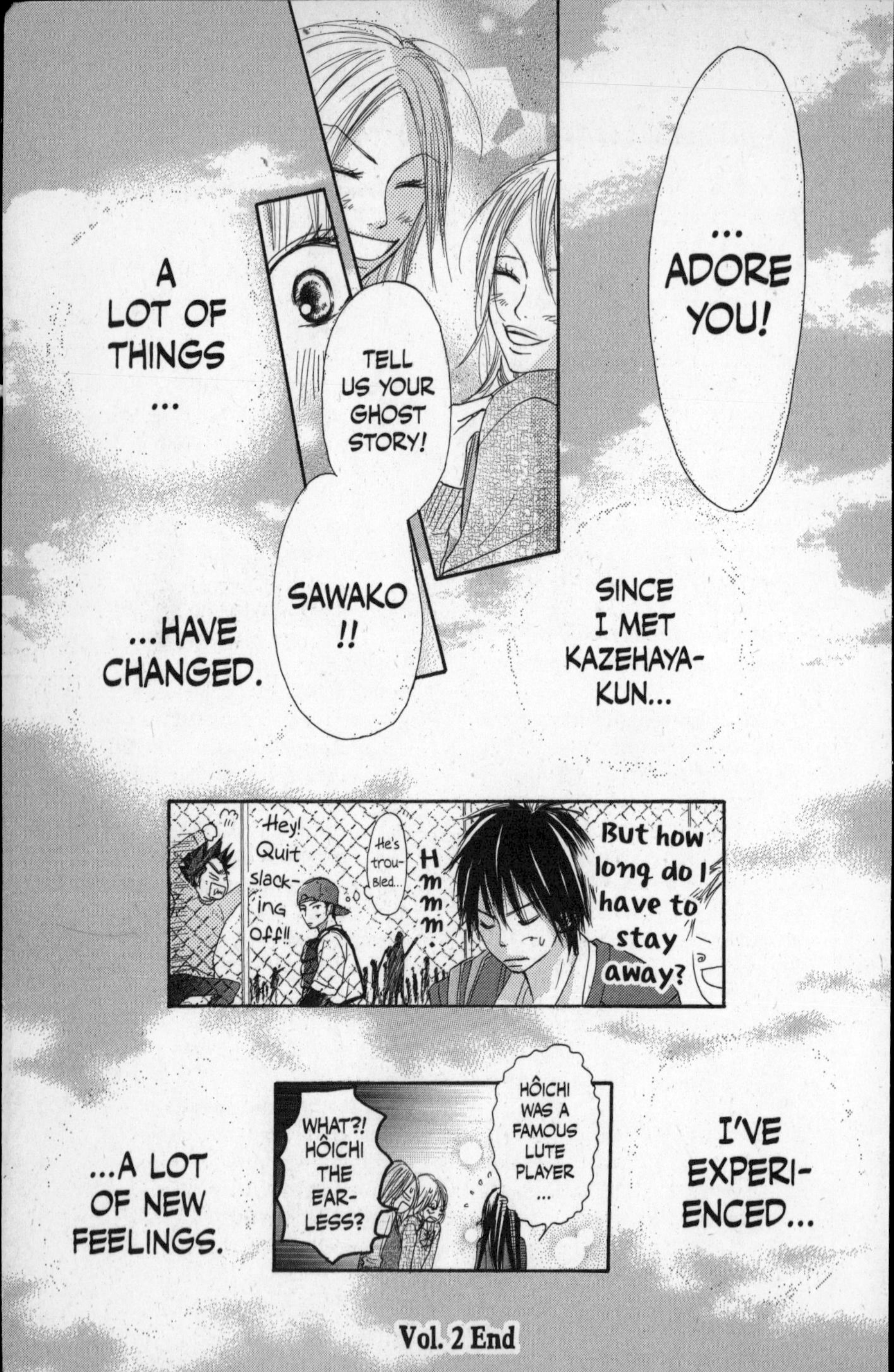
... ADORE YOU!
SINCE I MET KAZEHAYA-KUN...
TELL US YOUR GHOST STORY!
SAWAKO !!
A LOT OF THINGS ...
...HAVE CHANGED.
But how long do I have to stay away?
Hmmm.
He's troubled...
Hey! Quit slacking off!!
I'VE EXPERIENCED...
HÔICHI WAS A FAMOUS LUTE PLAYER ...
WHAT?! HÔICHI THE EARLESS?
...A LOT OF NEW FEELINGS.

Vol. 2 End

From me (the editor) to you (the reader).

Here are some Japanese culture explanations that will help you better understand the references in the *Kimi ni Todoke* world.

Honorifics:
When saying someone's name in Japanese, a suffix is often attached to indicate how familiar the speaker is with the person. Some are more polite and respectful, while others are endearing. Calling someone by just their first name is the most informal.
-*kun* is used for young men or boys, usually someone you are familiar with.
-*chan* is used for young women, girls or young children and can be used as a term of endearment.
-*san* is used for someone you respect or are not close to, or to be polite.

Page 7, Japanese bathtubs:
Bathtubs in Japan are typically a lot deeper and shorter in length than Western-style bathtubs. The water line will usually come up to your shoulders as you sit down, so it's not too hard to submerge yourself fully.

Page 10, *Glass Mask*:
Glass Mask is a long-running shojo classic by Suzue Miuchi. About aspiring actress Maya Kitajima and her stern drama coach, "The Crimson Goddess" is one of the original plays featured in the story.

Page 11, "Ladies":
In the '70s and '80s, female-only biker gangs were called "Ladies." Though they still exist, you're more likely to see Ladies out in the countryside rather than the big cities.

Page 48, Koji Matoba:
A Japanese actor known for playing tough guys.

Page 48, Yumiko Shaku:
A Japanese actress who got her start as a pinup girl.

Page 63, Aya Nakahara:
Aya Nakahara is the popular manga artist of *Love★Com*.

Page 119, Purifying salt:
Salt is often used in Japan as part of a purification ritual. One occasion would be purifying your house after an unpleasant or unwanted visitor has dropped by. Chizu has her salt ready because she doesn't want to accept that Ryu may be right.

Page 179, Namahage:
Namahage are ogres that are found in Akita folklore. (Akita is a prefecture in the northern area of the main island of Japan.) During New Year's, men will dress up in ogre masks and straw outfits and go around the neighborhood asking where the naughty children are.

Page 187, "Hôichi the Earless":
A frightening tale about the blind minstral player Hôichi and what happens when he encounters a supernatural audience who really want a piece of him. Literally...

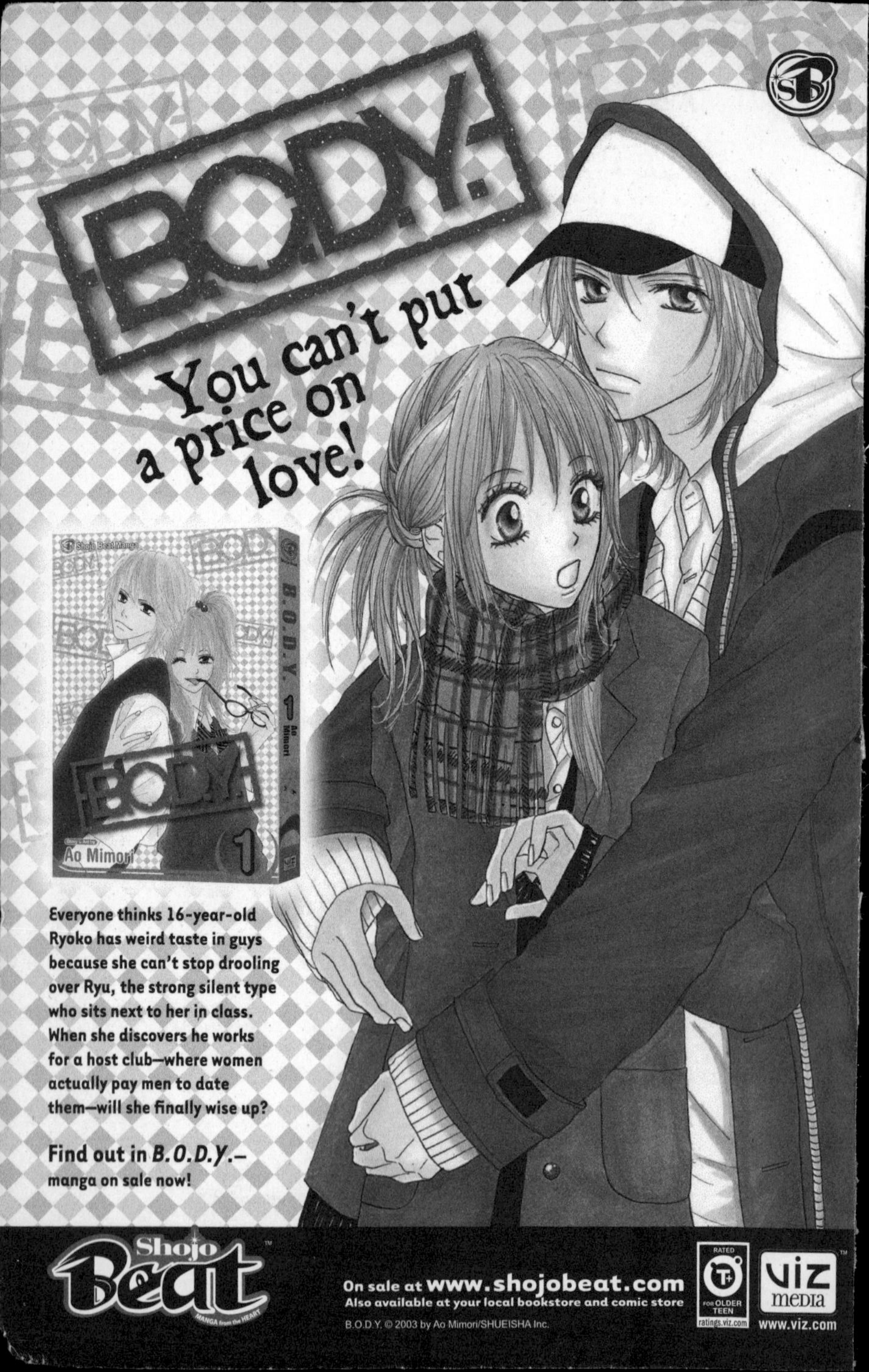
B.O.D.Y.
You can't put a price on love!
Shojo Beat Manga
B.O.D.Y.
1
Ao Mimori
Everyone thinks 16-year-old Ryoko has weird taste in guys because she can't stop drooling over Ryu, the strong silent type who sits next to her in class. When she discovers he works for a host club—where women actually pay men to date them—will she finally wise up?
Find out in B.O.D.Y.—manga on sale now!
Shojo Beat
MANGA from the HEART
On sale at www.shojobeat.com
Also available at your local bookstore and comic store
B.O.D.Y. © 2003 by Ao Mimori/SHUEISHA Inc.
RATED T+ FOR OLDER TEEN
ratings.viz.com
VIZ media
www.viz.com

I've been so overwhelmed with drawing this manga that it's already volume 2. For *Kimi ni Todoke*, I asked the designer to experiment with the background color on the covers. All of the versions they came up with were so pretty I had a really hard time choosing. The more I saw, the more I couldn't decide. After a lot of thought I finally went with light blue for the first volume and pink for the second volume. Just choosing the color for one cover was overwhelming. I'm already looking forward to choosing the background color for volume 3.

--Karuho Shiina

Karuho Shiina was born and raised in Hokkaido, Japan. Though *Kimi ni Todoke* is only her second series following many one-shot stories, it has already racked up accolades from various "Best Manga of the Year" lists. Winner of the 2008 Kodansha Manga Award for the shojo category, *Kimi ni Todoke* also placed fifth in the first-ever Manga Taisho (Cartoon Grand Prize) contest in 2008.

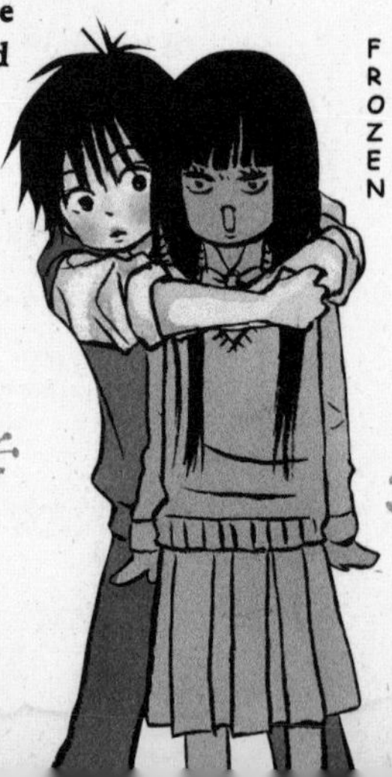
FROZEN

Shojo Beat

Kimi ni Todoke
VOL. 2

Shojo Beat Manga Edition

STORY AND ART BY
KARUHO SHIINA

Translation/JN Productions
Touch-up Art & Lettering/Vanessa Satone
Design/Yukiko Whitley
Editor/Yuki Murashige

VP, Production/Alvin Lu
VP, Publishing Licensing/Rika Inouye
VP, Sales & Product Marketing/Gonzalo Ferreyra
VP, Creative/Linda Espinosa
Publisher/Hyoe Narita

Printed in the U.S.A.

Published by VIZ Media, LLC
P.O. Box 77010
San Francisco, CA 94107

10 9 8 7 6 5 4 3 2 1
First printing, October 2009

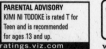